Living to Tell the Tale

LIVING TO
TELL THE TALE

Gabriel García Márquez

TRANSLATED FROM THE SPANISH
BY EDITH GROSSMAN

Alfred A. Knopf   New York
2003

THIS IS A BORZOI BOOK
PUBLISHED BY ALFRED A. KNOPF

Originally published in Spain as *Vivir para contarla* by
Mondadori (Grijalbo Mondadori, S.A.), Barcelona, and
subsequently in the United States by Alfred A. Knopf,
a division of Random House, Inc., in 2002.
Copyright © 2002 by Gabriel García Márquez
Copyright © 2002 by Mondadori (Grijalbo Mondadori, S.A.)

Portions appeared in *The New Yorker*, February 19, 2002, and
in *Zoetrope* vol. 2, no. 3 (Fall 1998).

Library of Congress Cataloging-in-Publication Data
García Márquez, Gabriel, [date]
[Vivir para contarla. English]
Living to tell the tale / Gabriel García Márquez ; translated by
Edith Grossman.
p.   cm.
ISBN 1-4000-4134-1
1. García Márquez, Gabriel, [date]—Childhood and youth.
2. Authors, Colombian—20th century—Biography.
I. Grossman, Edith, [date]   II. Title.

PQ8180.17.A73Z47813 2003
863'.64—dc22
[B]   2003058924

Manufactured in the United States of America
First Edition

Life is not what one lived, but what one remembers
and how one remembers it in order to recount it.

Caribbean Sea

Manaure

Riohacha

Santa
Marta

Ciénaga

Barranquilla   Riofrío

LA GUAJIRA

Cerrejón

Fonseca   Barrancas

Patillal   San Juan
del César

Aracataca   Villanueva

Valledupar

Fundación

COLOMBIA   La Paz

VENEZUELA

0   50 miles

Caribbean Sea

Cabo de la Vela

Cartagena
Bocagrande

Calamar

AREA OF
INSET

Tolú

Magangué

Sincelejo

Sincé   El Banco

Sucre

Ayapel   Achí
Majagual

Barrancabermeja

Puerto Berrío

Medellín

Puerto   Chiquinquirá
Quibdó   Salgar   BOYACÁ

Andagoya   Chía   Zipaquirá

★ Bogotá

Sevilla   Melgar   Quetame

Buenaventura   Apiay

Villarrica

COLOMBIA

Neiva

PANAMA

CHOCÓ

Pacific
Ocean

Magdalena River

VENEZUELA

Pasto

ECUADOR

BRAZIL

0   100   200 miles

PERU

Leticia

Living to Tell the Tale

1

MY MOTHER ASKED ME to go with her to sell the house. She had come that morning from the distant town where the family lived, and she had no idea how to find me. She asked around among acquaintances and was told to look for me at the Librería Mundo, or in the nearby cafés, where I went twice a day to talk with my writer friends. The one who told her this warned her: "Be careful, because they're all out of their minds." She arrived at twelve sharp. With her light step she made her way among the tables of books on display, stopped in front of me, looking into my eyes with the mischievous smile of her better days, and before I could react she said:

"I'm your mother."

Something in her had changed, and this kept me from recognizing her at first glance. She was forty-five. Adding up her eleven births, she had spent almost ten years pregnant and at least another ten nursing her children. She had gone gray before her time, her eyes seemed larger and more startled behind her first bifocals, and she wore strict, somber mourning for the death of her mother, but she still preserved the Roman beauty of her wedding portrait, dignified now by an autumnal air. Before anything else, even before she embraced me, she said in her customary, ceremonial way:

"I've come to ask you to please go with me to sell the house."

She did not have to tell me which one, or where, because for us only one existed in the world: my grandparents' old house in Aracataca, where I'd had the good fortune to be born, and where I had not lived again after the age of eight. I had just dropped out of the faculty of law after six semesters devoted almost entirely to reading whatever I could get my hands on, and reciting from memory the unrepeatable poetry of the Spanish Golden Age. I already had read, in translation, and in borrowed editions, all the books I would have needed to learn the novelist's craft, and had published six stories in newspaper supplements, winning the enthusiasm of my friends and the attention of a few critics. The following month I would turn twenty-three, I had passed the age of military service and was a veteran of two bouts of gonorrhea, and every day I smoked, with no foreboding, sixty cigarettes made from the most barbaric tobacco. I divided my leisure between Barranquilla and Cartagena de Indias, on Colombia's Caribbean coast, living like a king on what I was paid for my daily commentaries in the newspaper *El Heraldo*, which amounted to almost less than nothing, and sleeping in the best company possible wherever I happened to be at night. As if the uncertainty of my aspirations and the chaos of my life were not enough, a group of inseparable friends and I were preparing to publish without funds a bold magazine that Alfonso Fuenmayor had been planning for the past three years. What more could anyone desire?

For reasons of poverty rather than taste, I anticipated what would be the style in twenty years' time: untrimmed mustache, tousled hair, jeans, flowered shirts, and a pilgrim's sandals. In a darkened movie theater, not knowing I was nearby, a girl I knew told someone: "Poor Gabito is a lost cause." Which meant that when my mother asked me to go with her to sell the house, there was nothing to prevent me from saying I would. She told me she did not have enough money, and out of pride I said I would pay my own expenses.

At the newspaper where I worked, this was impossible to arrange. They paid me three pesos for a daily commentary and four for an editorial when one of the staff writers was out, but it was barely enough to live on. I tried to borrow money, but the manager reminded me that I already owed more than fifty pesos. That afternoon I was guilty of an abuse that none of my friends would have been capable of committing. At the door of the Café Colombia, next to the bookstore, I approached Don Ramón Vinyes, the old Catalan teacher and bookseller, and asked for a loan of ten pesos. He had only six.

Neither my mother nor I, of course, could even have imagined that this simple two-day trip would be so decisive that the longest and most diligent of lives would not be enough for me to finish recounting it. Now, with more than seventy-five years behind me, I know it was the most important of all the decisions I had to make in my career as a writer. That is to say: in my entire life.

Before adolescence, memory is more interested in the future than the past, and so my recollections of the town were not yet idealized by nostalgia. I remembered it as it was: a good place to live where everybody knew everybody else, located on the banks of a river of transparent water that raced over a bed of polished stones as huge and white as prehistoric eggs. At dusk, above all in December, when the rains had ended and the air was like a diamond, the Sierra Nevada de Santa Marta and its white peaks seemed to come right down to the banana plantations on the other side of the river. From there you could see the Arawak Indians moving in lines like ants along the cliffs of the sierra, carrying sacks of ginger on their backs and chewing pellets of coca to make life bearable. As children we dreamed of shaping balls of the perpetual snow and playing war on the parched, burning streets. For the heat was so implausible, in particular at siesta time, that the adults complained as if it were a daily surprise. From the day I was born I had heard it said, over and over again, that the rail lines and camps of the United Fruit Company had been built at night because during the day the sun made the tools too hot to pick up.

The only way to get to Aracataca from Barranquilla was by dilapidated motor launch through a narrow channel excavated by slave labor during colonial times, and then across the *ciénaga*, a vast swamp of muddy, desolate water, to the mysterious town that was also called Ciénaga. There you took the daily train that had started out as the best in the country and traveled the last stretch of the journey through immense banana plantations, making many pointless stops at hot, dusty villages and deserted stations. This was the trip my mother and I began at seven in the evening on Saturday, February 19, 1950—the eve of Carnival—in an unseasonable rainstorm and with thirty-two pesos that would be just enough to get us home if the house was not sold for the amount she had anticipated.

The trade winds were so fierce that night that I had trouble at the river port convincing my mother to board the boat. She was not being unreasonable. The launches were abbreviated imitations of the steamships out of New Orleans, but with gasoline motors that transmitted the tremors of a high fever to everything on board. There was a small salon that had hooks for hanging hammocks at different levels, and wooden benches where people elbowed their way to a seat with all their baggage, bundles of merchandise, crates of chickens, and even live pigs. There were a few suffocating cabins, each furnished with two army cots, almost always occupied by threadbare little whores who offered emergency services during the crossing. Since by now none of the cabins was free, and we had not brought hammocks, my mother and I took by storm two iron chairs in the central passageway, and there we prepared to spend the night.

Just as she had feared, the squall lashed the reckless ship as we crossed the Magdalena River, which has an oceanic temperament so close to its estuary. In the port I had bought a good supply of the least expensive cigarettes, made of black tobacco and a cheap paper that could have been used to wrap packages, and I began to smoke the way I did in those days, using the butt end of one cigarette to light the next, as I reread *Light in August:* at the time, William Faulkner was the most faithful of my tutelary demons. My mother clung to her rosary as if it were a capstan that could hoist a tractor or hold a plane in the air, and as always she requested nothing for herself but asked for the prosperity and long life of her eleven orphans. Her prayer must have gone where it was supposed to, because the rain became gentle when we entered the channel and the breeze almost was not strong enough to keep the mosquitoes away. Then my mother put away her rosary and for a long while observed in silence the tumultuous life going on around us.

She had been born to a modest family but grew up in the ephemeral splendor of the banana company, from which she at least had retained her rich girl's good education at the Colegio de la Presentación de la Santísima Virgen in Santa Marta. During Christmas vacations she would embroider with her friends, play the clavichord at charity bazaars, and, with an aunt as chaperone, attend the purest dances given by the timid local aristocracy, but as far as anyone knew she had no sweetheart until she married the town telegraph operator against her parents' wishes. Since that time her most conspicuous virtues had been a sense of humor and an iron good health that the sneak attacks of adversity would never defeat over the course of her long life. But her most surprising trait, and also since that time the least likely to be suspected, was the exquisite skill with which she hid her tremendous strength of character: a perfect Leo. This had allowed her to establish a matriarchal power whose domain extended to the most distant relatives in the most unexpected places, like a planetary system that she controlled from her kitchen with a subdued voice and almost without blinking, while the pot of beans was simmering.

Seeing her endure that brutal trip with equanimity, I asked myself how she had been able to subordinate the injustices of poverty with so much speed and mastery. That awful night tested her to the limit. The bloodthirsty mosquitoes, the dense heat, the nauseating reek of the channel mud churned up by the launch as it passed, the frantic back-and-forth of sleepless passengers who could find no place to sit in the crush of people—it all seemed intended to unhinge the most even-tempered nature. My mother bore everything, sitting motionless in her chair, while the girls for hire, dressed up as men or as *manolas*,* reaped the harvest of Carnival in the nearby cabins. One of them had entered and left her cabin, which was right next to my

*The *manolo* was to Madrid what the cockney was to London.

mother's chair, several times, and always with a different client. I thought my mother had not seen her. But the fourth or fifth time in less than an hour that the girl went in and came out, she followed her with a pitying eye to the end of the passageway.

"Poor things," she said with a sigh. "What they have to do to live is worse than working."

This is how matters stood until midnight, when the unbearable vibration and the dim lights in the passageway made me tired of reading, and I sat down beside her to smoke, trying to free myself from the quicksands of Yoknapatawpha County. I had left the university the year before with the rash hope that I could earn a living in journalism and literature without any need to learn them, inspired by a sentence I believe I had read in George Bernard Shaw: "From a very early age I've had to interrupt my education to go to school." I was not capable of discussing this with anyone because I felt, though I could not explain why, that my reasons might be valid only to me.

Trying to convince my parents of this kind of lunacy, when they had placed so much hope in me and spent so much money they did not have, was a waste of time. My father in particular would have forgiven me anything except my not hanging on the wall the academic degree he could not have. Our communication was interrupted. Almost a year later I was still planning a visit to explain my reasons to him when my mother appeared and asked me to go with her to sell the house. But she did not mention the subject until after midnight, on the launch, when she sensed as if by divine revelation that she had at last found the opportune moment to tell me what was, beyond any doubt, the real reason for her trip, and she began in the manner and tone and with the precise words that she must have ripened in the solitude of her sleepless nights long before she set out.

"Your papá is very sad," she said.

So there it was, the inferno I feared so much. She began as she always did, when you least expected it, in a soothing voice that nothing could agitate. Only for the sake of the ritual, since I knew very well what the answer would be, I asked:

"And why's that?"

"Because you've left your studies."

"I didn't leave them," I said. "I only changed careers."

The idea of a thorough discussion raised her spirits.

"Your papá says it amounts to the same thing," she said.

Knowing it was false, I told her:

"He stopped studying too, to play the violin."

"That was different," she replied with great vivacity. "He only played the violin at parties and serenades. If he left his studies it was because he didn't have enough money to eat. But in less than a month he learned telegraphy, which was a very good profession back then, above all in Aracataca."

"I earn a living, too, writing for newspapers," I said.

"You say that so as not to mortify me," she said. "But even from a distance anybody can see the state you're in. So bad I didn't even recognize you when I saw you in the bookstore."

"I didn't recognize you either," I told her.

"But not for the same reason," she said. "I thought you were a beggar." She looked at my worn sandals and added: "Not even any socks."

"It's more comfortable," I said. "Two shirts and two pairs of undershorts: you wear one while the other's drying. What else does anyone need?"

"A little dignity," she said. But she softened this at once by saying in a different tone: "I'm telling you this because of how much we love you."

"I know," I said. "But tell me something: wouldn't you do the same thing in my place?"

"I wouldn't," she said, "not if it meant upsetting my parents."

Recalling the tenacity with which she had broken down her family's opposition to her marriage, I said with a laugh:

"I dare you to look me in the eye."

But she was somber as she avoided my glance because she knew all too well what I was thinking.

"I didn't marry until I had my parents' blessing," she said. "Unwilling, I grant you, but I had it."

She interrupted the discussion, not because my arguments had defeated her but because she wanted to use the toilet and did not trust the state of its hygiene. I spoke to the bosun to find out if there was a more sanitary place, but he explained that he himself used the public lavatory. And concluded, as if he had just been reading Conrad: "At sea we are all equal." And so my mother submitted to the law of equality. Contrary to what I had feared, when she came out it was all she could do to control her laughter.

"Can you imagine," she said to me, "what your papá will think if I come back with a social disease?"

Sometime after midnight we were delayed for three hours because clumps of anemones growing in the channel slowed down the propellers, the launch ran aground in a thicket of mangroves, and many passengers had to stand on the banks and pull it free with the cords of their hammocks. The heat and mosquitoes became excruciating, but my mother eluded them with her instantaneous and intermittent catnaps, famous in our family, which allowed her to rest without losing the thread of the conversation. When we resumed our journey and a fresh breeze began to blow, she was wide awake.

"In any case," she said with a sigh, "I have to bring your papá some kind of answer."

"Don't worry about it," I said with the same innocence. "In December I'll go myself and explain everything to him."

"That's ten months from now," she said.

"Well, after all, it's too late this year to arrange anything at the university," I told her.

"Do you really promise you'll go?"

"I promise." And for the first time I detected a certain tension in her voice:

"Can I tell your papá that you're going to say yes?"

"No," was my categorical answer. "You can't."

It was clear that she was looking for another way out. But I did not give it to her.

"Then it's better if I tell him the whole truth right away," she said, "so it won't seem like a deception."

"All right," I said with relief. "Tell him."

We stopped there, and someone who did not know her very well would have thought it was over, but I knew this was only a pause so that she could catch her breath. A little while later she was sound asleep. A light wind blew away the mosquitoes and saturated the new air with a fragrance of flowers. Then the launch acquired the grace of a sailboat.

We were in the great swamp, the Ciénaga Grande, another of the myths of my childhood. I had crossed it several times when my grandfather, Colonel Nicolás Ricardo Márquez Mejía—his grandchildren called him Papalelo—took me from Aracataca to Barranquilla to visit my parents. "You shouldn't be afraid of the swamp, but you must respect it," he had told me, speaking of the unpredictable moods of its waters, which could behave like either a pond or an untameable ocean. In the rainy season it was at the mercy of storms that came down from the sierra. From December to April, when the weather was supposed to be calm, the north winds attacked it with so much force that each night was an adventure. My maternal grandmother, Tranquilina Iguarán—Mina—would not risk the crossing except in cases of dire emergency, after a terrifying trip when they'd had to seek shelter and wait until dawn at the mouth of the Riofrío.

That night, to our good fortune, it was a still water. From the windows at the prow, where I went for a breath of air a little before dawn, the lights of the fishing boats floated like stars in the water. There were countless numbers of them, and the invisible fishermen conversed as if they were paying a call, for their voices had a phantasmal resonance within the boundaries of the swamp. As I leaned on the railing, trying to guess at the outline of the sierra, nostalgia's first blow caught me by surprise.

On another night like this, as we were crossing the Ciénaga Grande, Papalelo left me asleep in the cabin and went to the bar. I don't know what time it was when, over the drone of the rusted fan and the clattering metal laths in the cabin, the raucous shouts of a crowd woke me. I could not have been more than five years old and was very frightened, but it soon grew quiet again and I thought it must have been a dream. In the morning, when we were already at the dock in Ciénaga, my grandfather stood shaving with his straight razor, the door open and the mirror hanging from the frame. The memory is exact: he had not yet put on his shirt, but over his undershirt he wore his eternal elastic suspenders, wide and with green stripes. While he shaved he kept talking to a man I could still recognize today at first glance. He had the unmistakable profile of a crow and a sailor's tattoo on his right hand, and he wore several solid gold chains around his neck, and bracelets and bangles, also of gold, on both wrists. I had just gotten dressed and was sitting on the bed, putting on my boots, when the man said to my grandfather:

"Don't doubt it for a second, Colonel. What they wanted to do with you was throw you into the water."

My grandfather smiled and did not stop shaving, and with his typical haughtiness he replied:

"Just as well for them they didn't try."

Only then did I understand the uproar of the previous night, and I was very shaken by the idea that someone would have thrown my grandfather into the swamp.

The recollection of this unexplained episode took me by surprise that dawn when I was going with my mother to sell the house, and was contemplating the sierra snows gleaming blue in the first rays of the sun. A delay in the channels allowed us to see in the full light of day the narrow bar of luminous sand that separates the sea from the swamp, where there were fishing villages with their nets laid out to dry in the sun and thin, grimy children playing soccer with balls made of rags. It was astounding to see on the streets the number of fishermen whose arms were mutilated because they had not thrown their sticks of dynamite in time. As the launch passed by, the children began to dive for the coins the passengers tossed to them.

It was almost seven when we dropped anchor in a pestilential marsh a short distance from the town of Ciénaga. Teams of porters, up to their knees in mud, took us in their arms and carried us to the dock, splashing through wheeling turkey buzzards that fought over the unspeakable filth in the quagmire. We were sitting at the tables in the port, eating an unhurried breakfast of delicious mojarra fish from the swamp and slices of fried green plantain, when my mother resumed the offensive in her personal war.

"So, tell me once and for all," she said, not looking up, "what am I going to tell your papá?"

I tried to gain some time to think.

"About what?"

"The only thing he cares about," she said with some irritation. "Your studies."

It was my good fortune that a presumptuous fellow diner, intrigued by the intensity of our conversation, wanted to know my reasons. My mother's immediate response not only intimidated me somewhat but also surprised me, for she was a woman who kept jealous watch over her private life.

"He wants to be a writer," she said.

"A good writer can earn good money," the man replied in all seriousness. "Above all if he works for the government."

I don't know if it was discretion that made my mother change the subject or fear of the arguments offered by this unexpected interlocutor, but the outcome was that the two of them sympathized with each other over the unpredictability of my generation and shared their nostalgic memories. In the end, by following the trail of names of mutual acquaintances, they discovered that we were doubly related through the Cotes and Iguarán lines. In those days this happened to us with two out of three people we met along the Caribbean coast, and my mother always celebrated it as an extraordinary event.

We drove to the railroad station in a one-horse victoria, perhaps the last of a legendary line already extinct in the rest of the world. My mother was lost in thought, looking at the arid plain calcinated by nitrate that began at the mudhole of the port and merged with the horizon. For me it was a historic spot: one day when I was three or four years old and making my first trip to Barranquilla, my grandfather had led me by the hand across that burning wasteland, walking fast and not telling me where we were going, and then, without warning, we found ourselves facing a vast extension of green water belching foam, where an entire world of drowned chickens lay floating.

"It's the ocean," he said.

Disenchanted, I asked him what was on the other shore, and without a moment's hesitation he answered:

"There is no shore on the other side."

Today, after seeing so many oceans front and back, I still

think that was one of his great responses. In any case, none of my earlier images of the ocean corresponded to that sordid mass of water with its nitrate-encrusted beach where the tangled branches of rotting mangroves and sharp fragments of shell made it impossible to walk. It was horrible.

My mother must have had the same opinion of the ocean at Ciénaga, for as soon as she saw it appear to the left of the carriage, she said with a sigh:

"There's no ocean like the one at Riohacha."

On that occasion I told her my memory of the drowned chickens, and like all adults, she thought it was a childhood hallucination. Then she continued her contemplation of each place along the way, and I knew what she thought of them by the changes in her silence. We passed the red-light district on the other side of the railroad tracks, with its little painted houses and rusty roofs and old parrots from Paramaribo that sat on rings hanging from the eaves and called out to clients in Portuguese. We passed the watering site for the locomotives, with its immense iron dome where migratory birds and lost seagulls took shelter to sleep. We rode around the edge of the city without entering it, but we saw the wide, desolate streets and the former splendor of one-story houses with floor-to-ceiling windows, where endless exercises on the piano began at dawn. Without warning, my mother pointed her finger.

"Look," she said. "That's where the world ended."

I followed the direction of her index finger and saw the station: a building of peeling wood, sloping tin roofs, and running balconies, and in front of it an arid little square that could not hold more than two hundred people. It was there, my mother told me that day, where in 1928 the army had killed an undetermined number of banana workers. I knew the event as if I had lived it, having heard it recounted and repeated a thousand times by my grandfather from the time I had a memory: the soldier reading the decree by which the striking laborers were declared a gang of lawbreakers; the three thousand men, women, and children motionless under the savage sun after the officer gave them five minutes to evacuate the square; the order to fire, the clattering machine guns spitting in white-hot bursts, the crowd trapped by panic as it was cut down, little by little, by the methodical, insatiable scissors of the shrapnel.

The train would arrive at Ciénaga at nine in the morning, pick up passengers from the launches and those who had come down from the sierra, and continue into the interior of the banana region a quarter of an hour later. My mother and I reached the station after eight, but the train had been delayed. Still, we were the only passengers. She realized this as soon as she entered the empty car, and she exclaimed with festive humor:

"What luxury! The whole train just for us!"

I have always thought it was a false gaiety to hide her disillusionment, for the ravages of time were plain to see in the condition of the cars. They were old second-class cars, but instead of cane seats or glass windowpanes that could be raised or lowered, they had wooden benches polished by the warm, unadorned bottoms of the poor. Compared to what it had been before, not only that car but the entire train was a ghost of itself. The train had once had three classes. Third class, where the poorest people rode, consisted of the same boxcars made of planks used to transport bananas or cattle going to slaughter, modified for passengers with long benches of raw wood. Second class had cane seats and bronze trim. First class, for government officials and executives of the banana company, had carpets in the corridor and upholstered seats, covered in red velvet, that could change position. When the head of the company took a trip, or his family, or his distinguished guests, a luxury car was coupled to the end of the train, with tinted glass in the windows and gilded cornices and an outdoor terrace with little tables for drinking tea on the journey. I never met a single mortal who had seen the inside of this unimaginable coach. My grandfather had twice been mayor and had a frivolous idea of money, but he traveled in second class only if he was with a female relative. And when asked why he traveled in third class, he would answer: "Because there's no fourth." However, at one time the most memorable aspect of the train had been its punctuality. Clocks in the towns were set by its whistle.

That day, for one reason or another, it left an hour and a half late. When it began to move, very slow and with a mournful creaking, my mother crossed herself but then made an immediate return to reality.

"This train needs to have its springs oiled," she said.

We were the only passengers, perhaps in the entire train, and so far nothing had been of any real interest to me. I sank into the lethargy of *Light in August*, smoking without pause, but with occasional, rapid glances to identify the places we were leaving behind. With a long whistle the train crossed the salt marshes of the swamp and raced at top speed along a bone-shaking corridor of bright red rock, where the deafening noise of the cars became intolerable. But after about fifteen minutes it slowed down and entered the shadowy coolness of the plantations with discreet silence, and the atmosphere grew denser and the ocean breeze was not felt again. I did not have to interrupt my reading to know we had entered the hermetic realm of the banana region.

The world changed. Stretching away on both sides of the track were the symmetrical, interminable avenues of the plantations, along which oxcarts loaded with green stalks of bananas were moving. In uncultivated spaces there were sudden red brick camps, offices with burlap at the windows and fans hanging from the ceilings, and a solitary hospital in a field of poppies. Each river had its village and its iron bridge that the train crossed with a blast of its whistle, and the girls bathing in the icy water leaped like shad as it passed, unsettling travelers with their fleeting breasts.

In the town of Riofrío several Arawak families got on the train carrying packs filled with avocados from the sierra, the most delicious in the country. They made their timid way up and down the car looking for a place to sit, but when the train started to move again the only people left were two white women with an infant, and a young priest. The baby did not stop crying for the rest of the trip. The priest wore an explorer's boots and helmet, and a rough linen cassock darned in square patches like a sail, and he spoke at the same time that the baby cried and always as if he were in the pulpit. The subject of his sermon was the possibility that the banana company would return. Ever since it left nothing else was talked about in the region, and opinion was divided between those who wanted it to come back and those who did not, but everyone considered it a certainty. The priest was against it and expressed his position with so personal an argument that the women thought it was nonsense:

"The company leaves ruin wherever it goes."

It was the only original thing he said but he was not able to explain it, and in the end the woman with the baby confounded him by saying that God could not be in agreement with him.

Nostalgia, as always, had wiped away bad memories and magnified the good ones. No one was safe from its onslaught. Through the train window you could see men sitting in the doorways of their houses, and you only had to look at their faces to know what they were waiting for. Women washing clothes on the gravel beaches watched the train go by with the same hope. They thought every stranger who arrived carrying a briefcase was the man from the United Fruit Company coming back to reestablish the past. At every encounter, on every visit, in every letter, sooner or later the sacramental sentence would make its appearance: "They say the company's coming back." Nobody knew who said it, or when, or why, but nobody doubted it was true.

My mother thought herself free of those ghosts, for when her parents died she had cut all connections to Aracataca. But her dreams betrayed her. At least, when she had one interesting enough to recount at breakfast, it was always related to her nostalgic memories of the banana region. She survived her most difficult times without selling the house, hoping to quadruple the price when the company came back. At last the irresistible pressure of reality had defeated her. But when she heard the priest on the train say that the company was about to return, she made a disconsolate gesture and whispered in my ear:

"What a shame we can't wait just a little longer and sell the house for more money."

While the priest was talking, we passed a town where a

crowd filled the square and a band played a lively concert under the oppressive sun. All those towns always appeared identical to me. When Papalelo would take me to Don Antonio Daconte's brand-new Olympia Cinema, I noticed that the railroad depots in cowboy movies looked like our stations. Later, when I began to read Faulkner, the small towns in his novels seemed like ours, too. And it was not surprising, for they had been built under the messianic inspiration of the United Fruit Company and in the same provisional style of a temporary camp. I remembered them all, with the church on the square and little fairy-tale houses painted in primary colors. I remembered the gangs of black laborers singing at twilight, the shanties on the estates where field hands sat to rest and watch freight trains go by, the ditches where morning found the cutters whose heads had been hacked off in drunken Saturday-night brawls. I remembered the private cities of the gringos in Aracataca and Sevilla, on the other side of the railroad tracks, surrounded, like enormous electrified chicken yards, by metal fences that on cool summer dawns were black with charred swallows. I remembered their slow blue lawns with peacocks and quail, the residences with red roofs and wire grating on the windows and little round tables with folding chairs for eating on the terraces among palm trees and dusty rosebushes. Sometimes, through the wire fence, you could see beautiful languid women in muslin dresses and wide gauze hats cutting the flowers in their gardens with golden scissors.

Even in my childhood it was not easy to distinguish some towns from others. Twenty years later it was even more difficult, because the boards with their idyllic names—Tucurinca, Guamachito, Neerlandia, Guacamayal—had fallen down from the station porticoes, and they were all more desolate than in memory. At about eleven-thirty in the morning the train stopped in Sevilla for fifteen interminable minutes to change locomotives and take on water. That was when the heat began. When we started to move again, the new locomotive kept sending back blasts of soot that blew in the paneless windows and left us covered in black snow. The priest and the women had gotten off in some town without our realizing it, and this heightened my feeling that my mother and I were traveling all alone in a ghost train. Sitting across from me, looking out the window, she had nodded off two or three times, but then she was wide awake and once again asked me the dreaded question:

"So, what shall I tell your papá?"

I thought she would never give up her search for the flank where she could break through my decision. Earlier she had suggested a few compromises that I rejected out of hand, but I knew her withdrawal would not last long. Even so, this new assault took me by surprise. Prepared for another long, fruitless battle, I answered with more calm than I had shown before:

"Tell him the only thing I want in life is to be a writer, and that's what I'm going to be."

"He isn't opposed to your being what you want to be," she said, "as long as you have a degree in something."

She spoke without looking at me, pretending to be less interested in our conversation than in the life passing by the window.

"I don't know why you insist so much when you know very well I won't give in," I said to her.

Then she looked into my eyes and asked, intrigued:

"Why do you believe I know that?"

"Because you and I are just alike," I said.

The train stopped at a station that had no town, and a short while later it passed the only banana plantation along the route that had its name written over the gate: *Macondo*. This word had attracted my attention ever since the first trips I had made with my grandfather, but I discovered only as an adult that I liked its poetic resonance. I never heard anyone say it and did not even ask myself what it meant. I had already used it in three books as the name of an imaginary town when I happened to read in an encyclopedia that it is a tropical tree resembling the ceiba, that it produces no flowers or fruit, and that its light, porous wood is used for making canoes and carving cooking implements. Later, I discovered in the *Encyclopaedia Britannica* that in Tanganyika there is a nomadic people called the Makonde, and I thought this might be the origin of the word. But I never confirmed it, and I never saw the tree, for though I often asked about it in the banana region, no one could tell me anything about it. Perhaps it never existed.

The train would go past the Macondo plantation at eleven o'clock, and stop ten minutes later in Aracataca. On the day I went with my mother to sell the house, the train was an hour and a half late. I was in the lavatory when it began to accelerate, and a dry burning wind came in the broken window, mixing with the din of the old cars and the terrified whistle of the locomotive. My heart pounded in my chest and an icy nausea froze my belly. I rushed out, driven by the kind of fear you feel in an earthquake, and I found my mother imperturbable in her seat, reciting aloud the places she saw moving past the window like instantaneous flashes of the life that once was and never would be again.

"That's the land they sold my father with the story that there was gold on it," she said.

The house of the Adventist teachers passed like a shooting star, with its flower garden and a sign in English over the door: *The sun shines for all.*

"That was the first thing you learned in English," my mother said.

"Not the first thing," I told her, "the only thing."

The cement bridge passed by, and the muddy waters of the irrigation ditch from the days when the gringos diverted the river to bring it to the plantations.

"The neighborhood of the easy women, where the men spent the whole night dancing the *cumbiamba* with rolls of bills burning instead of candles," she said.

The benches along the promenade, the almond trees rusted by the sun, the yard of the little Montessori school where I learned to read. For an instant the total image of the town on that luminous Sunday in February shone through the window.

"The station!" my mother exclaimed. "How the world has changed if nobody's waiting for the train."

Then the locomotive stopped whistling, slowed down, and came to a halt with a long lament.

The first thing that struck me was the silence. A material silence I could have identified blindfolded among all the other silences in the world. The reverberation of the heat was so intense that you seemed to be looking at everything through undulating glass. As far as the eye could see there was no recollection of human life, nothing that was not covered by a faint sprinkling of burning dust. My mother stayed in her seat for a few more minutes, looking at the dead town laid out along empty streets, and at last she exclaimed in horror:

"My God!"

That was the only thing she said before she got off.

While the train stood there I had the sensation that we were not altogether alone. But when it pulled away, with an immediate, heart-wrenching blast of its whistle, my mother and I were left forsaken beneath the infernal sun, and all the heavy grief of the town came down on us. But we did not say anything to each other. The old wooden station with its tin roof and running balcony was like a tropical version of the ones we knew from westerns. We crossed the deserted station whose tiles were beginning to crack under the pressure of grass, and we sank into the torpor of siesta as we sought the protection of the almond trees.

Since I was a boy I had despised those inert siestas because we did not know what to do. "Be quiet, we're sleeping," the sleepers would murmur without waking. Stores, public offices, and schools closed at twelve and did not open again until a little before three. The interiors of the houses floated in a limbo of lethargy. In some it was so unbearable that people would hang their hammocks in the courtyard or place chairs in the shade of the almond trees and sleep sitting up in the middle of the street. Only the hotel across from the station, with its bar and billiard room, and the telegraph office behind the church remained open. Everything was identical to my memories, but smaller and poorer, and leveled by a windstorm of fatality: the decaying houses themselves, the tin roofs perforated by rust, the levee with its crumbling granite benches and melancholy almond trees, and all of it transfigured by the invisible burning dust that deceived the eye and calcinated the skin. On the other side of the train tracks the private paradise of the banana company, stripped now of its electrified wire fence, was a vast thicket with no palm trees, ruined houses among the poppies, and the rubble of the hospital destroyed by fire. There was not a single door, a crack in a wall, a human trace that did not find a supernatural resonance in me.

My mother held herself very erect as she walked with her light step, almost not perspiring in her funereal dress, and in absolute silence, but her mortal pallor and sharpened profile revealed what was happening to her on the inside. At the end of the levee we saw the first human being: a tiny woman with an impoverished air who appeared at the corner of Jacobo Beracaza and walked beside us holding a small pewter pot whose ill-fitting lid marked the rhythm of her step. My mother whispered without looking at her:

"It's Vita."

I had recognized her. From the time she was a small girl she had worked in my grandparents' kitchen, and no matter how much we had changed she would have recognized us if she had deigned to look at us. But no: she walked in another world. Even today I ask myself if Vita had not died long before that day.

When we turned the corner, the dust burned my feet through the weave of my sandals. The feeling of being forsaken became unbearable. Then I saw myself and I saw my mother, just as I saw, when I was a boy, the mother and sister of the thief whom María Consuegra had killed with a single shot one week earlier, when he tried to break into her house.

At three in the morning the sound of someone trying to force the street door from the outside had wakened her. She got up without lighting the lamp, felt around in the armoire for an archaic revolver that no one had fired since the War of a Thousand Days, and located in the darkness not only the place where the door was but also the exact height of the lock. Then she aimed the weapon with both hands, closed her eyes, and squeezed the trigger. She had never fired a gun before, but the shot hit its target through the door.

He was the first dead person I had seen. When I passed by at seven in the morning on my way to school, the body was still lying on the sidewalk in a patch of dried blood, the face destroyed by the lead that had shattered its nose and come out one ear. He was wearing a sailor's T-shirt with colored stripes and ordinary trousers held up by a rope instead of a belt, and he was barefoot. At his side, on the ground, they found the homemade picklock with which he had tried to jimmy the lock.

The town dignitaries came to María Consuegra's house to offer her their condolences for having killed the thief. I went that night with Papalelo, and we found her sitting in an armchair from Manila that looked like an enormous wicker peacock, surrounded by the fervor of her friends who listened to the story she had repeated a thousand times. Everyone agreed with her that she had fired out of sheer fright. It was then that my grandfather asked her if she had heard anything after the shot, and she answered that first she had heard a great silence, then the metallic sound of the picklock falling on the cement, and then a faint, anguished voice: "Mother, help me!" María Consuegra, it seemed, had not been conscious of this heartbreaking lament until my grandfather asked her the question. Only then did she burst into tears.

This happened on a Monday. On Tuesday of the following week, during siesta, I was playing tops with Luis Carmelo Correa, my oldest friend in life, when we were surprised by the sleepers waking before it was time and looking out the windows. Then we saw in the deserted street a woman dressed in strict mourning and a girl about twelve years old who was carrying a bouquet of faded flowers wrapped in newspaper. They protected themselves from the burning sun with a black umbrella and were quite oblivious to the effrontery of the people who watched them pass by. They were the mother and younger sister of the dead thief, bringing flowers for his grave.

That vision pursued me for many years, like a single dream that the entire town watched through its windows as it passed, until I managed to exorcise it in a story. But the truth is that I did not become aware of the drama of the woman and the girl, or their imperturbable dignity, until the day I went with my mother to sell the house and surprised myself walking down the same deserted street at the same lethal hour.

"I feel as if I were the thief," I said.

My mother did not understand me. In fact, when we passed the house of María Consuegra she did not even glance at the door where you could still see the patched bullet hole in the wood. Years later, recalling that trip with her, I confirmed that she did remember the tragedy but would have given her soul to forget it. This was even more evident when we passed the house where Don Emilio, better known as the Belgian, had lived, a veteran of the First World War who had lost the use of both legs in a minefield in Normandy and who, one Pentecostal Sunday, had escaped the torments of memory with the aromatic fumes of gold cyanide. I was no older than six, but I remember as if it were yesterday the upheaval this news caused at seven in the morning. It was so memorable that when we returned to the town to sell the house, my mother at last broke her silence after twenty years.

"The poor Belgian," she said with a sigh, "just as you said, and he never played chess again."

Our intention was to go straight to the house. But when we were no more than a block away, my mother stopped without warning and turned the corner.

"It's better if we go this way," she said. And since I wanted to know why, she answered: "Because I'm afraid."

This was how I learned the reason for my nausea: it was fear, not only of confronting my ghosts but fear of everything. And so we walked down a parallel street, making a detour whose only purpose was to avoid passing our house. "I wouldn't have had the courage to see it without talking to somebody first," my mother would tell me afterward. That is what she did. Almost dragging me along, she walked unannounced into the pharmacy of Dr. Alfredo Barboza, a corner house less than a hundred paces from ours.

Adriana Berdugo, the pharmacist's wife, was so absorbed in working at her primitive hand-cranked Domestic sewing machine that she did not know my mother was standing in front of her; my mother said, almost in a whisper:

"Comadre."

Adriana looked up, her eyes rarefied by the thick lenses of

the farsighted, then she took off her glasses, hesitated for a moment, and jumped up with a sob, her arms open wide:

"Ay, Comadre!"

My mother was already behind the counter, and without saying anything else they embraced and wept. I stood watching them from the other side of the counter, not knowing what to do, shaken by the certainty that this long embrace with its silent tears was something irreparable that was happening forever in my own life.

The pharmacy had been the leading one in the days of the banana company, but all that was left of the old bottles and jars in the empty cabinets were a few porcelain flagons marked with gilt letters. The sewing machine, the pharmaceutical balance, the caduceus, the clock with the pendulum that still moved, the linocut of the Hippocratic Oath, the rickety rocking chairs, all the things I had seen as a boy were still the same, and in the same place, but transfigured by the rust of time.

Adriana herself was a victim. Although she wore a dress with large tropical flowers, as she once had, you could detect almost nothing of the impulsiveness and mischief that had made her famous well into her maturity. The only thing about her that was still intact was the odor of valerian that drove cats mad and that I continued to recall for the rest of my life with a feeling of calamity.

When Adriana and my mother had no more tears left, we heard a thick, short cough behind the thin wooden partition that separated us from the back of the store. Adriana recovered something of her charm from another time and spoke so that she could be heard through the partition.

"Doctor," she said, "guess who's here."

From the other side the rasping voice of a hard man asked without interest:

"Who?"

Adriana did not answer but signaled to us to go into the back room. A childhood terror paralyzed me on the spot, and my mouth filled with a livid saliva, but I walked with my mother into the crowded space that once had been the pharmacy's laboratory, and had been outfitted as an emergency bedroom. There was Dr. Alfredo Barboza, older than all the old men and animals on land and in the water, lying faceup on his eternal hemp hammock, without shoes, and wearing his legendary pajamas of raw cotton that looked more like a penitent's tunic. He was staring up at the ceiling, but when he heard us come in he turned his head and fixed his limpid yellow eyes on us until he recognized my mother at last.

"Luisa Santiaga!" he exclaimed.

He sat up in the hammock with the fatigue of an old piece of furniture, became altogether humanized, and greeted us with a rapid squeeze of his burning hand. He noticed my surprise and told me: "I've had a fever for a year." Then he left the hammock, sat on the bed, and said to us in a single breath:

"You cannot imagine what this town has gone through."

That single sentence, which summarized an entire life, was enough for me to see him as what he may always have been: a sad, solitary man. He was tall, thin, with beautiful hair, the color of metal, that had been cut with indifference, and intense yellow eyes that had been the most fearsome of my childhood terrors. In the afternoon, on our way home from school, we would go up to his bedroom window, attracted by the fascination of fear. There he was, swaying in the hammock with violent lurches to ease the heat he felt. The game consisted in staring at him until he realized we were there and turned without warning to look at us with his burning eyes.

I had seen him for the first time when I was five or six years old, one morning when I sneaked into the backyard of his house with some classmates to steal the enormous mangoes from his trees. Then the door of the wooden outhouse standing in one corner of the yard opened and out he came, fastening his linen underdrawers. I saw him as an apparition from the next world in his white hospital nightshirt, pale and bony and with those yellow hellhound's eyes that looked at me forever. The others escaped through openings in the fence, but I was petrified by his unmoving eyes. He stared at the mangoes I had just pulled from the tree and extended his hand toward me.

"Give them to me!" he ordered, and he added as he looked

me up and down with great contempt: "Miserable backyard thief!"

I tossed the mangoes at his feet and escaped in terror.

He was my personal phantom. If I was alone, I would go far out of my way not to pass by his house. If I was with adults, I dared a furtive glance at the pharmacy. I would see Adriana serving her life sentence at the sewing machine behind the counter, and I would see him through the bedroom window swinging with great lurches in the hammock, a sight that was enough to make my hair stand on end.

He had come to town at the beginning of the century, one of the countless Venezuelans who managed to escape the savage despotism of Juan Vicente Gómez by crossing the border in La Guajira. The doctor had been one of the first to be driven by two contrary forces: the ferocity of the despot in his country, and the illusion of the banana bonanza in ours. From the time of his arrival he acquired a reputation for his clinical eye—as they used to say then—and his soul's good manners. He was one of the most frequent visitors to my grandparents' house, where the table was always set without knowing who was arriving on the train. My mother was godmother to his oldest child, whom my grandfather taught to defend himself. I grew up among them, as I continued to grow up later among the exiles from the Spanish Civil War.

The last vestiges of fear that this forgotten outcast had caused in me as a child dissipated as my mother and I, sitting next to his bed, listened to the details of the tragedy that had crushed the town. He had a power of evocation so intense that each thing he recounted seemed to become visible in the room rarefied by heat. The origin of all the misfortunes, of course, had been the massacre of the workers by the forces of law and order, but doubts still persisted regarding the historical truth: three dead, or three thousand? Perhaps there had not been so many, he said, but people raised the number according to their own grief. Now the company had gone forever.

"The gringos are never coming back," he concluded.

The only certainty was that they took everything with them: money, December breezes, the bread knife, thunder at three in the afternoon, the scent of jasmines, love. All that remained were the dusty almond trees, the reverberating streets, the houses of wood and roofs of rusting tin with their taciturn inhabitants, devastated by memories.

The first time the doctor paid attention to me that afternoon was when he saw me surprised by the sharp crackle like a scattered rain shower on the tin roof. "It's the turkey buzzards," he told me. "They spend the whole day walking on the roofs." Then he pointed with a languid index finger toward the closed door and concluded:

"At night it's worse, because you can hear the dead wandering up and down those streets."

He invited us to lunch and there was no reason not to accept, since the sale of the house needed only to be formalized. The tenants were the buyers, and the details had been agreed upon by telegram. Would we have time?

"More than enough," said Adriana. "Now nobody even knows when the train comes back."

And so we shared with them a local meal whose simplicity had nothing to do with poverty but with a regimen of sobriety that he practiced and advocated not only for the table but for all of life's activities. From the moment I tasted the soup I had the sensation that an entire sleeping world was waking in my memory. Tastes that had been mine in childhood and that I had lost when I left the town reappeared intact with each spoonful, and they gripped my heart.

From the beginning of the conversation with the doctor I felt the same age I had been when I mocked him through the window, and so he intimidated me when he spoke to me with the same seriousness and affection he used with my mother. When I was a boy, in difficult situations, I tried to hide my confusion behind a rapid, continual blinking of my eyes. That uncontrollable reflex returned without warning when the doctor looked at me. The heat had become unbearable. I remained on the margins of the conversation for a while, asking myself how it was possible that this affable and nostalgic old man had been the terror of my childhood. Then, after a long pause and some trivial reference, he looked at me with a grandfather's smile.

"So you're the great Gabito," he said. "What are you studying?"

I hid my confusion with a spectral recounting of my studies: a secondary-school baccalaureate degree completed with good grades at a government boarding school, two years and a few months of chaotic law, and empirical journalism. My mother listened and immediately sought the doctor's support.

"Imagine, Compadre," she said, "he wants to be a writer."

The doctor's eyes shone in his face.

"Comadre, how wonderful!" he said. "It's a gift from heaven." And he turned to me: "Poetry?"

"Novels and stories," I told him, my heart in my mouth.

He became enthusiastic:

"Have you read *Doña Bárbara*?"

"Of course," I replied, "and almost everything else by Rómulo Gallegos."

As if revived by a sudden enthusiasm, he told us that he had met him when he delivered a lecture in Maracaibo, and he seemed a worthy author of his books. The truth is, at that moment, with my fever of 104 degrees for the sagas of Mississippi, I was beginning to see the seams in our native novel. But such easy and cordial communication with the man who had been the terror of my childhood seemed like a miracle to me, and I preferred to go along with his enthusiasm. I spoke to him about "La Jirafa," or "The Giraffe"—my daily commentary in *El Heraldo*—and offered him the news that very soon we intended to publish a magazine for which we had great hopes. Feeling more sure of myself, I told him about the project and even gave him its proposed name: *Crónica*.

He scrutinized me from head to toe.

"I don't know how you write," he said, "but you already talk like a writer."

My mother hurried to explain the truth: no one was opposed to my being a writer as long as I pursued academic studies that would give me a firm foundation. The doctor minimized everything and spoke about the writer's career. He too had wanted one, but his parents, with the same arguments she was using, had obliged him to study medicine when they failed to make him a soldier.

"And look, Comadre," he concluded. "I'm a doctor, and here I am, not knowing how many of my patients have died by the will of God and how many because of my medicines."

My mother felt lost.

"The worst thing," she said, "is that he stopped studying law after all the sacrifices we made to support him."

But the doctor thought this was splendid proof of an over-whelming vocation: the only force capable of competing with the power of love. And more than any other the artistic vocation, the most mysterious of all, to which one devotes one's entire life without expecting anything in return.

"It is something that one carries inside from the moment one is born, and opposing it is the worst thing for one's health," he said. And he put on the finishing touches with the enchanting smile of an irredeemable Mason: "A priest's vocation must be like this."

I was dazzled by the manner in which he explained what I had never been able to clarify. My mother must have felt it too, because she looked at me in slow silence and surrendered to her fate.

"What will be the best way to tell all this to your papá?" she asked me.

"The way we just heard it," I said.

"No, that won't do any good," she said. And after more reflection she concluded: "But don't you worry, I'll find a good way to tell him."

I do not know if she did, or if she did something else, but that was the end of the debate. The clock told the hour with two bell strokes like two drops of glass. My mother gave a start. "My God," she said. "I had forgotten why we came." And she rose to her feet:

"We have to go."

The first sight of the house, just across the street, had very little to do with my memory and nothing at all with my nostalgia. The two tutelary almond trees that for years had been an unequivocal sign of identity had been cut down to the roots and the house left exposed to the elements. What remained beneath the fiery sun had no more than thirty meters of facade: one half of adobe with a tile roof that made you think of a dollhouse, and the other half of rough planks. My mother gave a few slow taps on the closed door, then some louder ones, and she asked through the window:

"Is anybody home?"

The door opened just a little, in a very hesitant way, and from the shadows a woman asked:

"What can I do for you?"

My mother responded with an authority that may have been unconscious:

"I'm Luisa Márquez."

Then the street door opened all the way, and a pale, bony woman dressed in mourning looked out at us from another life. At the back of the living room, an older man rocked in an invalid's chair. These were the tenants who after many years had proposed buying the house, but they did not have the look of buyers, and the house was in no condition to interest anyone. According to the telegram my mother had received, the tenants agreed to pay half the price in cash, for which she would sign a receipt, and pay the rest when the deeds were signed over the course of the year, but nobody remembered arranging a visit. After a long conversation among the deaf, the only thing made clear was that no agreement existed. Overwhelmed by this folly and the dreadful heat, my mother, bathed in sweat, glanced around her and let escape with a sigh:

"This poor house can't last much longer."

"It's worse than that," said the man. "If it hasn't fallen down around us it's because of what we've spent to maintain it."

They had a list of pending repairs in addition to others that had been deducted from the rent, to the point where we were the ones who owed them money. My mother, who always cried without difficulty, was also capable of a fearsome courage in facing life's snares. She argued well, but I did not intervene because after the first stumbling block I understood that the buyers were right. Nothing was clear in the telegram regarding the date and manner of the sale, yet it was understood that it had been arranged. It was a situation typical of the family's conjectural vocation. I could imagine how the decision had been made, at the lunch table and at the very moment the telegram arrived. Not counting me, there were ten brothers and sisters with the same rights. In the end, my mother scraped together a few pesos here and a few there, packed her schoolgirl's bag, and left with nothing but her return passage.

My mother and the woman went over everything again from the beginning, and in less than half an hour we had reached the conclusion that there would be no deal. Among other irremediable reasons because we had not remembered a lien against the house that would not be taken care of until many years later, when a firm sale was made at last. And so when the woman tried to repeat one more time the same vicious argument, my mother used drastic measures in her unappealable manner.

"The house is not for sale," she said. "Let's remember that we were born here, and here we'll all die."

We spent the rest of the afternoon, until the return train arrived, collecting nostalgic memories in the spectral house. All of it was ours, but only the rented portion that faced the street, where my grandfather's offices had been, was in use. The rest was a shell of decaying walls and rusted tin roofs at the mercy of lizards. My mother, taken aback in the doorway, exclaimed in a categorical way:

"This isn't the house!"

But she did not say which one it was, for in the course of my childhood it was described in so many different ways that there were at least three houses that changed shape and direction according to the person who was speaking. The original, according to what I heard my grandmother say in her disparaging way, was an Indian hut. The second, constructed by my grandparents, was made of cane and mud with a roof of bitter palm, and it had a large, well-lit living room, a dining room like a terrace with gaily colored flowers, two bedrooms, a courtyard with a gigantic chestnut tree, a well-tended vegetable garden, and a corral where the goats lived in peaceful fellowship with the pigs and chickens. According to the most frequent version, this house was reduced to ashes by fireworks that fell on the palm roof during the celebrations one July 20, Independence Day, of who knows which year of so many different wars. All that remained were the cement floors and the suite of two rooms with a door to the street where Papalelo had his offices on the several occasions when he was a public official.

On the still-warm ruins the family built its definitive shelter. A linear house with eight successive rooms along a hallway with an alcove filled with begonias where the women in the family would sit to embroider on frames and talk in the cool of the evening. The rooms were simple and did not differ from one another, but a single glance was enough for me to know that in each of their countless details lay a crucial moment of my life.

The first room served as a reception room and personal office for my grandfather. It had a rolltop desk, a padded swivel chair, an electric fan, and an empty bookcase with a single enormous, tattered book: a dictionary of the Spanish language. Right next to it was the workshop where my grandfather spent his best hours making the little gold fish with articulated bodies and tiny emerald eyes, which provided him with more joy than food. Certain notable personages were received there, in particular politicians, unemployed public officials, and war veterans. Among them, on different occasions, two historic visitors: Generals Rafael Uribe Uribe and Benjamín Herrera, both of whom had lunch with the family. But what my grandmother remembered about Uribe Uribe for the rest of her life was his moderation at the table: "He ate like a bird."

Because of our Caribbean culture, the space shared by the office and workshop was forbidden to women, just as the town taverns were forbidden to them by law. Still, in time it was turned into a hospital room where Aunt Petra died and Wenefrida Márquez, Papalelo's sister, endured the last months of a long illness. That initiated the hermetic paradise of the many resident and transient women who passed through the house during my childhood. I was the only male who enjoyed the privileges of both worlds.

The dining room was simply a widened section of the hallway with the alcove where the women of the house sat to sew, and a table for sixteen expected or unexpected diners who would arrive every day on the noon train. From there my mother contemplated the broken pots of begonias, the rotted stubble, the trunk of the jasmine plant eaten away by ants, and she recovered her breath.

"Sometimes we couldn't breathe because of the jasmines' hot perfume," she said, looking at the brilliant sky, and she sighed with all her heart. "But what I've missed most since then is the three o'clock thunder."

That moved me, because I also remembered the single crash like a torrent of stones that woke us from our siesta, but I never had been aware that it happened only at three.

After the hallway there was a parlor reserved for special occasions, while ordinary visitors were greeted with cold beer in the office if they were men, or in the hallway with the begonias if they were women. Then began the mythic world of the bedrooms. First my grandparents' room, with a large door to the garden, and a woodcut of flowers with the date of construction: 1925. There, out of the blue, my mother gave me the most unexpected surprise with a triumphant emphasis:

"Here's where you were born!"

I had not known that before, or I had forgotten it, but in the next room we found the crib where I slept until I was four years old and that my grandmother kept forever. I had forgotten it, but as soon as I saw it I remembered myself in the overalls with little blue flowers that I was wearing for the first time, screaming for somebody to come and take off my diapers that were filled with shit. I could barely stand as I clutched at the bars of the crib that was as small and fragile as Moses' basket. This has been a frequent cause of discussion and joking among relatives and friends, for whom my anguish that day seems too rational for one so young. Above all when I have insisted that the reason for my suffering was not disgust at my own filth but fear that I would soil my new overalls. That is, it was not a question of hygienic prejudice but esthetic concern, and because of the manner in which it persists in my memory, I believe it was my first experience as a writer.

In that bedroom there was also an altar with life-size saints, more realistic and gloomy than those of the Church. Aunt Francisca Simodosea Mejía always slept there, a first cousin of my grandfather's whom we called Aunt Mama, who had lived in the house as its lady and mistress since the death of her parents. I slept in a hammock off to the side, terrified by the blinking of the saints in the light of the perpetual lamp that was not extinguished until everyone had died, and my mother slept there, too, when she was single, tormented by her terror of the saints.

At the end of the hallway there were two rooms that were forbidden to me. In the first lived my cousin Sara Emilia Márquez, a daughter my uncle Juan de Dios had fathered before he was married, who was brought up by my grandparents. In addition to a natural distinction that was hers from the time she was very little, she had a strong personality that woke my first literary appetites with a wonderful collection of stories, illustrated in full color and published by Calleja, to which she never gave me access for fear I would leave it in disarray. It was my first bitter frustration as a writer.

The last room was a repository for old furniture and trunks that sparked my curiosity for years but which I was never allowed to explore. Later I learned that also stored there were the seventy chamber pots my grandparents bought when my mother invited her classmates to spend their vacations in the house.

Facing these two rooms, along the same hallway, was the large kitchen with primitive portable ovens of calcinated stone, and my grandmother's large work oven, for she was a professional baker and pastry chef whose little candy animals saturated the dawn with their succulent aroma. This was the realm of the women who lived or served in the house, and they sang in a chorus with my grandmother as they helped her in her many tasks. Another voice was that of Lorenzo el Magnífico, the hundred-year-old parrot inherited from my great-grandparents, who would shout anti-Spanish slogans and sing songs from the War for Independence. He was so shortsighted that he had fallen into a pot of stew and was saved by a miracle because the water had only just begun to heat. One July 20, at three in the afternoon, he roused the house with shrieks of panic:

"The bull, the bull! The bull's coming!"

Only the women were in the house, for the men had gone to the local bullfight held on the national holiday, and they thought the parrot's screams were no more than a delirium of his senile dementia. The women of the house, who knew how to talk to him, understood what he was shouting only when a wild bull that had escaped the bull pens on the square burst into the kitchen, bellowing like a steamship and in a blind rage charging the equipment in the bakery and the pots on the stoves. I was going in the opposite direction when the gale of terrified women lifted me into the air and took me with them into the storeroom. The bellowing of the runaway bull in the kitchen and the galloping of his hooves on the cement floor of the hallway shook the house. Without warning he appeared at a ventilation skylight, and the fiery panting of his breath and his large reddened eyes froze my blood. When his handlers succeeded in taking him back to the bull pen, the revelry of the drama had already begun in the house and would last more than a week, with endless pots of coffee and sponge cakes to accompany the tale, repeated a thousand times and each time more heroic than the last, of the agitated survivors.

The courtyard did not seem very large, but it had a great variety of trees, an uncovered bath with a cement tank for rain-water, and an elevated platform that one reached by climbing a fragile ladder some three meters high. The two large barrels that my grandfather filled at dawn with a manual pump were located there. Beyond that was the stable made of rough boards and the servants' quarters, and at the very end the enormous backyard with fruit trees and the only latrine, where day and night the Indian maids emptied the chamber pots from the house. The leafiest and most hospitable tree was a chestnut at the edge of the world and of time, under whose ancient branches more than two colonels retired from the many civil wars of the previous century must have died while urinating.

The family had come to Aracataca seventeen years before my birth, when the United Fruit Company began its intrigues to take control of the banana monopoly. They brought their son Juan de Dios, who was twenty-one, and their two daughters, Margarita María Miniata de Alacoque, who was nineteen, and Luisa Santiaga, my mother, who was five. Before her they had lost twin girls by miscarriage four months into the pregnancy. When she had my mother, my grandmother announced that she had given birth for the last time, for she was now forty-two years old. Almost half a century later, at the same age and under identical circumstances, my mother said the same thing when her eleventh child, Eligio Gabriel, was born.

The move to Aracataca was seen by my grandparents as a journey into forgetting. In their service they brought two Goajiro Indians—Alirio and Apolinar—and an Indian woman—Meme—purchased in their own region for a hundred pesos each when slavery had already been abolished. The colonel, pursued by sinister remorse for having killed a man in an affair of honor, brought everything necessary for recreating the past as far away as possible from his bad memories. He had seen the area many years earlier in a campaign, when he passed through on his way to Ciénaga, and in his capacity as quartermaster general he was present at the signing of the Treaty of Neerlandia.

The new house did not give them back their tranquility, because his remorse was so pernicious it would still infect an errant great-great-grandson. The most frequent and intense evocations, with which we had shaped an ordered version of events, were those of my grandmother Mina, who by this time was blind and half crazed. However, in the midst of implacable gossip regarding the imminent tragedy, she was the only one who did not hear about the duel until after it had been fought.

The drama took place in Barrancas, a peaceful and prosperous town in the foothills of the Sierra Nevada, where the colonel learned the goldsmith's craft from his father and grandfather, and where he had returned to live when the peace treaties had been signed. His adversary was a giant sixteen years younger than he, a dyed-in-the-wool Liberal like him, a militant Catholic and a poor farmer who had recently married and had two children and a good man's name: Medardo Pacheco. The saddest thing for the colonel must have been that it was not any of the numerous faceless enemies he had confronted on battlefields but an old friend, ally, and fellow soldier in the War of a Thousand Days whom he had to fight to the death when both of them believed that peace had been won.

This was the first incident from real life that stirred my writer's instincts, and I still have not been able to exorcise it. Ever since I gained the use of my reason, I had been aware of the magnitude and weight that the drama had in our house, but its details remained foggy. My mother, who had just turned three, always remembered it as an improbable dream. In front of me the adults would complicate the story to confuse me, and I never could assemble the complete puzzle because everyone, on both sides, would place the pieces in their own way. The most reliable version was that Medardo Pacheco's mother had provoked him into avenging her honor, which had been offended by a base remark attributed to my grandfather. He denied it, saying it was a lie, and gave public explanations to those who had been offended, but Medardo Pacheco persisted in his ill will and then moved from offended to offender with a serious insult to my grandfather concerning his conduct as a Liberal. I never found out what it was. His honor wounded, my grandfather challenged him to a fight to the death, without a fixed date.

An exemplary indication of the colonel's nature was the time he allowed to pass between the challenge and the duel. He arranged his affairs with absolute discretion in order to guarantee his family's security in the only choice destiny offered him: death or prison. He began by selling without haste the little he had to live on after the last war: the goldsmith's workshop and a small farm he had inherited from his father, where he raised goats for slaughter and cultivated a field of sugarcane. After six months he put the money he had gotten at the back of a closet and waited in silence for the day he himself had chosen: October 12, 1908, the anniversary of the discovery of America.

Medardo Pacheco lived on the outskirts of town, but my grandfather knew he could not miss the procession of the Virgen del Pilar that afternoon. Before he went out to find him, he wrote a brief, tender letter to his wife in which he told her where he had hidden his money and gave her some final instructions concerning the children's future. He placed it under the pillow they shared, where his wife no doubt would find it when she lay down to sleep, and with no goodbyes of any kind he went out to the encounter with his evil hour.

Even the least valid versions agree that it was a typical Monday in a Caribbean October, with a sad rain, low clouds, and a funereal wind. Medardo Pacheco, dressed for Sunday, had just entered a dead-end alley when Colonel Márquez waylaid him. Both were armed. Years later, in her lunatic ramblings, my grandmother would say: "God gave Nicolasito the opportunity to pardon the life of that poor man, but he didn't know how to take it." Perhaps she thought this because the colonel told her he had seen a flash of regret in the eyes of his adversary, who had been taken by surprise. He also told her that when the enormous body, as big as a ceiba tree, collapsed into the underbrush it emitted a wordless sob, "like a wet kitten." Oral tradition attributed a rhetorical sentence to Papalelo at the moment he turned himself in to the mayor: "The bullet of honor conquered the bullet of power." It is a sentence faithful to the Liberal style of the time, but I have not been able to reconcile it with my grandfather's temperament. The truth is there were no witnesses. An authorized version would have been the legal testimony of my grandfather and his contemporaries from both factions, but if there ever was a file of documents, not even its shadow remains. Of the numerous versions I have heard so far, I have not found two that agreed.

The incident divided the families in town, even the dead man's. One side proposed avenging him, while the others took Tranquilina Iguarán and her children into their houses until the danger of retaliation subsided. These details made so strong an impression on me in my childhood that I not only assumed the weight of ancestral guilt as if it were my own, but even now, as I write this, I feel more compassion for the dead man's family than for my own.

Papalelo was moved to Riohacha for greater safety, and then to Santa Marta, where he was sentenced to a year in prison: the first half in solitary and the second half in the general population. As soon as he was free he traveled with the family for a brief time to the town of Ciénaga, then to Panama, where he had another daughter with a casual lover, and at last to the unhealthy and unwelcoming jurisdiction of Aracataca and a job as a tax collector for the departmental office of finance. Never again was he armed on the street, even in the worst times of the banana violence, and he kept his revolver under the pillow only to defend the house.

Aracataca was very far from being the still water they had dreamed of after the nightmare of Medardo Pacheco. It was born as a Chimila Indian settlement and entered history on its left foot as a remote district without God or law in the municipality of Ciénaga, more debased than enriched by the banana fever. It bears the name not of a town but of a river: *Ara* in the Chimila language, and *Cataca*, the word with which the community recognized its leader. Therefore we natives do not call it Aracataca but use its correct name: Cataca.

When my grandfather tried to awaken the family's enthusiasm with the fantasy that the streets were paved with gold there, Mina had said: "Money is the devil's dung." For my mother it was the kingdom of all terrors. The earliest one she remembered was the plague of locusts that devastated the fields while she was still very young. "You could hear them pass like a wind of stones," she told me when we went to sell the house. The terrorized residents had to entrench themselves in their rooms, and the scourge could be defeated only by the arts of witchcraft.

In any season we would be surprised by dry hurricanes that blew the roofs off houses and attacked the new banana crop and left the town covered in astral dust. In summer terrible droughts vented their rage on the cattle, or in winter immeasurable rains fell that turned the streets into turbulent rivers. The gringo engineers navigated in rubber boats among drowned mattresses and dead cows. The United Fruit Company, whose artificial systems of irrigation were responsible for the unrestrained waters, diverted the riverbed when the most serious of the floods unearthed the bodies in the cemetery.

The most sinister of the plagues, however, was the human one. A train that looked like a toy flung onto the town's burning sands a leaf storm of adventurers from all over the world who took control of the streets by force of arms. The sudden prosperity brought with it excessive population growth and extreme social disorder. It was only five leagues away from the Buenos Aires penal colony, on the Fundación River, whose inmates would escape on weekends to play at terrorizing Aracataca. From the time the palm and reed huts of the Chimilas began to be replaced by the wooden houses of the United Fruit Company, with their sloping tin roofs, burlap windows, and outhouses adorned with vines of dusty flowers, we resembled nothing so much as the raw towns in western movies. In the midst of that blizzard of unknown faces, of tents on public thoroughfares and men changing their clothes in the street, of women sitting on trunks with their parasols opened and mules and mules and mules dying of hunger in the hotel's stables, those who had arrived first became the last. We were the eternal outsiders, the newcomers.

The killings were not only because of Saturday brawls. One afternoon we heard shouts in the street and saw a headless man ride past on a donkey. He had been decapitated by a machete during the settling of accounts on the banana plantations, and his head had been carried away by the icy waters of the irrigation ditch. That night I heard my grandmother give her usual explanation: "Only a Cachaco could do something so horrible."

Cachacos were natives of the altiplano, and we distinguished them from the rest of humanity not only by their languid manners and depraved diction but by their presumption that they were the emissaries of Divine Providence. Their image became so hateful that after the ferocious repression of the banana strikes by soldiers from the interior, we called men in the military not soldiers but Cachacos. We viewed them as the sole beneficiaries of political power, and many of them behaved as if that were true. Only in this way can one explain the horror of the "Black Night of Aracataca," a legendary slaughter with such uncertain traces in popular memory that there is no certain evidence it ever really happened.

It began on a Saturday worse than the others when a respectable townsman whose identity did not pass into history went into a tavern to ask for a glass of water for a little boy whose hand he was holding. A stranger drinking alone at the bar wanted to force the boy to take a drink of rum instead of water. The father tried to stop him, but the stranger persisted until the frightened boy knocked over his drink without meaning to. Without hesitation, the stranger shot him dead.

It was another of the phantoms of my childhood. Papalelo would often remind me of it when we entered the taverns together to have a cold drink, but in a manner so unreal that not even he seemed to believe the story. It must have happened soon after he came to Aracataca, since my mother remembered it only because of the horror it caused in the adults. The only thing known about the aggressor was that he spoke with the affected accent of the Andeans, so that the town's reprisals were directed not only against him but any of the numerous despised strangers who spoke with that same accent. Bands of natives armed with harvesting machetes poured into the streets in the dark, seized the invisible shape they took by surprise in the gloom, and ordered:

"Speak!"

Only because of his diction they hacked him to pieces, not taking into account the impossibility of being accurate when there were so many different ways of speaking. Don Rafael Quintero Ortega, the husband of my aunt Wenefrida Márquez and the most boastful and beloved of Cachacos, was about to celebrate his hundredth birthday because my grandfather had locked him in a pantry until tempers had cooled.

Family misfortunes reached their culmination after two years of living in Aracataca with the death of Margarita María

Miniata, who was the light of the house. For years her daguerreotype hung in the living room, and her name has been repeated from one generation to the next as another of the many indications of family identity. Recent generations do not seem moved by that princess with the shirred skirts, little white boots, and a braid hanging down to her waist, which they will never make consonant with the rhetorical image of a great-grandmother, but I have the impression that beneath the weight of remorse and frustrated hopes for a better world, that state of perpetual alarm was the one that most resembled peace for my grandparents. Until their deaths they continued feeling like strangers no matter where they were.

They were, to be precise, but in the crowds the train brought to us from the world, it was difficult to make immediate distinctions. With the same impulse as my grandparents and their progeny, the Fergussons, the Duráns, the Beracazas, the Dacontes, the Correas had also come in search of a better life. In turbulent avalanches Italians, Canary Islanders, Syrians—whom we called Turks—continued to arrive, filtering through the borders of the Province in search of freedom and other ways of living that they had lost in their homelands. They were of every condition and class. Some were escapees from Devils Island—the French penal colony in the Guianas—persecuted more for their ideas than for common crimes. One of them, René Belvenoit, a French journalist condemned for political reasons, was a fugitive in the banana region and wrote a masterful book about the horrors of his captivity. Thanks to all of them—good and bad—Aracataca was from the beginning a country without frontiers.

But the unforgettable colony for us was the Venezuelan; in one of their houses two adolescent students on vacation would bathe with bucketsful of water from the icy cisterns of dawn: half a century later, Rómulo Betancourt and Raúl Leoni would be successive presidents of their country. Among the Venezuelans, the closest to us was Miz Juana de Freytes, a striking matron with a biblical gift for narration. The first formal story I knew was "Genoveva of Brabante," which I heard from her along with the masterpieces of world literature that she reduced to children's stories: the *Odyssey*, *Orlando Furioso*, *Don Quixote*, *The Count of Monte Cristo*, and many episodes from the Bible.

My grandfather's lineage was one of the most respectable but also the least powerful. But he was distinguished by a respectability recognized even by the native-born dignitaries of the banana company. It was that of the Liberal veterans of the civil wars who remained there after the last two treaties, following the good example of General Benjamín Herrera, on whose farm in Neerlandia one could hear in the afternoons melancholy waltzes from his peacetime clarinet.

My mother became a woman in that hellhole and filled the space in everybody's heart after typhus carried off Margarita María Miniata. She, too, was sickly. She had spent an uncertain childhood plagued by tertian fevers, but when she was treated for the last one the cure was complete and forever, and her health allowed her to celebrate her ninety-seventh birthday with eleven of her children and four more of her husband's, sixty-five grandchildren, eighty-eight great-grandchildren, and fourteen great-great-grandchildren. Not counting those no one ever knew about. She died of natural causes on June 9, 2002, at eight-thirty in the evening, when we were already preparing to celebrate her first century of life, and on the same day and almost at the same hour that I put the final period to these memoirs.

She was born in Barrancas on July 25, 1905, when the family was just beginning to recover from the disaster of the wars. She was given her first name in honor of Luisa Mejía Vidal, the colonel's mother, who had been dead for a month on the day she was born. She got her second name because it was the day of the apostle Santiago el Mayor, decapitated in Jerusalem. She hid this name for half her life because she thought it masculine and ostentatious, until a disloyal son betrayed her in a novel.

She was a diligent student except for the piano class that her mother imposed on her because she could not conceive of a respectable young lady who was not an accomplished pianist. Luisa Santiaga studied for three years out of obedience and dropped it in a day because of the tedium of daily exercises in the sultry heat of siesta. But the only virtue of use to her in the flower of her twenty years was the strength of her character when the family discovered that she was mad with love for the young and haughty telegraph operator from Aracataca.

The history of their forbidden love was another of the wonders of my youth. Having heard it told so often by my parents—sometimes by both of them together and sometimes by each one alone—I knew almost the entire story when I wrote *Leaf Storm*, my first novel, at the age of twenty-seven, even though I was also aware that I still had a good deal to learn about the art of writing novels. They were both excellent storytellers and had a joyful recollection of their love, but they became so impassioned in their accounts that when I was past fifty and had decided at last to use their story in *Love in the Time of Cholera*, I could not distinguish between life and poetry.

According to my mother's version, they met for the first time at the wake for a child that neither one could identify for me. She was singing in the courtyard with her friends, following the popular custom of singing love songs to pass the time during the nine nights of mourning for innocents. Out of nowhere, a man's voice joined the choir. All the girls turned to stare and were stunned by his good looks. "He's the one we're going to marry," they sang in chorus to the rhythm of their clapping hands. He did not impress my mother, and she said so: "He looked like just another stranger to me." And he was. He had just arrived from Cartagena de Indias after interrupting his medical and pharmaceutical studies for lack of funds, and had begun a somewhat commonplace life in several towns of the region in the recent profession of telegraph operator. A photograph from those days shows him with the equivocal air of an impoverished gentleman. He was wearing a suit of dark taffeta with a four-button jacket, very close-fitting in the style of the day, a high stiff collar and wide tie, and a flat-brimmed straw hat. He also wore fashionable round spectacles with thin wire frames and clear lenses. Those who knew him at the time saw him as a hard-living, womanizing bohemian who nonetheless never drank alcohol or smoked a cigarette in his long life.

That was the first time my mother laid eyes on him. He, on the other hand, had seen her the previous Sunday at eight o'clock Mass, guarded by her aunt, Francisca Simodosea, who had been her companion since her return from school. He had seen them again the following Tuesday, sewing beneath the almond trees at the door to the house, so that on the night of the wake he already knew she was the daughter of Colonel Nicolás Márquez, for whom he had several letters of introduction. After that night she also learned that he was a bachelor with a propensity for falling in love who had an immediate success because of his inexhaustible gift for conversation, his ease in writing verse, the grace with which he danced to popular music, and the premeditated sentimentality with which he played the violin. My mother would tell me that when you heard him playing in the small hours of the morning, the urge to weep was irresistible. His calling card in society had been "After the Ball Is Over," a waltz of consummate romanticism that was part of his repertoire and had become indispensable in his serenades. These amiable safe-conducts and his personal charm opened the doors of the house to him and earned him a frequent place at family lunches. Aunt Francisca, a native of Carmen de Bolívar, adopted him without reservation when she learned he had been born in Sincé, a town near her birthplace. Luisa Santiaga was entertained at social gatherings by his seducer's stratagems, but it never occurred to her that he would want anything more. On the contrary: their good relations were based above all on her serving as a screen for the secret love between him and a classmate of hers, and she had agreed to act as his godparent at the wedding. From then on he called her godmother and she called him godson. It is easy, then, to imagine Luisa Santiaga's surprise one night at a dance when the audacious telegraph operator took the flower from his buttonhole and said to her:

"I give you my life in this rose."

This was not a spontaneous gesture, he told me many times, but after meeting all the girls he had concluded that Luisa Santiaga was the one for him. She interpreted the rose as another of the playful gallantries he used with her friends. To the extent that when she left the dance, she also left the flower somewhere, and he knew it. She'd had only one secret suitor, a luckless poet and good friend who had never touched her heart with his ardent verses. But Gabriel Eligio's rose disturbed her sleep with inexplicable fury. In our first formal conversation about their love, when she already had a good number of children, she confessed to me: "I couldn't sleep because I was angry thinking about him, but what made me even angrier was that the angrier I became the more I thought about him." For the rest of the week it was all she could do to endure the terror that she might see him and the torment that she might not. From the godmother and godson they had once been, they began to treat each other as strangers. One afternoon, as they were sewing beneath the almond trees, Aunt Francisca teased her niece with mischievous guile:

"I heard somebody gave you a rose."

Well, as usual, Luisa Santiaga would be the last to know that the torments of her heart were already common knowledge. In the numerous conversations I had with her and my father, they both agreed that their explosive love had three decisive moments. The first was on a Palm Sunday during High Mass. She was sitting with Aunt Francisca on a bench on the side of the epistolary when she recognized the sound of his flamenco heels on the floor tiles and saw him pass so close that she felt the warm gust of his bridegroom's cologne. Aunt Francisca appeared not to have noticed him, and he appeared not to have noticed them either. But the truth was that it had all been premeditated by him, and he had been following them since they walked past the telegraph office. He remained standing next to the column closest to the door so that he could observe her from the back but she could not see him. After a few intense minutes Luisa Santiaga could not bear the suspense, and she looked over her shoulder toward the door. Then she thought she would die of rage because he was looking at her, and their eyes met. "It was just what I had planned," my father would say with pleasure when he repeated the story to me in his old age.

My mother, on the other hand, never tired of saying that for three days she had not been able to control her fury at falling into the trap.

The second moment was a letter he wrote to her. Not the kind she might have expected from a poet and violinist of furtive serenades, but an imperious note demanding a reply before he traveled to Santa Marta the following week. She did not reply. She locked herself in her room, determined to kill the worm that did not leave her enough breath to live, until Aunt Francisca tried to persuade her to capitulate once and for all before it was too late. In an effort to overcome her resistance, she told Luisa Santiaga the exemplary tale of Juventino Trillo, the suitor who stood guard every night from seven to ten under the balcony of his impossible beloved. She attacked him with every insult that occurred to her, and in the end she stood on the balcony night after night and emptied a chamberpot of urine on his head. But she could not drive him away. After every kind of baptismal assault—moved by the self-sacrifice of that invincible love—she married him. My parents' story did not reach those extremes.

The third moment in the siege was a grand wedding to which both had been invited as patrons of honor. Luisa Santiaga could find no excuse not to attend an event of such importance to her family. But Gabriel Eligio had the same thought, and he attended the celebration prepared for anything. She could not control her heart when she saw him crossing the room with the obvious intention of asking her to dance the first dance. "My blood was pounding so hard in my body I couldn't tell if it was from anger or fear," she told me. He realized this and delivered a brutal blow: "Now you don't have to say yes because your heart is saying it for you."

Without a word, she left him standing in the middle of the room while the music was still playing. But my father understood this in his own way.

"It made me happy," he told me.

Luisa Santiaga could not endure the rancor she felt toward herself when she was awakened before dawn by the strains of the poisoned waltz, "After the Ball Is Over." The first thing she did the next morning was to return all Gabriel Eligio's gifts to him. This undeserved rebuff, and the gossip about her walking away from him at the wedding, like feathers tossed into the air had no winds to bring them back. Everyone assumed it was the inglorious end of a summer storm. This impression was strengthened when Luisa Santiaga suffered a recurrence of the tertian fevers of her childhood, and her mother took her away to recuperate in the town of Manaure, an Edenic spot in the foothills of the sierra. Both always denied having any communication during those months, but this is not very credible, for when she returned, recovered from her ailments, both also seemed to have recovered from their misgivings. My father would say that he went to meet her at the station because he had read the telegram in which Mina announced their return, and when Luisa Santiaga shook his hand in greeting, he felt something like a Masonic sign that he interpreted as a message of love. She always denied this with the same modesty and shyness she brought to her evocations of those years. But the truth is that from then on they were less reticent about being seen together. All she needed was the ending that Aunt Francisca provided the following week while they were sewing in the hallway of begonias:

"Mina knows everything."

Luisa Santiaga always said it was her family's opposition that made her leap across the dikes of the torrent she had kept hidden in her heart since the night she left her suitor standing in the middle of the dance floor. It was a bitter war. The colonel attempted to stay on the sidelines, but he could not elude the blame that Mina threw in his face when she realized he was not as innocent as he appeared. It seemed clear to everyone that the intolerance was not his but hers, when in reality it was inscribed in the law of the tribe, for whom every suitor is an interloper. This atavistic prejudice, whose embers still smolder, has turned us into a vast community of unmarried women and men with their flies unzipped and numerous children born out of wedlock.

Friends were divided, for or against the lovers, according to age, and those who did not have a firm position had one imposed by events. The young became their enthusiastic accomplices. His above all, for he relished his position as the sacrificial victim of social prejudices. The majority of adults, however, viewed Luisa Santiaga as the precious jewel of a rich and powerful family whom a parvenu telegraph operator was courting not for love but self-interest. She herself, once obedient and submissive, confronted her opponents with the ferocity of a lioness that has just given birth. In the most corrosive of their many domestic disputes, Mina lost her temper and threatened her daughter with the bread knife. An impassive Luisa Santiaga stood her ground. When she became aware of the criminal impetus of her wrath, Mina dropped the knife and screamed in horror: "Oh my God!" And placed her hand on the hot coals of the stove as a brutal penance.

Among the powerful arguments against Gabriel Eligio was his status as the love child of an unmarried woman who had given birth to him at the tender age of fourteen after a casual misstep with a schoolteacher. She was called Argemira García Paternina, a slender, free-spirited white girl who had another five sons and two daughters by three different fathers whom she never married or lived with under the same roof. She resided in the town of Sincé, where she had been born, and scratched out a living for her offspring with an independent and joyful spirit that we, her grandchildren, might well have wanted for a Palm Sunday. Gabriel Eligio was a distinguished example of that ragged breed. Since the age of seventeen he'd had five virgin lovers, as he revealed to my mother in an act of penance on their wedding night aboard the hazardous Riohacha schooner as it was lashed by a squall. He confessed that with one of them, when he was eighteen and the telegraph operator in Achí, he'd had a son, Abelardo, who was almost three. With another, when he was twenty and the telegraph operator in Ayapel, he had a daughter a few months old, whom he had never seen and whose name was Carmen Rosa. He had promised the baby's mother that he would come back and marry her, and he had intended to fulfill the commitment until his life changed course because of his love for Luisa Santiaga. He had recognized his older child before a notary and later would do the same with his daughter, but these were no more than byzantine formalities without consequence in the eyes of the law. It is surprising that his irregular conduct could cause moral uneasiness in Colonel Márquez, who had fathered, in addition to his three official children, nine more with different mothers, both before and after his marriage, all of them welcomed by his wife as if they were her own.

It is not possible for me to establish when I first heard about these events, but in any case the transgressions of my forebears did not interest me in the slightest. On the other hand, the names in the family attracted my notice because they seemed unique. First those on my mother's side: Tranquilina, Wenefrida, Francisca Simodosea. Then that of my paternal grandmother: Argemira, and those of her parents: Lozana and Aminadab. Perhaps this is the origin of my firm belief that the characters in my novels cannot walk on their own feet until they have a name that can be identified with their natures.

The arguments against Gabriel Eligio were made worse because he was an active member of the Conservative Party, against which Colonel Nicolás Márquez had fought his wars. The peace declared by the signing of the Neerlandia and Wisconsin accords was only tenuous, for a fledgling centralism was still in power and a good deal of time would have to pass before the Goths and the Liberals stopped baring their teeth at one another. Perhaps the suitor's Conservatism was more a matter of familial contagion than ideological conviction, but for her family it outweighed other attributes of his good character, such as his always keen intelligence and proven integrity.

Papá was a difficult man to see into or to please. He was always very much poorer than he seemed and considered poverty a hateful enemy he could never accept and never defeat. With the same courage and dignity he endured the opposition to his love for Luisa Santiaga, in the back room of the telegraph office in Aracataca, where he hung a hammock for sleeping alone. But next to it he also had a bachelor's cot with well-oiled springs for whatever the night might offer him. At one time I was somewhat tempted by his furtive hunter's ways, but life taught me that it is the most arid form of solitude, and I felt great compassion for him.

Until a short while before his death I would hear him say that on one of those difficult days he had to go with several friends to the colonel's house, and everyone was invited to sit down except him. Her family always denied the story and attributed it to the embers of my father's resentment, or at least to a false memory, but once my grandmother let it slip in the confessional ravings of her almost one hundred years, which did not seem evoked so much as relived.

"There's that poor man standing in the doorway of the living room, and Nicolasito hasn't asked him to sit down," she said with true regret.

Always attentive to her dazzling revelations, I asked who the man was, and her simple reply was:

"García, the one with the violin."

Amid so many absurdities, the one most uncharacteristic of my father was his buying a revolver because of what might happen with a warrior at rest like Colonel Márquez. It was a venerable long-barreled Smith & Wesson .38, with who knows how many previous owners or how many deaths it was accountable for. The only certainty is that he never fired it, not even as a warning or out of curiosity. Years later his oldest children found it with its original five bullets in a cupboard full of useless trash, next to the violin of his serenades.

Gabriel Eligio and Luisa Santiaga were not intimidated by the harshness of her family. At first they met on the sly, in the houses of friends, but when the blockade was closed around her their only communication was by letters sent through ingenious channels. When she was not permitted to attend parties where he might be a guest, they saw each other at a distance. Then the repression became so severe that no one dared defy the wrath of Tranquilina Iguarán, and the lovers disappeared from public view. When not even a crack was left open for furtive letters, they invented the stratagems of the shipwrecked. She managed to hide a greeting card in a cake that someone had ordered for Gabriel Eligio's birthday, and he lost no opportunity to send her false and innocuous telegrams with the real message in code or written in invisible ink. Aunt Francisca's complicity then became so evident, despite her categorical denials, that for the first time her authority in the house was affected, and she was allowed to accompany her niece only when she was sewing in the shade of the almond trees. Then Gabriel Eligio sent messages of love from the window of Dr. Alfredo Barboza, whose house was across the street, using the manual telegraphy of deaf-mutes. She learned it so well that when her aunt's attention wandered she held intimate conversations with her sweetheart. It was only one of the countless tricks devised by Adriana Berdugo, a *comadre* of Luisa Santiaga's and her most inventive and daring accomplice.

These consoling devices would have been enough for them to survive over a slow fire, until Gabriel Eligio received an alarming letter from Luisa Santiaga that obliged him to think in a decisive way. She had written in haste, on toilet paper, giving him the bad news that her parents had resolved to take her to Barrancas, stopping in each town along the way, as a brutal cure for her lovesickness. It would not be the ordinary journey of one bad night aboard the schooner to Riohacha, but the barbarous route along the spurs of the Sierra Nevada, on mules and in carts, across the vast province of Padilla.

"I would rather have died," my mother told me on the day we went to sell the house. And she had in fact tried to die, barring her bedroom door and eating nothing but bread and water for three days, until she was overcome by the reverential terror she felt for her father. Gabriel Eligio realized that the tension had reached its limits, and he made a decision that was also extreme, but manageable. He strode across the street from Dr. Barboza's house to the shade of the almond trees and stopped in front of the two women who waited for him in terror, their work in their laps.

"Please leave me alone for a moment with the señorita," he said to Aunt Francisca. "I have something important to say that only she can hear."

"What insolence!" her aunt replied. "There's nothing that has to do with her that I can't hear."

"Then I won't say it," he said, "but I warn you that you will be responsible for whatever happens."

Luisa Santiaga begged her aunt to leave them alone and took responsibility. Then Gabriel Eligio expressed his view that she should take the trip with her parents, in the manner they chose and for the time it might take, but only on the condition that she give her promise as a solemn oath that she would marry him. She was happy to do so and added on her own account that only death could prevent their marriage.

They both had almost a year to demonstrate the seriousness of their promises, but neither one imagined how much it would cost them. The first part of the journey in a caravan of mule drivers, riding on muleback along the precipices of the Sierra Nevada, took two weeks. They were accompanied by Wenefrida's maid Chon—an affectionate diminutive of Encarnación—who joined the family after they left Barrancas. The colonel knew that steep, rocky route all too well, for he had left a trail of children there on the dissipated nights of his wars, but his wife had chosen it without knowing that, because she had bad memories of the schooner. For my mother, who was riding a mule for the first time, it was a nightmare of naked suns and ferocious downpours, her soul dangling by a thread in the soporific breath that rose from the gorges. The thought of an uncertain sweetheart, with his midnight clothes and sunrise violin, seemed like a trick of the imagination. By the fourth day, incapable of surviving, she warned her mother that she would throw herself over a cliff if they did not return home. Mina, more frightened than her daughter, agreed. But the head drover showed her on the map that returning or continuing would take the same amount of time. Relief came in eleven days, when they saw from the final cornice the radiant plain of Valledupar.

Before the first stage of the journey was over, Gabriel Eligio had secured permanent communication with his wandering sweetheart, thanks to the complicity of the telegraph operators in the seven towns where she and her mother would stay before reaching Barrancas. Luisa Santiaga made her own arrangements, too. The entire Province was saturated with people named Iguarán and Cotes, whose tribal consciousness had the strength of an impenetrable jungle, and she succeeded in bringing them over to her side. This allowed her to maintain a feverish correspondence with Gabriel Eligio from Valledupar, where she spent three months, until the trip ended almost a year later. She had only to pass by each town's telegraph office, and with the complicity of her young and enthusiastic kinswomen she would receive and respond to his messages. Chon, the silent one, played an invaluable role because she carried messages hidden in her clothes without making Luisa Santiaga uneasy or offending her modesty, for she could not read or write, and would die to keep a secret.

Almost sixty years later, when I tried to plunder these memories for *Love in the Time of Cholera*, my fifth novel, I asked my papá if in the professional jargon of telegraph operators there existed a specific word for the act of linking one office to another. He did not have to think about it: *pegging in*. The word is in the dictionary, though not with the specific meaning I needed, but it seemed perfect since communication between different offices was established by connecting a peg on a panel of telegraphic terminals. I never discussed it with my father. But not long before his death he was asked in a newspaper interview if he had ever wanted to write a novel, and he answered that he had but gave it up when I asked him about the verb *pegging in*, because he realized then that the book I was writing was the same one he had planned to write.

On that occasion he also revealed a secret that could have changed the course of our lives. And it was that after six months of traveling, when my mother was in San Juan del César, Gabriel Eligio was told in confidence that Mina had the responsibility of preparing for the definitive return of the family to Barrancas provided the rancor caused by the death of Medardo Pacheco had healed over. It seemed absurd to him, now that the bad times had been left behind and the absolute imperium of the banana company was beginning to resemble the dream of the promised land. But it was also reasonable that the intractability of the Márquez Iguarán family would lead them to sacrifice their own happiness if they could free their daughter from the talons of the hawk. Gabriel Eligio's immediate decision was to request a transfer to the telegraph office in Riohacha, some twenty leagues from Barrancas. The position was not open but they promised to keep his application in mind.

Luisa Santiaga could not determine her mother's secret intentions, but she did not dare deny them either, for she had noticed that the closer they came to Barrancas, the calmer and more peaceful Tranquilina Iguarán seemed. Chon, everyone's confidante, gave her no clues. To get to the truth, Luisa Santiaga told her mother that she would love to stay in Barrancas and live there. The mother had a moment's hesitation but decided not to say anything, and the daughter was left with the impression that she had come very close to the secret. Troubled, she escaped into the destiny of the cards with a street Gypsy who gave her no clues about her future in Barrancas. On the other hand, she did tell her that there would be no obstacle to a long and happy life with a distant man she did not know well, but who would love her until death. Her description of the man returned Luisa Santiaga's soul to her body, for she found many qualities in him that she saw in her beloved, above all in his temperament. At the end the Gypsy predicted without a shred of doubt that she would have six children with him. "I died of fright," my mother said the first time she told me the story, not even imagining that her children would number five more than that. The two of them accepted the prediction with so much enthusiasm that their telegraphic correspondence stopped being a concert of illusory intentions and became methodical, practical, and more intense than ever. They set dates, established means, and devoted their lives to the shared determination to marry without consulting anyone when they met again, wherever and however that might be.

Luisa Santiaga was so faithful to their commitment that in the town of Fonseca she did not think it correct to attend a gala ball without her sweetheart's consent. Gabriel Eligio was in the hammock sweating out a fever of 104 when he heard the signal for an urgent incoming telegram. It was his colleague in Fonseca. To guarantee complete security, she asked who was operating the key at the end of the chain of telegraph offices. More astonished than gratified, her sweetheart transmitted an identifying phrase: "Tell her I'm her godson." My mother recognized the password and stayed at the dance until seven in the morning, when she had to change her clothes in a rush so she would not be late for Mass.

In Barrancas they did not find the slightest trace of animosity toward the family. On the contrary, seventeen years after the misfortune, a Christian spirit of forgiving and forgetting prevailed among the relatives of Medardo Pacheco. They gave mother and daughter so warmhearted a welcome that now it was Luisa Santiaga who thought about the possibility of the family returning to that mountain oasis so different from the heat and dust, the bloodthirsty Saturdays, the decapitated phantoms of Aracataca. She managed to suggest this to Gabriel Eligio, provided he obtained his transfer to Riohacha, and he agreed. However, she also learned at this time that the story of the move was not only without foundation but that no one had wanted it except Mina. This was established in a letter Mina sent to her son Juan de Dios after he wrote to her, frightened of their returning to Barrancas when it was still not twenty years since Medardo Pacheco's death. For he was always so convinced of the inescapability of the law of La Guajira that half a century later he was opposed to his son Eduardo joining the public health service in Barrancas.

Despite all these fears, that was where every knot in the situation was untied in three days. On the Tuesday when Luisa Santiaga confirmed to Gabriel Eligio that Mina did not intend to move to Barrancas, he was informed that the position in Riohacha was now available due to the sudden death of the operator. The next day, Mina emptied the drawers in the pantry looking for poultry shears and happened to open the tin of English biscuits where her daughter hid her love telegrams. Her rage was so great that all she could say to her was one of the celebrated insults she would improvise at her worst moments: "God forgives everything except disobedience." That weekend they traveled to Riohacha to board the Sunday schooner to Santa Marta. Neither one was aware of the awful night of battering February gales: the mother devastated by defeat and the daughter terrified but happy.

Solid ground restored to Mina the composure she had lost when she discovered the letters. The next day she returned alone to Aracataca and left Luisa Santiaga under the protection of her son Juan de Dios, certain she had rescued her from the demons of love. The opposite was true: Gabriel Eligio traveled whenever he could from Aracataca to Santa Marta to see her. Uncle Juanito, who had endured the same intransigence from his parents in his love for Dilia Caballero, had resolved not to take sides in his sister's love affair, but at the moment of truth he found himself trapped between his adoration of Luisa Santiaga and his veneration for his parents, and he took refuge in a formula characteristic of his proverbial goodness: he allowed the sweethearts to see each other outside his house, but never alone or with his knowledge. Dilia Caballero, his wife, who forgave but did not forget, devised for her sister-in-law the same infallible coincidences and masterful stratagems she had used to undermine the vigilance of her in-laws. Gabriel and Luisa began by seeing each other in the houses of friends, but little by little they risked public places that were not very crowded. In the end they dared to talk through the window when Uncle Juanito was not at home, she in the living room and he in the street, faithful to their commitment not to see each other in the house. The window seemed to be made for the purpose of forbidden love, with Andalusian grillwork from top to bottom and a frame of climbing vines that even had its breath of jasmine in the torpor of the night. Dilia had anticipated everything, including the complicity of certain neighbors who would whistle in code to alert the lovers to imminent danger. One night, however, all the precautions failed, and Juan de Dios surrendered to the truth. Dilia took advantage of the occasion to invite the sweethearts to sit in the living room with the windows open so they could share their love with the world. My mother never forgot her brother's sigh: "What a relief!"

At this time Gabriel Eligio received his formal appointment to the telegraph office in Riohacha. Unsettled by a new separation, my mother appealed to Monsignor Pedro Espejo, the vicar of the diocese, in the hope that he would marry them without her parents' consent. The respectability of the monsignor had reached such proportions that many of the faithful confused it with saintliness, and some attended his Masses only to confirm if it was true that at the moment of the Elevation he rose several centimeters off the ground. When Luisa Santiaga asked for his help, he gave yet another indication that intelligence is one of the privileges of saintliness. He refused to interfere in the internal jurisdiction of a family so jealous of its privacy but chose instead to find out in secret about my father's family through the curia. The parish priest in Sincé ignored the liberties taken by Argemira García and responded with a benevolent formula: "This is a respectable though not very devout family." Then the monsignor spoke with the sweethearts, as a couple and as individuals, and wrote a letter to Nicolás and Tranquilina in which he expressed his heartfelt certainty that there was no human power capable of overcoming this obdurate love. My grandparents, defeated by the power of God, agreed to turn the painful page, and they granted Juan de Dios full power to arrange the wedding in Santa Marta. But they did not attend, although they sent Francisca Simodosea to be matron of honor.

My parents married on June 11, 1926, in the Cathedral of Santa Marta, forty minutes late because the bride forgot the date and had to be awakened after eight in the morning. That same night they again boarded the fearful schooner so that Gabriel Eligio could take possession of the telegraph office in Riohacha, and they passed their first night together in chastity, overcome by seasickness.

My mother was so nostalgic about the house where she spent her honeymoon that her older children could have described it room by room as if we had lived there, and even today it continues to be one of my false memories. Yet the first time I went to the peninsula of La Guajira in reality, not long before my sixtieth birthday, I was surprised that the telegraph office building had nothing to do with the one in my memory. And the idyllic Riohacha that I had carried in my heart since childhood, with its saltpeter streets going down to a sea of mud, was nothing more than fantasies borrowed from my grandparents. In fact, now that I know Riohacha, I cannot visualize it as it is but only as I constructed it stone by stone in my imagination.

Two months after the wedding, Juan de Dios received a telegram from my papá announcing that Luisa Santiaga was pregnant. The news shook the very foundations of the house in Aracataca, where Mina had not yet recuperated from her bitterness, and both she and the colonel laid down their weapons so that the newlyweds would come back to stay with them. It was not easy. After a noble, reasoned resistance of several months' duration, Gabriel Eligio agreed to his wife giving birth in her parents' house.

A short while later my grandfather greeted him at the train station with a sentence that remained like a gold frame around the family's historical record: "I am prepared to give you all the satisfactions that may be necessary." My grandmother renovated the bedroom that had been hers until then and installed my parents in it. Over the course of the year, Gabriel Eligio gave up his worthy profession of telegraph operator and devoted his autodidact's talent to a science on the decline: homeopathy. My grandfather, out of gratitude or remorse, arranged with the authorities for the street where we lived in Aracataca to bear the name it still has: Avenida Monsignor Espejo.

That was how and where the first of seven boys and four girls was born on Sunday, March 6, 1927, at nine in the morning and in an unseasonable torrential downpour, while the sky of Taurus rose on the horizon. I was almost strangled by the umbilical cord because the family midwife, Santos Villero, lost control of her art at the worst possible moment. But Aunt Francisca lost even more control, for she ran to the street door shouting as if there were a fire:

"A boy! It's a boy!" And then, as if sounding the alarm: "Rum, he's choking!"

The family supposes that the rum was not for celebrating but for rubbing on the newborn to revive him. Miz Juana de Freytes, who made her providential entrance into the bedroom, often told me that the most serious risk came not from the umbilical cord but from my mother's dangerous position on the bed. She corrected it in time, but it was not easy to revive me, and so Aunt Francisca poured the emergency baptismal water over me. I should have been named Olegario, the saint whose day it was, but nobody had the saints' calendar near at hand, and with a sense of urgency they gave me my father's first name followed by that of José, the Carpenter, because he was the patron saint of Aracataca and March was his month. Miz Juana de Freytes proposed a third name in memory of the general reconciliation achieved among families and friends with my arrival into the world, but in the formal rite of baptism three years later they forgot to include it: Gabriel José de la Concordia.

2

ON THE DAY I went with my mother to sell the house, I remembered everything that had made an impression on my childhood but was not certain what came earlier and what came later, or what any of it signified in my life. I was not really aware that in the midst of the false splendor of the banana company, my parents' marriage was already inscribed in the process that would put the final touches on the decadence of Aracataca. Once I began to remember, I heard—first with a good deal of discretion and then in a loud, alarmed voice—the fateful sentence repeated: "They say the company's leaving." But either nobody believed it, or nobody dared think of the devastation it would bring.

My mother's version had such meager numbers and a setting so abject for the imposing drama I had imagined that it caused a sense of frustration in me. Later, I spoke with survivors and witnesses and searched through newspaper archives and official documents, and I realized that the truth did not lie anywhere. Conformists said, in effect, that there had been no deaths. Those at the other extreme affirmed without a quaver in their voices that there had been more than a hundred, that they had been seen bleeding to death on the square, and that they were carried away in a freight train to be tossed into the ocean like rejected bananas. And so my version was lost forever at some improbable point between the two extremes. But it was so persistent that in one of my novels I referred to the massacre with all the precision and horror that I had brought for years to its incubation in my imagination. This was why I kept the number of the dead at three thousand, in order to preserve the epic proportions of the drama, and in the end real life did me justice: not long ago, on one of the anniversaries of the tragedy, the speaker of the moment in the Senate asked for a minute of silence in memory of the three thousand anonymous martyrs sacrificed by the forces of law and order.

The massacre of the banana workers was the culmination of others that had occurred earlier, but with the added argument that the leaders were marked as Communists, and perhaps they were. I happened to meet the most prominent and persecuted of them, Eduardo Mahecha, in the Modelo Prison in Barranquilla at about the time I went with my mother to sell the house, and I maintained a warm friendship with him after I introduced myself as the grandson of Nicolás Márquez. It was he who revealed to me that my grandfather was not neutral but had been a mediator in the 1928 strike, and he considered him a just man. So that he rounded out the idea I always had of the massacre, and I formed a more objective conception of the social conflict. The only discrepancy among everyone's memories concerned the number of dead, which in any event will not be the only unknown quantity in our history.

So many contradictory versions have been the cause of my false memories. The most persistent is of my standing in the doorway of the house with a Prussian helmet and a little toy rifle, watching the battalion of perspiring Cachacos marching past under the almond trees. One of the commanding officers in parade uniform greeted me as he passed:

"Hello, Captain Gabi."

The memory is clear, but there is no possibility that it is true. The uniform, the helmet, and the toy rifle coexisted, but some two years after the strike and when there no longer were military forces in Cataca. Multiple incidents like this one gave me a bad name in the house for having intrauterine memories and premonitory dreams.

That was the state of the world when I began to be aware of my family environment, and I cannot evoke it in any other way: sorrows, griefs, uncertainties in the solitude of an immense house. For years it seemed to me that this period had become a recurrent nightmare that I had almost every night, because I would wake in the morning feeling the same terror I had felt in the room with the saints. During my adolescence, when I was a student at an icy boarding school in the Andes, I would wake up crying in the middle of the night. I needed this old age without remorse to understand that the misfortune of my grandparents in the house in Cataca was that they were always mired in their nostalgic memories, and the more they insisted on conjuring them the deeper they sank.

In even simpler terms: they were in Cataca but continued living in the province of Padilla, which we still call the Province, with no other information, as if it were the only one in the world. Perhaps without even thinking about it, they had built the house in Cataca as a ceremonial replica of the house in Barrancas, from whose window you could see, on the other side of the street, the melancholy cemetery where Medardo Pacheco lay buried. In Cataca they were well liked and content, but their lives were subject to the servitude of the land where they had been born. They entrenched themselves in their preferences, their beliefs, their prejudices, and closed ranks against everything that was different.

Their closest friends were, before anyone else, those who came from the Province. Their domestic language was the one their grandparents had brought from Spain across Venezuela in the previous century, revitalized by Caribbean localisms, the Africanisms of slaves, and fragments of the Goajiro language that filtered into ours, drop by drop. My grandmother would use it to conceal things from me, not realizing I understood it better than she because of my direct dealings with the servants. I still remember many terms: *atunkeshi*, I'm sleepy; *jamusaitshi taya*, I'm hungry; *ipuwots*, the pregnant woman; *aríjuna*, the stranger, which my grandmother used in a certain sense to refer to the Spaniard, the white man, in short, the enemy. The Goajiro, for their part, always spoke a kind of boneless Castilian with

brilliant flashes, like Chon's own dialect, and a perverse precision that my grandmother forbade her to use because it always
led to an inescapable ambiguity: "The lips of the mouth."

The day was incomplete until they received the news of who
had been born in Barrancas, how many the bull had killed in
the arena in Fonseca, who had been married in Manaure or had
died in Riohacha, and the condition of General Socarrás, who
was very ill in San Juan del César. California apples wrapped in
tissue paper, red snapper frozen in ice, hams from Galicia,
Greek olives were all on sale at bargain prices in the commissary of the banana company. But nothing was eaten in the
house that was not seasoned in the broth of longing: *malanga*
for the soup had to be from Riohacha and corn for the breakfast *arepas* needed to come from Fonseca, goats were raised
with salt from La Guajira, and turtles and lobsters were
brought in live from Dibuya.

And so most of the visitors who arrived every day on the
train came from the Province or had been sent by someone
from there. Always the same family names: Riasco, Noguera,
Ovalle, often crossed with the sacramental tribes of Cotes and
Iguarán. They were passing through, with nothing but a knap-
sack on their back, and though their visits were not announced
it was expected that they would stay for lunch. I have never forgotten my grandmother's almost ritualized phrase when she
entered the kitchen: "We have to make everything, because we
don't know what the people who are coming will like."

That spirit of perpetual evasion was sustained by a geographical reality. The Province had the autonomy of a separate
world and a compact and ancient cultural unity in a fertile
canyon between the Sierra Nevada de Santa Marta and the
Sierra de Perijá, on the Colombian Caribbean. Its communication with the world was easier than with the rest of the country,
for its daily life was identified more with the Antilles because of
easy commerce with Jamaica or Curaçao, and was almost confused with Venezuela's because of a border of open doors that
made no distinctions of class or color. The rust of power barely
reached it from the interior of the country, stewing in its own
broth over a slow fire: laws, taxes, soldiers, bad news incubated

at an altitude of twenty-five hundred meters and eight days of navigation along the Magdalena River in a steamboat fueled by wood.

That insular nature had generated a watertight culture with its own character that my grandparents implanted in Cataca. More than a home, the house was a town. There were always several sittings at the table, but from the time I was three, the first two were sacred: the colonel at the head and I at the corner to his right. The remaining places were occupied first by the men and then by the women, but never at the same time. These rules were broken during the July 20 patriotic holiday, and lunch by shifts lasted until everyone had eaten. At night the table was not laid, but large cups of café con leche were given out in the kitchen, along with my grandmother's exquisite pastries. When the doors were closed, people hung their hammocks where they could, at different levels, even from the trees in the courtyard.

I lived one of the great fantasies of those years one day when a group of men came to the house, dressed alike in gaiters and spurs, and all of them with a cross of ash drawn on their foreheads. They were the sons fathered by the colonel across the entire length of the Province during the War of a Thousand Days, and they had come from their towns almost a month late to congratulate him on his birthday. Before coming to the house they had heard Ash Wednesday Mass, and the cross that Father Angarita drew on their foreheads seemed like a supernatural emblem whose mystery would pursue me for years, even after I became familiar with the liturgy of Holy Week.

Most of them had been born after my grandparents' marriage. After she had heard of their births, Mina wrote their first and family names in a notebook, and in the end, with an awkward indulgence, she included them with all her heart in the family records. But neither she nor anyone else found it easy to distinguish one from the other before that memorable visit, when each of them revealed his peculiar nature. They were serious and hardworking, family men, peaceable people, yet not afraid to lose their heads in the vertigo of drunken revelry. They broke dishes, trampled rosebushes chasing a calf in order to toss it in a blanket, shot chickens for the stew, and set loose a greased pig that ran over the women embroidering in the hallway, but no one lamented these mishaps because of the gusts of joy they brought with them.

With some frequency I continued to see Esteban Carrillo, Aunt Elvira's twin brother, who was skilled in the manual arts and traveled with a toolbox for making repairs as a favor in the houses he visited. With his sense of humor and good memory he filled in numerous gaps in the family history that had seemed impassable to me. In my adolescence I also visited my uncle Nicolás Gómez, an intense blond with reddish freckles who always held in very high esteem his respectable trade as a shopkeeper in the former penal colony at Fundación. Struck by my excellent reputation as a lost cause, he would say goodbye to me with a well-stocked shopping bag for my journey. Rafael Arias always arrived in a hurry on his way to somewhere else, on the back of a mule and in riding clothes, with only enough time to drink a cup of coffee standing in the kitchen. I found the others scattered among the towns in the Province on the nostalgic trips I made later to write my first novels, and I always missed the cross of ash on their foreheads as an incontrovertible sign of family identity.

Years after my grandparents had died and the family manor had been abandoned to its fate, I came to Fundación on the night train and sat at the only food stand open at that hour in the station. There was little left to eat, but the owner improvised a nice dish in my honor. She was witty and obliging, and behind these gentle virtues I thought I could detect the strong character of the women in the tribe. I confirmed this years later: the good-looking proprietor was Sara Noriega, another of my unknown aunts.

Apolinar, the small, solid former slave whom I always recalled as an uncle, disappeared from the house for years, and one afternoon he reappeared for no reason, dressed in mourning in a black suit and an enormous black hat pulled down to his melancholy eyes. As he passed through the kitchen he said that he had come for the funeral, but no one understood him until the next day, when the news arrived that my grandfather had just died in Santa Marta, where he had been taken with great urgency and in secret.

The only one of my uncles who achieved public recognition was the oldest and the only Conservative, José María Valdeblánquez, who had been a senator of the Republic during the War of a Thousand Days and in that capacity was present at the signing of the Liberal surrender at the nearby farm in Neerlandia. Facing him, on the side of the defeated, was his father.

I believe that the essence of my nature and way of thinking I owe in reality to the women in the family and to the many in our service who ministered to my childhood. They had strong characters and tender hearts, and they treated me with the naturalness of the Earthly Paradise. Of the many I remember, Lucía was the only one who surprised me with her youthful perversity when she took me to the alley of the toads and lifted her dress to her waist to show me her copper-colored thatch of hair. But what in reality attracted my attention was the patch of *pinta* that extended along her belly like a map of the world, with purple dunes and yellow oceans. The others seemed like archangels of purity: they changed their clothes in front of me, bathed me when they bathed, sat me on my chamber pot and sat on theirs facing me to relieve themselves of their secrets, their sorrows, their rancors, as if I did not understand, not realizing I knew everything because I tied up the loose ends that they themselves left dangling.

Chon belonged to the servants and to the street. She had come from Barrancas with my grandparents when she was still a girl, had grown up in the kitchen but was assimilated into the family, and had been treated like a chaperoning aunt ever since her pilgrimage to the Province with my infatuated mother. In her final years she moved to her own room in the poorest part of town, simply because she wanted to, and lived by selling on the street, starting at dawn, balls of ground corn for *arepas*, and her peddler's cry became familiar in the silence of the small hours: "Old Chon's chilled dough . . ."

She had a beautiful Indian color and always seemed nothing but skin and bones, and she went barefoot, wearing a white turban and wrapped in starched sheets. Her pace was very slow as she walked down the middle of the street with an escort of tamed, silent dogs who advanced as they circled around her. In the end she became part of the town's folklore. At a Carnival celebration someone appeared as Chon, with her sheets and her vendor's cry, although they could not train a guard of dogs like hers. Her cry of "chilled dough" became so popular that it was the subject of an accordion players' song. One ill-fated morning two wild dogs attacked hers, who defended themselves with so much ferocity that Chon fell to the ground with a fractured spine. She did not survive despite the numerous medical resources my grandfather provided for her.

Another revealing memory from that time was when Matilde Armenta gave birth; she was a laundress who worked in the house when I was about six years old. I went into her room by mistake and found her naked and lying with her legs spread on a canvas bed, howling with pain, surrounded by a disordered and irrational band of midwives who had divided up her body among themselves to help her give birth with tremendous shouts. One wiped the sweat from her face with a damp towel, others held down her arms and legs and massaged her belly to speed up the birth. Santos Villero, impassive in the midst of the disorder, murmured prayers for a calm sea with closed eyes as she seemed to dig between the thighs of the woman in labor. The heat was unbearable in the room filled with steam from the pots of boiling water they had brought in from the kitchen. I stayed in a corner, torn between fear and curiosity, until the midwife pulled out by the ankles something raw like an unborn calf with a bloody length of intestine hanging from its navel. Then one of the women discovered me in the corner and dragged me from the room.

"You're in mortal sin," she said. And ordered with a menacing finger: "Don't think again about what you saw."

On the other hand, the woman who in reality took away my innocence did not intend to and never knew she had. Her name was Trinidad, she was the daughter of someone who worked in the house, and one fatal spring she began to blossom. She was thirteen but still used the dresses she had worn when she was nine, and they were so tight to her body that she seemed more naked than if she had been undressed. One night we were alone in the courtyard, band music erupted without warning from the house next door, and Trinidad began to dance with me, and she held me so tight she took my breath away. I do not know what became of her, but even today I still wake up in the middle of the night agitated by the upheaval, and I know I could recognize her in the dark by the touch of every inch of her skin and her animal odor. In an instant I became conscious of my body with a clarity of instincts that I have never felt again, and that I dare to recall as an exquisite death. After that I knew in a confused and illusory fashion that there was an unfathomable mystery I did not know but that agitated me as if I did. The women of the family, however, always led me along the arid path of chastity.

The loss of innocence taught me at the same time that it was not Baby Jesus who brought us toys at Christmas, but I was careful not to say so. When I was ten, my father revealed this to me as a secret for adults because he assumed I already knew it, and he took me to the stores on Christmas Eve to select toys for my brothers and sisters. The same thing had happened with the mystery of childbirth even before I witnessed Matilde Armenta: I choked with laughter when people said that a stork brought babies from Paris. But I should confess that neither then nor now have I succeeded in connecting childbirth with sex. In any case, I think my intimacy with the maids could be the origin of a thread of secret communication that I believe I have with women and that throughout my life has allowed me to feel more comfortable and sure with them than with men. It may also be the source of my conviction that they are the ones who maintain the world while we men throw it into disarray with our historic brutality.

Sara Emilia Márquez, without knowing it, had something to do with my destiny. Pursued from the time she was very young by suitors she did not even deign to notice, she decided, and for the rest of her life, on the first one who looked all right to her. The chosen one had something in common with my father, for he was a stranger who arrived, no one knew how or from where, with a good background but no known resources. His name was José del Carmen Uribe Vergel, but at times he signed only J. del C. Some time passed before anyone knew who he was in reality and where he came from, until it was learned from the speeches he was hired to write for public functionaries, and from the love poems he published in his own cultural magazine whose frequency depended on the will of God. From the time he appeared in the house, I felt a great admiration for his fame as a writer, the first I had met in my life. On the spot I wanted to be like him and was not content until Aunt Mama learned to comb my hair like his.

I was the first one in the family who learned of their secret love, one night when he came into the house across the way where I was playing with friends. He called me aside, in a state of evident tension, and gave me a letter for Sara Emilia. I knew she was sitting in the door of our house waiting for one of her friends to visit. I crossed the street, hid behind one of the almond trees, and threw the letter with so much precision that it fell into her lap. Frightened, she raised her hands, but the scream remained in her throat when she recognized the handwriting on the envelope. Sara Emilia and J. del C. were my friends from then on.

Elvira Carrillo, the twin sister of my uncle Esteban, would twist and squeeze a stalk of cane with both hands and get out the juice with the strength of a sugar mill. She was better known for her brutal frankness than for the tenderness with which she treated children, above all my brother Luis Enrique, a year younger than I, for whom she was both sovereign and accomplice, and who gave her the inscrutable name of Aunt Pa. Impossible problems were always her specialty. She and Esteban were the first to come to the house in Cataca, but while he found his path in all kinds of fruitful trades and businesses, she remained as an indispensable aunt in the family without ever realizing that she was. She would disappear when she was not needed, but when she was, no one ever knew where she came from or how. In her bad moments she would talk to herself while she stirred the pot, and reveal in a loud voice the location of things that were thought to be lost. She stayed on in the house after she had buried the older people, while weeds devoured the place little by little, and animals wandered the bedrooms, and she was disturbed after midnight by a cough from beyond the grave in the next room.

Francisca Simodosea—Aunt Mama—the commander of the tribe, who died a virgin at the age of seventy-nine, differed from the others in her habits and language. For her culture was not from the Province but from the feudal paradise of the savannas of Bolívar, where her father, José María Mejía Vidal, had migrated from Riohacha with his silversmith's skills when he was very young. She had allowed her wiry dark hair, which resisted turning white until she was very old, to grow down to her knees. She would wash it with perfumed water once a week and sit to comb it in the doorway of her bedroom in a sacred ritual that took several hours, consuming without pause cigarettes made of harsh tobacco that she smoked backwards, with the lit end inside her mouth, as the Liberal troops did so as not to be seen by the enemy in the dark of night. Her style of dress was different, too, with underskirts and bodices of immaculate linen, and velveteen mules.

As opposed to the uncorrupted purism of my grandmother, Mama's language was the loosest popular slang. She did not hide it from anyone or under any circumstances, and she said what she thought to everyone's face. Including a nun, one of my mother's teachers at the boarding school in Santa Marta, whom she stopped short because of a trivial impertinence: "You're one of those women who doesn't know her ass from a day of fasting." But she always managed not to seem coarse or insulting.

For half her life she was the keeper of the keys to the cemetery, and she filled out and issued death certificates and made the hosts for Mass at home. She was the only person in the family, of either sex, who did not seem to have a heart pierced by the sorrow of thwarted love. We became aware of that one night when the doctor was preparing to insert a catheter, and she stopped him with an argument I did not understand at the time: "I want you to know, Doctor, that I've never known a man."

From then on I often heard her say this, yet it never seemed boastful or regretful to me but like a simple fact that left no trace at all in her life. On the other hand, she was an artful match-maker who must have suffered in her double game of acting as lookout for my parents without being disloyal to Mina.

I have the impression that she got along better with children than with adults. It was she who took care of Sara Emilia until she moved alone into the room with the Calleja books. Then, to replace her, she sheltered me and my sister Margot, though my grandmother was still in charge of my personal cleanliness and my grandfather concerned himself with my formation as a man.

My most unsettling memory of those times is Aunt Petra, my grandfather's older sister, who went to Riohacha to live with them when she lost her sight. She lived in the room next to the office, where the workshop was later, and she developed a magical skill for moving around in her darkness without any-one's help. I still remember her as if it were yesterday, walking without a stick as if she had both eyes, slow but without hesita-tion, guided only by different smells. She recognized her room by the vapor of muriatic acid in the workshop next door, the hallway by the perfume of jasmines in the garden, my grand-parents' bedroom by the smell of the wood alcohol they both would rub on their bodies before they went to sleep, Aunt Mama's room by the odor of oil in the lamps on the altar, and, at the end of the hallway, the succulent smell of the kitchen. She was slim and silent, with skin like withered lilies and shin-ing hair the color of mother-of-pearl, which she wore hanging down to her waist and cared for herself. Her green, limpid ado-lescent's eyes changed their light to match her states of mind. In any event these were casual walks, for she spent the entire day in her room with the door half closed, and she was almost always alone. Sometimes she sang in whispers to herself, and her voice could be confused with Mina's, but her songs were different and sadder. I heard someone say they were *romanzas* from Riohacha, but I discovered only as an adult that in reality she invented them herself as she sang them. Two or three times I could not resist the temptation of going into her room without anyone knowing, but I did not find her. Years later, during one of my vacations from secondary school, I recounted these memories to my mother, and she did all she could to persuade me of my error. Her reasoning was absolute, and I could confirm it beyond the shadow of a doubt: Aunt Petra had died before I was two years old.

We called Aunt Wenefrida Nana, and she was the happiest and most amiable of the tribe, but I can recall her only in her sickbed. She was married to Rafael Quintero Ortega—Uncle Quinte—a poor people's lawyer who had been born in Chía, some fifteen leagues from Bogotá and at the same altitude above sea level. But he adapted so well to the Caribbean that in the inferno of Cataca he needed hot-water bottles at his feet to sleep in the cool December weather. The family had already recovered from the misfortune of Medardo Pacheco when it was Uncle Quinte's turn to suffer his own for killing the opposing lawyer in a lawsuit. He had the image of being a good and peaceable man, but his adversary harassed him without letup, and he had no recourse but to arm himself. He was so small and thin that he wore children's shoes, and his friends made cordial jokes because the revolver bulged as big as a cannon under his shirt. My grandfather gave him a serious warning with his celebrated phrase: "You don't know how heavy a dead man is." But Uncle Quinte did not have time to think about it when his enemy, shouting like a lunatic, blocked his way in the antechamber of the court and rushed at him with his giant's body. "I didn't even know how I pulled out the revolver and shot into the air with both hands and my eyes closed," Uncle Quinte told me a short while before he died at the age of one hundred. "When I opened my eyes," he told me, "I could see him, big and pale and still standing, and then he began a slow collapse until he was sitting on the floor." Until that moment Uncle Quinte did not know he had hit him in the middle of his forehead. I asked him what he had felt when he saw him fall, and his frankness surprised me:

"Immense relief!"

My last memory of his wife, Wenefrida, was on a night of pouring rain when a sorceress exorcised her. This was not a conventional witch but an amiable woman, well dressed in stylish clothes, who used a branch of nettles to drive evil humors out of the body while she sang an incantation that was like a lullaby. All of a sudden Nana writhed in a deep convulsion, and a bird the size of a chicken and with iridescent feathers escaped from between the sheets. The woman caught it in midair with a masterful blow of her hand and wrapped it in a black cloth she had prepared. She ordered a fire lit in the backyard and without any ceremony tossed the bird into the flames. But Nana did not recover from her ailments.

A short while later, the fire in the courtyard was lit again when a hen laid a fantastic egg that looked like a Ping-Pong ball with an appendage like that on a Phrygian cap. My grandmother identified it on the spot: "It's a basilisk's egg." She threw it into the fire, murmuring prayers of conjuration.

I never could conceive of my grandparents as being an age different from the age they were in my memories of this period. The same is true of the pictures taken of them in the dawn of their old age, and whose fading copies have been transmitted like a tribal ritual over four prolific generations. Above all those of my grandmother Tranquilina, the most credulous and impressionable woman I have ever known, because of the terror the mysteries of daily life caused in her. She would try to lighten her chores by singing old love songs in full voice, but all of a sudden she would interrupt them with her war cry against calamity: *"Ave María Purísima!"*

For she saw that the rocking chairs rocked alone, that the phantom of puerperal fever was lurking in the bedrooms of women in labor, that the scent of jasmines from the garden was like an invisible ghost, that a cord dropped by accident on the floor had the shape of the numbers that might be the grand prize in the lottery, that a bird without eyes had wandered into the dining room and could be chased away by singing *La Magnífica*.* She believed she could decipher with secret keys the identity of the protagonists and places in the songs that reached her from the Province. She imagined misfortunes that happened

*A prayer, unauthorized by the Church, used by campesinos.

sooner or later, she foresaw who was going to come from Rio-hacha in a white hat, or from Manaure with a colic that could be cured only with the bile of a turkey buzzard, for in addition to being a prophet by trade she was a furtive witch doctor.

She had a very personal system for interpreting her own dreams and those of others, which governed the daily behavior of each one of us and controlled the life of the house. However, she almost died without any premonitions when she pulled the sheets off her bed in a single tug, and a revolver went off, one that the colonel kept hidden under his pillow so he would have it at hand when he slept. From the trajectory of the bullet embedded in the ceiling, it was established that it had passed very close to my grandmother's face.

From the time I had a memory I suffered the morning torture of Mina brushing my teeth, while she enjoyed the magical privilege of taking hers out to wash them and leaving them in a glass of water while she slept. Convinced they were her natural teeth that she took out and put in by Goajiro arts, I had her show me the inside of her mouth so I could see the back of her eyes, brain, nose, and ears from the inside, and I suffered the disappointment of not seeing anything but her palate. But no one deciphered the marvel for me, and for a long time I insisted that the dentist make the same thing for me that he had made for my grandmother so she could brush my teeth while I played on the street.

We had a kind of secret code by means of which we both communicated with an invisible universe. By day her magical world was fascinating, but at night it caused me terror, pure and simple: the fear of the dark, older than we are, that has pursued me my whole life on lonely roads and even in cheap dance halls all over the world. In my grandparents' house each saint had a room and each room had a dead person. But the only house known in an official way as "the dead man's house" was the one next door to ours, and its dead man was the only one identified by his human name at a séance: Alfonso Mora. Someone close to him took the trouble of identifying him in the registries of baptisms and deaths and found numerous homonyms, but none showed signs of being ours. For many years that house had been the priest's residence, and the lie flourished that the ghost was Father Angarita himself trying to frighten away the curious who spied on him during his nocturnal wanderings.

I never knew Meme, the Goajiro slave whom the family brought from Barrancas and who, one stormy night, ran away with Alirio, her adolescent brother, but I always heard that they were the ones who most peppered the language of the house with their native tongue. Her convoluted Castilian was the wonder of poets, ever since the memorable day when she found the matches that Uncle Juan de Dios had lost and returned them to him with her triumphant argot:

"Here I am, your match."

It was difficult to believe that my grandmother Mina, with her women gone astray, was the economic support of the house when resources began to fail. The colonel had some scattered properties occupied by Cachaco tenant farmers, but he refused to evict them. Obliged to save the honor of one of his children, he had to mortgage the house in Cataca, and it cost him a fortune not to lose it. When there was nothing left, Mina continued to support the family in her spirited way with the bakery, the little candy animals that were sold all over town, the spotted hens, the duck eggs, the vegetables from the backyard. She made a radical reduction in the number of servants and kept the most useful ones. Money as cash came to an end because it had no meaning in the oral tradition of the house. So that when they had to buy a piano for my mother when she returned from school, Aunt Pa made an exact calculation in domestic currency: "A piano costs five hundred eggs."

In the midst of that troop of evangelical women, my grandfather was complete security for me. My doubts disappeared only with him, and I felt I had my feet on the ground and was well established in real life. The strange thing, as I think about it now, is that I wanted to be like him, realistic, valiant, and sure, but I never could resist the constant temptation to peer into my grandmother's world. I remember him as thickset and ruddy, with a few white hairs on his shining skull, a well-trimmed brush mustache, and round spectacles with gold wire frames. His speech was deliberate, understanding, and conciliatory in times of peace, but his Conservative friends remembered him as an enemy to be feared in the tribulations of war.

He never used a military uniform, for his rank was revolutionary and not academic, but long after the wars he still wore the *liquilique*, a cotton shirt with pockets, in common use among veterans from the Caribbean. When the law on war pensions was passed he filled out the forms to obtain his, and he as well as his wife and closest heirs continued to wait for it until his death. My grandmother Tranquilina, who died far from that house, blind, decrepit, and half senile, told me in her final moments of lucidity: "I can die in peace because I know all of you will receive Nicolasito's pension."

It was the first time I heard the mythic word that sowed the seed of eternal illusions in the family: retirement. It had come into the house before my birth, when the government established pensions for the veterans of the War of a Thousand Days. My grandfather in person organized the file with a surfeit of sworn testimonies and probative documents, and he took them himself to Santa Marta to sign the payment protocol. According to the least happy calculations, the amount would be sufficient for him and his descendants to the second generation. "Don't worry," my grandmother would tell us, "the retirement money will take care of everything." Then the mail, which had never been anything urgent in the family, was transformed into an envoy of Divine Providence.

With the burden of uncertainty I carried inside, I never could avoid it. On occasion, however, Tranquilina was in a mood that in no way corresponded to her name. In the War of a Thousand Days, my grandfather had been imprisoned in Riohacha by a first cousin of hers who was an officer in the Conservative army. Her Liberal relations, and she herself, understood this as an act of war before which familial power was of no avail. But when my grandmother learned that they had her husband in the stocks like a common criminal, she confronted her cousin with a whip and forced him to turn my grandfather over to her safe and sound.

My grandfather's world was quite different. Even in his final years he seemed very agile when he walked around with his toolbox making repairs to the house, or when he made water for the bath come up by spending hours at the manual pump in the backyard, or when he climbed tall ladders to see how much water was in the water barrels. On the other hand, he would ask me to tie his bootlaces for him because when he tried to do it himself it left him breathless. It was a miracle he did not die one morning when he tried to catch the shortsighted parrot, who had climbed as high as the water barrels. He had succeeded in grasping him by the neck when he slipped on the catwalk and fell to the ground from a height of four meters. Nobody could explain how he survived with his ninety kilos of weight and his fifty-some years. That was for me the memorable day when the doctor examined him from head to toe as he lay naked on the bed, and asked about the old half-inch scar that he found in his groin.

"That's a bullet wound from the war," my grandfather said.

I still have not recovered from my emotion. As I have not recovered from the day when he looked out into the street through his office window to see a famous ambler horse somebody wanted to sell him, and without warning he felt his eye filling with water. He tried to protect it with his hand and a few drops of transparent liquid were left on his palm. He not only lost his right eye, but my grandmother did not permit him to buy a horse inhabited by the devil. For a long time he wore a pirate's patch over the clouded socket until the oculist changed it for a pair of graduated glasses and prescribed a walking stick of carreto wood that in the end became a sign of his identity, like the vest pocket watch with the gold chain whose cover was opened to unexpected music. It was always common knowledge that the betrayals of age that were beginning to disturb him did not in any way affect his arts as a secret seducer and admirable lover.

In the ritual bath at six in the morning, which in his final years he always took with me, we would pour water from the tank over ourselves with a calabash and finish by splashing on the Agua Florida from Lanman & Kemps, which the smugglers from Curaçao delivered by the case to the home, like brandy and shirts of Chinese silk. Once he was heard to say that it was the only scent he used because only the person wearing it could smell it, but he did not believe that again when someone recognized him on another person's pillow. Another story that I heard repeated for years had to do with the night when the light had gone out and my grandfather poured a bottle of ink on his head thinking it was his Agua Florida.

For his daily tasks inside the house he wore drill trousers and his usual elastic suspenders, soft shoes, and a cloth cap with a visor. For Sunday Mass, which he almost never missed and only in unavoidable circumstances, or for any weekday anniversary or memorial, he wore a three-piece suit of white linen, with a celluloid collar and a black tie. Beyond any doubt these rare occasions earned him his reputation as a spendthrift and an arrogant man. The impression I have today is that the house and everything in it existed only for him, for it was an exemplary machista marriage in a matriarchal society, in which the man is absolute king of his house but the one who rules is his wife. In short, he was the macho. That is: in private a man of exquisite tenderness that he was ashamed of in public, while his wife burned to make him happy.

My grandparents made another trip to Barranquilla when the first centenary of the death of Simón Bolívar was celebrated in December 1930, in order to be present at the birth of my sister Aida Rosa, the fourth child in the family. They brought Margot, who was a little more than a year old, back to Cataca with them, and my parents stayed in Barranquilla with Luis Enrique and the newborn. It was hard for me to get used to the change, because Margot came to the house like a creature from another life, rachitic and wild, and with an impenetrable interior world. When Abigaíl—the mother of Luis Carmelo Correa—saw her she could not understand why my grandparents had assumed the burden of that commitment. "The girl is dying," she said. In any case, they had said the same thing about me, because I ate very little, because I blinked, because the things I recounted seemed so outrageous that they thought they were lies, not thinking that most of them were true in another way. I learned only years later that Dr. Barboza was the only one who had defended me with a wise argument: "Children's lies are signs of great talent."

A good deal of time passed before Margot surrendered to family life. She would sit in her little rocking chair to suck her finger in the most unexpected corner. Nothing attracted her attention except the chimes of the clock, which she looked at every hour with her large, hallucinatory eyes. For several days she would not eat. She rejected the food without dramatics, or sometimes she threw it into the corners. No one understood how she was still alive without eating, until they realized that she only liked the damp earth of the garden and the pieces of lime that she scratched off the walls with her nails. When my grandmother found out, she put cow bile in the most appetizing parts of the garden and hid hot peppers in the flowerpots. Father Angarita baptized her in the same ceremony with which he ratified the emergency baptism that had been performed on me when I was born. I received it standing on a chair and bore with courage the kitchen salt the priest put on my tongue and the pitcher of water he poured over my head. Margot, on the other hand, resisted for the two of us with the shriek of a wounded animal and a rebellion of her entire body that godfathers and godmothers barely managed to control over the baptismal font.

Today I think that she, in her relationship to me, was more rational than the adults were with one another. Our complicity was so unusual that on more than one occasion we could each guess what the other was thinking. One morning she and I were playing in the garden when the train whistle blew, as it did every day at eleven. But this time when I heard it I experienced an inexplicable revelation: the doctor from the banana company, who months earlier had given me a rhubarb concoction that brought on a crisis of vomiting, was on that train. I ran through the house shouting the alarm, but no one believed it. Except my sister Margot, who remained hidden with me until the doctor had finished lunch and left on the return train. *"Ave María Purísima!"* my grandmother exclaimed when they found us hiding under her bed, "with these kids you don't need telegrams."

I never could overcome my fear of being alone, above all in the dark, but it seems to me it had a concrete origin, which is that at night my grandmother's fantasies and premonitions materialized. At the age of seventy I still glimpsed in dreams the ardor of the jasmines in the hallway and the phantom in the gloomy bedrooms, and always with the same feeling that ruined my childhood: terror of the night. Often I have had a foreboding, in my worldwide attacks of insomnia, that I too carry the curse of that mythical house in a happy world where we died every night.

The strangest thing is that my grandmother sustained the house with her sense of unreality. How was it possible to maintain so comfortable a life with such meager resources? The figures do not add up. The colonel had learned his father's trade, who in turn had learned it from his, and in spite of the celebrity of his little gold fish that were seen everywhere, it was not a profitable business. Even more: when I was a boy I had the impression that he plied his trade only for short periods or when he was preparing a wedding gift. My grandmother used to say that he worked in order to give presents. Still, his reputation as a good functionary was well established when the Liberal Party came to power, and he was treasurer for years and a finance administrator several times.

I cannot imagine a family environment more favorable to my vocation than that lunatic house, in particular because of the character of the numerous women who reared me. My grandfather and I were the only males, and he initiated me into the sad reality of adults with tales of bloody battles and a scholar's explanations of the flight of birds and claps of thunder at dusk, and he encouraged me in my fondness for drawing. At first I drew on the walls until the women in the house created an uproar: walls are the paper of the rabble. My grandfather was furious and had a wall in his workshop painted white, and he bought me colored pencils and later a box of watercolors so that I could paint as much as I pleased while he made his celebrated little gold fish. Once I heard him say that his grandson was going to be a painter, and I paid no particular attention because I believed that painters were people who only painted doors.

Those who knew me when I was four say that I was pale and introverted, and spoke only to recount absurdities, but for the most part my stories were simple episodes from daily life that I made more attractive with fantastic details so that the adults would notice me. My best sources of inspiration were the conversations older people had in my presence because they thought I did not understand them, or the ones in intentional code in order to prevent my understanding them. Just the opposite was true: I soaked them up like a sponge, pulled them apart, rearranged them to make their origins disappear, and when I told them to the same people who had told the stories earlier, they were bewildered by the coincidence between what I said and what they were thinking.

At times I did not know what to do with my thoughts and I tried to hide them with rapid blinking. This happened so often that some rationalist in the family decided I should be seen by an eye doctor, who attributed my blinking to a problem with my tonsils and prescribed a syrup of iodized radish that worked very well to assuage the adults. For her part, my grandmother came to the providential conclusion that her grandson was a fortune-teller. This turned her into my favorite victim until the day she suffered a dizzy spell because I really did dream that a live bird had come out of my grandfather's mouth. The fear that she would die because of me was the first moderating element in my precocious lack of restraint. Now I believe these were not a child's mean tricks, as one might think, but a budding narrator's rudimentary techniques to make reality more entertaining and comprehensible.

My first passage into real life was the discovery of soccer in the middle of the street or in some nearby gardens. My teacher was Luis Carmelo Correa, who was born with a natural instinct for sports and an inborn talent for mathematics. I was five months older, but he made fun of me because he was growing taller and faster than me. We began to play with balls made of cloth and I managed to become a good goalie, but when we moved on to a regulation ball I was hit in the stomach by a kick of his so powerful that my vanity could go no further. On the occasions we have met as adults, I have confirmed with great joy that we continue to treat each other as we did when we were boys. But my most striking memory from that time was the swift passage of the superintendent of the banana company in a luxurious open car, beside a woman with long golden hair that blew in the wind, and a German shepherd sitting like a king in the seat of honor. They were instantaneous apparitions from a remote, unimaginable world forbidden to us mortals.

I began to assist at Mass without too much belief but with a rigor that perhaps was interpreted as an essential ingredient of faith. It must have been on account of those virtues that I was taken at the age of six to Father Angarita to be initiated into the mysteries of First Communion. It changed my life. They began to treat me like an adult, and the principal sacristan taught me how to assist at Mass. My only problem was that I could not understand at what moment I was supposed to ring the bell, and I would ring it when it occurred to me as the result of inspiration pure and simple. The third time I did this the priest turned around and told me in a severe way not to ring it again. The best part of the service was when the other altar boy, the sacristan, and I were left alone to straighten up the sacristy and would eat the leftover Hosts with a glass of wine.

On the eve of my First Communion the priest heard my confession with no preambles, sitting like a real pope on the thronelike chair while I knelt in front of him on a plush cushion. My awareness of good and evil was rather simple, but the priest assisted me with a dictionary of sins so that I could say which ones I had committed and which ones I had not. I believe I responded well until he asked me if I had done impure things with animals. I had the confused notion that some men committed some sin with she-donkeys that I had never understood, but not until that night did I learn that it was also possible with hens. And so my first step for my First Communion was another great stride forward in the loss of my innocence, and I did not find any reason to continue as an altar boy.

My test by fire was when my parents moved to Cataca with

Luis Enrique and Aida, my brother and other sister. Margot, who barely remembered Papá, was terrified of him. I was too, but with me he always was more wary. Only once did he take off his belt to whip me, and I stood firm, bit my lips, and looked him in the eye, prepared to endure anything in order not to cry. He lowered his arm and began to put his belt back on while he mumbled reproaches for what I had done. In our long conversations as adults, he confessed that it hurt him a great deal to hit us, but perhaps he did it because of his terror that we would turn out to be crooks. In his good moments he was amusing. He loved to tell jokes at the table, and some were very good, but he repeated them so often that one day Luis Enrique stood up and said:

"Let me know when all of you finish laughing."

The historic whipping, however, took place on the night Luis Enrique did not show up at my parents' house or my grandparents' house, and they looked for him all over town until they found him at the movies. Celso Daza, who sold cold drinks, had served him one made of sapodilla fruit at eight o'clock, and Luis Enrique had disappeared without paying and with the glass. The woman who prepared fried food sold him an empanada and saw him a short while later talking to the doorman at the movie, who let him in without paying because he had said his papá was waiting for him inside. The picture was *Drácula*, with Carlos Villarías and Lupita Tovar, directed by George Melford. For years Luis Enrique would tell me about his terror at the moment the lights went on in the theater as Count Dracula was about to sink his vampire's fangs into the neck of the beautiful girl. He was in the most remote seat he could find in the balcony, and from there he saw Papá and our grandfather searching row by row in the orchestra seats, along with the owner of the theater and two police officers. They were about to give up when Papalelo caught sight of him in the last row of the top balcony and pointed with his walking stick:

"There he is!"

Papá pulled him out by the hair, and the beating he gave him in the house became a legendary punishment in the history of the family. My terror and my admiration for my brother's act of independence remained forever vivid in my memory. But he seemed to survive everything and become more and more heroic. Yet today I am intrigued that his rebelliousness was not expressed during those rare times when Papá was not in the house.

I took refuge more than ever in the shadow of my grandfather. We were always together, in the mornings in his workshop or his finance administrator's office, where he assigned me a happy task: to draw the brands of the cows that were going to be slaughtered, and I did this with so much seriousness that he gave me his place at the desk. When it was time for lunch, with all the guests, we always sat at the head of the table, he with his large aluminum pitcher of ice water and I with a silver spoon that I used for everything. People were surprised to see that if I wanted a piece of ice, I would put my hand into the pitcher to pick it out, and a skim of grease was left on the water. My grandfather defended me: "He has every right."

At eleven we went to meet the train, for his son Juan de Dios, who still lived in Santa Marta, sent him a letter every day with the conductor, who would charge five centavos. For another five centavos my grandfather sent an answer on the return train. In the afternoon, as the sun was going down, he led me by the hand to tend to his personal errands. We went to the barber shop—the longest quarter of an hour in my childhood; to see the fireworks on patriotic holidays—which terrified me; to Holy Week processions—with a dead Christ who I had always thought was flesh and blood. I wore a Scotch plaid cap, just like one my grandfather had, which Mina had bought for me so I would look more like him. She was so successful that Uncle Quinte viewed us as a single person with two different ages.

At any hour of the day my grandfather would take me shopping at the banana company's succulent commissary. There I discovered red snapper, and placed my hand on ice for the first time and was shaken to discover that it was cold. I was happy eating whatever I wanted, but his chess games with the Belgian and his political conversations bored me. Now I realize, however, that on those long excursions we would see two different worlds. My grandfather saw his on his horizon, and I saw mine at eye level. He greeted his friends on their balconies, and I longed for the peddler's toys displayed on the sidewalks.

In the early evening we would linger in the universal din of Las Cuatro Esquinas, he conversing with Don Antonio Daconte, who received him standing in the doorway of his colorful establishment, and I marveling at the latest from all over the world. I was driven wild by carnival magicians who pulled rabbits out of hats, fire-eaters, ventriloquists who made animals talk, accordion players who shouted out songs about the things happening in the Province. Today I realize that one of them, very old and with a white beard, may have been the legendary Francisco el Hombre.

Each time he thought the film appropriate, Don Antonio Daconte would invite us to the early show at the Olympia, to the consternation of my grandmother, who considered it debauchery unsuitable for an innocent grandson. But Papalelo persisted, and the next day he would have me recount the film at the table, correcting my oversights and errors and helping me to reconstruct the difficult episodes. These were early indications of dramatic art that no doubt were of benefit to me, above all when I began to draw comic strips before I learned to write. At first I was praised for my childish achievements, but I liked the easy applause of the adults so much that they began to avoid me when they heard me coming. Later the same thing happened with the songs I was obliged to sing at weddings and birthday parties.

Before we went to sleep we spent a long while in the studio of the Belgian, the terrifying old man who appeared in Aracataca after the First World War, and I do not doubt he was Belgian because of the recollection I have of his bewildering accent and his sailor's nostalgic memories. The other living creature in his house was a Great Dane, who was deaf and a pederast and named for a president of the United States: Woodrow Wilson. I met the Belgian when I was four years old and my grandfather would go to play silent, interminable games of chess with him. Beginning on the first night, I was astounded that there was nothing in the house whose use I could determine. For he was an artist of everything that survived in the disorder of his own works: pastel seascapes, photographs of children on birthdays and First Communions, copies of Asian jewels, figures made of cow horn, furniture of disparate periods and styles, one piece stacked on the other.

I was struck by his skin, which adhered to his bones and was the same sunny yellow color as his hair, and the lock of hair that fell over his face and got in the way when he spoke. He smoked an old sea wolf's pipe that he lit only for chess, and my grandfather said it was a trick to distract his opponent. He had a bulging glass eye that seemed more interested in his interlocutor than the healthy eye. He was crippled from the waist down, hunched forward and twisted to his left, but he navigated like a fish among the reefs of his workshops, hanging from rather than leaning on his wooden crutches. I never heard him speak about his voyages, which were, it seemed, numerous and intrepid. The only passion he was known to have outside his house was for the movies, and on weekends he never missed a film no matter what kind it was.

I never liked him, least of all during the chess games when it took him hours to move a single piece while I was collapsing with exhaustion. One night he looked so helpless that I was assaulted by the premonition that he would die very soon, and I felt sorry for him. But over time he began to think so much about his moves that I ended up wishing with all my heart that he would die.

During this time my grandfather hung in the dining room the picture of the Liberator Simón Bolívar at his funeral. It was difficult for me to understand why he did not have the corpse's shroud I had seen at wakes, but lay stretched out on a desk wearing the uniform of his days of glory. My grandfather cleared up my doubts with a categorical statement:

"He was different."

Then, in a tremulous voice that did not seem to be his, he read me a long poem that hung next to the picture, of which I remembered only and forever the final verses: "Thou, Santa Marta, wert charitable, and in thy lap thou gavest him that piece of the ocean's strand to die." From then on, and for many years afterward, I had the idea that Bolívar had been found dead on the beach. It was my grandfather who taught me and asked me never to forget that he was the greatest man ever born in the history of the world. Confused by the discrepancy between his statement and another that my grandmother had made to me with equal emphasis, I asked my grandfather if Bolívar was greater than Jesus Christ. He replied, shaking his head without his earlier conviction:

"One thing has nothing to do with the other."

I know now that it had been my grandmother who insisted that her husband take me with him on his twilight excursions, for she was certain they were pretexts for visiting his real or hypothetical lovers. It is probable that at times I served as his alibi, but the truth is that he never took me anywhere that was not on the anticipated itinerary. I have a clear image, however, of a night when I was holding somebody's hand and happened to pass a strange house and saw my grandfather sitting like the lord and master in the living room. I never could understand why I was shaken by the intuition that I should not tell this to anyone. Until the sun rose today.

It was also my grandfather who gave me my first contact with the written word when I was five, and he took me one afternoon to see the animals in a circus passing through Cataca, under a tent as large as a church. The one that attracted my attention was a battered, desolate ruminant with the expression of a frightening mother.

"It's a camel," my grandfather told me.

Someone standing nearby interrupted:

"Excuse me, Colonel, but it's a dromedary."

I can imagine now how my grandfather must have felt when someone corrected him in the presence of his grandson. Without even thinking about it, he went him one better with a worthy question:

"What's the difference?"

"I don't know," the other man said, "but this is a dromedary."

My grandfather was not an educated man and did not pretend to be one, for he had dropped out of the public school in Riohacha to go and shoot a gun in one of the countless civil wars along the Caribbean. He never studied again, but all his life he was conscious of the gaps, and he had an avid desire for immediate knowledge that more than compensated for his deficiencies. That afternoon he returned dejected to his office and consulted the dictionary with childish attention. Then he and I learned for the rest of our lives the difference between a dromedary and a camel. In the end he placed the glorious tome in my lap and said:

"This book not only knows everything, but it's also the only one that's never wrong."

It was a huge illustrated book, on its spine a colossal Atlas holding the vault of the universe on his shoulders. I did not know how to read or write, but I could imagine how correct the colonel was if the book had almost two thousand large, crowded pages with beautiful drawings. In church I had been surprised by the size of the missal, but the dictionary was thicker. It was like looking out at the entire world for the first time.

"How many words does it have?" I asked.

"All of them," said my grandfather.

The truth is that I did not need the written word at this time because I expressed everything that made an impression on me in drawings. At the age of four I had drawn a magician who cut off his wife's head and put it back on again, just as Richardine had done in his act at the Olympia. The graphic sequence began with the decapitation by handsaw, continued with the triumphant display of the bleeding head, and ended with the wife, her head restored, thanking the audience for its applause. Comic strips had already been invented but I only saw them later in the color supplement to the Sunday papers. Then I began to invent graphic stories without dialogue. But when my grandfather gave me the dictionary, it roused so much curiosity in me about words that I read it as if it were a novel, in alphabetical order, with little understanding. That was my first contact with what would be the fundamental book in my destiny as a writer.

When children are told the first story that in reality appeals to them, it is very difficult to get them to listen to another. I believe this is not true for children who are storytellers, and it was not true for me. I wanted more. The voracity with which I listened to stories always left me hoping for a better one the next day, above all those that had to do with the mysteries of sacred history.

Everything that happened to me in the street had an enormous resonance in the house. The women in the kitchen would tell the stories to the strangers arriving on the train, who in turn brought other stories to be told, and all of it was incorporated into the torrent of oral tradition. Some events were first learned through the accordion players who sang about them at fairs, and travelers would retell them and enhance them. But the most striking story of my childhood occurred very early one Sunday, on our way to Mass, in an ill-advised sentence spoken by my grandmother:

"Poor Nicolasito is going to miss Pentecost Mass."

I was happy, because Sunday Mass was too long for a boy my age, and the sermons of Father Angarita, whom I loved so much as a child, seemed soporific. But it was a vain illusion, for my grandfather almost dragged me to the Belgian's studio, in the green velveteen suit I had been dressed in for Mass and that was too tight for me in the crotch. The police officers recognized my grandfather from a distance and opened the door for him with the ritual formula:

"Go in, Colonel."

Only then did I learn that the Belgian had inhaled a solution of gold cyanide—which he shared with his dog—after seeing *All Quiet on the Western Front*, the picture by Lewis Milestone based on the novel by Erich Maria Remarque. Popular intuition, which always finds the truth even when it seems impossible, understood and proclaimed that the Belgian had not been able to endure the shock of seeing himself crushed with his decimated patrol in a morass of mud in Normandy.

The small reception room was in darkness because of the closed windows, but the early light from the courtyard illuminated the bedroom, where the mayor and two more police officers were waiting for my grandfather. There was the body covered with a blanket on a campaign cot, the crutches within reach, where their owner had left them before he lay down to die. Beside him, on a wooden stool, was the tray where he had vaporized the cyanide, and a sheet of paper with large letters written in pencil: "Don't blame anyone, I'm killing myself because I'm a fool." The legal formalities and the details of the funeral, soon resolved by my grandfather, did not take more than ten minutes. For me, however, they were the most affecting ten minutes I would remember in my life.

The first thing that shook me when I came in was the smell in the bedroom. I learned only much later that it was the bitter almond smell of the cyanide that the Belgian had inhaled in order to die. But not that or any other impression would be more intense and long-lasting than the sight of the corpse when the mayor moved the blanket aside to show him to my grandfather. He was naked, stiff and twisted, his rough skin covered with yellow hair, his eyes like still pools looking at us as if they were alive. That horror of being seen by the dead shook me for years afterward whenever I passed the graves without crosses of suicides buried outside the cemetery by order of the Church. But what I remembered with greatest clarity, along with a charge of horror when I saw the body, was the boredom of nights in his house. Perhaps that was why I said to my grandfather when we left the house:

"The Belgian won't be playing chess anymore."

It was a simple idea, but my grandfather told it to the family as if it were a brilliant witticism. The women repeated it with so much enthusiasm that for some time I ran from visitors for fear they would say it in front of me or oblige me to repeat it. This also revealed to me a characteristic of adults that would be very useful to me as a writer: each of them told the story with new details that they added on their own, until the various versions became different from the original. No one can imagine the compassion I have felt since then for the poor children whose parents have declared them geniuses, who make them sing for visitors, imitate birds, even lie in order to entertain. Today I realize, however, that this simple sentence was my first literary success.

That was my life in 1932, when it was announced that Peruvian troops, under the military regime of General Luis Miguel Sánchez Cerro, had taken the undefended town of Leticia, on the banks of the Amazon River in the extreme south of Colombia. The news resounded throughout the country. The government ordered national mobilization and a public drive that would go from house to house and collect the most valuable family jewels. Patriotism exacerbated by the duplicitous attack of the Peruvian troops provoked an unprecedented popular response. The collectors could not cope with the number of voluntary contributions from all the houses, above all the wedding rings, as esteemed for their real price as for their symbolic value.

For me, on the other hand, it was one of the happiest times because of its disorder. The sterile rigor of schools was broken and replaced by popular creativity on the streets and in the houses. A civic battalion was formed from the cream of the young boys without distinctions of class or color, the feminine brigades of the Red Cross were created, anthems of war to the death against the evil aggressor were improvised, and a unanimous shout resounded throughout the country: "Long live Colombia, down with Peru!"

I never knew how these epic achievements ended because after a certain period of time spirits calmed without sufficient explanations. Peace was achieved with the assassination of General Sánchez Cerro at the hands of someone opposed to his bloody rule, and the war cry became routine when celebrating soccer victories at school. But my parents, who had contributed their wedding rings for the war, never recovered from their naïveté.

As far as I can remember, my vocation for music was revealed in those years by the fascination I felt for the accordion players with their travelers' songs. I knew some of them by heart, like the ones the women in the kitchen sang in secret because my grandmother considered them vulgar. Still, my need to sing in order to feel alive was inspired by the tangos of Carlos Gardel that infected half the world. I would dress like him, with a felt hat and silk scarf, and I did not need too many requests to burst into a tango at the top of my voice. Until the ill-fated morning when Aunt Mama woke me with the news that Gardel had died in the collision of two planes in Medellín. Months earlier I had sung "Cuesta abajo" at a charitable evening, accompanied by the Echeverri sisters, pure Bogotáns who were the teachers of teachers and the soul of every charitable evening and patriotic commemoration celebrated in Cataca. And I sang with so much character that my mother did not dare contradict me when I told her I wanted to learn the piano instead of the accordion that had been repudiated by my grandmother.

That same night she took me to the Señoritas Echeverri for lessons. While they were talking I looked at the piano from the other side of the room with the devotion of a stray dog, estimated if my feet could reach the pedals, and wondered if my thumb and little finger would be able to stretch for extraordinary intervals, or if I would be capable of deciphering the hieroglyphics of the staff. It was a visit of beautiful hopes that lasted for two hours. But in vain, for in the end the teachers told us that the piano was out of service and they did not know for how long. The idea was postponed until the return of the annual tuner, but it was not mentioned again until half a lifetime later, when in a casual conversation I reminded my mother of the sorrow I had felt at not learning the piano. She sighed.

"And the worst thing," she said, "is that there was nothing wrong with it."

Then I learned that she had arranged the excuse of the damaged piano with the teachers to spare me the torture she had suffered during five years of imbecilic exercises at the Colegio de la Presentación. The consolation was that during this time the Montessori school had opened in Cataca, and its teachers stimulated the five senses by means of practical exercises, and taught singing. With the talent and beauty of the director, Rosa Elena Fergusson, studying was something as marvelous as the joy of being alive. I learned to appreciate my sense of smell, whose power of nostalgic evocation is overwhelming. And taste, which I refined to the point where I have had drinks that taste of window, old bread that tastes of trunk, infusions that taste of Mass. In theory it is difficult to comprehend subjective pleasures, but those who have experienced them will understand right away.

I do not believe there is a method better than the Montessorian for making children sensitive to the beauties of the world and awakening their curiosity regarding the secrets of life. It has been rebuked for encouraging a sense of independence and individualism, and perhaps in my case this was true, but on the other hand I never learned to divide or find a square root or handle abstract ideas. We were so young that I remember only two classmates. One was Juanita Mendoza, who died of typhus at the age of seven, soon after the school opened, and this made so strong an impression on me that I have never been able to forget her wearing a crown and bridal veil in her coffin. The other is Guillermo Valencia Abdala, my friend since our first recess, and my infallible physician for Monday hangovers.

My sister Margot must have been very unhappy in that school, though I do not remember her ever mentioning it. She would sit in her chair in the elementary class and remain there without speaking—even during recess—and not moving her eyes from an indeterminate point until the last bell rang. I never knew at the time that while she was alone in the empty room she chewed on earth from the garden at home that she had hidden in the pocket of her pinafore.

It was very hard for me to learn how to read. It did not seem logical for the letter *m* to be called *em*, and yet with some vowel following it you did not say *ema* but *ma*. It was impossible for me to read that way. At last, when I went to the Montessori school, the teacher did not teach me the names of the consonants but their sounds. In this way I could read the first book I found in a dusty chest in the storeroom of the house. It was tattered and incomplete, but it involved me in so intense a way that Sara's fiancé had a terrifying premonition as he walked by: "Damn! This kid's going to be a writer."

Said by someone who earned his living as a writer, it made a huge impression on me. Several years went by before I knew that the book was *The Thousand and One Nights*. The story I liked best—one of the shortest, and the simplest one I read—continued to seem the best one for the rest of my life, though now I am not sure that was where I read it, something no one has been able to clarify for me. The story is this: a fisherman promised a neighbor that he would give her the first fish he caught if she would lend him a lead weight for his casting net, and when the woman opened the fish to fry it, she found a diamond the size of an almond.

I have always related the war with Peru with the decadence of Cataca, for once peace was declared my father became lost in a labyrinth of uncertainties that ended at last with the family moving to his hometown of Sincé. For Luis Enrique and me, who accompanied him on his exploratory trip, it was in reality a new school of life, with a culture so different from ours that they seemed to come from two different planets. Beginning on the day after our arrival, we were taken to nearby farms, and there we learned to ride burros, milk cows, geld calves, set traps for quail, fish with a baited hook, and understand why male and female dogs became stuck together. Luis Enrique was always far ahead of me in discovering the world that Mina had forbidden to us, and that my grandmother Argemira told us about in Sincé without the least malice. So many uncles and aunts, so many cousins of varying colors, so many relatives with strange last names speaking so many different argots at first conveyed more confusion than surprise, until we understood it as another way to love. Papá's papá, Don Gabriel Martínez, a legendary schoolteacher, received Luis Enrique and me in his courtyard with its immense trees and the most famous mangoes in town for their taste and size. He counted them one by one every day from the beginning of the annual harvest, and he picked them one by one with his own hand at the moment he sold them at the fabulous price of a centavo each. When he said goodbye to us after a friendly chat about his good teacher's memory, he picked a mango from the leafiest tree for the two of us.

Papá had sold us that trip as an important step in familial unification, but after we arrived we realized that his secret purpose was to open a pharmacy on the large main square. My brother and I were matriculated in the school of Maestro Luis Gabriel Mesa, where we felt freer and better integrated into a new community. We rented an enormous house on the best corner in town, with two stories and a running balcony facing the square, and desolate bedrooms where the invisible ghost of a stone curlew spent the entire night singing.

Everything was ready for the joyous landing of my mother and sisters when the telegram arrived with the news that my grandfather Nicolás Márquez had died. He had been caught off guard by a throat ailment that was diagnosed as terminal cancer, and there was almost no time to take him to Santa Marta to die. The only one of us he saw as he was dying was my brother Gustavo, born six months earlier, whom someone had put into my grandfather's bed so that he could say goodbye. My dying grandfather gave him a farewell caress. I needed many years before I realized what that inconceivable death meant to me.

The move to Sincé was made in any event, not only with all the children but with my grandmother Mina and Aunt Mama, who was already ill, both of them in the good care of Aunt Pa. But the joy of the change and the failure of the project occurred almost at the same time, and in less than a year we all returned to the old house in Cataca, "flogging our hats," as my mother would say in hopeless situations. Papá stayed in Barranquilla studying the way to set up his fourth pharmacy.

My final memory of the house in Cataca during those awful days was the fire in the courtyard where they burned my grandfather's clothes. His *liquiliques* and the white linen he wore as a civilian colonel resembled him as if he were still alive inside them while they burned. Above all the many cloth caps of different colors that had been the identifying sign that best distinguished him at a distance. Among them I recognized my Scotch plaid one, burned by mistake, and I was shaken by the revelation that this ceremony of extermination had conferred upon me a certain role in my grandfather's death. Today it seems clear: something of mine had died with him. But I also believe, beyond any doubt, that at that moment I was already an elementary-school writer who needed only to learn how to write.

It was the same state of mind that encouraged me to go on living when my mother and I left the house we could not sell. Since the return train could arrive at any time, we went to the station without even thinking about seeing anyone else. "We'll come back another day when we have more time," she said, using the only euphemism she could think of to say she would never come back. As for me, I knew then that for the rest of my life I would never stop missing the thunder at three in the afternoon.

We were the only phantoms at the station, apart from the employee in overalls who sold the tickets as well as doing what in our time had required twenty or thirty hurried men. The heat was merciless. On the other side of the tracks there were only the remains of the forbidden city of the banana company, its old mansions without their red tile roofs, the withered palms among the weeds, the ruins of the hospital, and at the far end of the promenade, the Montessori schoolhouse abandoned among decrepit almond trees, and the little square of gravel facing the station without the slightest trace of historical greatness.

Each thing, just by looking at it, aroused in me an irresistible longing to write so I would not die. I had suffered this on other occasions, but only on that morning did I recognize it as a crisis of inspiration, that word, abominable but so real, that demolishes everything in its path in order to reach its ashes in time.

I do not remember if we spoke further, not even on the return train. When we were already on the launch, in the small hours of Monday and with the cool breeze of the sleeping swamp, my mother realized I was not asleep either, and she asked me:

"What are you thinking about?"

"I'm writing," I answered. And I rushed to be more amiable: "I mean, I'm thinking about what I'm going to write when I get to the office."

"Aren't you afraid your papá will die of grief?"

I eluded the charge with a long pass of the cape.

"He's had so many reasons to die, this one must be the least fatal."

It was not the most propitious time for me to attempt a second novel, after having been mired in the first one and attempting other forms of fiction, with luck or without it, but that night I imposed it on myself like a vow made in war: I would write it or die. Or as Rilke had said: "If you think you are capable of living without writing, do not write."

From the taxi that took us to the dock for launches, my old city of Barranquilla looked strange and sad in the first light of that providential February. The captain of the launch *Eline Mercedes* invited me to accompany my mother to the town of Sucre, where the family had lived for the past ten years. I did not even think about it. I said goodbye to her with a kiss, and she looked into my eyes, smiled at me for the first time since the previous afternoon, and asked me with her usual mischievousness:

"So, what shall I tell your papá?"

I answered with my heart in my hand:

"Tell him I love him very much and that thanks to him I'm going to be a writer." And without compassion I anticipated any other alternatives: "Nothing but a writer."

I liked saying it, sometimes as a joke and sometimes in all seriousness, but never with so much conviction as on that day. I remained on the dock responding to the slow goodbyes my mother waved to me from the railing, until the launch disappeared among the debris of other ships. Then I hurried to the office of *El Heraldo*, excited by the yearning that gnawed in my belly, and almost without breathing I began the new novel with my mother's sentence: "I've come to ask you to please go with me to sell the house."

My method back then was different from the one I adopted later as a professional writer. I typed only with my index fingers—as I still do—but did not break each paragraph until I was satisfied with it—as I do now—but poured out everything, rough and raw, that was inside me. I think this system was imposed by the size of the sheets of paper, vertical strips cut from the rolls for printing, that could be five meters long. The result was originals as long and narrow as papyrus cascading out of the typewriter and extending along the floor as one wrote. The editor-in-chief did not assign articles by the page, or by words or letters, but by centimeters of paper. "A piece a meter and a half long," he would say. In my maturity I began to miss this format until I realized that in practice it was the same as the computer screen.

The impetus with which I began the novel was so irresistible that I lost my sense of time. At ten in the morning I must have had more than a meter written when all of a sudden Alfonso Fuenmayor pushed open the main door and stood there like stone, with the key still in the lock, as if he had confused it with the key to the bathroom. Until he recognized me.

"What the hell are you doing here at this time of day?" he said to me in surprise.

"I'm writing the novel of my life," I told him.

"Another one?" Alfonso said with his irreverent humor. "You have more lives than a cat."

"It's the same one, but in another way," I said in order not to give him useless explanations.

We did not use the familiar *tú* with each other because of the strange Colombian custom of using *tú* from the first greeting and changing to *usted* only when greater intimacy is achieved— as married couples do.

He took books and papers out of his shabby briefcase and put them on the desk. In the meantime, he listened with his insatiable curiosity to the emotional upheaval I tried to convey to him with the frenetic story of my trip. At last, by way of synthesis, I could not avoid my unfortunate tendency to reduce to an irreversible phrase what I am not capable of explaining.

"It's the biggest thing that's happened to me in my life," I said.

"Let's hope it won't be the last," said Alfonso.

He did not even think that, for he, too, was not capable of accepting an idea without first having reduced it to its proper size. Still, I knew him well enough to realize that perhaps my emotion regarding the trip had not moved him as much as I had hoped, but it had no doubt intrigued him. That was true: beginning the next day he began to ask me all sorts of casual but very lucid questions about how the writing was going, and a simple facial expression of his was enough to make me think that something ought to be corrected.

While we were talking I had gathered my papers together in order to clear the desk, since that morning Alfonso had to write the first editorial for *Crónica*. But he had news that cheered my day: the first issue, expected for the following week, was being postponed a fifth time because of inadequate supplies of paper. With luck, Alfonso said, we would have the first issue in three weeks.

I thought this providential delay would be enough time for me to complete the beginning of the book, for I was still too green to realize that novels do not begin the way you want them to, but the way they want to. In fact, six months later, when I believed I was working on the final version, I had to do a complete rewrite of the first ten pages so that the reader would believe them, and today they still do not seem valid to me. The delay must have been a relief for Alfonso as well, because instead of complaining about it he took off his jacket and sat down at the desk to continue correcting the recent edition of the *Dictionary of the Royal Academy of the Language*, which we had received during this time. It had been his favorite pastime since he happened to come across an error in an English dictionary and had sent the documented correction to the publishers in London, perhaps with no other gratification than including one of our jokes in his letter: "At last England owes us, the Colombians, a favor." The publishers responded with a very cordial letter in which they recognized their mistake and asked him to continue collaborating with them. He did, for several years, and he not only found more slips in the same dictionary but in others as well, in various languages. When that relationship ended, he had already contracted the solitary vice of correcting dictionaries in Spanish, English, or French, and if someone was late, or he had to wait for a bus or stand in any of the other lines that fill our lives, he passed the time in the millimetric task of hunting down errors in the thickets of languages.

By twelve o'clock the heat was unbearable. The smoke from our cigarettes had clouded the small amount of light that came in through the two windows, but neither of us took the trouble to ventilate the office, perhaps because of the secondary addiction to smoking the same smoke over again until you died. With the heat it was different. I have the inherent good fortune of being able to ignore it until it is ninety degrees in the shade. Alfonso, on the other hand, without interrupting his work, was taking off his clothing piece by piece as the heat began to press in on him: tie, shirt, undershirt. With the added advantage that his clothing remained dry while he was drowning in perspiration, and he could put it on again when the sun went down, as unwrinkled and fresh as it had been at breakfast. This must have been the secret that allowed him to always appear anywhere with his linen white, his ties knotted, and his coarse Indian hair divided in the center of his skull by a mathematical line. That is how he looked at one o'clock, when he walked out of the bathroom as if he had just awakened from a restorative sleep. When he walked past me he asked:

"Shall we have lunch?"

"Not hungry, Maestro," I said.

In the code of the tribe it was a direct reply: if I said yes it was because I was in dire straits, perhaps after two days of bread and water, and in that case I would go with him without further commentary, and it was clear that he would arrange to pay for me. My answer—"not hungry"—could mean anything, but it was my way of telling him that lunch was not a problem. We agreed to see each other in the evening, as always, at the Librería Mundo.

A short while after midday a young man came in who looked like a movie star. He was very blond, his skin was tanned, his eyes were a mysterious blue, and he had the warm voice of a harmonium. As we spoke about the magazine that would soon appear, he drew the outline of a fighting bull on the cover of the desk in six masterful lines and signed it with a message for Fuenmayor. Then he tossed the pencil onto the table and took his leave with a slam of the door. I was so absorbed in my writing that I did not even look at the name on the drawing. I wrote for the rest of the day without eating or drinking, and when the afternoon light faded I had to grope my way out with the first sketches of my new novel, happy in the certainty that I at last had found a path different from what I had been writing without hope for more than a year.

I did not learn until that night that the afternoon visitor was the painter Alejandro Obregón, who had just returned from another of his many trips to Europe. He was not only one of the great painters in Colombia but one of the men most loved by his friends, and he had come home early to participate in the launching of *Crónica*. I found him with his intimates in a nameless tavern on La Luz, a lane in the middle of Barrio Abajo, which Alfonso Fuenmayor had baptized with the title of a recent book by Graham Greene: *El tercer hombre—The Third Man*. Alejandro's returns were always historic, and the one that night culminated with the performance of a trained cricket that obeyed its owner's orders as if it were human. It would stand on two legs, extend its wings, sing with rhythmic whistles, and recognize applause with theatrical bows. Finally, when its trainer was intoxicated by a salvo of applause, Obregón picked up the cricket by its wings, held it with his fingertips, and to the astonishment of everyone put it in his mouth and chewed the live insect with sensual delight. It was not easy to make amends to the inconsolable trainer with all kinds of flattery and gifts. Later I learned it was not the first cricket that Obregón had eaten alive at a public performance, and it would not be the last.

Never did I feel, as I did in those days, so much a part of that city and the half-dozen friends who were beginning to be known as the Barranquilla Group in the journalistic and intellectual circles of the country. They were young writers and artists who exercised a certain leadership in the cultural life of the city, guided by the Catalan master Don Ramón Vinyes, a legendary dramatist and bookseller who had been consecrated in the *Espasa Encyclopedia* since 1924.

I had met them in September of the previous year when I came from Cartagena—where I lived then—on the urgent recommendation of Clemente Manuel Zabala, the editor-in-chief of *El Universal*, the paper where I had written my first editorials. We spent one night talking about everything and established so enthusiastic and constant a communication, exchanging books and literary jokes, that I ended up working with them. Three of the original group were distinguished by their independence and the strength of their vocations: Germán Vargas, Alfonso Fuenmayor, and Álvaro Cepeda Samudio. We had so many things in common that vindictive people would say we all had the same father, but we were marked and disliked in certain quarters because of our independence, our irresistible vocations, a creative determination that elbowed its way forward, and a timidity that each one resolved in his own way, not always with good fortune.

Alfonso Fuenmayor was an excellent writer and journalist of twenty-eight who for a long time had written a topical column in *El Heraldo*—"Wind of the Day"—using the Shakespearian pseudonym Puck. The more familiar we became with his informality and sense of humor, the less we understood how he had read so many books in four languages on every imaginable topic. His last indispensable experience, when he was almost fifty years old, was an enormous and battered automobile that he would drive at great risk to everyone at twenty kilometers an hour. Cabdrivers, his great friends and most perceptive readers, recognized him from a distance and moved away to clear the street for him.

Germán Vargas Cantillo was a columnist for the evening paper *El Nacional,* and a knowledgeable and biting literary critic whose prose was so amiable he could convince the reader that things had happened only because he recounted them. He was one of the best commentators on radio and no doubt the best educated in those times that were so good for new professions, and an inimitable example of the natural reporter I would have liked to be. He was blond and big-boned, with eyes of a dangerous blue; it was never possible to understand when he had the time to be up-to-date on everything worth reading. He did not back down for an instant from his early obsession with discovering literary values hidden in remote corners of the forgotten Province and bringing them to light. It was lucky he never learned to drive in that brotherhood of the distracted, for we were afraid he would not resist the temptation to read while he was at the wheel.

Álvaro Cepeda Samudio, on the other hand, was more than anything a dazzling driver—of automobiles as well as letters, a wonderful storyteller when he felt like sitting down to write them, a masterful film critic, and no doubt the best educated among them, and an instigator of reckless polemics. He looked like a Gypsy from the Ciénaga Grande, with tanned skin, a beautiful head of tousled black curls, and a madman's eyes that did not hide his tender heart. His favorite footwear was the cheapest cloth sandals, and between his teeth he clenched an enormous cigar that was almost always unlit. He had written his first pieces as a journalist, and published his first stories, in *El Nacional*. That year he was in New York finishing a graduate degree in journalism at Columbia University.

An itinerant member of the group, and the most distinguished, along with Don Ramón, was José Félix Fuenmayor, Alfonso's father. A historic journalist and one of the great narrators, he had published a book of poems, *Tropical Muses*, in 1910, and two novels: *Cosme*, in 1927, and *A Sad Adventure of Fourteen Wise Men*, in 1928. None of them was a commercial success, but specialized critics always considered José Félix one of the best storytellers, one who had been smothered by the Province's foliage.

I had not heard of him when I met him, one midday when we happened to be the only people in the Café Japy, and I was dazzled on the spot by the learning and simplicity of his conversation. He was a veteran and a survivor of a sordid prison in the War of a Thousand Days. He did not have the education of Vinyes, but he was closer to me because of his nature and his Caribbean culture. But what I liked best about him was his strange ability to convey his learning as if it were child's play. He was an invincible conversationalist and a teacher of life, and his mode of thinking was different from everything I had known until then. Álvaro Cepeda and I spent hours listening to him, above all because of his basic tenet that the essential differences between life and literature were simple errors of form. Later, I don't remember where, Álvaro wrote in an accurate flash of intuition: "We all come from José Félix."

The group had formed in a spontaneous fashion, almost through the power of gravity, by virtue of an affinity that was indestructible but difficult to understand at first glance. We were often asked why we always agreed when we were so different, and we had to improvise some kind of answer in order not to tell the truth: we did not always agree, but we understood the reasons. We were conscious of the fact that outside our circle we had an image as arrogant, narcissistic, and anarchic. Above all because of our political positions. Alfonso was viewed as an orthodox liberal, Germán as a reluctant freethinker, Álvaro as an arbitrary anarchist, and I as an unbelieving Communist and potential suicide. But I believe without any doubt at all that our greatest good fortune was that even in the most extreme difficulties we might lose our patience but never our sense of humor.

We discussed our few serious disagreements only among ourselves, and at times they reached dangerous temperatures, but even so they were forgotten as soon as we got up from the table or a friend not in the group came over. I learned the least forgettable lesson, forever, in the Los Almendros bar, one night soon after I had arrived, when Álvaro and I became embroiled in a discussion of Faulkner. The only witnesses at the table were Germán and Alfonso, and they kept to the sidelines, maintaining a stony silence that reached unbearable extremes. I do not remember at what moment, full of rage and a raw *aguardiente*, I challenged Álvaro to settle the argument with our fists. We both were ready to get up from the table and go out into the middle of the street, when the impassive voice of Germán Vargas stopped us short with an eternal lesson:

"Whoever stands up first has lost."

None of us had turned thirty at the time. At the age of twenty-three, I was the youngest of the group, and had been adopted by them after I came to stay in December. But at the table of Don Ramón Vinyes, the four of us behaved as the advocates and postulators of the faith, always together, talking about the same things, mocking everything, and so much in agreement about taking a contrary position that we came to be viewed as only one person.

The only woman we considered part of the group was Meira Delmar, who had already been initiated into the poetic passion, but we conversed with her only on the few occasions when we went outside our sphere of disreputable behavior. Evenings at her house were memorable, with famous writers and artists who were passing through the city. Another friend with less

time, whom we saw with less frequency, was the painter Cecilia
Porras, who on occasion visited from Cartagena and accompanied us on our nocturnal rounds, because she did not care at all
that women were looked at askance in drunkards' cafés and
houses of ill repute.

The group would meet twice a day in the Librería Mundo,
which became a literary meeting place. It was a peaceful still
water in the midst of the din of Calle San Blas, the noisy and
feverish commercial thoroughfare along which the center of
the city emptied out at six in the afternoon. Alfonso and I, like
diligent students, would write until early evening in our office
next to the newsroom at *El Heraldo*, he composing his judicious
editorials and I my untidy articles. Often we would exchange
ideas from one typewriter to the other, lend each other adjectives, trade information back and forth, until it was difficult to
know in some cases which paragraph belonged to whom.

Our daily life was almost always predictable, except on Friday nights when we were at the mercy of inspiration and sometimes went on until breakfast on Monday. If interest waylaid
us, the four of us would undertake a literary pilgrimage without
restraint or moderation. It would begin at El Tercer Hombre
with the artisans from the neighborhood and the mechanics
from a car repair shop, in addition to dissolute public officials
and others who were a little less so. The strangest one of all was
a residential thief who arrived a little before midnight in the
uniform of his trade: ballet tights, tennis shoes, a baseball cap,
and a satchel of lightweight tools. Someone who caught him
robbing his house managed to take his picture and published
the photograph in the press in case anyone could identify him.
The only thing he obtained were several letters from readers
indignant at the dirty trick that had been played on poor sneak
thieves.

The thief had a strong literary vocation, he did not miss a
word of our conversations about art and books, and we knew he
was the shamefaced author of love poems that he declaimed for
the other patrons when we were not there. After midnight he
went out to rob in the wealthy neighborhoods, as if it were his
job, and three or four hours later he would bring us a gift of

some trinkets taken from his larger haul. "For your girls," he would say, not even asking if we had any. When a book caught his eye he would bring it to us as a gift, and if it was worthwhile we would donate it to the departmental library directed by Meira Delmar.

Those itinerant pontifications had earned us a turbid reputation among the good *comadres* whom we would see as they left five o'clock Mass, and they would cross the street in order not to pass too close to those who were drunk at dawn. But the truth is there was no drunken carousing more honorable and fruitful. If anyone knew this right away I did, for I joined them in their shouting in the brothels about the work of John Dos Passos or the goals missed by the Deportivo Junior team. In fact, one of the charming hetaeras at El Gato Negro, fed up with an entire night of arguments at no charge, had yelled at us as we left:

"If you guys fucked as much as you shouted, we girls would be bathed in gold!"

We often went to see the new sun at a nameless brothel in the red-light district where Orlando Rivera (Figurita) had lived for years while he painted a history-making mural. I do not remember anyone wilder, with his lunatic eyes, his goatee, and his orphan's kindness. In elementary school he had been bitten by the mad idea that he was Cuban and became more of a Cuban, and a better Cuban, than if he really had been one. He spoke, ate, painted, dressed, fell in love, danced, and lived his life as a Cuban, and he died a Cuban without ever visiting Cuba.

He did not sleep. When we visited him at dawn he would jump down from the scaffolding, daubed with more paint than the mural, and blaspheming in the language of the *Mambises**
in a marijuana hangover. Alfonso and I would bring him articles and stories to illustrate, and we had to tell him about them because he did not have the patience to understand them when they were read. He did his drawings in an instant using the techniques of caricature, which were the only ones he believed

*A *Mambí* (plural *Mambises*) was a Cuban rebel against Spanish rule of the island.

in. He almost always liked them, though Germán Vargas would say in a good-humored way that they were much better when he didn't.

This was how Barranquilla was, a city that resembled no other, above all from December to March, when the northern trade winds compensated for infernal days with nocturnal gales that whirled around the courtyards of houses and carried chickens through the air. Only the transient hotels and the sailors' taverns around the port remained alive. Some little nocturnal birds would wait whole nights for an always uncertain clientele from the riverboats. A brass band would play a languid waltz on the alameda but no one heard it because of the shouts of the drivers arguing about soccer among the taxis parked facing into the sidewalk along the Paseo Bolívar. The only possible place was the Café Roma, which was frequented by Spanish refugees and never closed for the simple reason that it had no doors. It also had no roof, in a city of sacramental rainstorms, but you never heard of anyone who stopped eating a potato omelet or closing a deal on account of the rain. It was a retreat from the weather, with little round tables painted white and iron chairs under the foliage of flowering acacias. At eleven, when the morning papers—*El Heraldo* and *La Prensa*—went to press, the night editors would meet there to eat. The Spanish refugees were there from seven on, after listening at home to the spoken newspaper of Professor Juan José Pérez Domenech, who continued to report on the Spanish Civil War twelve years after it had been lost. One fateful night, the writer Eduardo Zalamea anchored there on his way back from La Guajira, and he shot himself in the chest with a revolver without serious consequences. The table became a historic relic that the waiters showed to tourists, who were not permitted to sit at it. Years later, Zalamea published the testimony of his adventure in *Cuatro años a bordo de mí mismo*—*Four Years Aboard Myself*—a novel that opened unsuspected horizons for our generation.

I was the most destitute of the brotherhood, and often I took refuge in the Café Roma to write until dawn in an isolated corner, for my two jobs together had the paradoxical virtue of being important and ill-paid. Dawn found me there, reading without mercy, and when hunger pursued me I would have thick hot chocolate and a sandwich of good Spanish ham, and stroll with the first light of dawn beneath the flowering *matarratón* trees on the Paseo Bolívar. During the first weeks I wrote until very late in the newsroom, and slept a few hours in the empty offices or on the rolls of newsprint, but in time I found myself obliged to look for a less original place.

The solution, like so many others in the future, was given to me by the good-natured cabdrivers along the Paseo Bolívar: a transient hotel a block from the cathedral, where you could sleep alone or with a companion for a peso and a half. The building was very old but well maintained, at the expense of the solemn little whores who plundered the Paseo Bolívar after six in the evening, lying in wait for loves gone astray. The concierge was named Lácides. He had a crossed glass eye, and he stammered because of shyness, and I still remember him with an immense gratitude that began the first night I went there. He tossed the peso and fifty centavos into the drawer behind the counter, already filled with the loose, wrinkled bills of early evening, and he gave me the key to room number six.

I had never been in so peaceful a place. The most I heard were muffled steps, an incomprehensible murmur, and every once in a while the anguished creak of rusted springs. But not a whisper, not a sigh: nothing. The only difficulty was the ovenlike heat because the window was sealed shut with wooden crosspieces. Still, on the first night I read William Irish very well, almost until dawn.

It had been the mansion of former shipowners, with columns overlaid in alabaster and gaudy friezes around an interior courtyard covered by pagan stained glass that radiated the splendor of a greenhouse. The city's notary offices were on the ground floor. On each of the three stories of the original house there were six large marble chambers, converted into cardboard cubicles—just like mine—where the nightwalkers of the area reaped their harvest. That joyful bawdy house once had the name Hotel New York, and Alfonso Fuenmayor later called it the Skyscraper, in memory of the suicides who in those years were throwing themselves off the top of the Empire State Building.

In any case, the axis of our lives was the Librería Mundo at twelve noon and at six in the evening, on the busiest block of Calle San Blas. Germán Vargas, an intimate friend of the owner, Don Jorge Rondón, was the one who convinced him to open the store that soon became the meeting place for young journalists, writers, and politicians. Rondón lacked business experience, but he soon learned, and with an enthusiasm and a generosity that soon turned him into an unforgettable Maecenas. Germán, Álvaro, and Alfonso were his advisors in ordering books, above all the new books from Buenos Aires, where publishers had begun the translation, printing, and mass distribution of new literature from all over the world following the Second World War. Thanks to them we could read in a timely way books that otherwise would not have come to the city. The publishers themselves encouraged their patrons and made it possible for Barranquilla to again become the center of reading it had been years earlier, until Don Ramón's historic bookstore ceased to exist.

It was not too long after my arrival when I joined the brotherhood that waited for the traveling salesmen from the Argentine publishers as if they were envoys from heaven. Thanks to them we were early admirers of Jorge Luis Borges, Julio Cortázar, Felisberto Hernández, and the English and North American novelists who were well translated by Victoria Ocampo's crew. Arturo Barea's *The Making of a Rebel*—was the first hopeful message from a remote Spain silenced by two wars. One of those travelers, the punctual Guillermo Dávalos, had the good habit of sharing our nocturnal binges and giving us as presents the samples of his new books after he had finished his business in the city.

The group, who lived far from the center of the city, did not go to the Café Roma at night unless they had concrete reasons to do so. For me, on the other hand, it was the house I did not have. In the morning I worked in the peaceful editorial offices of *El Heraldo*, had lunch how, when, and where I could, but almost always as the guest of somebody in the group of good friends and interested politicians. In the afternoon I wrote "La Jirafa," my daily commentary, and any other occasional text. At twelve noon and six in the evening I was the most punctual at the Librería Mundo. The aperitif at lunch, which the group drank for years at the Café Colombia, later moved to the Café Japy, across the street, because it was the busiest and most spirited one on Calle San Blas. We used it to see visitors, as an office and place of business, to conduct interviews, and as an easy place for all of us to meet.

Don Ramón's table at the Japy had inviolable laws imposed by custom. He was the first to arrive because of his schedule of teaching until four in the afternoon. No more than six of us fit at the table. We had chosen our places in relation to his, and it was considered bad taste to squeeze in other chairs where they did not fit. Because of the duration and quality of their friendship, from the first day Germán sat on his right. He took care of Don Ramón's material affairs. He resolved them even if he was not asked to, because the scholar had an innate vocation for not understanding practical life. In those days, the principal concern was the sale of his books to the departmental library and wrapping up other matters before he traveled to Barcelona. More than a secretary, Germán seemed like a good son.

Don Ramón's relations with Alfonso, on the other hand, were based on more difficult literary and political problems. As for Álvaro, it always seemed to me that he was inhibited when he found Don Ramón alone at the table and needed the presence of others to begin navigating. The only human being who had an absolute right to a place at the table was José Félix. At night, Don Ramón did not go to the Japy but to the nearby Café Roma, with his friends the Spanish exiles.

I was the last to join his table, and from the first day I sat, with no right of my own to it, in Álvaro Cepeda's chair while he was in New York. Don Ramón received me like one more disciple because he had read my stories in *El Espectador*. But I never would have imagined that I would become close enough to him to ask to borrow money for my trip to Aracataca with my mother. A short while later, in an inconceivable coincidence, we had our first and only conversation in private when I went to the Japy before the others in order to pay him, without witnesses, the six pesos he had lent me.

"Cheers, Genius," he greeted me as usual. But something in my face alarmed him: "Are you sick?"

"I don't believe so, Señor," I said with some uneasiness. "Why?"

"You look all in," he said, "but don't pay attention to me; these days we're all *fotuts del cul*."

He put the six pesos into his wallet with a reluctant gesture, as if the money were ill-gotten gains.

"I accept this," he explained, blushing, "as a memento of a very poor young man who was capable of paying a debt without being asked."

I did not know what to say, submerged in silence like a leaden well that I endured in the chatter of the room. I never dreamed how fortunate that meeting was. I had the impression that when the group talked, each one brought his grain of sand to the disorder, and the virtues and defects of each person were confused with those of the others, but it never occurred to me that I could talk alone about art and glory with a man who had lived for years in an encyclopedia. Often, late at night, when I was reading in the solitude of my room, I imagined exciting conversations I would have liked to have with him about my literary doubts, but they melted away without a trace in the light of the sun. My shyness grew even worse when Alfonso erupted with one of his extraordinary ideas, or Germán condemned one of the maestro's hurried opinions, or Álvaro shouted out a project that drove us out of our minds.

To my good fortune, that day in the Japy it was Don Ramón who took the initiative and asked me how my reading was going. At the time I had read everything I could find by the Lost Generation, in Spanish, with special attention to Faulkner, whom I probed into with the bloodthirsty stealth of a straight razor because of my strange fear that in the long run he might be nothing more than an astute rhetorician. After saying this I was shaken by the apprehension that it would seem a provocation, and I tried to soften it, but Don Ramón did not give me time.

"Don't worry, Gabito," he answered in an impassive way. "If Faulkner were in Barranquilla he would be at this table."

On the other hand, he found it noteworthy that Ramón Gómez de la Serna interested me so much that I quoted him in "La Jirafa" together with others who were indisputable novelists. I explained that I did not do it because of his novels, since except for *The Chalet of the Roses,* which I had liked very much, what interested me about him were the audacity of his mind and his verbal talents, but only as a kind of rhythmic gymnastics for learning to write. In that sense, I do not recall a more intelligent genre than his famous *greguerías,* his vivid metaphoric images in prose. Don Ramón interrupted me with his mordant smile:

"The danger for you is that without realizing it you can also learn to write badly."

However, before changing the subject he admitted that in the midst of his phosphorescent disorder, Gómez de la Serna was a good poet. His replies were like that, immediate and learned, and I was so blinded by fear that someone would interrupt this unique occasion that my nerves almost did not allow me to assimilate them. But he knew how to manage the situation. His usual waiter brought him his eleven-thirty Coca-Cola, and he seemed to be unaware of it yet sipped at it through a paper straw without interrupting his explanations. Most of the patrons greeted him in a loud voice from the door: "How are you, Don Ramón?" And he would respond, not looking at them, with a wave of his artist's hand.

As he spoke, Don Ramón directed furtive glances at the leather briefcase I clutched at with both hands as I listened to him. When he finished drinking the first Coca-Cola, he twisted the straw as if it were a screwdriver and ordered the second. I asked for mine knowing very well that at this table each man paid his own bill. At last he asked about the mysterious briefcase to which I clung as if it were a life raft.

I told him the truth: it was the rough draft of the first chapter of the novel I had begun when I returned from Cataca with my mother. With an audacity I would never be capable of again at any crossroads in life or death, I placed the open briefcase on the table in front of him as an innocent inducement. He stared at me with his clear eyes of a dangerous blue and asked with some astonishment:

"May I?"

It was typed with countless corrections, on strips of newsprint folded like the bellows of an accordion. Without haste he put on his reading glasses, unfolded the strips of paper with professional skill, and arranged them on the table. He read without a variation in expression, without his skin changing color, without an alteration in his breathing, his cockatoo's tuft of hair unmoved by the rhythm of his thoughts. When he finished two complete strips he refolded them in silence, with medieval art, and closed the briefcase. Then he put his glasses in their case and placed it in his breast pocket.

"It is evident that the material is still raw, which is logical," he said with great simplicity. "But it's going well."

He made some marginal comments on my handling of time, which was my life-or-death problem and without a doubt the most difficult, and he added:

"You must be aware that the drama has already occurred and the characters are there only to evoke it, and so you have to contend with two different times."

After a series of precise technical comments that I could not appreciate because of my inexperience, he advised me not to call the city in the novel Barranquilla, as I had done in the rough draft, because it was a name so restricted by reality that it would leave the reader with very little room for dreaming. And he concluded in his mocking tone:

"Or play the innocent and wait for it to drop from heaven. After all, the Athens of Sophocles was never the same as the city of Antigone."

But what I followed to the letter forever after was the sentence with which he said goodbye to me that afternoon:

"I thank you for your courtesy, and I'm going to reciprocate with a piece of advice: never show anybody the rough draft of anything you're writing."

It was my only conversation alone with him, but it was worth all of them, because he left for Barcelona on April 15, 1950, as had been anticipated for more than a year, rarefied in his black woolen suit and magistrate's hat. It was like seeing off a schoolboy. At the age of sixty-eight he was in good health and his lucidity was intact, but those of us who accompanied him to the airport said goodbye as if he were someone returning to his native land to attend his own funeral.

Only on the following day, when we came to our table in the Japy, did we realize the void left by his chair, which no one would occupy until we agreed it should be Germán. We needed a few days to become accustomed to the new rhythm of our daily conversation, until the first letter from Don Ramón arrived, which was like hearing his voice written in a meticulous hand in purple ink. In this way a frequent and intense correspondence with all of us was initiated through Germán, in which he recounted very little of his life and a great deal about a Spain that he would continue to consider an enemy country as long as Franco lived and maintained Spanish dominion over Cataluña.

The idea for the weekly was Alfonso Fuenmayor's and had originated long before this time, but I have the impression it was hastened along by the departure of the Catalan scholar. When we were at the Café Roma three nights later, Alfonso informed us that he had everything ready for the launch. It would be a weekly twenty-page journalistic and literary tabloid whose name—*Crónica*—would not say much to anyone. To us it seemed insane that after four years of not acquiring funds from places that had more than enough money, Alfonso Fuenmayor had obtained backing from artisans, automobile mechanics, retired magistrates, and even complicit tavern owners who agreed to pay for their advertisements with rum. But there were reasons to think it would be well received in a city that, in the midst of its industrial drive and civic conceits, kept alive its devotion to its poets.

Other than ourselves there would be few regular contributors. The only professional with extensive experience was Carlos Osío Noguera—El Vate Osío, or Osío the Bard—a poet and journalist with a very personal amiability and an enormous body, who was a government functionary and a censor at *El Nacional*, where he had worked with Álvaro Cepeda and

German Vargas. Another would be Roberto (Bob) Prieto, a strange, erudite member of the upper class who could think in English or French as well as he did in Spanish, and play various works by the great masters from memory on the piano. The least comprehensible person on the list thought up by Alfonso Fuenmayor was Julio Mario Santodomingo. He imposed him without reservation because of Santodomingo's intention to be a different kind of man, but what few of us understood was why he would appear on the list for the editorial board when he seemed destined to be a Latin Rockefeller, intelligent, educated, cordial, but condemned without appeal to the fog of power. Very few knew, as we four promoters of the magazine did, that the secret dream of his twenty-five years was to be a writer.

The publisher, by his own right, would be Alfonso. German Vargas would be more than anything else the great reporter with whom I hoped to share the position, not when I had time—we never had it—but when I achieved my dream of learning how to do it. Álvaro Cepeda would send contributions in his free time at Columbia University, in New York. At the end of the line, no one was freer and more eager than I to be named managing editor of an independent and uncertain weekly, and I was.

Alfonso had reserves in his files going back many years, and a good deal of advance work from the last six months, including editorial commentaries, literary materials, masterful articles, and promises of commercial advertising from his wealthy friends. The managing editor, with no fixed schedule and a salary better than that of any journalist in my category, but dependent on future earnings, was also prepared to put out a magazine that would be worthwhile and on time. At last, on Saturday of the following week, when I walked into our cubicle at *El Heraldo* at five in the afternoon, Alfonso Fuenmayor did not even look up to finish his editorial.

"Look over all your stuff, Maestro," he said. "*Crónica*'s coming out next week."

I was not frightened because I had already heard the same statement twice before. But it happened on the third try.

The biggest journalistic event of the week—by overwhelming odds—had been the arrival of the Brazilian soccer player Heleno de Freitas to play for Deportivo Junior, yet we would not cover it in competition with the specialized press but treat it as major news of cultural and social interest. *Crónica* would not allow itself to be pigeonholed by those kinds of distinctions, least of all when dealing with something as popular as soccer. The decision was unanimous and the work efficient.

We had prepared so much material in advance that the only last-minute item was the article about Heleno, written by Germán Vargas, a master of the genre and a soccer fanatic. The first issue was right on time and appeared on the newsstands on Saturday, April 29, 1950, the day of St. Catherine of Siena, the writer of blue letters on the most beautiful square in the world. *Crónica* was printed with a last-minute slogan of mine under the name: "Su mejor weekend," "Your Best Weekend." We knew we were defying the indigestible purism that prevailed in the Colombian press during those years, but what we wanted to say with the slogan had no equivalent with the same nuances in Spanish. The cover was an ink drawing of Heleno de Freitas by Alfonso Melo, the only portrait artist among our three draftsmen.

The edition, in spite of last-minute rushing and a lack of publicity, was sold out long before the entire editorial staff reached the municipal stadium on the following day—Sunday, April 30—where a stellar match was being played between Deportivo Junior and Sporting, both teams from Barranquilla. The magazine itself was divided because Germán and Álvaro were fans of Sporting, and Alfonso and I supported Junior. However, the mere name of Heleno and the excellent article by Germán Vargas sustained the mistaken notion that *Crónica* was, at last, the great sports magazine that Colombia had been waiting for.

The stadium was crowded all the way up to the pennants. After six minutes of the first period, Heleno de Freitas scored his first goal in Colombia with a left rebound from the center of the field. Although in the end Sporting won 3–2, the afternoon belonged to Heleno, and after him, to us, because of the success of the premonitory cover. Yet there was no power human or divine capable of making any public understand that *Crónica* was not a sports magazine but a cultural weekly that had honored Heleno de Freitas as one of the great news stories of the year.

It was not beginners' luck. Three of us were in the habit of dealing with soccer topics in general interest columns, including Germán Vargas, of course. Alfonso Fuenmayor was an avid soccer fan, and for years Álvaro Cepeda had been the Colombia correspondent for *The Sporting News* in St. Louis, Missouri. But the readers we longed for did not welcome the subsequent issues with open arms, and the fans in the stadiums abandoned us without a pang.

Trying to repair the break, we decided on the editorial board that I would write the main article about Sebastián Berascochea, another of the Uruguayan stars on Deportivo Junior, in the hope I would reconcile soccer and literature as I so often had tried to do with other occult sciences in my daily column. The soccer fever that Luis Carmelo Correa had infected me with in the fields of Cataca had subsided almost to zero. Besides, I was one of the early fans of Caribbean baseball—or *el juego de pelota*, as we called it in the vernacular. Yet I took up the challenge.

My model, of course, was the reporting of Germán Vargas. I backed this up by reading some other sportswriters, and felt relieved after a long conversation with Berascochea, an intelligent, amiable man with a very clear sense of the image he wanted to give to his public. The problem was that I identified and described him as an exemplary Basque, only because of his last name, not bothering to consider the detail that he was a very dark-skinned black with the finest African lineage. It was the greatest blunder of my life, at the very worst moment for the magazine. In fact, I identified with all my heart with the letter from a reader who defined me as a sportswriter incapable of telling a soccer ball from a trolley car. Germán Vargas himself, so meticulous in his judgments, affirmed years later in a commemorative book that the article on Berascochea was the worst thing I had ever written. I believe he exaggerated, but not too much, because no one knew the profession as well as he did, with his reports and articles written in so fluid a tone that they seemed to have been dictated to the linotypist.

We did not give up soccer or baseball because both were popular along the Caribbean coast, but we increased the current topics and new works of literature. It was all in vain: we never could overcome the mistaken assumption that *Crónica* was a sports magazine, but the stadium fans overcame theirs and abandoned us to our fate. And so we continued to publish it as we had intended, although after the third week it was still floating in the limbo of its own ambiguity.

I was not disheartened. The trip to Cataca with my mother, my historic conversation with Don Ramón Vinyes, and my deep connection to the Barranquilla Group had filled me with an encouragement that lasted for the rest of my life. From then on I did not earn a centavo except with the typewriter, and this seems more meritorious to me than one might think, because the first royalties that allowed me to live on my stories and novels were paid to me when I was in my forties, after I had published four books with the most abject earnings. Before that, my life was always agitated by a tangle of tricks, feints, and illusions intended to outwit the countless lures that tried to turn me into anything but a writer.

3

WHEN THE DISASTER of Aracataca had been con-
summated, and my grandfather was dead, and
what might have remained of his uncertain pow-
ers was extinguished, those of us who had lived by them were at
the mercy of nostalgic longings. Not a soul was left in the
house when no one came back on the train. Mina and Francisca
Simodosea remained there under the protection of Elvira Carrillo, who took care of them with a servant's devotion. When,
in the end, my grandmother lost her sight and her reason, my
parents took her with them so that she would at least have a
better life for her dying. Aunt Francisca, virgin and martyr,
continued to be the same woman of uncommon self-assurance
and gruff aphorisms, who refused to give up the keys to the
cemetery and the preparation of Hosts for consecration, arguing that God would have called her if that was His will. One
day she sat down in the doorway of her room with several of
her immaculate sheets and sewed her own made-to-measure
shroud with such fine workmanship that death waited for more
than two weeks until she had finished it. That night she lay
down without saying goodbye to anyone, without any kind of
disease or pain, and prepared to die in the best of health. Only
later did people learn that on the previous night she had filled
out the death certificates and taken care of the formalities for

her own funeral. Elvira Carrillo, who also had never known a man, by her own choice, was left alone in the immense solitude of the house. At midnight the ghost with the eternal cough in the neighboring bedrooms would wake her, but it never mattered because she was accustomed to also sharing the afflictions of supernatural life.

Her twin brother Esteban Carrillo, on the contrary, remained lucid and dynamic until he was very old. Once when I was having breakfast with him, I recalled with all its visual details that people on the Ciénaga launch had tried to throw his father overboard, that he had been lifted onto the shoulders of the crowd and tossed in a blanket like Sancho Panza being tossed by the mule drivers. By then Papalelo had died, and I recounted the memory to Uncle Esteban because I thought it was amusing. But he leaped to his feet, furious because I had not told anyone about it as soon as it happened, and eager for me to identify in my memory the man who had been talking to my grandfather on that occasion, so that he could tell my uncle who the men were who had tried to drown his father. He could not understand either why Papalelo had not defended himself, when he was a good shot who during two civil wars had often been in the line of fire, who slept with a revolver under his pillow, and who in peaceful times had killed an enemy in a duel. In any case, Esteban told me, it would never be too late for him and his brothers to punish the affront. It was the Guajiran law: an insult to a member of the family had to be paid for by all the males in the aggressor's family. Uncle Esteban was so determined that he took his revolver from his belt and placed it on the table so as not to lose time while he finished questioning me. From then on, whenever we met in our wanderings his hope returned that I had remembered. One night he appeared in my cubicle at the newspaper, during the time I was investigating the family's past for a first novel I never finished, and he proposed that we look into the assault together. He never gave up. The last time I saw him in Cartagena de Indias, when he was old and his heart had cracked, he said goodbye to me with a sad smile:

"I don't know how you can be a writer with such a bad memory."

When there was nothing more to do in Aracataca, my father took us to live in Barranquilla again, to open another pharmacy without a centavo of capital but with good credit from the wholesalers who had been his partners in earlier businesses. It was not the fifth drugstore, as we used to say in the family, but the same old one that we took from city to city depending on Papá's commercial hunches: twice in Barranquilla, twice in Aracataca, and once in Sincé. In all of them he'd had precarious profits and salvageable debts. The family without grandparents or uncles or aunts or servants was reduced then to parents and children—there were six of us, three boys and three girls—in nine years of marriage.

I felt very uneasy about this change in my life. I had been in Barranquilla several times to visit my parents, as a boy and always in passing, and my memories of that time are very fragmentary. The first visit took place when I was three and had been brought there for the birth of my sister Margot. I remember the stink of mud in the port at dawn, the one-horse carriage whose coachman used his whip to drive away the porters who tried to climb onto the driver's seat on the deserted, dusty streets. I remember the ocher walls and the green wood of doors and windows in the maternity hospital where the baby was born, and the strong smell of medicine in the room. The infant was in a very simple iron bed at the rear of a desolate room, with a woman who no doubt was my mother, but I can recall only a faceless presence who held out a languid hand to me and said with a sigh:

"You don't remember me anymore."

Nothing more. The first concrete image I have of her is from several years later; it is clear and certain, but I have not been able to situate it in time. It must have been on a visit she made to Aracataca after the birth of Aida Rosa, my second sister. I was in the courtyard, playing with a newborn lamb that Santos Villero had carried in her arms from Fonseca for me, when Aunt Mama came running and told me with a shout that I thought came from fear:

"Your mamá's here!"

She almost dragged me to the living room, where all the women in the house and some female neighbors were sitting in chairs lined up along the walls, as if it were a wake. The conversation was interrupted by my sudden entrance. I stood petrified in the door, not knowing which of all those women was my mother, until she opened her arms to me and said in the most loving voice I can remember:

"But you've grown into a man!"

She had a beautiful Roman nose, and she was dignified and pale, and more distinguished than ever because of that year's fashion: a silk dress the color of marble with a waist dropped to the hips, several loops of a pearl necklace, silver shoes with an instep strap and high heels, and a hat of fine straw in the shape of a bell like the ones in silent movies. Her embrace surrounded me in the particular scent I always smelled on her, and a lightning flash of guilt shook me body and soul because I knew that my duty was to love her but I felt that I did not.

On the other hand, the oldest memory I have of my father is clear and confirmed on December 1, 1934, the day he turned thirty-three. I saw him walking with rapid, joyful strides into my grandparents' house in Cataca, wearing a three-piece white linen suit and a straw boater. Someone who congratulated him with a hug asked him how old he was. I never forgot his answer because at the time I did not understand it:

"The age of Christ."

I have always wondered why that memory seems so old to me, when it is certain that by then I had been with my father many times.

We had never lived in the same house, but after Margot's birth my grandparents adopted the custom of taking me to Barranquilla, so that when Aida Rosa was born it was less strange to me. I believe it was a happy house. They had a pharmacy there, and later they opened another in the business center. We saw my grandmother Argemira—Mamá Gime—again, and two of her children, Julio and Enga, who was very beautiful but famous in the family for her bad luck. She died at the age of twenty-five, no one knows of what, and people still say it was because of a rejected suitor's curse. As we grew up, Mamá Gime seemed more amiable and foulmouthed to me.

During this same period my parents were responsible for an emotional mishap that left me with a scar difficult to erase. It happened one day when my mother suffered an attack of nostalgia and sat down at the piano to play "After the Ball Is Over," the historic waltz of her secret love, and Papá had the romantic idea of dusting off his violin to accompany her, even though it was missing a string. She adjusted without difficulty to his romantic middle-of-the-night style and played better than ever, until she looked at him with pleasure over her shoulder and realized that his eyes were wet with tears. "Who are you remembering?" my mother asked with ferocious innocence. "The first time we played this together," he answered, inspired by the waltz. Then my mother slammed both fists down on the keyboard in a rage.

"It wasn't with me, you Jesuit!" she shouted at the top of her voice. "You know very well who you played it with and you're crying for her."

She did not say her name, not then and not ever, but her shout petrified all of us with panic wherever we were in the house. Luis Enrique and I, who always had secret reasons to be afraid, hid under our beds. Aida ran to the house next door, and Margot contracted a sudden fever that kept her delirious for three days. Even the younger children were accustomed to my mother's explosions of jealousy, her eyes in flames and her Roman nose sharpened like a knife. We had seen her take down the pictures in the living room with strange serenity and smash them one after the other on the floor in a noisy hailstorm of glass. We had caught her sniffing every article of Papá's clothing before tossing them in the laundry basket. Nothing else happened after the night of the tragic duet, but the Florentine tuner took away the piano to sell it, and the violin—along with the revolver— ended up rotting in the closet.

At that time Barranquilla was an outpost of civil progress, gentle liberalism, and political coexistence. Decisive factors in its growth and prosperity were the end of more than a century of civil wars that had devastated the country since its independence from Spain, and then the collapse of the banana region that had been wounded beyond measure by the fierce repression unleashed on it after the great strike.

Still, until that time nothing could resist the enterprising spirit of its people. In 1919, the young industrialist Mario Santodomingo—the father of Julio Mario—had won civic glory by inaugurating the national air-mail service with fifty-seven letters in a canvas sack that he threw on the beach of Puerto Colombia, five leagues from Barranquilla, from a primitive airplane piloted by a North American, William Knox Martin. At the end of the First World War a group of German aviators—including Helmuth von Krohn—came to the country and established air routes with Junker F-13s, the first amphibious planes that traveled the Magdalena River like providential grasshoppers carrying six intrepid passengers and large sacks of mail. This was the embryo of the Colombian-German Air Transport Company, or SCADTA, one of the oldest firms of its kind in the world.

Our last move to Barranquilla was, for me, not a simple change of city and house but a change of Papá at the age of eleven. The new one was a fine man, but with a sense of paternal authority very different from the one that had made Margarita and me happy in my grandparents' house. Accustomed to being our own masters, we found it very difficult to adjust to another regime. Among his most admirable and moving qualities, Papá was an absolute autodidact and the most voracious reader I have ever known, though he was also the least systematic. After he left medical school he dedicated himself to studying homeopathy on his own, for at that time academic training was not required, and he obtained his license with honors. On the other hand, he did not have my mother's courage in facing crises. He spent the worst ones in the hammock in his room, reading every piece of printed paper he came across and solving crossword puzzles. But his problem with reality was insoluble. He had an almost mythical devotion to the rich, not those who could not be explained but men who had made their money by dint of talent and integrity. Restless in his hammock even in the middle of the day, he would accumulate vast fortunes in his imagination with undertakings so simple he could not understand how they had not occurred to him before. He liked to cite as an example the strangest riches he knew of in Darién: two hundred leagues of sows that had just given birth. Nonetheless, those extraordinary enterprises were not to be found in the places where we lived but in lost paradises he had heard of in his wanderings as a telegraph operator. His fatal impracticality kept us suspended between setbacks and relapses, but there were also long periods when not even the crumbs of our daily bread fell from heaven. In any case, in good times and bad, our parents taught us to celebrate the one and endure the other with the submission and dignity of old-style Catholics.

The only trial left for me was to travel alone with my papá, and I had the experience in its entirety when he took me to Barranquilla to help him set up the pharmacy and prepare for the arrival of the family. I was surprised that when we were alone he treated me as an older person, with affection and respect, and even assigned me tasks that did not seem easy for someone my age, but I did them well and was pleased, though he did not always agree. He was in the habit of telling us stories about his childhood in his hometown, but he repeated them year after year for each new child, so that they began to lose their charm for those of us who already knew them. In fact, we older ones would get up from the table when he began to recount them after meals. Luis Enrique, in another of his attacks of frankness, offended him when he said as he walked away:

"Let me know when our grandfather dies again."

Those outbursts that were so impulsive exasperated my father and were added to the reasons he had already assembled for sending Luis Enrique to the reformatory in Medellín. But with me in Barranquilla he became a different man. He filed away his repertoire of popular anecdotes and told me interesting stories about his arduous life with his mother, the legendary miserliness of his father, the difficulties he had being a student. Those memories allowed me to better tolerate some of his capriciousness and understand some of his incomprehension.

During that time we talked about books we had read and were going to read, and in the leprous stalls of the public market we reaped a good harvest of comic books about Tarzan and detectives and wars in space. But I was also about to be a victim of his practical sense, above all when he decided that we would eat only one meal a day. We suffered our first setback when he caught me filling the hollows of twilight with sodas and sweet rolls seven hours after lunch, and I could not tell him where I had gotten the money to buy them. I did not dare confess that my mother had given me a few pesos in secret as a precaution against the Trappist regimen he imposed when he traveled. That complicity with my mother lasted for as long as she had access to funds. When I was a boarder in secondary school she packed various bath and toilet items in my bag, and a fortune of ten pesos inside a box of Reuter soap, in the hope that I would open it at a moment of great need. I did, for while I was studying far from home, any moment was an ideal time to find ten pesos.

Papá arranged not to leave me alone at night in the pharmacy in Barranquilla, but his solutions were not always the most amusing for a boy of twelve. Visits at night to his friends' families were exhausting, because the ones that had children my age obliged them to go to bed at eight, leaving me tormented by boredom and sleepiness in a wasteland of social small talk. One night I must have fallen asleep during a visit to the family of a physician who was a friend of his, and I did not know how or at what time I woke walking down a strange street. I had no idea where I was, or how I had gotten there, and it could only be understood as an episode of sleepwalking. There was no precedent for it in the family, and it was never repeated again, but this is still the only possible explanation. The first thing that surprised me when I woke was the store window of a barber shop with gleaming mirrors where three or four patrons were being waited on under a clock that read ten after eight, which was an unthinkable hour for a boy my age to be alone on the street. Dazed with fright, I confused the names of the family we were visiting and could not remember their address, but some passersby were able to tie up the loose ends and take me to the right house. I found the neighborhood in a state of panic brought on by all kinds of conjectures regarding my disappearance. The only thing they knew about me was that I had gotten out of my chair in the middle of the conversation, and they thought I had gone to the bathroom. The sleepwalking explanation did not convince anyone, least of all my father, who without hesitation understood it as a piece of mischief that had not turned out well for me.

By a stroke of luck I was able to make amends some days later at another house, where he left me one night while he attended a business dinner. The entire family was interested only in a popular quiz show on the Atlántico radio station, and that night the question seemed unanswerable: "What animal changes its name when it rolls over?" By a strange miracle I had read the answer that very afternoon in the latest edition of the *Almanaque Bristol* and thought it was a bad joke: the only animal that changes its name is the *escarabajo*, because when it rolls over it turns into an *escararriba*.* I told this in secret to one of the girls in the house, and the oldest one rushed to the telephone and gave the answer to the Atlántico radio station. She won first prize, enough to pay the rent for three months: a hundred pesos. The living room filled with boisterous neighbors who had listened to the program and hurried to congratulate the winners, but what interested the family more than the money was the victory itself in a contest that had made radio history along the Caribbean coast. No one remembered I was there. When Papá came to pick me up, he joined the family celebration and drank a toast to their victory, but no one told him who the real winner had been.

Another victory at that time was my father's permission to go alone to the Sunday matinee at the Colombia Theater. For the first time they were showing serials, one episode each Sunday, and a tension was created that did not give you a moment's peace during the week. *La invasión de Mongo* was the first interplanetary epic, replaced in my heart only years later by Stanley

*The wordplay is based on *escarabajo* [beetle], *abajo* [below], and *arriba* [above]. *Escararriba* is an invented word.

Kubrick's *2001: A Space Odyssey.* But Argentine cinema, with the films of Carlos Gardel and Libertad Lamarque, defeated all the rest in the end.

In less than two months we finished setting up the pharmacy and rented and furnished the family's residence. The pharmacy was on a very active corner in the middle of the business center and only four blocks from the Paseo Bolívar. The residence, on the other hand, was on a marginal street in the impoverished and lively area known as Barrio Abajo, but the rent did not correspond to what it was but what it aspired to be: a Gothic manor house with gingerbread painted yellow and red, and two battle minarets.

On the same day that we acquired the site for the pharmacy, we hung our hammocks from the hooks in the back of the store and slept there, simmering in a soup of perspiration. When we occupied the residence we discovered there were no hooks for hammocks, but we laid the mattresses on the floor and slept as well as we could after we managed to borrow a cat to chase away the mice. When my mother arrived with the rest of the troops, the furnishings were still not complete and there were no kitchen utensils or many other things that we needed to live.

In spite of its artistic pretensions, the house was ordinary and not really big enough for us, with a living room, dining room, two bedrooms, and a small paved courtyard. The fact was it should not have cost a third of the rent we were paying. My mother was horrified when she saw it, but her husband reassured her with the lure of a golden future. They were always this way. It was impossible to conceive of two creatures so different who got along so well and loved each other so much.

My mother's appearance made an impression on me. She was pregnant for the seventh time, and it seemed to me that her eyelids and ankles were as swollen as her waist. She was thirty-three years old at the time, and this was the fifth house she had furnished. I was struck by her low state of mind that became worse after the first night, for she was terrified by the idea, which she herself invented with no foundation at all, that

Madame X had lived there before she was knifed to death. The crime had been committed seven years earlier, the last time my parents had lived in Barranquilla, and it was so terrifying that my mother had proposed not living in the city again. Perhaps she had forgotten it when she returned this time, but it came back to her on the first night she spent in a gloomy house where, on the spot, she had detected a certain resemblance to Dracula's castle.

The first news about Madame X had been the discovery of her naked body made unrecognizable by its advanced state of decomposition. It was established with difficulty that she had been younger than thirty, with black hair and attractive features. It was believed that she had been buried alive because her left hand was over her eyes in a gesture of terror, and her right arm was raised above her head. The only possible clues to her identity were two blue ribbons and an ornamental comb in what might have been a braided hairdo. Among many hypotheses, the one that seemed most probable was that she was a French dancer of easy virtue who had disappeared after the possible date of the crime.

Barranquilla had the well-deserved reputation of being the most hospitable and peaceful city in the country, but it was afflicted with an atrocious crime each year. Still, there was no precedent for one that had shaken public opinion as much and for as long as the crime of the nameless knifing victim. *La Prensa*, one of the most important newspapers in the country at the time, was considered the pioneer in Sunday comic strips— *Buck Rogers, Tarzan of the Apes*—but from its earliest years it had made its mark as one of the great precursors in crime reporting. For several months it kept the city in suspense with large headlines and surprising revelations that, with reason or without it, made the now-forgotten reporter famous throughout the country.

The authorities tried to restrict his reports with the argument that they were interfering with the investigation, but readers believed the authorities less than the revelations in *La Prensa*. The confrontation kept readers fascinated, and on at least one occasion investigators were obliged to change direction. The image of Madame X was implanted so deeply in the popular imagination that in many houses the doors were locked with chains and special vigilance was maintained at night on the assumption that the murderer, who was still at large, would attempt to continue his program of atrocious crimes, and it was decided that adolescent girls should not leave their houses alone after six in the evening.

The truth, however, was not discovered by anyone but was revealed sometime later by the perpetrator of the crime, Efraín Duncan, who confessed to having killed his wife, Ángela Hoyos, on the date calculated by the coroner's office, and burying her in the place where the stabbed body had been found. Family members recognized the blue ribbons and the comb that Ángela wore when she left the house with her husband on April 5 for a supposed trip to Calamar. The case was closed in a conclusive way by a final, inconceivable coincidence that seemed to have been pulled out of his sleeve by an author of fantastic novels: Ángela Hoyos had an identical twin sister, which permitted her to be identified beyond any doubt.

The myth of Madame X degenerated into an ordinary crime of passion, but the mystery of her identical twin still floated through the houses because people began to think she was Madame X herself come back to life through the arts of witchcraft. Doors were closed with crossbars and blocked with ramparts of furniture to prevent the murderer from coming in at night, for he had escaped prison with the aid of magic. In wealthy neighborhoods, it became the fashion to have hunting dogs trained to attack murderers capable of walking through walls. In reality, my mother could not overcome her fear until the neighbors convinced her that the house in Barrio Abajo had not yet been built in the days of Madame X.

On July 10, 1939, my mother gave birth to a little girl with the beautiful profile of an Indian, who was baptized Rita on account of the inexhaustible devotion felt in the house for St. Rita of Casia, founded, among many other graces, on the patience with which she endured the wicked character of her wayward husband. My mother would tell us that he had returned home one night maddened by alcohol, a minute after a hen left her droppings on the dining-room table. Without time to clean the immaculate tablecloth, the wife managed to cover the waste with a plate so that her husband would not see it, and hastened to distract him with the obligatory question:

"What would you like to eat?"

The man growled:

"Shit."

Then his wife lifted the plate and said with saintly sweetness:

"Here you are."

The story says that the husband then became convinced of his wife's holiness and converted to the faith of Christ.

The new drugstore in Barranquilla was a spectacular failure, undiminished by the speed with which my father foresaw it. After several months of defending himself in bits and pieces, opening two holes in order to fill one, he revealed himself to be more erratic than he had seemed so far. One day he packed his knapsacks and went to seek the fortunes lying buried in the most unexpected towns along the Magdalena River. Before he left he took me to his associates and friends and informed them with a certain solemnity that in his absence I would be there. I never knew if he said it as a joke, as he liked to do even on solemn occasions, or if he said it in all seriousness, as he enjoyed doing on ordinary occasions. I suppose that each of them understood him in his own way, for at the age of twelve I was rachitic and pale and almost unfit for even drawing and singing. The woman who sold us milk on credit told my mother in front of everyone, including me, without a hint of malice:

"You'll forgive me for saying so, Señora, but I don't believe this boy will grow up."

For a long time afterward my fear left me expecting a sudden death, and I often dreamed that when I looked in the mirror I did not see myself but an unborn calf. The school doctor diagnosed me as suffering from malaria, tonsillitis, and black bile on account of my abuse of unguided readings. I did not try to relieve anyone's alarm. On the contrary, I would exaggerate my condition as an invalid to avoid chores. My father, however, paid no attention to science and before he left he proclaimed that I was responsible for the house and family during his absence:

"As if he were me."

On the day he left he gathered us together in the living room and gave us instructions and preventive reprimands for what we might not do well in his absence, but we realized they were stratagems to keep from crying. He gave each of us a five-centavo coin, which was a small fortune for any child in those days, and he promised to exchange each of them for two identical ones if they were still intact when he returned. Then he addressed me in an evangelical tone:

"I leave them in your hands, may I find them in your hands."

It broke my heart to see him leave the house in his riding gaiters with his knapsacks over his shoulder, and I was the first who gave in to tears when he looked at us for the last time before turning the corner and waved goodbye. Only then, and for the rest of my life, did I realize how much I loved him.

It was not difficult to carry out his charge to me. My mother was becoming accustomed to inopportune and uncertain times alone, and she managed them with reluctance, but with great facility. Cooking and keeping the house in order made it necessary for even the youngest children to help in domestic duties, which they did well. During this time I felt like an adult for the first time when I realized that my brothers and sisters had begun to treat me like an uncle.

I never could overcome my shyness. When I had to confront the raw responsibility our wandering father had left with us, I learned that shyness is an invincible phantom. Each time I had to ask for credit, even when it had been agreed to ahead of time in stores owned by friends, I put it off for hours in the vicinity of the house, repressing my desire to cry and the cramps in my stomach, until at last I dared to go in with my jaws clenched so tight I could not speak. There was always some heartless shopkeeper who would leave me in utter confusion: "You moronic kid, you can't talk with your mouth shut." More than once I returned home with empty hands and some excuse I had invented. But never again was I as wretched as the first time I tried to talk on the telephone in the store at the corner. The owner helped me with the operator, for automatic service did not exist yet. I felt the winds of death when he gave me the receiver. I was hoping for an obliging voice and what I heard was the barking of someone who spoke into the darkness at the same time I did. I thought my interlocutor could not understand me either and I raised my voice as loud as I could. In a fury, he raised his too:

"What the hell are you shouting at me for?"

I hung up, terrified. I must admit that despite my fever to communicate I still have to repress my fear of telephones and airplanes, and I do not know if it is something left over from those days. How did I ever do anything? It was my good fortune that Mamá often repeated the answer: "You must suffer in order to serve."

Our first news of Papá came two weeks later in a letter intended more to entertain than to inform us about anything. My mother understood it in this way and she sang that day as she washed the dishes to raise our morale. Without my papá she was different: she identified with her daughters as if she were an older sister. She fit in with them so well that she was the best at their children's games, even dolls, and would lose her temper and fight with them as equals. Another two letters in the same vein as the first came from my papá, and they were filled with such promising projects that they helped us to sleep better.

A serious problem was the speed with which we outgrew our clothes. No one got hand-me-downs from Luis Enrique, it would not even have been possible because he would come home in miserable condition, his clothes ruined, and we never knew why. My mother said it was if he had walked through barbed wire. My sisters—seven and nine years old—helped each other with miracles of ingenuity, and I always have believed that the pressing needs of those days turned them into premature adults. Aida was resourceful and Margot had, for the most part, overcome her shyness and was affectionate and obliging with her newborn sister. I was the most difficult, not only because I had to perform distinctive tasks but because my mother, protected by everyone's enthusiasm, took the risk of reducing the household funds in order to matriculate me in the Cartagena de Indias School, a ten-block walk from the house.

In accordance with the notification we had received, some

twenty applicants showed up at eight in the morning for the admissions procedure. To our good fortune it was not a written examination, but three teachers called us in the order we had enrolled the previous week and gave us a brief examination based on our certificates of previous study. I was the only one who did not have any, since there had not been time to request them from the Montessori and elementary schools in Aracataca, and my mother thought I would not be admitted without papers. But I decided to take a chance. One of the teachers removed me from the line when I confessed I did not have them, but another took charge of my fate and led me to his office to examine me without prerequisites. He asked me what quantity was a gross, how many years were in a lustrum and a millennium, he had me repeat the departmental capitals, the principal rivers of the nation, and the countries that bordered it. Everything seemed routine until he asked me what books I had read. He found it noteworthy that at my age I cited so many and so great a variety of books, and had read *The Thousand and One Nights* in an adult edition that had not suppressed some of the scabrous episodes that scandalized Father Angarita. It surprised me to learn that it was an important book, for I always had thought that serious adults could not believe that genies came out of bottles or doors opened at the incantation of magic words. The applicants who had gone before me had taken no more than a quarter of an hour, and were admitted or rejected, but I spent more than half an hour conversing with the teacher about all kinds of subjects. Together we looked at a bookcase that stood behind his desk and was crowded with volumes, and there, distinguished by their number and splendor, was the series *The Young Person's Treasury*, which I had heard about, but the teacher convinced me that at my age, *Don Quixote* was more useful. He did not find it in his library but promised to lend it to me later. After half an hour of rapid commentaries on *Sinbad the Sailor* or *Robinson Crusoe*, he accompanied me to the exit without telling me if I had been admitted. I thought I had not been, of course, but on the terrace he shook my hand and said goodbye until Monday at eight in the morning, when I would matriculate in the most advanced course in the primary school: the fourth year.

He was the headmaster. His name was Juan Ventura Casalins and I remember him as a friend of my childhood, with nothing of the fearsome image that people had of teachers at the time. His unforgettable virtue was treating all of us as equal adults, though I still think he paid particular attention to me. In classes he would ask me more questions than he did the others, and he helped me so that my answers would be accurate and fluid. He allowed me to take books from the school library to read at home. Two of them, *Treasure Island* and *The Count of Monte Cristo*, were my happiness drug during those rocky years. I devoured them letter by letter, longing to know what happened in the next line and at the same time longing not to know in order not to break the spell. With them, as with *The Thousand and One Nights*, I learned and never forgot that we should read only those books that force us to reread them.

On the other hand, my reading of *Don Quixote* always deserved a separate chapter, because it did not cause the upheaval in me foreseen by Maestro Casalins. The long learned speeches of the knight errant bored me, I did not find the stupidities of the squire at all amusing, and I even began to think it was not the same book that people talked so much about. But I told myself that a teacher as learned as ours could not be mistaken, and I forced myself to swallow it like spoonfuls of a purgative. I made other attempts in secondary school, where I was obliged to study it as a requirement, and I had an irremediable aversion to it until a friend advised me to put it on the back of the toilet and try to read it while I took care of my daily needs. Only in this way did I discover it, like a conflagration, and relish it forward and back until I could recite entire episodes by heart.

That providential school also left me historic memories of an irretrievable city and time. It was the only building at the top of a green hill, and from its terrace the two ends of the world were visible. To the left, the Prado, the most distinguished and expensive district, which at first sight seemed a faithful copy of the electrified henhouse of the United Fruit Company. This was not a coincidence: a firm of American urban planners was building it with their imported tastes and norms and prices, and it was an infallible tourist attraction for the rest of the country. To the right, on the other hand, was the slum of our Barrio Abajo, with its streets of burning dust and houses of cane and mud with palm roofs, always reminding us that we were nothing more than flesh-and-blood mortals. It was our good fortune that from the terrace of the school we had a panoramic vision of the future: the historic delta of the Magdalena River, which is one of the great rivers of the world, and the gray ocean of Bocas de Ceniza.

On May 28, 1935, we saw the oil tanker *Taralite*, flying a Canadian flag and under the command of Captain D. F. McDonald, which entered along the canals cut out of rock to roars of jubilation and dropped anchor in the port of the city to the noise of music and fireworks. This was the culmination of a great civic achievement that had cost many years and many pesos and had converted Barranquilla into the only sea-and-river port in the country.

Not long afterward, a plane piloted by Captain Nicolás Reyes Manotas skimmed over the rooftops in search of a clear space for an emergency landing, to save not only his own skin but that of the souls he might hit in his fall. He was one of the pioneers of Colombian aviation. The primitive airplane had been given to him as a gift in Mexico, and he flew it solo from one end of Central America to the other. The crowd gathered at the airport in Barranquilla had prepared a triumphant welcome for him with handkerchiefs and flags and a band, but Reyes Manotas wanted to fly over the city another two times as a greeting, and his engine failed. He managed to recover with miraculous skill and land on the roof of a building in the business center, but the plane was caught in electric cables and was dangling from a post. My brother Luis Enrique and I followed him in a tumultuous crowd as far as we could, but we managed to see the pilot only after they got him out with great difficulty, though he was safe and sound and had a hero's ovation.

The city also had its first radio station, a modern aqueduct that became a touristic and pedagogical attraction for displaying the new process of water purification, and a fire department whose sirens and bells were a fiesta for children and adults from the first moment they were heard. At about the same time the first convertible automobiles came in, racing along the streets at lunatic velocities and smashing into smithereens on the new paved highways. The undertaking establishment La Equitativa, inspired by the humor of death, set up an enormous sign at the exit from the city: "Take your time, we're waiting for you."

At night, when there was no other refuge but the house, my mother would gather us together to read us Papá's letters. Most of them were masterpieces of distraction, but one was very explicit about the enthusiasm that homeopathy awakened in older people along the lower Magdalena. "There are cases here that would seem like miracles," my father said. At times he left us with the impression that very soon he would reveal something wonderful, but what followed was another month of silence. During Holy Week, when two of my younger brothers contracted pernicious cases of chicken pox, we had no way to communicate with him because not even the most expert scouts could pick up his trail.

It was during those months that I understood in real life one of the words used most by my grandparents: poverty. I interpreted it as the situation we experienced in their house when the banana company began to be dismantled. They were always complaining about it. There were no longer two or even three shifts at the table, as there once had been, but only one. In order not to renounce the sacred ritual of lunches, even when they no longer had the resources to maintain them, they began to buy food prepared at the stands in the market, which was good and much cheaper and had the added surprise that we children liked it better. But the lunches ended forever when Mina learned that some frequent guests had resolved not to return to the house because the food was not as good as it once had been.

The poverty of my parents in Barranquilla, on the contrary, was exhausting, but it allowed me the good fortune of establishing an exceptional relationship with my mother. More than the expected filial love, I felt an astounding admiration for her because she had the character of a lioness, silent but fierce when faced with adversity, and a relationship with God that seemed more combative than submissive: two exemplary virtues that imbued her life with a confidence that never failed. At the worst moments she would laugh at her own providential resources. Like the time she bought an ox knee and boiled it day after day for our increasingly watery daily broth until it had no more to give. One night during a terrifying storm she used up the month's supply of lard to make rag candles, because the electricity was off until dawn and she herself had inculcated a fear of the dark in the younger ones to keep them from leaving their beds.

At first my parents visited families they knew who had emigrated from Aracataca because of the banana crisis and the decline of public order. They were circular visits that always revolved around the topic of the misfortunes that had raged through the town. But when poverty squeezed us in Barranquilla we did not complain again in anyone else's house. My mother reduced her reticence to a single phrase: "You can see poverty in the eyes."

Until I was five, death had been for me a natural end that happened to other people. The delights of heaven and the torments of hell seemed only lessons to be memorized in Father Astete's catechism class. They had nothing to do with me, until I learned in passing at a wake that lice were escaping from the hair of the dead man and wandering along the pillows. What disturbed me after that was not the fear of death but embarrassment that lice would escape my head too in the presence of all my relatives at my wake. But in primary school in Barranquilla, I did not realize I was crawling with lice until I had infected the entire family. Then my mother gave yet another proof of her character. She disinfected her children one by one with insecticide for cockroaches, in thorough cleansings that she baptized with a name of noble lineage: the police. The problem was that no sooner were we clean than we began to crawl again, because I became reinfected at school. Then my mother decided to use drastic remedies and she forced me to have my head shaved. It was an act of heroism to appear at school on Monday wearing a cloth cap, but I survived the mockery of my classmates with honor and completed the final year with the highest grades. I never saw Maestro Casalins again, but my eternal gratitude remained.

A friend of my papá's whom we never met got me a vacation job at a printing shop near the house. The salary was just a little more than nothing, and my only incentive was the idea of learning the trade. But I did not have a minute to look at the press because my work, in another section, consisted of arranging lithographed plates for binding. A consolation was that my mother authorized me to use my salary to buy the Sunday supplement of *La Prensa* that had the comic strips of *Tarzan*, *Buck Rogers*, called *Rogelio el Conquistador*, and *Mutt and Jeff*, called *Benitín y Eneas*. During my leisure time on Sundays I learned to draw them from memory and would continue the week's episodes on my own. I managed to waken the enthusiasm of some adults on the block and sold them for as much as two centavos.

The job was tiring and sterile, and no matter how many pains I took, the reports of my superiors accused me of a lack of enthusiasm in my work. It must have been out of consideration for my family that they relieved me of the routine of the shop and made me a street distributor of illustrated advertisements for a cough syrup recommended by the most famous movie stars. That seemed fine to me because the fliers were attractive with full-color photographs of the actors on glossy paper. From the beginning, however, I realized that handing them out was not as easy as I thought, since people viewed them with suspicion because they were being given away, and most contorted and twitched as if they had been electrified in order not to accept them. On the first few days I went back to the shop with what I had left over so that they would make up the amount I had distributed. Until I ran into some school friends from Aracataca, whose mother was horrified to see me doing what she considered work for beggars. She was almost shouting when she berated me for walking around the street in cloth sandals that my mother had bought so I would not wear out my full-dress half boots.

"You tell Luisa Márquez," she said, "to think about what her parents would say if they saw their favorite grandchild in the market handing out advertisements for consumptives."

I did not give my mother the message in order to spare her the grief, but I cried into my pillow with rage and shame for several nights. The end of the drama was that I did not hand out fliers again but tossed them into the gutters in the market, not foreseeing that the water was gentle and the glossy papers stayed afloat until they formed a quilt of beautiful colors on the surface, a very unusual sight from the bridge.

My mother must have received a message from her beloved dead in a revelatory dream, because in less than two months she took me out of the printing shop without any explanations. I resisted because I did not want to miss the Sunday edition of *La Prensa* that we received in the family like a blessing from heaven, but my mother continued buying it even when she had to put one less potato in the soup. Another means of salvation was the consolatory sum that Uncle Juanito sent to us during the harshest months. He still lived in Santa Marta on his scant earnings as a certified accountant, and he imposed upon himself the duty of sending us a letter every week with two one-peso bills inside. The captain of the launch *Aurora*, an old friend of the family, would give it to me at seven in the morning, and I would go home with basic foodstuffs for several days.

One Wednesday I could not run the errand and my mother entrusted it to Luis Enrique, who could not resist the temptation of multiplying the two pesos in the slot machine in a Chinese tavern. He did not have the resolve to stop when he lost the first two slugs, and he kept trying to get them back until he was down to the last one. "I was in such a panic," he told me as an adult, "that I decided never to go home again." He knew very well that two pesos bought basic food for a week. By a stroke of luck, with the last slug something happened in the machine, it shuddered with the metal earthquake in its gut, and in an unstoppable stream it vomited up all the slugs for the two lost pesos. "Then the devil inspired me," Luis Enrique told me, "and I dared risk another slug." He won. He risked another and won, and another and another and he won. "The terror I felt then was worse than when I was losing, and my guts turned to water," he told me, "but I went on playing." In the end he won twice the original two pesos in five-centavo coins, and he did not dare exchange them for bills at the register for fear the Chinese owner would involve him in some deceit. They were so bulky in his pockets that before he gave Mamá the two pesos from Uncle Juanito in five-centavo coins, he buried the four he had won at the back of the courtyard where he hid every stray centavo he found. Little by little he spent them without confessing the secret to anyone until many years later, in torment for having fallen into the temptation of risking his last five centavos in the Chinese shop.

His relationship with money was very personal. Once when my mother caught him scratching at the money for the market in her purse, his defense was somewhat savage but lucid: the money one takes without permission from the purses of one's parents cannot be a theft because the money belongs to everybody in common and they deny it to us out of envy because they can not do with it what their children do. I defended his argument to the extreme of confessing that I, too, had sacked her domestic hiding places when the need was urgent. My mother lost her temper. "Don't be so stupid," she almost shouted at me. "You and your brother don't steal anything from me, because I leave the money where I know you'll find it when you're in trouble." In an attack of rage I once heard her murmur in despair that God ought to allow the theft of certain things in order to feed one's children.

Luis Enrique's natural talent for mischief was very useful in solving mutual problems, but he never made me an accomplice in his misconduct. On the contrary, he always arranged matters so that not even the slightest suspicion would fall on me, which strengthened a true affection for him that has lasted my whole life. On the other hand, I never let him know how much I envied his audacity and suffered on account of the beatings Papá gave him. My behavior was very different from his, though at times it was hard for me to temper my envy. But I was troubled by Mamá's parents' house in Cataca, where they took me to sleep only when they were going to give me purges for worms, or castor oil. To the point where I despised the twenty-centavo coins they paid me for the dignity with which I took them.

I believe the height of my mother's desperation was sending me with a letter to a man who had a reputation for being the richest man and at the same time the most generous philanthropist in the city. Talk of his good heart was as widespread as news of his financial triumphs. My mother wrote him an anguished and direct letter to request urgent financial assistance, not in her name, because she was capable of enduring anything, but for love of her children. Only someone who knew her would understand what that humiliation meant in her life, but circumstances demanded it. She warned me that the secret had to remain between the two of us, and it did, until this moment when I am writing about it.

I knocked at the large front door of the house, which somehow resembled a church, and almost without delay a small window opened and a woman looked out; all I remember about her was the ice in her eyes. She took the letter without saying a word and shut the window again. It must have been eleven in the morning, and I waited, sitting against the doorjamb, until three in the afternoon, when I decided to knock again and try to get an answer. The same woman opened the window, recognized me in surprise, and asked me to wait a moment. The answer was that I should come back at the same time on Tuesday of the following week. I did, but the only answer was that there would be no answer for another week. I had to go back three more times, always receiving the same answer, until a month and a half later, when a woman even harsher than the first responded, on behalf of her employer, that this was not a charitable establishment.

I walked around the burning streets trying to find the courage to bring my mother an answer that would deliver her from her illusions. It was already dark when I faced her with an aching heart and said that the good philanthropist had died several months earlier. What grieved me most was the rosary my mother said for the eternal rest of his soul.

Four or five years later, when we heard the factual report on the radio that the philanthropist had died the day before, I was petrified as I waited for my mother's reaction. But I will never understand how it was that she heard it with sympathetic attention and said with a heartfelt sigh:

"God keep him in His holy kingdom!"

A block from the house we made friends with the Mosqueras, a family that spent fortunes on comic books and kept them piled to the ceiling in a shed in their courtyard. We were the only privileged beings who could spend entire days there reading *Dick Tracy* and *Buck Rogers*. Another fortunate discovery was an apprentice who painted movie posters for the nearby Las Quintas Theater. I helped him for the sheer pleasure of painting letters, and he got us in free two or three times a week for the good films with gun battles and fistfights. The only luxury that was missing was a radio so that we could listen to music at any time of day with just the touch of a button. Today it is difficult to imagine how rare they were in the houses of the poor. Luis Enrique and I would sit on a bench at the store on the corner where idle patrons could sit and chat, and we spent entire afternoons listening to the programs of popular music, which is what most of the programs were. In time we learned by heart a complete repertoire of Miguelito Valdés and the Casino de la Playa Orchestra, Daniel Santos and the Sonora Matancera, and the boleros of Agustín Lara in the voice of Toña la Negra. Our amusement at night, above all on the two occasions when they cut off our electricity for lack of payment, was to teach the songs to my mother and brothers and sisters, Ligia and Gustavo in particular, who learned them like parrots without understanding them and entertained us no end with their lyrical bits of nonsense. There were no exceptions. We all inherited from our father and mother a special memory for music and a good ear for learning a song the second time we heard it. Above all Luis Enrique, who was born a musician and specialized on his own in guitar solos for serenades of unrequited love. It did not take us long to discover that all the children without radios in the neighboring houses also learned the songs from my brothers and sisters, and most of all from my mother, who became one more sister in that house of children.

My favorite program was *The Little Bit of Everything Hour*, with the composer, singer, and conductor Angel María Camacho y Cano, who held his audience captive starting at one in the afternoon with an ingenious miscellany, in particular his amateur hour for children under fifteen. All you had to do was register at the offices of La Voz de la Patria—The Voice of the Nation—and come to the program half an hour early. Maestro Camacho y Cano in person accompanied on the piano, and one of his assistants carried out the unappealable sentence of interrupting the song with a church bell when the amateur made the slightest mistake. The prize for the best-sung song was more than we could dream of—five pesos—but my mother was explicit: the most important thing was the glory of singing well on so prestigious a program.

Until that time I had identified myself only with my father's family name—García—and my two baptismal names—Gabriel José—but on that historic occasion my mother asked me to register with her family name too—Márquez—so that no one could have any doubt about my identity. It was an event at home. They made me dress in white as if it were my First Communion, and before I went out they gave me a dose of potassium bromide. I arrived at La Voz de la Patria two hours early, and the effect of the sedative soon passed as I waited in a nearby park because no one was allowed to enter the studios until a quarter of an hour before the program. As each minute passed I felt the spiders of terror growing inside me, and when I went in at last my heart was pounding. I had to make a supreme effort not to return home with the story that for some reason or other they had not allowed me to participate. The maestro did a quick test with me on the piano to establish my key. They called seven in the order in which they had registered, they rang the bell for three because of various mistakes, and they announced me with the simple name of Gabriel Márquez. I sang "El cisne," a sentimental song about a swan whiter than a snowflake killed along with his lover by a pitiless hunter. After the first measures I realized that the key was very high for me in some notes that had not been tested in rehearsal, and I had a moment of panic when the assistant's expression became doubtful and he got ready to pick up the bell. I do not know where I found the courage to make an energetic sign to him not to ring it, but it was too late: the bell rang without mercy. The five-peso prize, along with several gifts from advertisers, went to a very beautiful blonde who had massacred a selection from *Madame Butterfly*. I returned home crushed by defeat, and I never could console my mother for her disappointment. Many years passed before she confessed to me that the reason for her chagrin was that she had told her relatives and friends to listen to me sing and did not know how to avoid them.

In the midst of that regimen of laughter and tears, I never missed school. Even when I had not eaten. But my time for reading at home was spent in household chores, and we did not have a budget for electricity that would allow reading until midnight. In any event, I resolved the problem. On the way to school there were several garages for passenger buses, and I would spend hours at one of them watching how they painted signs on the sides announcing routes and destinations. One day I asked the painter to let me paint a few letters to see if I could do it. Surprised by my natural aptitude, he sometimes allowed me to assist him for a few pesos that helped the family budget a little. Another hopeful thing was my casual friendship with the three García brothers, the children of a sailor on the Magdalena River, who had organized a popular-music trio to enliven their friends' parties for pure love of the art. I joined them to form the García Quartet that would compete in the amateur hour on the Atlántico radio station. We won the first day to thunderous applause, but they did not pay us the prize of five pesos because of an irreparable error in our registration. We continued rehearsing together for the rest of the year and singing as a favor at family parties, until life at last dispersed us.

I never shared the malicious view that the patience with which my father dealt with poverty showed a good deal of irresponsibility. On the contrary: I believe these were Homeric tests of an unfailing complicity between him and his wife that allowed them to maintain their courage even at the edge of the abyss. He knew that she managed panic even better than despair, and that this was the secret of our survival. What he did not think of, perhaps, is that she alleviated his sorrows while leaving the best of her life behind her. We never could understand the reason for his trips. It would often happen that we would be awakened at midnight on a Saturday and taken to the local office of an oil encampment on the Catatumbo, where a call from my father was waiting for us on the radiotelephone. I will never forget my mother bathed in tears during a conversation made more difficult by technology.

"Oh, Gabriel," my mother said, "look how you've left me with this army of children, when it's so bad sometimes we have nothing to eat."

He replied with the bad news that he had an enlarged liver. It often happened to him, but my mother did not worry too much because on occasion he used it to hide his cheating.

"That always happens to you when you don't behave," she said to him as a joke.

She spoke looking at the microphone as if Papá were there, and at the end she became confused trying to send him a kiss and kissed the microphone. She herself could not control her giggles, and she never could tell the entire story because she always ended up bathed in tears of laughter. However, that day she was distracted, and at last she said at the table as if talking to no one in particular:

"I noticed something strange in Gabriel's voice."

We explained that the radio system not only distorts voices but masks personalities. The next night she said when she was half asleep: "In any event, his voice sounded as if he were much thinner." Her nose had grown sharper because of those bad times, and she asked herself between sighs what those towns without God or laws were like where her man was wandering untethered. Her hidden motives were more apparent in a second conversation by radio, when she made my father promise that he would return home without delay if nothing was resolved in two weeks. But before the time was up, we received a dramatic one-word telegram from Altos del Rosario: "Undecided." My mother saw in the message a confirmation of her most lucid forebodings, and she dictated her unappealable verdict:

"Either you come home before Monday, or I'm going there right now with all our offspring."

A holy remedy. My father knew the power of her threats, and before the week was out he was back in Barranquilla. We were struck by the way he came in, dressed without care, his skin greenish and unshaved, so that my mother thought he was ill. But it was a momentary impression, because in two days' time he salvaged his youthful project of opening a multipurpose pharmacy in the town of Sucre, an idyllic and prosperous corner that was a night and a day's sail from Barranquilla. He had been there in his youth as a telegraph operator, and his heart stood still when he remembered the trip through crepuscular canals and golden swamps, and the eternal dances. At one time he had persisted in trying to obtain the store there, but without the luck he had in obtaining others he had wanted even more, like Aracataca. He thought about it again some five years later, during the third banana crisis, but he found it had been taken over by wholesalers from Magangué. However, a month before returning to Barranquilla, he happened to meet one of them who not only described a different reality but offered him good credit for Sucre. He did not accept because he was about to achieve the golden dream of Altos del Rosario, but when he was surprised by his wife's sentence, he found the wholesaler from Magangué, who was still wandering the river towns, and they concluded the deal.

After some two weeks of studies and arrangements with wholesalers who were friends of his, he left with his appearance and disposition reestablished, and his impression of Sucre was so intense that he wrote in his first letter: "The reality was better than the memory." He rented a house with a balcony on the main square, and from there he regained his friends from long ago, who opened their doors wide to him. The family had to sell what it could, pack up the rest, which was not very much, and take it along on one of the steamboats that made a regular trip along the Magdalena River. In the same letter he sent a money order well calculated to cover immediate expenses and announced another for the costs of the trip. I cannot imagine more attractive news for my mother's illusory character, so that her reply was intended not only to sustain her husband's spirits but to sugarcoat the news that she was pregnant for the eighth time.

I filled out the forms and made the reservations on the *Capitán de Caro*, a legendary ship that traveled the distance between Barranquilla and Magangué in a night and half a day. Then we would continue to our destination by motor launch along the San Jorge River and the idyllic Mojana Channel.

"As long as we leave here, even if it's for hell," exclaimed my mother, who always distrusted the Babylonian reputation of Sucre. "You shouldn't leave a husband alone in a town like that."

She imposed so much haste on us that three days before the trip we were sleeping on the floor because we had already auctioned off the beds and all the furniture we could sell. Everything else was in boxes, and the money for our passage safe in one of my mother's hiding places, counted and recounted a thousand times over.

The clerk who took care of me in the shipping offices was so charming that I did not have to clench my jaws to get along with him. I have the absolute certainty that I made meticulous notes of the fares he quoted in the clear, proper diction of obliging Caribbean people. What made me most happy and what I remembered best was that under the age of twelve you paid only half the regular fare. In other words, all the children except me. On that basis, my mother set aside the money for the trip and spent all the rest dismantling the house.

On Friday I went to buy the tickets and the clerk greeted me with the startling news that the discount for children under twelve was not half but only thirty percent, which made an irreparable difference to us. He claimed I had written it down wrong, because the information was printed on an official notice that he placed in front of me. I went home devastated, and my mother made no comment but put on the dress she had worn when she was in mourning for her father, and we went to the riverboat agency. She wanted to be fair: someone had made a mistake and it very well might have been her son, but that did not matter. The fact was that we had no more money. The agent explained that there was nothing he could do.

"You must realize, Señora," he said, "that it isn't a question of wanting or not wanting to serve you, but these are the regulations of a serious firm that cannot be run like a weather vane."

"But they're only babies," said my mother, and she pointed at me as an example. "Imagine, this one's the oldest, and he just turned twelve." And with her hand she indicated:

"They're this big."

It was not a question of height, claimed the agent, but age. No one paid any less except newborns, who traveled free. My mother looked to a higher authority:

"Whom do I have to see to straighten this out?"

The clerk did not have the chance to answer. The manager, an older man with a maternal belly, came to the door of the office in the middle of the discussion, and the clerk rose to his feet when he saw him. He was immense, and his appearance respectable, and his authority, even in shirtsleeves and soaked with perspiration, was more than evident. He listened to my mother with attention and responded in a serene voice that a decision of this kind was possible only through a revision of regulations at a meeting of the partners.

"Believe me, I am very sorry," he concluded.

My mother sensed a moment of power and refined her argument.

"You are correct, Señor," she said, "but the problem is that your clerk did not explain it with care to my son, or my son did not understand him, and I proceeded on that error. Now I have everything packed and ready to go on board, we are sleeping on the blessed floor, our money for the market will be finished today, and on Monday I turn the house over to the new tenants." She realized that the clerks in the room were listening to her with great interest, and then she addressed them: "What can this mean to so important a company?" And without waiting for an answer, she asked the manager, looking him straight in the eye:

"Do you believe in God?"

The manager became confused. The entire office was in suspense during a silence that lasted too long. Then my mother stirred in her chair, pressed together her knees, which had begun to tremble, held her handbag in her lap with both hands, and said with a determination typical of her great causes:

"Well, I'm not moving until this is resolved."

The manager was horrified, and the entire staff stopped working to look at my mother. She was impassive, her nose sharp, her skin pale and pearly with sweat. She had stopped wearing mourning for her father, but had put it back on because it seemed the most suitable dress for the task. The manager did not look at her again but looked at his employees without knowing what to do, and at last he exclaimed to everyone:

"This is unprecedented!"

My mother did not blink. "I had a knot of tears in my throat but I had to resist because it would have ended in disaster," she told me. Then the manager asked the clerk to bring the documents to his office. He did, and in five minutes he came out again, grumbling and furious, but with all the tickets in order for the trip.

The following week we disembarked in the town of Sucre as if we had been born there. It must have had some sixteen thousand inhabitants, like so many of the country's municipalities in those days, and they all knew one another, not so much by their names as by their secret lives. Not only the town but the entire region was a sea of gentle water that changed colors on account of the blankets of flowers that covered it according to the time, the place, and our own state of mind. Its splendor recalled that of the dreamlike still waters in Southeast Asia. During the many years the family lived in Sucre there was not a single automobile. It would have been impractical, since the unswerving streets of flattened earth seemed drawn in a straight line for bare feet, and many houses had a private dock in the kitchen with household canoes for local transportation.

My first emotion was of inconceivable liberty. Everything that we children had not had or had longed for was soon within reach. We ate when we were hungry or slept when we wanted to, and it was not easy to worry about anyone, for despite the harshness of their laws, adults were so caught up in their own time that they did not have enough left over to even worry about themselves. The only condition for the safety of children was that they learn to swim before they walked, for the town was divided in two by a channel of dark waters that served as both aqueduct and sewer. From the time they turned one they were tossed from the balconies of the kitchens, first with life preservers so they would lose their fear of the water, and then without life preservers so they would lose their respect for death. Years later, my brother Jaime and my sister Ligia, who survived the dangers of initiation, excelled in children's swimming championships.

What made Sucre an unforgettable town for me was the feeling of freedom we children had moving through the streets. In two or three weeks we knew who lived in each house, and we behaved as if we had always known them. Social customs—simplified by use—were those of modern life within a feudal culture: the wealthy—cattle ranchers and sugar industrialists—lived on the main square, and the poor wherever they could. As for ecclesiastical administration, it was a territory of missions with jurisdiction and control in a vast lacustrine empire. In the center of that world, the parish church on the main square of Sucre was a pocket version of the Cologne cathedral, copied from memory by a Spanish priest doubling as architect. The wielding of power was immediate and absolute. Every night, after the rosary, they rang the bells in the church tower the number of times that corresponded to the moral classification of the film being shown in the nearby theater, in accordance with the catalogue of the Catholic Office for Films. The missionary on duty, sitting in the door of his office, watched those who entered the theater across the street so that transgressors would be sanctioned.

My great frustration was my age when I came to Sucre. I still had three months to go before crossing the fateful line of thirteen, and in the house they no longer tolerated me as a child but neither did they recognize me as an adult, and in that limbo of my age I turned out to be the only one of my brothers and sisters who did not learn to swim. They did not know whether to seat me at the children's table or with the grownups. The maids no longer changed their clothes in front of me, even with the lights out, but one of them slept naked in my bed several times without disturbing my sleep. I had not had time to become sated with that excess of free will when I had to go back to Barranquilla in January of the following year in order to begin my baccalaureate, because in Sucre there was no secondary school good enough for the excellent grades of Maestro Casalins.

After long discussions and consultations, with very scant participation from me, my parents decided on the Colegio San José de la Compañía de Jesús in Barranquilla. I cannot explain where they found so many resources in so few months, when the pharmacy and homeopathic consulting room were still in the future. My mother always gave a reason that required no proofs: "God is very great." In the expenses of the move there must have been provision for the installation and support of the family, but not for my school fees. From having only one pair of torn shoes and one change of clothes that I wore while the other was being washed, my mother furnished me with new clothes in a trunk the size of a catafalque, not foreseeing that in six months I would have grown a span. She was also the one who decided on her own that I would begin to wear long pants, in opposition to the social provision respected by my father that they could not be worn until one's voice started to change.

The truth is that in the discussions regarding the education of each child, I was always sustained by the hope that Papá, in one of his Homeric rages, would decree that none of us would go back to school. It was not impossible. He was self-taught because of the overwhelming force of his poverty, and his father had been inspired by the steel morality of Fernando VII, who proclaimed individual instruction at home in order to preserve the integrity of the family. I feared secondary school as if it were jail, the mere idea of living subjected to a regimen of bells frightened me, but it also was my only chance to enjoy a free life after I was thirteen, to have good relations with the family but far from its discipline, its demographic enthusiasm, its unsettled days, and to read without stopping for breath for as long as the light lasted.

My only argument against the Colegio San José, one of the most demanding and expensive schools in the Caribbean, was its martial discipline, but my mother stopped me with a premonition: "They make governors there." When retreat was no longer possible, my father washed his hands of the matter:

"It should be noted that I didn't say either yes or no."

He would have preferred the Colegio Americano so that I would learn English, but my mother rejected it with the perverse argument that it was a den of Lutherans. Today I have to admit, to be fair to my father, that one of the defects in my life as a writer has been not speaking English.

Seeing Barranquilla again from the bridge of the same *Capitán de Caro* on which we had traveled three months earlier troubled my heart, as if I had sensed that I was only returning to real life. It was fortunate that my parents had arranged room and board for me with my cousin José María Valdeblánquez and his wife Hortensia, who were young and amiable, and who shared their peaceful life with me in a simple living room, a bedroom, and a paved courtyard that was always in shadow because of the clothes hung out to dry on the lines. They slept in the bedroom with their six-month-old daughter. I slept in the living room on the sofa, which turned into a bed at night.

The Colegio San José was about six blocks away, in a park with almond trees where the oldest cemetery in the city had been located and where unattached bones and scraps of corpses' clothing could still be found level with the paving stones. On the day I entered the main courtyard there was a ceremony for the first-year students, wearing the Sunday uniform of white trousers and blue flannel jacket, and I could not control my terror that they knew everything I did not. But I soon realized they were as raw and frightened as I was facing the uncertainties of the future.

My personal phantom was Brother Pedro Reyes, prefect of the elementary division, who was bent on convincing the superiors of the academy that I was not prepared for the baccalaureate. He became the nightmare who would waylay me in the most unexpected places and give me instant examinations with diabolical pitfalls: "Do you believe God can make a stone so heavy He cannot carry it?" he asked and gave me no time to think. Or this other cursed trap: "If we placed a gold belt fifty centimeters thick around the equator, how much would the weight of Earth increase?" I could not get a single question right, even if I had known the answers, because my tongue stumbled in terror the way it had my first day on the telephone. The terror was well founded because Brother Reyes was right. I was not prepared for the baccalaureate, but I could not give up the good fortune of having been admitted without an examination. The mere sight of him made me tremble. Some classmates gave malicious interpretations to the siege but I had no reason to think they were true. Besides, my conscientiousness helped me because I passed my first oral exam with no opposition when I recited Fray Luis de León like flowing water, and with colored chalks drew a Christ that looked alive on the blackboard. The panel was so pleased it also forgot about arithmetic and national history.

The problem with Brother Reyes was settled because during Holy Week he needed some drawings for his botany class, and I made them for him without blinking. He not only called a halt to his siege but at times spent recess periods teaching me the well-founded answers to the questions I had not been able to answer, or to some even stranger that then appeared as if by accident on my next first-year exams. But whenever I was in a group he would joke, weak with laughter, that I was the only student in the third year of elementary who was doing well in his baccalaureate. Today I realize he was right. Above all on account of spelling, which was my Calvary throughout my time in school and continues to astound the people who proofread my originals. The most benevolent console themselves with the belief that they are typing errors.

A relief for my fears and alarms was the appointment of the painter and writer Héctor Rojas Herazo to the position of drawing teacher. He must have been about twenty. He came into the classroom accompanied by Father Prefect, and his greeting echoed like a slammed door in the stupor of three in the afternoon. He had the beauty and easy elegance of a movie star, in a very close-fitting camel's hair jacket with gold buttons, multicolored vest, and print silk tie. But the most extraordinary thing was his melon-shaped hat when the temperature was ninety degrees in the shade. He was as tall as the lintel, so that he had to bend down to draw on the blackboard. Standing beside him, Father Prefect seemed abandoned by the hand of God.

From the beginning it was evident he did not have a method or the patience for teaching, but his mischievous humor kept us in suspense, just as we were astounded by the masterful drawings he put on the board with colored chalks. He did not last more than three months in the position, we never knew why, but one could assume that his secular pedagogy was not compatible with the mental order of the Company of Jesus.

From the start I won fame as a poet at the *colegio*, first because of the facility with which I could memorize and recite at the top of my lungs the poems by Spanish classic and romantic poets in our textbooks, and then because of the rhymed satires I dedicated to my classmates in the *colegio* magazine. I would not have written them or would have paid a little more attention to them if I had imagined they were going to deserve the glory of being in print. For in reality they were affable satires that circulated on furtive scraps of paper around the soporific two-in-the-afternoon classrooms. Father Luis Posada—prefect of the second division—captured one, read it with a severe frown, reprimanded me as required, but kept it in his pocket. Then Father Arturo Mejía called me to his office to propose that the confiscated satires be published in the magazine *Juventud*, the official organ of the students at the *colegio*. My immediate reaction was a stomach cramp of surprise, embarrassment, and joy, which I resolved with a not very convincing refusal:

"They're just dumb things of mine."

Father Mejía made note of my reply, and with the authorization of the victims he published the verses under that title—"Dumb Things of Mine"—and signed *Gabito*, in the next issue of the magazine. In two successive issues I had to publish another series at the request of my classmates. So those youth-ful verses—for better or worse—are, to be precise, my *opera prima*.

The vice of reading anything that came my way occupied my free time and almost all my class time. I could recite entire poems from the popular repertoire in common use at the time in Colombia, and the most beautiful ones of the Golden Age and Spanish romanticism, many of them learned from the *colegio*'s textbooks. This extemporaneous knowledge at my age exasperated my teachers, for whenever they asked me a lethal question in class I would answer with a literary quotation or some bookish idea that they were in no position to evaluate. Father Mejía said: "He's an affected child," in order not to call me unbearable. I never had to force my memory, because poems and certain passages of good classic prose were etched in my mind after three or four readings. The first fountain pen I ever had was given to me by Father Prefect because I recited without any mistakes the fifty-seven ten-line stanzas of "Ver-tigo" by Gaspar Núñez de Arce.

I would read in my classes, the book open on my knees, with so much brazenness that my impunity seemed possible only through the complicity of the teachers. The one thing I could not achieve with my well-rhymed glibness was to have them excuse me from daily Mass at seven in the morning. In addition to writing those "dumb things of mine," I was a soloist in the choir, drew comic caricatures, recited poems at solemn ses-sions, and did so many other extracurricular things that no one could understand when I studied. The answer was as simple as could be: I did not study.

In the midst of so much excessive dynamism, I still do not understand why my teachers concerned themselves so much with me but did not cry out in horror at my bad spelling. Unlike my mother, who hid some of my letters from Papá in order to keep him alive, and returned others to me corrected, at times with her compliments on my grammatical progress and good use of words. But at the end of two years there were no improvements in sight. Today my problem is still the same: I never could understand why silent letters are allowed, or two

different letters with the same sound, and so many other pointless rules.

This was how I discovered a vocation that would accompany
me all my life: the pleasure I took in conversing with students
who were older than I. Even today, at gatherings of young people who could be my grandchildren, I have to make an effort
not to feel younger than they. And so I became friends with two
older students who would later be my companions in historic
periods of my life. One was Juan B. Fernández, son of one of
the three founders and owners of the newspaper *El Heraldo*, in
Barranquilla, where I got my feet wet as a reporter, and he had
been trained from the time he learned his ABCs all the way to
the management offices. The other was Enrique Scopell, son
of a Cuban photographer who was legendary in the city, and
himself a graphic reporter. However, my gratitude toward him
was not so much for our common work in the press as for his
occupation as a tanner of wild-animal skins that he exported all
over the world. On one of my first trips out of the country he
gave me a caiman skin that was three meters long.

"This skin is worth a fortune," he said without melodrama,
"but I advise you not to sell it unless you think you're going to
die of hunger."

I still ask myself how well the wise Quique Scopell knew he
was giving me an eternal amulet, for in reality I would have had
to sell it many times over during my years of recurrent famine.
But I still have it, dusty and almost petrified, because since I
began carrying it all around the world in my suitcase, I never
again lacked the money to eat.

The Jesuit teachers, so severe in the classroom, were different during recess periods, when they taught us what was not
said inside and confided what they really would have liked to
teach. As far as it was possible at my age, I believe I remember
that the difference was very noticeable and helped us even
more. Father Luis Posada, a young Cachaco with a progressive
mentality who worked for many years in labor union circles,
had a file of cards with all kinds of condensed encyclopedic
clues, in particular about books and authors. Father Ignacio
Zaldívar was a mountain Basque whom I continued to see in

Cartagena until his honorable old age in the convent of San Pedro Claver. Father Eduardo Núñez was already well along in his monumental history of Colombian literature, whose fate I never learned. The aged Father Manuel Hidalgo, the singing teacher who was already very old, detected vocations on his own and permitted unexpected incursions into pagan music.

I had a few casual chats with Father Pieschacón, the rector, and as a result I was certain he viewed me as an adult, not only because of the topics he raised but on account of his daring explanations. He was decisive in my life in clarifying my conception of heaven and hell, which I could not reconcile with the information in the catechism because of simple geographical obstacles. The rector assuaged the effect of those dogmas with his bold ideas. Heaven was, without further theological complications, the presence of God. Hell, of course, was its opposite. But on two occasions he confessed to me that for him the problem was that "in any event there was fire in hell," but he could not explain it. More because of these lessons during recess periods than formal classes, when I finished the year my chest was armored with medals.

My first vacation in Sucre began on a Sunday at four in the afternoon, on a dock decorated with garlands and colored balloons, and in a square transformed into a Christmas bazaar. As soon as I stepped on solid ground, a very beautiful blond girl threw her arms around my neck with an overwhelming spontaneity and smothered me with kisses. It was my sister Carmen Rosa, Papá's daughter before he married, who had come to spend some time with her unknown family. Another son of Papá's had also arrived on that occasion: Abelardo, a good professional tailor who opened his shop on one side of the main square and, in my puberty, taught me about life.

The new house with its new furniture had a party air and a new brother: Jaime, born in May under the auspicious sign of Gemini, and three months premature. I did not know about him until I arrived, for my parents seemed determined to moderate the annual births, but my mother hastened to explain that this was a tribute to St. Rita for the prosperity that had come into the house. She was rejuvenated and happy, more of a singer than ever, and Papá was floating on an air of good humor, the consulting room full and the pharmacy well stocked, in particular on Sundays when patients came from the nearby mountains. I do not know if he ever found out that this affluence was due in fact to his fame as a healer, though the country people did not attribute this to the homeopathic virtues of his little sugar drops and prodigious amounts of water but to his superior arts as a sorcerer.

Sucre was better than in memory because of the tradition that during the Christmas holidays the town divided into its two great districts: Zulia, to the south, and Congoveo, to the north. Apart from other secondary challenges, there was a competition among allegorical floats that represented the historic rivalry between the districts in artistic tournaments. At last, on Christmas Eve, they gathered in the main square in the midst of great debates, and the public decided which of the two districts was the year's winner.

From the moment of her arrival, Carmen Rosa contributed to a new holiday splendor. She was modern and flirtatious, and she became mistress of the dances with a train of impetuous suitors. My mother, so watchful of her daughters, was not that way with her; on the contrary, she facilitated the courtships that introduced a new note into the house. Theirs was a relationship between accomplices, the kind my mother never had with her own daughters. For his part, Abelardo resolved his life in another way, in a shop that was a single room divided by a folding partition. Things went well for him as a tailor, but not as well as they did for him as a circumspect stud, for he spent more time well accompanied in the bed behind the partition than alone and bored at the sewing machine.

During that vacation my father had the strange idea of preparing me for business. "Just in case," he told me. The first thing was to teach me how to collect pharmacy bills at people's houses. One day he sent me to collect several at La Hora, a brothel without prejudices on the outskirts of town.

I went up to the half-closed door of a room that opened onto the street, and I saw one of the women from the house, barefoot and wearing a slip that did not cover her thighs, taking a nap on an air mattress. Before I could speak to her she sat up on the mattress, looked at me half asleep, and asked me what I wanted. I told her I had a message from my father for Don Eligio Molina, the proprietor. But instead of giving me directions she told me to come in and bar the door, and with an index finger that said everything she signaled to me:

"Come here."

I went there, and as I approached, her heavy breathing filled the room like a river in flood, until she grasped my arm with her right hand and slipped her left inside my fly. I felt a delicious terror.

"So you're the son of the doctor with the little drops," she said as she handled me inside my trousers with five agile fingers that felt like ten. She took off my trousers and did not stop whispering warm words in my ear as she pulled her slip over her head and lay faceup on the bed wearing only her red-flowered panties. "This is something you have to take off," she told me. "It's your duty as a man."

I pulled down the zipper but in my haste I could not remove her panties, and she had to help me by extending her legs and making a swimmer's rapid movement. Then she lifted me by my armpits and put me on top of her in the academic missionary position. The rest she did on her own, until I died alone on top of her, splashing in the onion soup of her filly's thighs.

She lay in silence, on her side, staring into my eyes, and I looked back at her with the hope of beginning again, this time without fear and with more time. All of a sudden she said she would not charge me the fee of two pesos for her services because I had not come prepared. Then she lay on her back and scrutinized my face.

"Besides," she said, "you're Luis Enrique's big brother, aren't you? You both have the same voice."

I was innocent enough to ask her how she knew him.

"Don't be an idiot," she said with a laugh. "I even have a pair of his shorts here that I had to wash for him the last time."

It seemed an exaggeration considering my brother's age, but when she showed them to me I realized it was true. Then she jumped out of bed naked, with a balletic grace, and as she dressed she explained that Don Eligio Molina's was the next door in the building, on the left. At last she asked:

"It's your first time, isn't it?"

My heart skipped a beat.

"What do you mean?" I lied, "I've done it at least seven times."

"Anyway," she said with an ironic expression, "you ought to tell your brother to teach you a couple of things."

My initiation triggered a vital force in me. Vacation lasted from December to February, and I wondered how many times I would be able to get two pesos so I could go back to her. My brother Luis Enrique, already a veteran of the body, burst his sides laughing at the idea that someone our age would have to pay for something that two people did at the same time and that made them both happy.

Within the feudal spirit of La Mojana, the lords of the land enjoyed initiating the virgins from among their vassals, and after a few nights of abuse they would leave them to their fates. There were plenty to choose from when the girls came out to hunt on the square after dances. On that vacation, however, they filled me with the same fear as the telephone, and I watched them pass by like clouds in the water. I did not have an instant of tranquility because of the desolation my first casual adventure had left in my body. Even today I do not think it is exaggerated to believe it was the cause of my surly state of mind when I returned to the *colegio* bedazzled through and through by an inspired piece of nonsense by the Bogotán poet Don José Manuel Marroquín, which drove listeners mad beginning with the first stanza:

> *Now that barks dog, now that crows cock,*
> *now that dawning sounds the high rings bell;*
> *and the brays burro and the warbles bird,*
> *and the whistles watchmen and the grunts swine,*
> *and the dawny rose fields the broad gilds,*
> *pearling liquids poury as I tear sheds*
> *and colding with shiver though the burn souls,*
> *I come to sigh my heaves window your beneaths.*

I not only introduced disorder wherever I went reciting the interminable lines of the poem, but I learned to speak the language with the fluency of a native from who knows where. It happened with some frequency: I would give an answer to any question, but almost always it was so strange or amusing that the teachers would retreat. Someone must have worried about my mental health when I gave him a correct but at first hearing indecipherable answer on an exam. I do not remember there being any bad faith in these easy jokes that made everyone laugh.

I was surprised that the priests talked to me as if they had lost their minds, and I followed their lead. Another reason for alarm was that I invented parodies of sacred chorales with pagan words that, to my good fortune, no one understood. My counselor, with my parents' permission, took me to a specialist who gave me a thorough but very amusing examination, because in addition to his mental quickness he had an irresistible personal sympathy and methodology. He had me read a card of nonsensical sentences that I had to put in proper order. I did this with so much enthusiasm that the doctor could not resist the temptation of becoming involved in my game, and we thought up such ingenious tests that he took notes in order to incorporate them into future examinations. At the end of a detailed interrogation regarding my habits, he asked how often I masturbated. I answered the first thing that occurred to me: I never had dared to do it. He did not believe me but remarked in an offhand way that fear was a negative factor in sexual health, and his very incredulity seemed more like an incitement to me. I thought he was a splendid man, whom I tried to see as an adult when I was a reporter on *El Heraldo*, so that he could tell me the private conclusions he had drawn from my examination, and the only thing I learned was that he had moved to the United States years before. One of his old friends was more explicit and told me with great affection that there was nothing strange about his being in a mental hospital in Chicago, because he always thought he was in worse shape than his patients.

His diagnosis was nervous fatigue aggravated by reading after meals. He recommended absolute rest for two hours during digestion, and physical activity more demanding than the required sports. I am still surprised by the seriousness with which my parents and teachers took his orders. They regulated my reading and more than once took away the books they found me reading in class under the desk. They excused me from difficult subjects and obliged me to have more physical activity for several hours a day. And so while the others were in class, I played alone on the basketball court making simple-minded baskets and reciting from memory. My classmates were divided from the beginning: those who in reality thought I always had been crazy, those who believed I played at being crazy in order to enjoy life, and those whose dealings with me continued to be based on the assumption that the crazy people were the teachers. This is the period that gave rise to the story that I was expelled from school because I threw an inkwell at the arithmetic teacher as he was writing exercises on the rule of three on the blackboard. It was fortunate that Papá understood this in a simple manner and decided I should return home without finishing the year or wasting any more of his time and money on an ailment that might only be a liver complaint.

For my brother Abelardo, on the other hand, there were no problems in life that could not be resolved in bed. While my sisters treated me with compassion, he told me the magic prescription as soon as he saw me come into his shop:

"What you need is a good woman."

He was so serious about this that almost every day he would go to the billiard parlor on the corner for half an hour, leaving me behind the partition in the tailor shop with girlfriends of his of every stripe, and never with the same one. It was a period of creative excess that seemed to confirm Abelardo's clinical diagnosis, because the next year I went back to school in my right mind.

I never forgot the joy with which they welcomed me back at the Colegio San José, and the admiration with which they celebrated my father's little drops. This time I did not go to live with the Valdeblánquez family, who no longer had room in the house because of the birth of their second child, but went instead to the house of Don Eliécer García, a brother of my paternal grandmother who was famous for his kindness and integrity. He worked in a bank until his retirement, and what touched me most was his eternal passion for the English language. He studied it throughout his life, beginning at dawn and then very late at night, singing the exercises in a very good voice and with a good accent for as long as his age permitted. On holidays he would go to the port and hunt for tourists to talk to, and he came to have as good a command of English as he always had of Castilian, but his shyness prevented him from speaking it to anyone he knew. His three sons, all older than I, and his daughter Valentina, never could hear him.

Through Valentina—my close friend and an inspired reader—I discovered the existence of the Arena y Cielo, the Sand and Sky movement, formed by a group of young poets who had proposed renovating the poetry of the Caribbean coast following the good example of Pablo Neruda. In reality they were a local replica of the Piedra y Cielo, Stone and Sky, a group that reigned during those years in the poets' cafés in Bogotá and in the literary supplements edited by Eduardo Carranza in the shadow of the Spaniard Juan Ramón Jiménez, with the salutary determination to clear away the dead leaves of the nineteenth century. They were no more than half a dozen people just out of adolescence, but they had burst into the literary supplements along the coast with so much force that they were beginning to be seen as a great artistic promise.

The captain of Sand and Sky, named César Augusto del Valle, was about twenty-two years old and had brought his renovating impulse not only to the subjects and sentiments but also to the orthography and grammatical rules of his poems. To purists he seemed a heretic, to academics he seemed an imbecile, and to classicists he seemed a madman. The truth, however, was that in spite of his contagious militancy—like Neruda—he was an incorrigible romantic.

One Sunday my cousin Valentina took me to the house where César lived with his parents, in the San Roque district, the most boisterous in the city. He was big-boned, dark, and skinny, and had large rabbit teeth and the disheveled hair of the poets of his day. Above all, he was a roisterer and a womanizer. His house was lower middle class and lined with books, without room for one more. His father was a serious, somewhat melancholy man, who had the air of a retired functionary and seemed distressed by his son's sterile vocation. His mother welcomed me with a certain compassion, as if I were another son suffering from the same ailment that had made her shed so many tears for her own.

That house was for me the revelation of a world I had perhaps intuited when I was fourteen but never had imagined how much. After that first day I became its most assiduous visitor, and I took up so much of the poet's time that even today I cannot explain how he could stand me. I have come to think that he used me to try out his literary theories, arbitrary, perhaps, but dazzling, on an astonished but inoffensive interlocutor. He lent me books by poets I had never heard of, and I talked to him about them without the slightest awareness of my audacity. Above all Neruda, whose "Poem Twenty" I memorized in order to infuriate one or two Jesuits who did not travel those byways of poetry. At that time the cultural ambience of the city was excited by Meira Delmar's poem to Cartagena de Indias, which saturated all the media along the coast. The mastery of diction and voice with which César del Valle read it to me was so great that I learned it by heart after the second reading.

On many other occasions we could not talk because César was writing, in his own fashion. He walked through rooms and hallways as if he were in another world, and every two or three minutes he would pass in front of me like a sleepwalker, and then without warning he would sit at the typewriter, write a line, a word, a semicolon, perhaps, and go back to his walking. I observed him, dazzled by the celestial emotion of discovering the only and secret way to write poetry. He was always like that during my years at Colegio San José, which gave me the rhetorical basis for setting free my demons. The last news I had of that unforgettable poet, two years later in Bogotá, was a telegram from Valentina with the only two words she did not have the heart to sign: "César died."

My first emotion in a Barranquilla without my parents was an awareness of free will. I had friendships that I maintained outside of school. Among them Álvaro del Toro—who played second voice in my declamations during recess—and the Arteta tribe, with whom I would escape to bookstores and the movies. For the only restriction imposed on me in the house of Uncle Eliécer, in deference to his responsibility, was that I not come home after eight at night.

One day when I was waiting for César del Valle, reading in the living room of his house, a surprising woman came to visit him. Her name was Martina Fonseca, a white cast in the mold of an intelligent, autonomous mulatta, who may well have been the poet's lover. For two or three hours I lived to the full the pleasure of conversing with her, until César came home and they left together without saying where they were going. I heard nothing more about her until Ash Wednesday of that year, when I left High Mass and found her waiting for me on a bench in the park. I thought she was an apparition. She was wearing a dress of embroidered linen that purified her beauty, a bead necklace, and a flower of living fire in her low-cut neckline. Still, what I now appreciate most in memory is the way she invited me to her house without the slightest indication of pre-meditation, and without our considering the holy sign of the ashen cross that we both had on our foreheads. Her husband, a ship's pilot on the Magdalena River, was on his regular twelve-day voyage. What was strange about his wife inviting me on a casual Saturday for hot chocolate and crullers? Except that the ritual was repeated for the rest of the year when her husband was away on his ship, and always from four to seven, which was the time of the children's program at the Rex Theater, which in the house of Uncle Eliécer served as my excuse for being with her.

Her professional specialty was preparing elementary-school teachers for promotions. She attended the best qualified in her free hours with hot chocolate and crullers, so that the new pupil on Saturdays did not attract the attention of her talkative neighbors. The fluidity of the secret love that burned over a blazing fire from March to November was surprising. After the first two Saturdays I thought I would not be able to endure my raging desire to be with her all the time.

We were safe from all danger because her husband would

announce his arrival in the city with a code so that she would know he was coming into port. That is what happened on the third Saturday of our affair, when we were in bed and the distant howl was heard. She became tense.

"Be still," she said to me and waited for two more howls. She did not jump out of bed, as I expected on account of my own fear, but she continued, undaunted: "We still have more than three hours of life left."

She had described him to me as a "huge black over two meters tall with an artilleryman's tool." I was about to break the rules of the game because of an attack of jealousy, and not in a casual way: I wanted to kill him. Her maturity resolved everything, and from then on she led me by the halter past the pitfalls of real life as if I were a wolf cub in sheep's clothing.

I was doing very poor work in school and did not want to hear anything about it, but Martina took charge of my student's Calvary. She was surprised by the childishness of neglecting classes in order to humor the demon of an irresistible vocation for life. "It's logical," I told her. "If this bed were the academy and you were the teacher, I'd be number one not only in class but in the whole school." She took this as a good example.

"That's just what we're going to do," she said.

Without too many sacrifices she undertook the task of my rehabilitation with a fixed schedule. She organized assignments for me and prepared me for the following week between tumbles in bed and a mother's reprimands. If my homework was not correct and on time, she would punish me with the interdiction of one Saturday for every three failures. I never went past two. The change began to be noticed at school.

However, what she taught me in practice was an infallible formula that was of use to me, sad to say, only in the last year of my baccalaureate: if I paid attention in classes and did the assignments myself instead of copying them from my classmates, I would get a good grade and be able to read as much as I liked in my free hours, and lead my own life without exhausting all-night study sessions or useless fears. Thanks to this magical prescription I was first in the class that year of 1942 and received a medal of excellence and all kinds of honorable mentions. But confidential gratitude went to the doctors for how well they had cured me of my madness. At the celebration I realized that there was a bad dose of cynicism in the emotion with which I had expressed my thanks in earlier years for the recognition of merits that were not mine. In my last year, when it was deserved, it seemed to me decent not to thank anyone. But I responded with all my heart with the poem "The Circus," by Guillermo Valencia, which I recited in its entirety without a prompter in the final ceremony, more frightened than a Christian facing the lions.

During the vacation of that good year I had planned to visit my grandmother Tranquilina in Aracataca, but she had to go to Barranquilla for urgent surgery on her cataracts. The happiness of seeing her again was made complete by my grandfather's dictionary, which she brought to me as a gift. She had never been aware that she was losing her sight, or had refused to admit it, until she could no longer leave her room. The operation at the Caridad Hospital was quick and had a good prognosis. When the bandages were removed, while she was sitting on the bed, she opened the shining eyes of her renewed youth and summarized her joy in three words:

"I can see."

The surgeon tried to determine just what she could see, and she swept the room with her new eyes and enumerated each thing with admirable precision. The doctor was astounded, but only I knew that the things my grandmother enumerated were not the ones in front of her in the hospital room but the ones in her bedroom in Aracataca, which she knew by heart and remembered in their correct order. She never recovered her sight.

My parents insisted that I spend the vacation with them in Sucre and bring my grandmother with me. Much older than her age warranted, and with her mind adrift, the beauty of her voice had been refined and my grandmother sang more and with more inspiration than ever. My mother made certain she was kept clean and dressed, like an enormous doll. It was evident she was aware of the world but referred everything to the past. Above all radio programs, which awakened a childish interest in her. She recognized the voices of various announcers whom she identified as friends of her youth in Riohacha, because she had never had a radio in her house in Aracataca. She contradicted or criticized some commentaries by the announcers, discussed the most varied subjects with them or reproached them for grammatical errors, as if they were present in the flesh beside her bed, and she refused to have her clothes changed until they took their leave. Then she would respond with her good manners intact:

"Have a very pleasant evening, Señor."

Many mysteries regarding lost objects, secrets that had been kept, or forbidden subjects were clarified in her monologues: who hid the water basin that disappeared from the house in Aracataca in her trunk and then made off with it, who really had been the father of Matilde Salmona, who had been riddled with bullets when his brothers confused him with someone else.

My first vacation in Sucre without Martina Fonseca was not easy, but there was not even the slightest possibility that she would go away with me. The mere idea of not seeing her for two months had seemed unreal to me. But not to her. On the contrary, when I brought up the subject she was already, as usual, three steps ahead of me.

"I wanted to talk to you about that," she said without any mystery. "The best thing for both of us would be if you went to study somewhere else now that we're both raving mad. Then you'll realize that what we have will never be more than what it already was."

I thought she was joking.

"I'll leave tomorrow and be back in three months to stay with you."

She replied with tango music:

"Ha, ha, ha, ha!"

Then I learned that Martina was easy to persuade when she said yes but never when she said no. And so I accepted the challenge, bathed in tears, and proposed being another person in the life she planned for me: another city, another school, another group of friends, even another way of living. I barely thought about it. With the authority of my many medals, the first thing I said to my father with a certain solemnity was that I would not return to the Colegio San José. Or to Barranquilla.

"God be praised!" he said. "I've always wondered where you got the romantic idea of studying with the Jesuits."

My mother ignored his comments.

"If it's not there, it has to be in Bogotá," she said.

"Then it won't be anywhere," replied Papá without delay, "because no money is ever enough for the Cachacos."

It is strange, but the mere idea of not continuing to study, which had been the dream of my life, now seemed unimaginable. To the point where I had recourse to a dream that never had seemed attainable.

"There are scholarships," I said.

"Lots," said Papá, "but for the rich."

In part this was true, not because of favoritism but because the application procedures were difficult and the requirements not well publicized. As a result of centralism, everyone who aspired to a scholarship had to go to Bogotá, a distance of a thousand kilometers in eight days of travel that cost almost as much as three months at a good boarding school. But even so it might be pointless. My mother became exasperated:

"When you start scheming about money, you know where it begins but not where it ends."

Besides, there were other obligations that had not yet been paid. Luis Enrique, a year younger than I, had matriculated in two local schools and had dropped out of both of them after a few months. Margarita and Aida were doing well at the nuns' primary school, but they had already begun thinking about a cheaper city nearby for their baccalaureates. Gustavo, Ligia, Rita, and Jaime were not yet a pressing concern, but they were growing at an alarming rate. They, as well as the three who were born after them, treated me like someone who always arrived only to leave again.

It was my decisive year. The greatest attraction of each float were the girls chosen for their grace and beauty, and dressed like queens, who recited verses that alluded to the symbolic war between the two halves of the town. Still half an outsider, I enjoyed the privilege of being neutral, which is how I behaved.

That year, however, I gave in to the pleas of the captains of Congoveo to write the verses for my sister Carmen Rosa, who would be the queen of a monumental float. I was delighted to oblige, but because of my ignorance of the rules of the game, I went too far in my attacks on the adversary. I had no other recourse but to rectify the transgression with two poems of peace: one of atonement for the beauty from Congoveo and another of reconciliation for the beauty from Zulia. The incident became public. The anonymous poet, almost unknown in town, was the hero of the day. The episode introduced me into society and earned me the friendship of both bands. From then on I did not have enough time to help at children's plays, charity bazaars, philanthropic fairs, and even the speech of a candidate for the municipal council.

Luis Enrique, who was already showing signs of the inspired guitarist he would become, taught me to play the *tiple*, the treble guitar. With him and Filadelfo Velilla we became the kings of serenades, the first prize being that some of the serenaded girls dressed in a hurry, opened the house, woke the girls next door, and we continued the party until breakfast. That year the group was enhanced when it was joined by José Palencia, the grandson of a wealthy and generous landowner. José was a born musician capable of playing any instrument he came across. He looked like a movie star, was a stellar dancer, had a dazzling intelligence, and luck more envied than enviable in transient loves.

I, on the other hand, did not know how to dance and could not learn even in the house of the Señoritas Loiseau, six sisters, invalids from birth, who nonetheless gave classes in fine dancing without getting up from their rocking chairs. My father, never insensitive to reputation, approached me with a new point of view. For the first time we spent long hours talking. We almost did not know each other. In reality, looking back on it, I did not live with my parents for a total of more than three years, adding up the time with them in Aracataca, Barranquilla, Cartagena, Sincé, and Sucre. It was a very agreeable experience that allowed me to know them better. My mother said to me: "How nice that you've become friends with your papá." Days later, while she was preparing coffee in the kitchen, she said even more:

"Your papá is very proud of you."

The next day she tiptoed in to wake me and breathed in my ear: "Your papá has a surprise for you." In fact, when he came down for breakfast, he himself gave me the news in the presence of everyone, and said with a solemn emphasis:

"Get your stuff together, you're going to Bogotá."

The initial impact was one of great frustration, because what I would have wanted then was to remain submerged in perpetual carousing. But innocence prevailed. There was no problem about clothes for cold weather. My father had a black cheviot twill suit and another of corduroy, and he could not button either one at the waist. We went to Pedro León Rosales, called the tailor of miracles, and he altered them to fit me. My mother also bought me the camel's hair overcoat of a dead senator. When she was measuring it on me at home, my sister Ligia— who is a natural clairvoyant—warned me in secret that the ghost of the senator was wandering through his house at night wearing the overcoat. I paid no attention to her, but I should have, because when I put it on in Bogotá, I saw the face of the dead senator in the mirror. I pawned it for ten pesos and never redeemed it.

The domestic atmosphere had improved so much that I was on the verge of tears when we said our goodbyes, but the plan was followed in a precise way, without sentimentality. In the second week of January, in Magangué, I embarked on the *David Arango*, the flagship of the Colombian Shipping Company, after spending one night as a free man. My cabinmate was an angel who weighed two hundred twenty pounds and whose entire body was hairless. He had usurped the name Jack the Ripper, and he was the last survivor of a family of circus knife throwers from Asia Minor. At first glance he looked capable of strangling me in my sleep, but in the days that followed I realized he was only what he seemed: a giant baby with a heart too big for his body.

There was an official party on the first night, with an orchestra and a gala supper, but I escaped to the deck, contemplated for the last time the lights of the world I was preparing to forget without sorrow, and cried my eyes out until dawn. Today I can dare to say that the only reason I would want to be a boy again is to enjoy that voyage once more. I had to take the trip back and forth several times during the four years of the baccalaureate and another two at the university, and each time I learned more about life than I did in school, and learned it better than I did in school. At the time of year when the water was high, it was a five-day trip from Barranquilla to Puerto Salgar, where you then had to travel by train to Bogotá. In times of drought, when sailing was more amusing if you were not in a hurry, it could take up to three weeks.

The ships had easy, basic names: *Atlántico, Medellín, Capitán de Caro, David Arango.* Their captains, like those of Conrad, were authoritarian, good-natured men who ate like savages and did not know how to sleep alone in their regal cabins. The voyages were slow and surprising. We passengers sat in the galleries all day in order to see the forgotten villages, the coffin-shaped caimans, their jaws open waiting for unwary butterflies, the flocks of herons that took flight, startled by the wake of the ship, the coveys of ducks from the interior swamps, the manatees that sang on the wide beaches as they suckled their babies. During the whole voyage you woke at dawn dazed by the clamoring of monkeys and cockatoos. Often, your siesta was interrupted by the nauseating stench of a drowned cow, motionless in the trickle of water, a solitary turkey buzzard perched on its belly.

Now it is unusual to meet anyone on a plane. On the riverboats we students ended up seeming like one family, because every year we would arrange to make the trip at the same time. At times the ship would be stranded for up to fifteen days on a sandbar. No one cared, because the fiesta continued, and a letter from the captain sealed with his signet ring served as an excuse for arriving late at school.

From the first day I was struck by the youngest member of a family group who played the *bandoneón* as if half asleep, strolling for days on end along the deck in first class. I could not endure my envy, because ever since I heard the first accor-

dion players of Francisco el Hombre on the July 20 celebrations in Aracataca I had urged my grandfather to buy me an
accordion, but my grandmother always blocked us with the
usual absurdities about the accordion being a vulgar instrument for the lower classes. Some thirty years later in Paris I
thought I recognized the elegant accordionist from the ship at
an international conference of neurologists. Time had done its
work: he had grown a bohemian beard and his clothes were
larger by a couple of sizes, but the memory of his artistry was
so vivid I could not be mistaken. His reaction, however, could
not have been colder when I asked him without introducing
myself:

"How's the *bandoneón*?"

He replied in surprise:

"I don't know what you're talking about."

I felt the earth swallowing me, and I gave him my humble
excuses for having confused him with a student who played the
bandoneón on the *David Arango* early in January of 1944. Then
he gleamed with the memory. He was the Colombian Salomón
Hakim, one of the great neurologists in this world. The disappointment was that he had exchanged the *bandoneón* for medical engineering.

Another passenger attracted my attention because of his
distance. He was young, robust, with a ruddy complexion,
glasses for nearsightedness, and a premature baldness that
he carried off very well. He seemed the perfect image of the
Cachaco tourist. From the first day he cornered the most comfortable armchair, placed several towers of new books on an
end table, and read without blinking from the morning until he
was distracted by the carousing at night. Every day he appeared
in the dining room wearing a different flowered beach shirt,
and he ate breakfast, lunch, and supper, and continued reading alone at the most isolated table. I do not believe he had
exchanged a single greeting with anyone. In my mind I baptized him "the insatiable reader."

I did not resist the temptation of sneaking a look at his
books. Most were indigestible treatises on public law, which he
read in the mornings, underlining and making notes in the

margins. When the afternoons grew cool he read novels. Among them, one that astonished me: Dostoyevsky's *The Double*, which I had tried without success to steal from a bookstore in Barranquilla. I was mad to read it. In fact, I would have asked to borrow it but did not have the courage. One day he showed up with *The Great Meaulnes*, which I had not heard of but which very soon became one of my favorite masterpieces. On the other hand, I carried only unrepeatable books that I had already read: *Jeromín*, by Father Coloma, that I never finished reading; *The Vortex*, by José Eustasio Rivera; *From the Apennines to the Andes*, by Edmundo de Amicis, and my grandfather's dictionary, which I read for hours. The implacable reader, on the contrary, did not have enough time for all the books he had. What I mean to say and have not said is that I would have given anything to be him.

The third traveler, of course, was Jack the Ripper, my roommate, who talked in his sleep in a barbaric tongue for hours on end. His speeches had a melodic quality that gave a new depth to my readings in the middle of the night. He told me he was not aware of it and did not know what language he could be dreaming in, because as a boy he could talk with the acrobats in his circus in six Asian dialects but had forgotten all of them when his mother died. All that was left was Polish, his original language, but we were able to establish that this was not what he was speaking in his sleep. I do not recall a creature more lovable as he oiled and tested the edges of his sinister knives on his rosy tongue.

His only problem had been on the first day in the dining room, when he protested to the waiters that he could not survive the voyage if they did not serve him four portions. The bosun explained that it would be fine if he paid for them as a supplement with a special discount. He claimed that he had traveled the oceans of the world and on all of them they had recognized his human right not to die of hunger. The case went all the way to the captain, who decided in very Colombian fashion that he should be served two portions, and that the waiters could be distracted enough to let two more slip from their hands. He also helped himself by picking with his fork at the plates of his table companions and a few neighbors without appetite who took pleasure in his ideas. You had to be there to believe it.

I did not know what to do with myself until La Gloria, where a group of students boarded and formed trios and quartets at night and sang beautiful serenades of romantic boleros. When I discovered that they had an extra *tiple*, I took it over and rehearsed with them in the afternoons, and we would sing until dawn. The tedium of my free time found a remedy in a solution that came from the heart: whoever does not sing cannot imagine the pleasure of singing.

One night when there was a full moon we were awakened by a heartrending lament from the riverbank. The captain, Climaco Conde Abello, one of the greatest of them, gave an order to use searchlights to find the origin of the weeping: it was a manatee female who had become entangled in the branches of a fallen tree. Launches went into the water, and they moored her to a capstan and managed to free her. She was a fantastic, touching creature, half woman and half cow, almost four meters long. Her skin was livid and tender, and her large-breasted torso was that of a biblical matriarch. It was this same Captain Conde Abello whom I heard say, for the first time, that the world would come to an end if people kept killing the animals in the river, and he prohibited shooting from his boat.

"Whoever wants to kill somebody can go kill him in his own house!" he shouted. "Not on my ship!"

January 19, 1961, seventeen years later, I remember as a hateful day because a friend called me in Mexico to tell me that the steamship *David Arango* had caught fire and burned to ashes in the port of Magangué. I hung up with the terrible realization that my youth had ended that day, and the little still left to us of our river of nostalgic memories had gone to hell. Today the Magdalena River is dead, its waters polluted, its animals annihilated. The work of restoration talked about so much by successive governments that have done nothing would require the planting by experts of some sixty million trees on ninety percent of privately owned lands whose owners would have to give up, for sheer love of country, ninety percent of their current incomes.

Each voyage taught great lessons about life that connected us in an ephemeral but unforgettable way to the life of the towns we passed through, and many of us became forever caught up in their destinies. A renowned medical student went to a wedding dance uninvited, danced without permission with the prettiest woman at the party, and was shot to death by her husband. Another, in an epic bout of drinking, married the first girl he liked in Puerto Berrío and is still happy with her and their nine children. José Palencia, our friend from Sucre, won a cow in a drummers' competition in Tenerife and sold it on the spot for fifty pesos: a fortune at the time. In the immense red-light district in Barrancabermeja, the oil capital, we were astounded to find Angel Casij Palencia, José's first cousin who had disappeared without a trace from Sucre the previous year, singing with the band in a brothel. The band took care of the bill for the dancing and carousing that lasted until dawn.

My ugliest memory is of a gloomy tavern in Puerto Berrío, where the police drove four of us passengers out with clubs, not giving or listening to any explanations, and arrested us on the charge of having raped a female student. When we reached police headquarters they already had the real culprits—some local thugs who had nothing to do with our boat—behind bars, without a scratch.

At the final port of call, Puerto Salgar, we had to disembark at five in the morning dressed for the high country. Men in black wool with vests and mushroom-shaped hats and topcoats over their arms had changed identities surrounded by the psaltery of the toads and the pestilential stink of the river over-flowing with dead animals. When it was time to go ashore I had an unexpected surprise. An eleventh-hour friend had convinced my mother to make me a Corroncho, or coastal *petate*, with its narrow string hammock, wool blanket, and an emergency chamber pot, all of it wrapped in a mat made of esparto grass and tied into a cross with the cords of the hammock. My musical companions could not contain their laughter at seeing me with that kind of baggage in the cradle of civilization, and the most determined of them did what I would not have dared to do: he threw it into the water. My final vision of that unforgettable trip was the sight of the *petate* returning to its origins as it rolled in the current.

During the first four hours the train from Puerto Salgar climbed the rock cornices as if it were crawling. On the steepest sections it would slide back in order to gather momentum and attempt the ascent again, breathing as hard as a dragon. At times it was necessary for the passengers to get out to lighten the load and climb to the next cornice on foot. The towns along the way were sad and ice-cold, and in the deserted stations all that waited for us were the women who were lifelong vendors and offered through the train windows fat yellow chickens cooked whole and some snowy potatoes that tasted like heaven. That was where I felt for the first time an unknown and invisible physical state: cold. It was fortunate that at dusk, the immense savannas, as green and beautiful as a sea in heaven, opened without warning toward the horizon. The world became tranquil and fast-moving. The atmosphere in the train changed.

I had forgotten altogether about the insatiable reader when he appeared all of a sudden and sat across from me with a look of urgency. It was incredible. He had been impressed by a bolero that we sang at night on the ship, and he asked me to copy it down for him. Not only did I do that, but I taught him how to sing it. I was surprised by his good ear and the brilliance of his voice when he sang it alone the first time, without mistakes.

"That woman's going to die when she hears it!" he exclaimed, radiant.

Then I understood his urgency. When he heard us sing the bolero on the ship, he felt it would be a revelation for the sweetheart who had said goodbye to him three months earlier in Bogotá and was waiting for him that afternoon in the station. He had heard it again two or three times, and was able to reconstruct it in bits and pieces, but when he saw me sitting alone on the train, he had resolved to ask the favor. Then I also felt bold enough to tell him, with some malice, though it had nothing to do with anything, how surprised I had been to see on his table a book that was so difficult to find. His surprise was authentic:

"Which one?"

"*The Double.*"

He laughed with satisfaction.

"I haven't finished it yet," he said. "But it's one of the strangest things I've come across."

He went no further. He thanked me in every way possible for the bolero and said goodbye with a firm handshake.

It was beginning to grow dark when the train slowed, passed by a shed filled with rusted scrap iron, and anchored at a gloomy dock. I grasped my trunk by the handle and dragged it toward the street before the crowd could knock me down. I was almost there when someone shouted:

"Young man! *¡Joven!*"

I turned around, as did several young men and others less young who were running along with me, and the insatiable reader passed me and handed me a book without stopping.

"Enjoy it!" he shouted, and disappeared into the crowd.

The book was *The Double.* I was so stunned I did not realize what had just happened to me. I put the book into the pocket of my overcoat, and the icy wind of dusk struck me when I walked out of the station. About to perish, I put the trunk on the platform and sat on it to breathe in the air I needed. There was not a soul on the streets. The little I managed to see was the corner of a sinister, glacial avenue under a light rain mixed with soot, at an altitude of two thousand four hundred meters, in polar air that made respiration difficult.

Dying of the cold, I waited no less than half an hour. Someone had to come, because my father had sent an urgent telegram to Don Eliécer Torres Arango, a relative of his who would be my host. But what concerned me then was not if someone was coming or not coming, but my fear of sitting on a sepulchral trunk not knowing anyone on the other side of the world. Then a distinguished man got out of a taxi, carrying a silk umbrella and wearing a camel's hair coat that came down to his ankles. I understood that he was my host, though he only glanced at me and walked by, and I did not have the audacity to signal him in any way. He hurried into the station and came out again minutes later with no expression of hope. At last he saw me and pointed with his index finger:

"You're Gabito, right?"

I answered him with all my heart:

"Almost, now."

4

AT THAT TIME Bogotá was a remote, lugubrious city where an insomniac rain had been falling since the beginning of the sixteenth century. I noticed that on the street there were too many hurrying men, dressed like me when I arrived, in black wool and bowler hats. On the other hand, not a single consolatory woman could be seen, for they, like priests in cassocks and soldiers in uniform, were not permitted to enter the gloomy cafés in the business district. In the streetcars and public urinals there was a melancholy sign: "If you don't fear God, fear syphilis."

I was struck by the gigantic Percherons that pulled the beer wagons, the pyrotechnical sparks made by the streetcars when they turned corners, and the stopping of traffic to allow funeral processions to make their way on foot through the rain. They were the most mournful, with luxurious carriages, and horses decked out in velvet and headpieces with large black feathers, and corpses from good families who behaved like the inventors of death. In the atrium of the Church of Las Nieves I caught a glimpse from the taxi of the first woman I had seen on the streets: slim and reserved, as elegant as a queen of mourning, but I was left forever with only half an illusion because her face was covered by an impassable veil.

It was a moral collapse. The house where I spent the night

was large and comfortable, but it seemed spectral to me because of its gloomy garden with dark roses and a cold that crushed one's bones. It belonged to the Torres Gamboa family, relatives of my father whom I knew, but at supper, wrapped in sleeping blankets, they looked like strangers to me. My greatest shock was when I slipped between the sheets and shouted in horror because they felt soaked in an icy liquid. They explained that it was like this the first time and little by little I would become accustomed to the oddities of the climate. I wept for long hours in silence before falling into an unhappy sleep.

This was my state of mind four days after I had arrived, as I walked at top speed, as a defense against the cold and drizzle, to the Ministry of Education, where they were about to open registration for the national scholarship competition. The line began on the third floor of the ministry, facing the actual door to the registration offices, and snaked down the stairs to the main entrance. The spectacle was disheartening. By the time the sky cleared, at about ten in the morning, the line stretched two more blocks to the Avenida Jiménez de Quesada and did not include the applicants who had taken refuge in doorways. It seemed impossible to win anything in a competition like that one.

A little after noon I felt two taps on my shoulder. It was the insatiable reader from the ship, who had recognized me among the last people in line, but it was hard for me to identify him in the mushroom-shaped hat and funereal clothing the Cachacos wore. He was perplexed, too, and he asked me:

"But what the hell are you doing here?"

I told him.

"That's really funny!" he said, weak with laughter. "Come with me." And he led me by the arm to the ministry. Then I found out that he was Dr. Adolfo Gómez Támara, national director of scholarships for the Ministry of Education.

It was the least plausible coincidence, and one of the most fortunate of my life. With a joke of pure student ancestry, Gómez Támara introduced me to his assistants as the most inspired singer of romantic boleros. They served me coffee and registered me with no further formalities, though they told me first that they were not showing contempt for application forms but paying tribute to the unfathomable gods of chance. They informed me that the general examination would take place the following Monday in the Colegio de San Bartolomé. They estimated there were some thousand applicants from all over the country for three hundred scholarships, which meant the battle would be long, difficult, and perhaps a mortal blow to my hopes. The recipients would learn the results in a week, along with information about the school to which they had been assigned. This was something new and serious for me, because they could just as well send me to Medellín as to Vichada. They explained that the geographical lottery was intended to stimulate cultural mobility among the various regions. When they finished the application forms, Gómez Támara shook my hand with the same enthusiastic energy he had shown when he thanked me for the bolero.

"Be smart, now," he said. "Your life is in your hands."

As I left the ministry, a little man of clerical appearance offered to obtain a sure scholarship for me to the school of my choice, without any exams, for a fee of fifty pesos. To me that was a fortune, but I believe that if I'd had it I would have paid it to avoid the terror of the examination. Days later I recognized the charlatan in a newspaper photograph as the head of a gang of swindlers who dressed like priests to arrange illicit deals in official institutions.

I did not unpack my trunk, certain they would send me somewhere else. My pessimism was so intense that on the eve of the examination I went with the musicians from the boat to a rough tavern in the rundown Las Cruces district. We sang for our drinks at the price of one song for a glass of *chicha*, the barbaric drink of fermented corn that exquisite drunkards refined with gunpowder. And so I came to the exam late, with a throbbing head and not even a memory of where I had been or who brought me home the night before, but for charity's sake they received me in an immense hall crowded with applicants. A quick glance at the questions was enough for me to know I was defeated before I even began. To fool the monitors, I whiled away the time on the social sciences, where the questions seemed the least cruel. But then I felt possessed by an aura of inspiration that allowed me to improvise credible answers and miraculous lucky guesses. Except in mathematics, which not even God could make me understand. The exam in drawing, which I did in haste, but with success, was a relief. "It must have been a miracle of the *chicha*," my musicians told me. In any case, I finished in a state of final surrender, determined to write a letter to my parents regarding my rights and my reasons for not returning home.

I fulfilled my duty to request the results a week later. The clerk at the reception desk must have recognized some mark in my file because without saying a word she took me to the director. I found him in a very good mood, in shirtsleeves and wearing fancy red suspenders. He reviewed the grades on my examination with professional attention, hesitated once or twice, and at last took a breath.

"Not bad," he said to himself. "Except in math, but you scraped by thanks to the five in drawing."

He leaned back in his swivel chair and asked me what school I had in mind.

It was one of my historic shocks, but I did not hesitate:

"San Bartolomé, here in Bogotá."

He placed the palm of his hand on a pile of papers on his desk.

"All these are letters from very influential people recommending children, relatives, and friends to secondary schools here," he said. He realized he had not been obliged to say this, and he went on: "If you'll permit me to help you, what would be best for you is the Liceo Nacional de Zipaquirá an hour away by train."

The only thing I knew about that historic city was that it had salt mines. Gómez Támara explained that it was a colonial secondary school expropriated from a religious community by a recent liberal reform, and it now had a splendid faculty of young, liberal teachers. I thought it was my duty to clarify matters.

"My papá's a Goth," I told him.

He burst into laughter.

"Don't be so serious," he said. "I mean liberal in the sense of being broad-minded."

He recovered his own style right away and decided that my fate lay in that old seventeenth-century convent that had been transformed into a school of unbelievers in a sleepy town where there were no distractions other than studying. The old cloister, in fact, remained impassive before eternity. In its earlier period it had a legend cut into the stone portico: *El principio de la sabiduría es el temor de Dios*—"The beginning of wisdom is the fear of God." But the device was exchanged for the seal of Colombia when the Liberal government of President Alfonso López Pumarejo nationalized education in 1936. At the entrance, as I recovered from the asphyxia caused by the weight of my trunk, I was depressed by the small courtyard with colonial arches carved out of living rock, with wooden balconies painted green and melancholy pots of flowers on the railings. Everything seemed subjected to a confessional order, and you could see with far too much clarity that in more than three hundred years nothing there had known the indulgence of a woman's hands. Brought up in the lawless spaces of the Caribbean, I was assaulted by the terror of spending the four decisive years of my adolescence in that time that had run aground.

Even today it seems impossible that two floors surrounding a taciturn courtyard, and another masonry building improvised on a plot of land in the rear, could house the residence and office of the rector, the administrative offices, the kitchen, the dining room, the library, six classrooms, the physics and chemistry laboratory, the storeroom, the sanitary facilities, and the dormitory with iron beds arranged in rows for fifty pupils dragged in from the most depressed suburbs in the nation, but very few from the capital. To my good fortune, that state of exile was one more favor from my lucky star. Because of it, I soon learned the nature of the country I had won in the world's raffle. The dozen Caribbean compatriots who claimed me as one of their own as soon as I arrived, and I as well, of course, made impassable distinctions between ourselves and the others: the natives and the outsiders.

The various groups distributed among the corners of the

courtyard, beginning with recess on the first evening, were a rich sampling of the nation. There were no rivalries as long as each group stayed on its own terrain. My immediate relationships were with people from the Caribbean coast, for we had a well-deserved reputation for being noisy, fanatics about group solidarity, and wild carousers at dances. I was an exception, but Antonio Martínez Sierra, a rumba dancer from Cartagena, taught me to dance to popular tunes during the nighttime recreational periods. Ricardo González Ripoll, my great accomplice in furtive courtships, became a famous architect who nonetheless never interrupted the same almost inaudible song that he hummed to himself and danced to alone until the end of his days.

Mincho Anaya, a born pianist who became the conductor of a national dance orchestra, founded the school band with any students who wanted to learn an instrument, and he taught me the secret of the second voice in boleros and *vallenatos*. His greatest feat, however, was training Guillermo López Guerra, a pure Bogotán, in the Caribbean art of playing the claves, which is a question of three-two, three-two.

Humberto Jaimes, from El Banco, was a relentless student who was never interested in dancing and who sacrificed his weekends to stay at school studying. I believe he had never seen a soccer ball or read an account of any kind of game, until he graduated as an engineer in Bogotá and joined *El Tiempo* as an apprentice sportswriter, where he became editor of his section and one of the fine soccer reporters in the country. In any event, the strangest case I remember was without a doubt that of Silvio Luna, a dark-skinned black from Chocó who graduated as a lawyer and then as a physician, and seemed ready to initiate his third career when I lost track of him.

Daniel Rozo (Pagocio) always behaved like an adept in all the human and divine sciences, and he was prodigal with them in class and during recess. We always came to him to learn about the state of the world during the Second World War, which we just managed to follow through rumors, since the regular entrance of newspapers or magazines into the school was not authorized, and we used the radio only to dance with one another. We never had the opportunity to determine where Pagocio found his historic battles in which the Allies were always victorious.

Sergio Castro—from Quetame—was perhaps the best student in all the grades at the *liceo*, and from his first day he always received the highest grades. I think his secret was the same one Martina Fonseca had advised me to use at the Colegio San José: he did not miss a word the teacher said or any of his classmates' remarks, he took notes even on his instructors' breathing, and he arranged them in a perfect notebook. Perhaps for the same reason he did not need to spend time preparing for exams, and he would read adventure novels on the weekends while the rest of us burned ourselves out cramming.

My most constant companion during recreational periods was the pure Bogotán Álvaro Ruiz Torres, who exchanged daily reports with me on our girlfriends during the nighttime recess as we marched with a military step around the courtyard. Others were Jaime Bravo, Humberto Guillén, and Álvaro Vidales Barón. I was very close to all of them at school, and for years we continued seeing one another in real life. Álvaro Ruiz went to Bogotá every weekend with his family and returned well supplied with cigarettes and news about girlfriends. It was he who encouraged me in both vices during the time we studied together, and who in these past two years has lent me his best recollections to give new vigor to these memoirs.

I do not know what in fact I learned during my captivity in the Liceo Nacional, but the four years of harmonious coexistence with everyone instilled a unitary vision of the nation in me, I discovered how diverse we were and what we were good for, and I learned and never forgot that the entire country was in fact the sum total of each one of us. Perhaps this was what they meant at the ministry regarding the regional mobility that the government was fostering. When I was already mature and had been invited into the cockpit of a transatlantic plane, the first words the captain said to me were to ask where I was from. I only had to hear him to answer:

"I'm as much from the coast as you are from Sogamoso."

He had the same way of being, the same expression, the

same quality of voice as Marco Fidel Bulla, who sat next to me in the fourth year at the *liceo*. This flash of intuition taught me to navigate the swamps of that unpredictable community, even without a compass and against the current, and may well have been a master key in my occupation as a writer.

I felt as if I were living a dream, for I had not aspired to a scholarship because I wanted to study but in order to maintain my independence from any other involvement and remain on good terms with my family. The certainty of three meals a day was enough to suppose that in this refuge for the poor we lived better than in our own houses, under a regime of supervised autonomy less obvious than domestic power. A market system functioned in the dining room that allowed each student to arrange his portions as he chose. Money had no value. The two eggs at breakfast were the most sought-after coin, because with them you could buy at a profit any other dish from the three meals. Each thing had its exact equivalent, and nothing disturbed that legitimate commerce. Even more: I do not remember a single fistfight for any reason during the four years I boarded there.

The teachers, who ate at another table in the same room, were not adverse to personal exchanges, for they still carried with them the habits of their own recent schools. The majority were bachelors, or lived there without their wives, and their salaries were almost as meager as the allowances from our families. They complained about the food with as much volubility as we did, and in a dangerous crisis the possibility arose of our conspiring with some of them on a hunger strike. Only when they received gifts or had guests from outside did they permit themselves inspired dishes that broke down our equality on that one occasion. That was the case, in the fourth year, when the school doctor promised us an ox heart to study in his anatomy course. The next day he sent it, still fresh and bloody, to the refrigerators in the kitchen, but it was not there when we went to get it for class. It was learned that at the last minute, for lack of an ox heart, the doctor had sent the heart of a bricklayer who had been killed when he slipped and fell from a fourth floor. Since there was not enough for everyone, the cooks prepared it with exquisite sauces, believing it was the ox heart they had been told would be served at the teachers' table. I believe these fluid relationships between teachers and students were the result in part of the recent reform in education, of which little remained in history, but that did serve at least to simplify protocols for us. Age differences were reduced, the rules about wearing a tie were relaxed, and no one was ever alarmed again because teachers and students had a few drinks together and attended the same Saturday dances with girls.

This atmosphere was possible only because of the kind of instructors who, in general, permitted easy personal relationships. Our mathematics teacher, with his learning and harsh sense of humor, turned classes into a terrifying fiesta. His name was Joaquín Giraldo Santa, and he was the first Colombian to obtain a doctorate in mathematics. To my misfortune, and despite my great efforts and his, I never succeeded in integrating into his class. People used to say in those days that poetic vocations interfered with mathematics, and in the end I not only believed it but was shipwrecked in the discipline. Geometry was more merciful, perhaps on account of its literary prestige. Arithmetic, on the other hand, behaved with hostile simplicity. Even today, in order to do a mental calculation, I have to break numbers into their easiest components, in particular seven and nine, whose tables I never could memorize. So in order to add seven and four, I take two from seven, add four to the five I have left, and then I add on the two: eleven! Multiplication always failed me because I never could remember the numbers I had in mind. I dedicated my best efforts to algebra, not only out of respect for its classical heritage but because of my affection for and terror of the teacher. It was useless. I failed each trimester, made it up twice, and failed in another illicit attempt that they conceded to me out of charity.

Three of the most self-sacrificing instructors taught languages. The first was the English teacher, Mister Abella, a pure Caribbean with perfect Oxonian diction and a somewhat ecclesiastical fervor for *Webster's Dictionary*, which he would recite with his eyes closed. His successor was Héctor Figueroa, a good young teacher with a feverish passion for the boleros that we would sing in harmony during recess. I did the best I could in the stupor of classes and on the final examination, but I believe my good grade was not because of Shakespeare so much as Leo Marini and Hugo Romani, the Argentine singers of boleros responsible for so many paradises and so many suicides of love. The fourth-year French teacher, Monsieur Antonio Yelá Alban, found me intoxicated by detective novels. His classes bored me as much as all the rest, but his opportune references to street French helped me to not die of hunger in Paris ten years later.

The majority of the teachers had been trained at the Normal Superior under the direction of Dr. José Francisco Socarrás, a psychiatrist from San Juan del César bent on replacing the clerical pedagogy of a century of Conservative governments with a humanistic rationalism. Manuel Cuello del Río was a radical Marxist who, perhaps for that reason, admired Lin Yutang and believed in apparitions of the dead. The library of Carlos Julio Calderón, presided over by his countryman José Eustasio Rivera, author of *The Vortex*, was divided into equal parts of Greek classics, Latin American members of Stone and Sky, and romantics from everywhere. Thanks to all of them, the few of us who were assiduous readers read St. John of the Cross or José María Vargas Vila, as well as the apostles of the proletarian revolution. Gonzalo Ocampo, the social sciences instructor, had a good political library in his room that circulated without malice in the classrooms of the older students, but I never understood why *The Origin of the Family, Private Property, and the State* by Friedrich Engels was studied in the arid afternoons of political economy and not in literature classes as the epic poem of a beautiful human adventure. During recreation periods Guillermo López Guerra read *Anti-Dühring*, also by Engels, lent to him by Professor Gonzalo Ocampo. But when I asked him for it so I could discuss it with López Guerra, Ocampo said he would not do me that bad turn with a great tome fundamental to the progress of humanity but so long and boring it might not pass into history. Perhaps this ideological swapping contributed to the *liceo*'s bad reputation as a laboratory of political perversion. But I needed half a lifetime to realize it might have been more of a spontaneous experiment to frighten away the weak and immunize the strong against all kinds of dogmatisms.

My most direct relationship was always with Professor Carlos Julio Calderón, the teacher of Spanish in the lower grades, of world literature in the fourth year, Spanish literature in the fifth, and Colombian literature in the sixth. And of something odd in his formation, considering his tastes: accounting. He had been born in Neiva, the capital of the department of Huila, and he never tired of proclaiming his patriotic admiration for José Eustasio Rivera. He had been obliged to interrupt his studies of medicine and surgery, and he remembered this as the frustration of his life, but his passion for arts and letters was irresistible. He was the first teacher to demolish my rough drafts with pertinent observations.

In any case, relations between students and teachers were exceptional for their naturalness, not only in classes but, in a special way, in the recess yard after supper, which permitted a kind of behavior different from what we were accustomed to and no doubt favored the climate of respect and camaraderie in which we lived.

I owe a terrifying adventure to the complete works of Freud, which were in the library. I did not understand anything of his scabrous analyses, of course, but his clinical cases, like the fantasies of Jules Verne, kept me in suspense to the end. Professor Calderón asked us to write a story on any subject in Spanish class. One occurred to me about a mental patient, a girl of seven, with a pedantic title that was just the opposite of poetry: "A Case of Obsessive Psychosis." The teacher had it read in class. The boy next to me, Aurelio Prieto, rejected without reservations the presumptuousness of writing about so twisted a subject without the slightest scientific or literary training. I explained, with more rancor than humility, that I had taken it from a clinical case described by Freud in his memoirs, and my only intention had been to use it for the assignment. Maestro Calderón, perhaps believing I was resentful because of acid criticism from several of my classmates, called me aside during recess to encourage me to continue along the same path. He pointed out that in my story it was evident I knew nothing about the techniques of modern fiction, but I had the instinct and the desire. He thought it was well written, and at least it intended something original. For the first time he spoke to me of rhetoric. He gave me some practical thematic and metrical devices for versifying without pretensions, and he concluded that in any event I ought to continue writing even if only for my mental health. That was the first of the long conversations we held at recreational periods and other free times during my years at the *liceo*, to which I owe a great deal in my life as a writer.

It was an ideal climate for me. Beginning at the Colegio San José, the vice of reading everything I came across was so deep-seated that I spent my free time and almost all my time in classes doing just that. When I was sixteen, with good spelling or without it, I could repeat without pausing for breath the poems I had learned at the Colegio San José. I read and reread them with no help or order, and almost always in secret during classes. I believe I had read the entire indescribable library of the *liceo*, made up of the castoffs of other less useful ones: official collections, legacies of indifferent teachers, unsuspected books washed ashore from who knows what remnants of shipwrecks. I cannot forget the Aldeana Library of the Editorial Minerva, sponsored by Don Daniel Samper Ortega and distributed in elementary and secondary schools by the Ministry of Education. It consisted of one hundred volumes that contained all the good and all the worst written in Colombia until that time, and I proposed reading them in numerical order for as long as my heart could stand it. What still terrifies me today is that I almost achieved my goal in my last two years at the *colegio*, and for the rest of my life I have not been able to establish if it was of any use to me.

Dawns in the dormitory had a suspicious resemblance to happiness, except for the lethal bell that sounded the alarm—as we used to say—at six in the middle of the night. Only two or three mental defectives would jump out of bed to be first in line for the six showers of icy water in the dormitory bathroom. The rest of us used the time to squeeze out the last drops of sleep until the teacher on duty walked the length of the room pulling the blankets off the sleepers. It was an hour and a half of open intimacy for putting our clothes in order, polishing our shoes, taking a shower in the liquid ice from the pipe without a showerhead, while each of us shouted out his frustrations and made fun of those of the rest, violated romantic secrets, aired deals and disagreements, and agreed on the bartering in the dining room. The morning subject of constant discussions was the chapter read the night before.

Starting at dawn, Guillermo Granados gave free rein to his virtues as a tenor with an inexhaustible repertoire of tangos. With Ricardo González Ripoll, my neighbor in the dormitory, we would sing duets of Caribbean *guarachas* to the rhythm of the rag we used to polish our shoes at the head of the bed, while my *compadre* Sabas Caravallo walked from one end of the dormitory to the other as naked as the day he was born, a towel hanging from his penis of reinforced concrete.

If it had been possible, a good number of us would have escaped in the middle of the night to keep dates planned on weekends. There were no night guards or dormitory monitors except for the teacher on duty for the week. And the eternal porter, Riveritos, who in reality always slept while he was awake and carrying out his daily duties. He lived in a room in the attic and did his work well, but at night we could unbar the heavy church doors, move them without any noise, enjoy the night in another house, and return a short while before dawn along the glacial streets. No one ever knew if Riveritos really slept like the dead man he seemed to be, or if it was his gallant way of being an accomplice to his boys. Not many escaped, and their secrets decayed in the memory of their faithful accomplices. I knew some who did this as a matter of routine, others who dared go once with a courage that filled them with the tension of the adventure, and returned exhausted by terror. We never knew of anyone who was caught.

My only social difficulty at school were the sinister nightmares inherited from my mother, which burst into other people's sleep like howls from beyond the grave. Students in the beds near me knew all about my nightmares and feared them only for the terror of the first howl in the silence of the night.

The teacher on duty, who slept in a chamber made of cardboard, sleepwalked from one end of the dormitory to the other until calm was restored. The dreams not only were uncontrollable but had something to do with my bad conscience, because on two occasions they happened to me in bawdy houses. They were also indecipherable, because they did not occur in terrifying visions but in joyful episodes with ordinary persons or places that all at once revealed sinister information in an innocent glance. A nightmare that could not compare to one of my mother's, who held her own head in her lap and rid it of the nits and lice that did not allow her to sleep. My shouts were not cries of fear but calls for help so that someone would be kind enough to wake me. In the dormitory of the *liceo* there was no time for anything, because at the first moan the pillows thrown from nearby beds fell all over me. I would awake panting and with my heart in an uproar, but happy to be alive.

The best thing at the *liceo* were the books read aloud before we went to sleep. The readings had begun through the initiative of Professor Carlos Julio Calderón, with a story by Mark Twain that the fifth-year students had to study for an emergency exam first thing the next day. He read the four pages aloud in his cardboard cubicle so that the students who had not had time to read it could take notes. Interest was so great that from then on the custom was established of reading aloud every night before going to sleep. It was not easy at first, because some sanctimonious teacher had imposed the requirement that he choose and expurgate the books that would be read, but the danger of a rebellion left that to the judgment of the older students.

They began with half an hour. The teacher on duty would read in his well-lit room at the entrance to the general dormitory, and at first we would silence him with mocking snores, real or feigned, but almost always deserved. Later the readings were extended to an hour, depending on the interest of the story, and teachers were relieved by students in weekly shifts. The good times began with Nostradamus and *The Man in the Iron Mask*, which pleased everyone. What I still cannot explain is the thundering success of Thomas Mann's *The Magic Moun-*

tain, which required the intervention of the rector to keep us from spending the whole night awake, waiting for Hans Castorp and Clavdia Chauchat to kiss. Or the rare tension of all of us sitting up on our beds in order not to miss a word of the disordered philosophical duels between Naptha and his friend Settembrini. The reading that night lasted for more than an hour and was celebrated in the dormitory with a round of applause.

The only teacher who remained one of the great unknown quantities of my youth was the rector, whom I had met when I arrived. His name was Alejandro Ramos, a stern, solitary man who had eyeglasses with thick lenses that resembled a blind man's, and an unostentatious power that carried the weight of an iron fist in every one of his words. He came down from his refuge at seven in the morning to inspect our personal grooming before we went into the dining room. He wore impeccable clothes in vivid colors, a shirt collar starched as stiff as celluloid with bright ties, and resplendent shoes. He recorded any defect in our personal cleanliness with a grunt that was an order to return to the dormitory to correct it. The rest of the day he spent behind closed doors in his office on the second floor, and we did not see him again until the following morning at the same time, or as he walked the twelve paces between his office and the sixth-year classroom, where he taught his one mathematics class three times a week. His students said he was a genius with numbers and amusing in his classes, and he left them amazed at his knowledge and trembling with fear of his final examination.

A short while after my arrival, I had to write the inaugural address for some official ceremony at the *liceo*. Most of the teachers approved the topic but agreed that in such cases the rector had the final word. He lived at the top of the stairs on the second floor, but I suffered the distance as if it were a trip on foot around the world. I had not slept well the night before, I put on my Sunday tie, and I had no appetite for breakfast. My knocking on the rectory door was so slow that the rector did not open it until my third knock, and he stepped aside for me without a greeting. Just as well, because I would not have had the voice to reply, not only because of his brusqueness but because of the grandness, order, and beauty of his office with its furniture of noble woods and velvet upholstery, and its walls lined with astonishing bookcases filled with leatherbound volumes. The rector waited with formal solemnity until I caught my breath. Then he pointed to the visitor's easy chair in front of the desk, and he sat down in his.

I had prepared the explanation for my visit with almost as much attention as the address. He listened in silence, approved each sentence with a nod of his head, still not looking at me but at the paper trembling in my hand. At some point that I thought amusing I tried to win a smile from him, but it was useless. Even more: I am sure he already knew the reason for my visit but made me comply with the ritual of explaining it to him.

When I finished he extended his hand over the desk and accepted the paper. He removed his glasses in order to read it with profound attention, and he stopped only to make two corrections with his pen. Then he put on his glasses and spoke, not looking me in the eye, in a stony voice that made my heart pound.

"There are two problems here," he said to me. "You wrote: 'In harmony with the exhuberant flora of our country, which the learned Spaniard José Celestino Mutis revealed to the world in the eighteenth century, in this *liceo* we live in a paradisíacal environment.' But the fact is that exuberant is spelled without an h and paradisiacal has no accent mark."

I felt humiliated. I had no answer for the first objection but I had no doubt about the second, and without delay I replied with what remained of my voice:

"Excuse me, Señor Rector, the dictionary allows paradisiacal with or without an accent mark, but the dactyl seemed more sonorous to me."

He must have felt as assaulted as I did, because he still did not look at me but took the dictionary from the shelf without saying a word. My heart skipped a beat because it was the same Atlas that had belonged to my grandfather, but new and shining and perhaps unused. At the first try he opened it to the exact page, read and reread the entry, and asked me without looking up from the page:

"What year are you in?"

"Third," I said.

He slammed the dictionary shut with a bang and looked me in the eye for the first time.

"Bravo," he said. "Keep it up."

From that day on the only thing missing was for my class-mates to proclaim me a hero, and with all the sarcasm possible they began to call me "the kid from the coast who talked to the rector." However, what affected me most in the interview was having confronted once again my personal drama with spelling. I never could understand it. One of my teachers tried to give me the coup de grace with the news that Simón Bolívar did not deserve his glory because of his terrible orthography. Others consoled me with the excuse that it is a problem for many peo-ple. Even today, when I have published seventeen books, my proofreaders honor me with the courtesy of correcting my spelling atrocities as if they were simple typographical errors.

Social gatherings in Zipaquirá corresponded in general to the vocation and nature of each person. The salt mines, active when the Spaniards found them, were a tourist attraction on weekends, which were finished off with a brisket baked in the oven and snowy potatoes in large pans of salt. The boarders from the coast, with our well-deserved reputation for rowdiness and ill-breeding, had the good manners to dance like artists to popular music and the good taste to fall in love forever.

I became so spontaneous that on the day the end of the war was announced, we took to the streets in a show of jubilation with flags, placards, and shouts of victory. Someone asked for a volunteer to make a speech, and without giving it a second thought I went out to the balcony of the social club facing the main square and improvised one with bombastic shouts that many people thought had been memorized.

It was the only speech I found myself obliged to improvise in the first seventy years of my life. I ended with a lyrical tribute to each of the Big Four, but the one that attracted attention in the square was for the president of the United States, who had died a short while before: "Franklin Delano Roosevelt who, like El Cid, knows how to win battles after death." The sentence remained afloat in the city for several days and was reproduced on street posters and on portraits of Roosevelt in the windows of some stores. And so my first public success was not as a poet or a novelist but as an orator, and what is even worse, as a political orator. From then on there was no public ceremony at the *liceo* when they did not put me on a balcony, but now I had written speeches that had been corrected down to the last breath.

With time, that brazenness served to give me a case of stage fright that brought me to the point of an absolute inability to speak, whether at large weddings, or in taverns filled with Indians in ponchos and hemp sandals where we would end up on the floor, or at the house of Berenice, who was beautiful and free of prejudices and who had the good fortune not to marry me because she was mad with love for someone else, or at the telegraph office, whose unforgettable Sarita would send anguished telegrams on credit when my parents were late with their remittances for my personal expenses, and more than once would advance me money orders to get me out of difficulty. But the least forgettable girl was not anyone's love but the nymph of the poetry addicts. Her name was Cecilia González Pizano, and she had a quick intelligence, personal charm, and a free spirit in a family whose tradition was conservative, and a supernatural memory for all poetry. She lived across from the entrance to the *liceo* with an aristocratic, unmarried aunt in a colonial mansion that surrounded a garden of heliotropes. At first it was a relationship confined to poetic competitions, but Cecilia became a true comrade in life, always filled with laughter, who in the end managed to sneak into Professor Calderón's literature classes with everyone's complicity.

In my days in Aracataca I had dreamed about the good life, going from fair to fair and singing with an accordion and a good voice, which always seemed to me to be the oldest and happiest way to tell a story. If my mother had renounced the piano in order to have children, and my father had hung up his violin in order to support us, it was not at all fair that the oldest of those children would set the good precedent of dying of hunger on account of music. My eventual participation as a singer and *tiple* player in the group at school proved that I had the ear to learn a more difficult instrument, and that I could sing.

There was no patriotic evening or solemn ceremony at the *liceo* in which I was not involved in some way, always through the grace of Maestro Guillermo Quevedo Zornosa, composer and leading citizen of the city, eternal conductor of the municipal band who wrote "Amapola"—the poppy on the road, as red as one's heart—a song of youth that in its time was the soul of soirées and serenades. On Sundays after Mass I was one of the first to cross the park and attend his band concert, always with *La gazza ladra* at the beginning, and the Anvil Chorus, from *Il trovatore*, at the end. The maestro never knew, and I did not dare tell him, that the dream of my life during those years was to be like him.

When the *liceo* asked for volunteers for a class in music appreciation, Guillermo López Guerra and I were the first to raise our hands. The course would meet on Saturday mornings, led by Professor Andrés Pardo Tovar, director of the first program of classical music on The Voice of Bogotá. We did not occupy even a fourth of the dining room that had been arranged to accommodate the class, but we were seduced on the spot by his apostle's fluency. He was the perfect Cachaco, with a dark-blue blazer, a satin vest, a sinuous voice, and deliberate gestures. What would be noteworthy today because of its antiquity was the windup phonograph that he managed with the skill and love of a seal trainer. He began with the supposition—correct in our case—that we were utter novices. And so he began with Saint-Saëns's *Carnival of the Animals*, outlining with erudite facts the nature of each animal. Then he played—of course!—Prokofiev's *Peter and the Wolf*. The bad thing about that Saturday party was that it inculcated in me the embarrassed feeling that the music of the great masters is an almost secret vice, and it took me many years not to make arrogant distinctions between good and bad.

I had no further contact with the rector until the following year, when he took over the teaching of geometry in the fourth year. He walked into the classroom on the first Tuesday at ten in the morning, said good day with a growl, not looking at anyone, and cleaned the board with the eraser until there was no trace of dust. Then he turned to us, and still without having called roll, he asked Álvaro Ruiz Torres:

"What is a point?"

There was no time to answer, because the social sciences teacher opened the door without knocking and told the rector he had an urgent call from the Ministry of Education. The rector hurried out to answer the telephone and did not return to class. Never again, because the call was to inform him that he had been relieved of his position, which he had fulfilled with dedication for five years after a lifetime of devoted service.

His successor was the poet Carlos Martín, the youngest of the good poets from the Stone and Sky group that César del Valle had helped me to discover in Barranquilla. He had published thirty-three books. I knew poems of his and had seen him once in a bookstore in Bogotá, but I never had anything to say to him, and I did not own any of his books so I could not ask him to sign one. One Monday he appeared unannounced at the lunchtime recess. We had not expected him so soon. He looked more like a lawyer than a poet, with his pinstripe suit, high forehead, and pencil-thin mustache that had a formal rigor also notable in his poetry. Placid and always somewhat distant, he walked with a measured step toward the closest groups and extended his hand to us:

"Hello, I'm Carlos Martín."

During that time I was fascinated by the lyrical prose pieces that Eduardo Carranza was publishing in the literary section of *El Tiempo* and in the magazine *Sábado*. I thought it was a genre inspired by Juan Ramón Jiménez's *Platero and I*, popular with the young poets who aspired to wipe the myth of Guillermo Valencia off the face of the map. The poet Jorge Rojas, heir to an ephemeral fortune, sponsored with his name and money the publication of some original chapbooks that aroused great interest in his generation, and unified a group of good, well-known poets.

This was a profound change in domestic relations. The spectral image of the former rector was replaced by a concrete presence who maintained the proper distance but was always within reach. He did away with the routine inspection of our personal grooming and other useless regulations, and at times he would converse with students during the nighttime recreational period.

The new style set me on my path. Perhaps Calderón had spoken about me to the new rector, because on one of the first nights he probed in an oblique way into my relationship to poetry, and I let out everything I had inside. He asked me if I had read *The Literary Experience*, a book by Don Alfonso Reyes that had been the subject of much discussion. I confessed that I had not, and he brought it to me the next day. I devoured half of it under cover of my desk in three successive classes, and the rest at recreation periods on the soccer field. It made me happy that so prestigious an essayist would take the time to study the songs of Agustín Lara as if they were poems by Garcilaso, with the pretext of an ingenious phrase: "The popular songs of Agustín Lara are not popular songs."* For me it was like finding poetry dissolved into the soup of daily life.

Martín gave up the magnificent apartment in the rectory. He installed his office with open doors in the main courtyard, and this brought him even closer to our conversations after supper. He moved with his wife and children, intending to stay, into a well-maintained colonial mansion on a corner of the main square, with a study whose walls were lined with all the books a reader attentive to the renovative tastes of those years could dream of. On weekends his friends from Bogotá would visit him there, in particular his comrades from Stone and Sky. One

*The ingenuity of the phrase *(Las populares canciones de Agustín Lara no son canciones populares)* is based on the position of the adjective, which gives rise to the two meanings of *popular*: widespread and well liked, and of the people, or folk (as opposed to learned or courtly).

Sunday I had to go to his house with Guillermo López Guerra on an errand, and Eduardo Carranza and Jorge Rojas, the two great stars, were there. With a rapid gesture the rector had us sit down so we would not interrupt the conversation, and we were there for half an hour without understanding a word because they were discussing a book by Paul Valéry, whom we had not even heard of. I had seen Carranza more than once in bookstores and cafés in Bogotá, and I would have been able to identify him just by the timbre and fluidity of his voice, which corresponded to his casual clothes and way of being: a poet. On the other hand, I could not have identified Jorge Rojas because of his ministerial attire and style until Carranza addressed him by name. I longed to be present at a discussion about poetry among three of the greatest, but it did not happen. When they had finished with their subject, the rector put his hand on my shoulder and said to his guests:

"This is a great poet."

He said it as a courtesy, of course, but I felt struck by lightning. Carlos Martín insisted on taking our picture with the two great poets, and he did, in fact, but I knew nothing more about it until half a century later in his house on the Catalan coast, where he retired to enjoy his honorable old age.

The *liceo* was shaken by a renovatory wind. The radio, which we had used only for dancing with one another, was transformed under Carlos Martín into an instrument for disseminating information, and for the first time the evening news was listened to and discussed in the recreational courtyard. Cultural activity increased with the creation of a literary center and the publication of a newspaper. When we made up a list of possible candidates based on their well-defined literary interests, the number gave us the name: the literary center of the Thirteen. It seemed a stroke of luck as well because it challenged superstition. The initiative came from the students themselves, and it consisted simply in our meeting once a week to talk about literature, though in reality that was all we did in our free time, both in and out of school. Each of us brought his own writing, read it, and submitted it to the judgment of the rest. Astounded by that example, I contributed the reading of sonnets that I had signed with the pseudonym Javier Garcés, which I used not to distinguish myself but only to hide. They were simple technical exercises without inspiration or aspiration, to which I attributed no poetic value because they did not come from my soul. I had begun with imitations of Quevedo, Lope de Vega, and even García Lorca, whose octosyllables were so spontaneous that it was enough just to begin in order to continue through inertia. I went so far in that fever of imitation that I set myself the task of parodying in order each of Garcilaso de la Vega's forty sonnets. I also wrote ones that some students requested so they could claim them as their own when they gave them to their Sunday girlfriends. One of the girls, in absolute secrecy, was very moved when she read me the verses her suitor had dedicated to her as if he had written them himself.

Carlos Martín gave us a small storeroom in the school's second courtyard, its windows sealed for security. There were about five of us who would give ourselves assignments for the next meeting. None of them had set writing as a career, though it was not a question of that but of testing each person's possibilities. We discussed the works of the other members and began to anger one another as if the meetings were soccer matches. One day Ricardo González Ripoll had to leave in the middle of a debate and surprised the rector with his ear at the door, listening to the discussion. His curiosity was legitimate because it did not seem credible to him that we would dedicate our free hours to literature.

Toward the end of March we heard the news that the former rector, Don Alejandro Ramos, had put a bullet through his head in the Parque Nacional in Bogotá. No one was willing to attribute this to his solitary and perhaps depressive character, and no one could find a reasonable motive for his committing suicide behind the monument to General Rafael Uribe Uribe, a fighter in four civil wars and a Liberal politician who was assassinated with an ax by two fanatics in the atrium of the Capitolio. A delegation from the *liceo* headed by the new rector attended the funeral of Maestro Alejandro Ramos, who remained in everyone's memory as the farewell to another time.

Interest in national politics was rather thin at school. In my grandparents' house I had heard it said too often that the only difference between the two parties after the War of a Thousand Days was that the Liberals went to five o'clock Mass so that no one would see them and the Conservatives went to Mass at eight so that people would believe they were believers. Still, the real differences began to be felt again thirty years later, when the Conservative Party lost power and the first Liberal presidents tried to open the country to the new winds blowing in the world. The Conservative Party, defeated by the rust of its absolute power, ordered and cleaned its own house under the distant brilliance of Mussolini in Italy and the dark shadows of General Franco in Spain, while the first administration of President Alfonso López Pumarejo, with a pleiad of well-educated young men, had tried to create the conditions for a modern liberalism, perhaps not realizing that he was carrying out the historic fatalism of splitting us into the two halves into which the world was divided. It was unavoidable. In one of the books the teachers lent us I found a citation attributed to Lenin: "If you do not become involved in politics, politics will eventually become involved in you."

But after forty-six years of a reactionary hegemony of Conservative presidents, peace began to seem possible. Three young presidents with modern ways of thinking had opened a liberal perspective that seemed ready to dissipate the mists of the past. Alfonso López Pumarejo, the most notable of the three, and a bold reformer, was reelected in 1942 for a second term, and nothing seemed to disturb the rhythm of the changing of the guard. So that in my first year at the *liceo* we were absorbed in the news of the European war, which kept us in suspense as national politics never had. Newspapers did not come into the school except in very special circumstances, because we were not in the habit of thinking about the press. Portable radios did not exist, and the only radio in the *liceo* was the old console in the teachers' room that we played at full volume at seven in the evening in order to dance. We were far from thinking that the bloodiest and most turbulent of all our wars was incubating at that very moment.

Politics forced its way into the *liceo*. We divided into groups of Liberals and Conservatives, and for the first time we knew which side each person was on. An internal militancy arose, cordial and somewhat academic at first, but it degenerated into the same state of mind that was beginning to rot the country. The first tensions at school were almost imperceptible, but no one doubted the good influence of Carlos Martín at the head of a faculty of teachers who had never hidden their ideologies. If the new rector was not an obvious militant, he at least authorized listening to the evening news on the radio in the teachers' room, and from then on political news prevailed over dance music. It was said without confirmation that in his office he had a portrait either of Lenin or of Marx.

The only threat of riot that ever took place at the *liceo* must have been the fruit of that rarefied atmosphere. In the dormitory pillows and shoes flew to the detriment of reading and sleep. I have not been able to establish the motive, but I think I remember—and several classmates agree with me—that it was because of an episode in the book being read aloud that night: *Cantaclaro*, by Rómulo Gallegos. A strange call to combat.

Summoned for an emergency, Carlos Martín came into the dormitory and walked from one end to the other several times in the immense silence caused by his appearance. Then, in an attack of authoritarianism unusual in a character like his, he ordered us to leave the dormitory in pajamas and slippers and assemble in the icy courtyard. There he delivered an oration in the circular style of Catiline, and we returned in perfect order and went back to sleep. It was the only incident of the kind that I can remember in our years at the *liceo*.

Mario Convers, a student who had entered the sixth-year class that year, kept us in a state of excitement with the idea of creating a newspaper different from the conventional ones in other schools. One of his first contacts was with me, and he seemed so convincing that I agreed, flattered but with no clear idea of my function, to be his editor-in-chief. Final preparations for the paper coincided with the arrest of President López Pumarejo on July 8, 1944, by a group of high-ranking officers in the Armed Forces, while he was on an official visit in the south of the country. The story, as he himself recounted it, was spare and to the point. Perhaps without intending to, he had told a stupendous tale to the investigators, according to which he had not known what had happened until he was freed. It was so close to the truths of real life that the Pasto coup became one more of many absurd episodes in our national history.

Alberto Lleras Camargo, in his position as first deputy, lulled the country with his perfect voice and diction for several hours on Radio Nacional until President López was freed and order was reestablished. But rigorous martial law, with censorship of the press, was imposed. The prognosis was uncertain. The Conservatives had governed the country from the time of our independence from Spain, in 1830, until the election of Olaya Herrera a century later, and they still gave no sign of liberalizing. The Liberals, on the other hand, were becoming more and more conservative in a country that was leaving scraps of itself behind in its history. At that moment they had an elite of young intellectuals fascinated by the lure of power, whose most radical and viable example was Jorge Eliécer Gaitán. He had been one of the heroes of my childhood because of his actions against repression in the banana zone, which I had heard about, without understanding them, ever since I gained the use of my reason. My grandmother admired him, but I believe she was concerned by his similarities at the time to the Communists. I had stood behind him when he gave a thundering speech from a balcony overlooking the square in Zipaquirá, and I was struck by his melon-shaped skull, the straight coarse hair and complexion of a pure Indian, his booming voice with its accent of the street urchins in Bogotá, perhaps exaggerated for political reasons. In his speech he did not talk about Liberals and Conservatives or the exploiters and the exploited, like everyone else, but about the poor and the oligarchs, a word I heard then for the first time as it was hammered into every sentence, and I hurried to look it up in the dictionary.

He was a distinguished lawyer, an outstanding pupil in Rome of the great Italian penologist Enrico Ferri. He had studied the oratorical arts of Mussolini there, and on the rostrum he had something of his theatrical style. Gabriel Turbay, his rival in the party, was an educated and elegant physician, with thin gold-rimmed glasses that gave him a certain air of a movie actor. At a recent Communist Party congress he had delivered an unexpected speech that surprised many and disturbed some of his middle-class party colleagues, but he did not believe he was contradicting by word or deed either his liberal formation or his aristocratic vocation. His familiarity with Russian diplomacy dated from 1936, when in his role as Colombian ambassador to Italy he established relations in Rome with the Soviet Union. Seven years later he formalized them in Washington as Colombian minister to the United States.

His relations with the Soviet embassy in Bogotá were very cordial, and he had some friends in the leadership of the Colombian Communist Party who would have been able to establish an electoral alliance with the Liberals, something often talked about in those days but never realized. During that period as well, when he was ambassador in Washington, an insistent rumor circulated in Colombia that he was the secret lover of a great Hollywood star—perhaps Joan Crawford or Paulette Goddard—but he also never renounced his career as an uncorruptible bachelor.

The supporters of Gaitán and of Turbay together could have formed a Liberal majority and opened new directions within the party itself, but neither of the two separate halves could defeat a united and armed Conservatism.

Our *Gaceta Literaria* appeared during those evil days. Even those of us who had already printed the first issue were surprised by its professional presentation as a well-formatted and well-printed eight-page tabloid. Carlos Martín and Carlos Julio Calderón were the most enthusiastic, and during recreation periods both of them commented on some of the articles. The most important of them was one written by Carlos Martín at our request, in which he established the need for a courageous awareness of the struggle against those who peddled the interests of the state, the ambitious politicians and speculators who interfered with the free progress of the country. It was published with a large photograph of him on the first page. There was an article by Convers about Hispanicism, and a lyrical prose piece by me and signed Javier Garcés. Convers announced that his friends in Bogotá were very enthusiastic, and there were possibilities for subventions to launch it on a large scale as an interscholastic paper.

The first issue had not yet been distributed when the Pasto coup took place. On the same day that a breakdown of public order was declared, the mayor of Zipaquirá burst into the *liceo* at the head of an armed squad and confiscated the copies we had ready for circulation. It was a cinematic assault, explainable only as the result of a calculated denunciation that the newspaper contained subversive material. That same day notification came from the press office of the presidency of the Republic stating that the paper had been printed without undergoing the censorship required by martial law, and Carlos Martín was stripped of the rectorship with no prior notification.

For us it was a nonsensical decision that made us feel humiliated and important at the same time. The print run was no more than two hundred copies, intended for distribution among friends, but they told us that the censorship requirement was unavoidable under martial law. Our license was canceled until the issuance of a new order that never arrived.

More than fifty years went by before Carlos Martín revealed to me, for these memoirs, the mysteries of that absurd episode. On the day the *Gaceta* was confiscated, the same education minister who had appointed him—Antonio Rocha—called him to his office in Bogotá to request his resignation. Carlos Martín found him with a copy of the *Gaceta Literaria* in which numerous phrases considered subversive had been underlined in red pencil. The same had been done to his editorial, and the one by Mario Convers, and even a poem by a known author that was suspected of being written in code. "Even the Bible underlined in that malicious way could express the opposite of its authentic meaning," Carlos Martín told him with so much blatant fury that the minister threatened to call the police. He was named publisher of the magazine *Sábado*, which for an intellectual like him should have been considered a stellar promotion. But he always had the impression that he had been the victim of a right-wing conspiracy. He was the object of an attack in a Bogotá café that he almost repelled with a gun. A new minister later named him chief counsel of the judicial section, and he had a brilliant career that culminated in a retirement surrounded by books and memories in his oasis in Tarragona.

At the same time that Carlos Martín was removed—with no connection to him, of course—an anonymous story made the rounds of the *liceo* and the houses and taverns of the city, according to which the war with Peru, in 1932, was a deception of the Liberal governor to stay in power despite the unrestrained opposition of the Conservatives. The story, which was even distributed on mimeographed sheets, claimed that the drama had begun without the slightest political intention when a Peruvian second lieutenant crossed the Amazon River with a military patrol and on the Colombian side kidnapped the secret girlfriend of the intendant of Leticia, an exciting mulatta called Pila, a diminutive of Pilar. When the Colombian intendant discovered the abduction he crossed that natural frontier with a group of armed peons and rescued Pila on Peruvian territory. But General Luis Sánchez Cerro, the dictator of Peru, took advantage of the dispute to invade Colombia and attempt to change the Amazonian boundaries in favor of his country.

Olaya Herrera—under the ferocious hounding of the Conservative Party that had been defeated after half a century of absolute rule—declared a state of war, established a national mobilization, purged the army and put in men he trusted, and sent troops to liberate the territories violated by the Peruvians. A battle cry shook the country and fired our childhood: "Long live Colombia, down with Peru!" In the paroxysm of the war the rumor circulated that civilian airplanes from SCADTA were militarized and armed as fighting squadrons, and that one of them, lacking bombs, dispersed a Holy Week procession in the Peruvian town of Guepí with a bombardment of coconuts.

The great writer Juan Lozano y Lozano, called upon by President Olaya to keep him informed of the truth in a war of reciprocal lies, wrote the truth of the incident in his masterful prose, but the false version was considered valid for a long time.

General Sánchez Cerro, of course, found a golden opportunity in the war to strengthen his iron regime. For his part, Olaya Herrera named as commander of the Colombian forces a Conservative general, Alfredo Vásquez Cobo, who happened to be in Paris. The general crossed the Atlantic in an armed ship and penetrated the mouths of the Amazon River all the way to Leticia, when the diplomats on both sides had already begun to extinguish the war.

With no connection at all to the Pasto coup or the incident of the newspaper, Carlos Martín was replaced as rector by Oscar Espitia Brand, a career educator and eminent physicist. The appointment aroused all kinds of suspicions in the school. I was shaken by reservations about him from our first greeting because of the absolute astonishment with which he stared at my poet's mane and untamed mustache. He had a hard face, and he looked straight into your eyes with a severe expression. The news that he would be our teacher of organic chemistry made my fear complete.

One Saturday during that year we were at the movies, in the middle of an evening show, when an agitated voice announced over the loudspeakers that a student at the *liceo* had died. This made so great an impression that I have not been able to remember what film we were watching, but I never forgot the intensity of Claudette Colbert about to throw herself into a torrential river from the railing of a bridge. The dead student, seventeen years old, was in the second year and had just arrived from his remote city of Pasto, near the border with Ecuador. He had suffered respiratory failure in the course of a run organized by the gym teacher as a weekend penance for his lazy students. It was the only instance of a student dying for any reason during my stay, and it caused great consternation not only in the *liceo* but in the city as well. My classmates chose me to say a few words of farewell at the funeral. That same night I requested an appointment with the new rector in order to show him my speech, and going into his office shook me like a super-natural repetition of the only interview I'd had with the late rector. Maestro Espitia read my manuscript with a tragic expression, and he approved it without comment, but when I stood to leave he indicated that I should sit down again. He had read notes and verses of mine, some of the many that circulated in secret during recreational periods, and he had thought a few of them deserved to be published in a literary supplement. I was just attempting to overcome my pitiless timidity when he expressed what was beyond a doubt his real purpose. He advised me to cut my poet's curls, inappropriate in a serious man, trim my bushy mustache, and stop wearing shirts with birds and flowers on them that were better suited to Carnival. I never expected anything like that, and to my good fortune I was too nervous to respond with an impertinence. He noticed this and adopted a sacramental tone to explain his fear that my style would be adopted by the younger students because of my reputation as a poet. I left the office affected by the recognition of my poetic customs and talent at so high a level, and disposed to satisfy the rector with a change in my appearance for so solemn a ceremony. To the point where I interpreted as a personal failure the cancellation of posthumous tributes at the request of the boy's family.

The ending was sinister. When the casket was on view in the school library, someone discovered that the glass looked foggy. Álvaro Ruiz Torres opened the casket at the request of the family and confirmed that it was, in fact, damp inside. Searching by touch for the cause of vapor in a sealed coffin, he applied light pressure to the chest with his fingertips and the corpse emitted a heartrending lament. The family was horrified at the idea that he was alive until the doctor explained that the lungs had retained air because of respiratory failure and had expelled it with pressure on the chest. Despite the simplicity of the diagnosis, or perhaps for that very reason, some were still afraid he had been buried alive. In that frame of mind, I left for my fourth-year vacation, longing to soften up my parents so I would not have to go on with my studies.

I disembarked in Sucre under an invisible drizzle. The

retaining wall at the port seemed different from the one in my memory. The square was smaller and barer than I recalled, and the church and promenade had a forsaken light under the pruned almond trees. The colored wreaths on the streets announced Christmas, but this did not awaken in me the emotion it once had, and I did not recognize any of the handful of men with umbrellas waiting on the dock, until one of them said as I passed, in an unmistakable accent and tone:

"What's the story?"

It was my papá, somewhat worn and pale from loss of weight. He was not wearing the white linen suit that had identified him from a distance ever since he was a young man, but a pair of house trousers, a short-sleeved tropical shirt, and a strange overseer's hat. He was accompanied by my brother Gustavo, whom I did not recognize because of his nine-year-old growth spurt.

It was fortunate that the family had retained the enterprising spirit of the poor, and the early supper seemed to have been prepared with the intention of letting me know that this was my house and there was no other. The good news at the table was that my sister Ligia had won the lottery. The story—which she told herself—began when our mother dreamed that her papá had fired a gun into the air to frighten away a thief he caught robbing the old house in Aracataca. My mother recounted the dream at breakfast, following a family custom, and suggested that they buy a lottery ticket ending in seven, because the number had the same shape as my grandfather's revolver. Their luck failed with a ticket my mother bought on credit, planning to pay for it with the prize money. But Ligia, who was eleven at the time, asked Papá for thirty centavos to pay for the ticket that did not win, and another thirty so that the following week she could play the same peculiar number again: 0207.

Our brother Luis Enrique hid the ticket to frighten Ligia, but his fright was greater the following Monday, when he heard her come into the house shouting like a madwoman that she had won the lottery. In his haste to do his mischief, our brother forgot where the ticket was, and in the confusion of the search, they had to empty closets and trunks and turn the house upside down from the living room to the toilets. But most disquieting of all was the cabalistic amount of the prize: 770 pesos.

The bad news was that my parents had at last realized their dream of sending Luis Enrique to the Fontidueño Reformatory in Medellín, convinced it was a school for disobedient children and not what it was in reality: a prison for the rehabilitation of very dangerous juvenile delinquents.

Papá made the final decision when he sent his wayward son to collect a bill owed to the pharmacy, and instead of handing over the eight pesos that they paid him, he bought a good-quality *tiple* that he learned to play like a master. My father made no comment when he discovered the instrument in the house, and he continued asking his son to collect the debt, but he always answered that the shopkeeper did not have the money to pay. Some two months had gone by when Luis Enrique found Papá accompanying himself on the *tiple* as he sang an improvised song: "Look at me, here I am, playing a *tiple* that cost me eight pesos."

We never found out how Papá had learned its origin, or why he had pretended to ignore his son's shabby trick, but the boy disappeared from the house until my mother had calmed her husband. That was when we heard Papá's first threats to send Luis Enrique to the reformatory in Medellín, but no one paid attention to him, for he had also announced his intention to send me to the seminary at Ocaña, not to punish me for anything but for the honor of having a priest in the house, and it took him longer to conceive the idea than to forget it. The *tiple*, however, was the last straw.

Admission to the house of correction was possible only by the decision of a judge for juveniles, but Papá overcame the lack of this requirement with a letter of recommendation from the archbishop of Medellín, Monsignor García Benítez, obtained through the mediation of mutual friends. Luis Enrique, for his part, gave yet another demonstration of his good nature and allowed himself to be taken away, as jubilant as if he were going to a party.

Vacation without him was not the same. He could accompany Filadelfo Velilla, the magical tailor and masterful *tiple* player, like a professional, and Maestro Valdés, of course. It was easy. When we left those rousing dances of the rich, flocks of furtive apprentice birds would assail us in the shadows of the park with all kinds of temptations. By mistake I proposed to one who passed close by, but who was not one of them, that she come with me, and she responded with exemplary logic that she could not because her husband was sleeping at home. But two nights later she told me she would leave the street door unbarred three times a week so I could come in without knocking when her husband was not there.

I remember her first name and family names, but I prefer to call her what I called her then: Nigromanta, or Necromancer. She would turn twenty at Christmas, and she had an Abyssinian profile and cocoa skin. Her bed was joyful and her orgasms rocky and agonized, and she had an instinct for love that seemed to belong more to a turbulent river than to a human being. Beginning with the first assault we went mad in bed. Her husband—like Juan Breva—had the body of a giant and the voice of a little girl. He had been a police officer in the south of the country, and he brought with him a bad reputation for killing Liberals just to keep up his marksmanship. They lived in a room divided by a cardboard partition, with a door to the street and another to the cemetery. The neighbors complained that she disturbed the peace of the dead with her howls of a happy dog, but the louder she howled the happier the dead must have been to be disturbed by her.

During the first week I had to escape the room at four in the morning because we had confused the date and the officer could come in at any moment. I went out by the door to the cemetery, among will-o'-the-wisps and the barking of necrophiliac dogs. On the second bridge across the channel I saw a huge shape coming toward me that I did not recognize until we had passed. It was the sergeant in person, who would have found me in his house if I had left five minutes later.

"Good morning, white boy," he said in a cordial tone.

I answered without conviction:

"God keep you, Sergeant."

Then he stopped to ask me for a light. I gave it to him, standing very close to protect the match from the early-morning wind. When he moved away with his cigarette lit, he said in a good-humored way:

"You have a stink of whore on you that's really awful."

My fear lasted less time than I had expected, because the following Wednesday I fell asleep again and when I opened my eyes I found my injured rival contemplating me in silence from the foot of the bed. My terror was so intense that it was difficult for me to continue breathing. She, who was naked, too, tried to place herself between us, but her husband moved her away with the barrel of his revolver.

"You stay out of this," he said. "Cheating in bed is settled with lead."

He put the revolver on the table, opened a bottle of cane rum, put it next to the revolver, and we sat facing each other to drink without speaking. I could not imagine what he was going to do, but I thought that if he wanted to kill me he would have done it already without all the rigamarole. A short while later Nigromanta appeared, wrapped in a sheet and with a festive air, but he pointed the revolver at her.

"This is men's business," he told her.

She gave a start and hid behind the partition.

We had finished the first bottle when the storm broke. He opened the second, pressed the muzzle against his temple, and stared at me with ice-cold eyes. Then he squeezed the trigger hard, but it clicked. He could not control the trembling of his hand when he gave me the revolver.

"It's your turn," he said.

It was the first time I had held a revolver, and I was surprised that it was so heavy and warm. I did not know what to do. I was soaked in glacial sweat, and my belly was full of a burning foam. I tried to say something but had no voice. It did not occur to me to shoot him, but I returned the revolver to him without realizing it was my only chance.

"What, did you shit yourself?" he asked with a joyful contempt. "You might have thought about that before you came here."

I could have told him that even machos shit, but I realized I did not have the balls for fatal jokes. Then he opened the cylinder of the revolver, took out the only cartridge, and threw it on the table: it was empty. What I felt was not relief but a terrible humiliation.

The rainstorm eased before four o'clock. We both were so exhausted by tension that I cannot remember at what moment he ordered me to dress, and I obeyed with a certain mournful solemnity. Only when he sat down again did I realize that he was the one who was crying. In abundance, without shame, almost as if he were showing off his tears. At last he wiped them away with the back of his hand, blew his nose with his fingers, and stood up.

"Do you know why you're leaving here alive?" he asked. And he answered his own question: "Because your papá was the only one who cured me of a case of the clap that nobody else could take care of for three years."

He gave me a man's pat on my back and pushed me into the street. It was still raining, and the town was flooded, so I walked along the stream in water up to my knees, astounded at being alive.

I do not know how my mother learned about the confrontation, but in the days that followed she undertook an insistent campaign to keep me from leaving the house at night. In the meantime, she treated me as she would have treated Papá, with distracted methods that did little good. She looked for signs that I had taken off my clothes outside the house, she discovered traces of perfume where none existed, she prepared heavy meals for me before I went out, following the popular superstition that her husband and sons would not dare make love during the sluggishness of digestion. At last, one night when she had no more pretexts for holding me, she sat in front of me and said:

"They're saying you're involved with the wife of a policeman and he's sworn he'll shoot you."

I managed to convince her it was not true, but the rumor persisted. Nigromanta sent word that she was alone, that her man was on an assignment, that she had not seen him for a long time. I always did everything possible not to run into him, but he would hurry to greet me from a distance with a gesture that could have been either a sign of reconciliation or of menace. During vacation the following year I saw him for the last time, on a drunken night when he offered me a drink of brutal rum I did not dare refuse.

I do not know by what conjuring arts my teachers and classmates, who had always viewed me as introverted, began to see me in the fifth year as a *poete maudit*, heir to the informal atmosphere that had thrived during the time of Carlos Martín. Was it in order to be more like that image that I began to smoke in the *liceo* when I was fifteen? My first attempt was horrible. I spent half the night agonizing in my own vomit on the bathroom floor. In the morning I was exhausted, but my tobacco hangover, instead of repelling me, provoked an irresistible desire to keep smoking. This was how I started my life as a diehard tobacco addict, to the point where I could not think of a sentence if my mouth was not full of smoke. At the *liceo* smoking was permitted only during recess, but I asked permission to go to the bathroom two and three times in each class, just to stave off the craving. I began smoking three packs of twenty cigarettes a day, and went up to four depending on the wildness of the night. Once, when I was already out of school, I thought I would go mad because of the dryness of my throat and the pain in my bones. I decided to give it up but could stand no more than two days of longing.

I do not know if this was what freed my hand in the prose of Professor Calderón's assignments, which grew more and more daring, and in the books of literary theory that he almost forced me to read. Today, as I review my life, I remember that my conception of the story was elementary despite the many I had read since I was first astonished by *The Thousand and One Nights*. I even dared to think that the marvels recounted by Scheherazade really happened in the daily life of her time, and stopped happening because of the incredulity and realistic cowardice of subsequent generations. By the same token, it seemed impossible that anyone from our time would ever believe again that you could fly over cities and mountains on a carpet, or that a slave from Cartagena de Indias would live for two hundred years in a bottle as a punishment, unless the author of the story could make his readers believe it.

I found classes tedious, except for literature—which I memorized—and in them I played a unique role. Bored with studying, I left everything to the mercy of chance. I had a natural instinct for predicting the important points in each subject, almost guessing the ones that most interested the teachers in order not to study the rest. The reality is that I did not understand why I had to sacrifice my talents and my time on courses that did not move me and therefore would be of no use to me in a life that was not mine.

I have dared to think that most of my teachers graded me more for my nature than my exams. What saved me were my unexpected answers, my lunatic notions, my irrational inventions. When I finished the fifth year, however, with academic shocks I did not feel capable of overcoming, I became aware of my limitations. Until then the baccalaureate had been a road paved with miracles, but my heart warned me that at the end of the fifth year an insurmountable wall was waiting for me. The unadorned truth is that I lacked the will, the vocation, the orderliness, the money, and the orthography to embark on an academic career. In other words: the years were flying by and I did not have the slightest idea what I was going to do with my life, for much more time would still have to go by before I realized that even that state of defeat was propitious, because there is nothing in this world or the next that is not useful to a writer.

Things were going no better for the country. Hounded by the fierce opposition of reactionary Conservatism, Alfonso López Pumarejo resigned the presidency of the Republic on July 31, 1945. He was succeeded by Alberto Lleras Camargo, appointed by Congress to complete the last year of the presidential term. Starting with the speech he gave when he assumed office, with his soothing voice and elegant prose style, Lleras began the illusory task of moderating tempers in the country for the election of the next officeholder.

Through the intercession of Monsignor López Lleras, the new president's cousin, the rector of the *liceo* obtained a special audience to request help from the government for a study trip to the Atlantic coast. I never knew why the rector chose me to accompany him to the audience on the condition that I arrange my disheveled hair and unruly mustache just a little. The other guests were Guillermo López Guerra, a friend of the president's, and Álvaro Ruiz Torres, the nephew of Laura Victoria, a famous poet of bold themes in the generation of Los Nuevos—the New Ones—to which Lleras Camargo also belonged. I had no alternative: on Saturday night, while Guillermo Granados read a novel that had nothing to do with my case to the dormitory, an apprentice barber in the third year gave me a recruit's haircut and carved out a tango mustache for me. For the rest of the week I endured the teasing of boarders and day students because of my new style. The mere idea of entering the Palacio Presidencial froze my blood, but my heart was mistaken because the only sign of the mysteries of power that we found there was a celestial silence. After a short wait in an anteroom with tapestries and satin curtains, a uniformed soldier led us to the office of the president.

Lleras Camargo's appearance had little in common with his portraits. I was struck by his triangular shoulders in an impeccable suit of English gabardine, his prominent cheekbones, his parchmentlike pallor, his teeth like those of a mischievous boy which were the delight of caricaturists, the slowness of his gestures, and his way of shaking hands and looking right into your eyes. I do not remember what idea I had of what presidents were like, but it did not seem to me that they were all like him. In time, when I knew him better, I realized that perhaps he himself never knew that, more than anything else, he was a writer gone astray.

After listening to the rector's words with too obvious an attention, he made some opportune comments but did not decide until he had also heard from the three students. He listened with the same attention, and it flattered us to be treated with the same respect and courtesy as the rector. The final two minutes were enough for us to be certain that he knew more about poetry than about river navigation and no doubt found it more interesting.

He granted everything we asked for, and also promised to attend the *liceo*'s closing ceremonies for the year, four months later. He did, as if they were the most serious government proceedings, and he laughed more than anyone at the farcical play we put on in his honor. At the final reception he enjoyed himself as if he were a student, an image different from his own, and he did not resist the studentlike temptation of putting his leg in the way of the one serving drinks, who just managed to avoid it.

In the festive mood of graduation celebrations, I went to spend fifth-year vacation with the family, and the first thing they told me was the very happy news that my brother Luis Enrique was back after a year and six months in the house of correction. Once again I was surprised by his good nature. He did not feel the slightest resentment against anyone for his sentence, and he recounted his misfortunes with invincible humor. In his meditations during confinement he reached the conclusion that our parents had imprisoned him in good faith. But the bishop's protection did not save him from the hard trials of daily life in prison, which instead of corrupting him enriched his character and his good sense of humor.

His first job when he returned was that of secretary to the mayor of Sucre. A short while the mayor suffered a sudden gastric upset, and someone recommended a magical remedy that had just come on the market: Alka-Seltzer. The mayor did not dissolve it in water but swallowed it like an ordinary pill, and through some miracle he did not choke on the uncontrollable effervescence in his stomach. Not yet recovered from the shock, he prescribed a few days' rest for himself, but he had political reasons for not having any of his legitimate deputies substitute for him, and he gave interim authority to my brother. Through that strange turn of events—and not having reached the prescribed age—Luis Enrique went down in the history of the city as the youngest mayor.

The only thing that really disturbed me during this vacation was the certainty that in the depths of their hearts my family was basing their future on what they were hoping for from me, and only I knew with certainty that these were vain illusions.

Two or three casual remarks of my father's halfway through the meal indicated to me that there was much to say about our common fate, and my mother hurried to confirm this. "If things go on this way," she said, "sooner or later we'll have to go back to Cataca." But a rapid glance from my father induced her to correct that:

"Or wherever we go."

Then it was clear: the possibility of a new move anywhere was a topic that had already been introduced in the family, not because of the moral atmosphere but in order to find a larger future for the children. Until that moment I had consoled myself with the idea of attributing to the city and its people, and even to my family, the spirit of defeat I suffered from myself. But my father's drama revealed once again that it is always possible to find someone who is guilty so you do not have to take the blame.

What I perceived in the air was something much more dense. My mother seemed to care only about the health of Jaime, her youngest, who had not managed to overcome his premature birth. She spent most of the day lying with him in her bedroom hammock, oppressed by sadness and humiliating heat, and the house began to resent her neglect. My brothers and sisters seemed to have no supervision. The order of our meals had relaxed so much that we ate without schedule whenever we were hungry. My father, the most home-loving of men, spent the day contemplating the square from the pharmacy and the evenings playing idle games at the billiard club. One day I could not bear the tension any longer. I lay down next to my mother in the hammock, as I had not been able to do when I was a child, and asked her what the mystery was that we were breathing in along with the air in the house. She swallowed an entire sigh so that her voice would not tremble and opened her heart to me:

"Your papá has a son by another woman."

From the relief I detected in her voice I realized the disquiet with which she had been waiting for my question. She had discovered the truth through the clairvoyance of jealousy, when a young maid came home filled with excitement because she had seen Papá talking on the phone in the telegraph office. A jealous woman did not need to know anything else. It was the one telephone in town, employed only for long-distance calls arranged ahead of time, and it had uncertain delays and minutes so expensive that it was used only in cases of extreme gravity. Each call, no matter how simple, aroused a malicious alarm in the community of the square. And so when Papá came home my mother watched him without saying anything to him, until he tore up a piece of paper he was carrying in his pocket that was the announcement of a judicial complaint because of professional abuse. My mother waited for the chance to ask him point-blank whom he had been talking to on the telephone. The question was so revealing that my papá could not find an immediate answer more credible than the truth:

"I was talking to a lawyer."

"I know that already," said my mother. "What I need is for you to tell me about it with the frankness I deserve."

My mother admitted afterward that she was the one who was terrified at the can of worms she might have opened without realizing it, for if he dared tell her the truth it was because he thought she already knew everything, or that he would have to tell her everything.

That was the case. Papá confessed that he had received notification of a criminal complaint against him for having abused in his consulting room a sick woman whom he had drugged with an injection of morphine. It must have happened in a forgotten jurisdiction where he had spent brief periods of time to attend patients without money. And he gave immediate proof of his rectitude: the melodramatic tale of anesthesia and rape was a criminal slander by his enemies, but the boy was his, conceived under normal circumstances.

It was not easy for my mother to avoid the scandal, because someone very influential was standing in the shadows and manipulating the strings of the plot. There was the precedent of Abelardo and Carmen Rosa, who had lived with us at various times and had everyone's affection, but both of them had been born before her marriage. Yet my mother overcame her rancor at the bitter pill of a new child and her husband's infidelity, and fought at his side in a public way until they had discredited the lie about the rape.

Peace returned to the family. However, a short while later, confidential news came from the same region about a little girl with a different mother whom Papá had recognized as his, and who was living in deplorable conditions. My mother wasted no time on quarrels and suppositions, but did battle to bring her to the house. "Mina did the same thing with all of Papá's scattered children," she said on that occasion, "and she never had any reason to regret it." And so she succeeded on her own in having the girl sent to her, with no public furor, and she mixed her into the already numerous family.

All of this was past history when my brother Jaime met a boy identical to our brother Gustavo at a party in another town. It was the son who had caused the legal complaint, well brought up and pampered by his mother. But our mother took all kinds of measures and brought him home to live with the family—when there already were eleven of us—and helped him to learn a trade and become established in life. Then I could not hide my astonishment that a woman whose jealousy was hallucinatory could have been capable of such actions, and she herself responded with a sentence that I have preserved ever since as if it were a diamond:

"Well, the same blood that's in my children's veins just can't go wandering around out there."

I saw my brothers and sisters only on my annual vacations. After each trip it was harder for me to recognize them and take a new memory away with me. In addition to our baptismal name, we all had another that the family gave us to make daily life easier, and it was not a diminutive but a casual nickname. From the moment I was born they called me Gabito—an unusual diminutive of Gabriel along the Guajira coast—and I have always felt it was my given name, and that Gabriel is the diminutive. Someone surprised by this capricious saints' calendar used to ask why our parents had not decided once and for all to baptize all their children with nicknames.

However, this liberal feeling of my mother's seemed contrary to her attitude toward her two oldest daughters, Margot and Aida, on whom she tried to impose the same severity that her mother had imposed on her because of her obstinate love for my father. She wanted to move to another town. Papá, on the other hand, who did not need to hear that twice to pack his suitcases and begin roaming the world, was reluctant this time. Several days went by before I learned that the problem was that the two oldest girls were in love with two different men, of course, but who both had the same name: Rafael. When I heard about it I could not control my laughter because of the memory of the horror novel that Papá and Mamá had lived through, and I told her so.

"It's not the same," she said.

"It is the same," I insisted.

"All right," she conceded, "it is the same, but two at the same time."

As had been the case in her day, reasons and arguments were of no use. No one ever learned how our parents found out, because each sister, on her own, had taken precautions not to be discovered. But the witnesses were the most unexpected ones, because these same sisters had sometimes arranged to be accompanied by younger siblings who could vouch for their innocence. Most surprising of all was that Papá also participated in the ambush, not with direct actions but with the same passive resistance that my grandfather Nicolás had used against his daughter.

"We would go to a dance and my papá would come in and take us home if he found that the Rafaels were there," Aida Rosa has recounted in a newspaper interview. They did not have permission to take a walk in the country or go to the movies, or they were sent with people who would not let them out of their sight. Each girl, on her own, invented useless pretexts for keeping their romantic appointments, and that was where an invisible phantom appeared and betrayed them. Ligia, who was younger than they, earned a reputation as a spy and an informer, but she excused herself with the argument that jealousy among siblings is another form of love.

During that vacation I tried to intercede with my parents so they would not repeat the mistakes that my mother's parents had made with her, and they always found complicated reasons for not understanding. The most terrible was the one about the *pasquines*, the anonymous scandal sheets that were posted in public and disclosed horrifying secrets—real or invented—even in the least suspect families. They revealed hidden paternities, shameful adulteries, perversions in bed that somehow had entered the public domain by paths less straightforward than the *pasquines*. But none of them had ever denounced anything that in some way was not known, no matter how hidden it had been kept, or that was not bound to happen sooner or later. "You yourself make your own *pasquines*," one of their victims used to say.

What my parents did not foresee was that their daughters would defend themselves with the same means they had used. They sent Margot to study in Montería, and Aida made the decision to go to Santa Marta. They were boarders, and on their free days there was someone who had been forewarned to accompany them, but they always arranged to communicate with their distant Rafaels. But my mother achieved what her parents did not achieve with her. Aida spent half her life in the convent and lived there without grief or glory until she felt safe from men. Margot and I were always united by memories of our shared childhood when I would keep an eye on the adults so they would not catch her eating dirt. In the end she became like a second mother to everyone, in particular Cuqui, the one who needed her most, and she kept him with her until his last breath.

Only today do I realize how much my mother's unhappy state of mind and the internal tensions in the house were in accord with the fatal contradictions in the country that had not surfaced yet but did exist. President Lleras would have to hold elections in the new year, and the future looked dark. The Conservatives, who had managed to bring down López, played a double game with his successor: they flattered him for his mathematical impartiality but fomented discord in the Province in order to regain power either by persuasion or by force.

Sucre had remained immune to violence, and the few cases that anyone recalled had nothing to do with politics. One had been the murder of Joaquín Vega, a very sought-after musician who played the saxhorn in the local band. They were playing at seven in the evening at the entrance to the movie theater, and a relative of his cut his throat when it was puffed out by the pressure of the music he was playing, and he bled to death on the ground. Both men were well loved in the town, and the only known but unconfirmed explanation was that it had been an affair of honor. The birthday of my sister Rita was being celebrated at the same time, and the shock of the bad news ruined the party that had been scheduled to last for many more hours.

The other duel, which occurred much earlier but was indelible in the town's memory, was the one between Plinio Balmaceda and Dionisiano Barrios. The first was a member of an old and respectable family, an enormous, charming man but also a troublemaker with a wicked temper when he crossed paths with alcohol. In his right mind he had the airs and graces of a gentleman, but when he drank too much he was transformed into a bully with an easy revolver and a riding whip in his belt to use on anyone he took a dislike to. Even the police tried to keep him at a distance. The members of his good family, tired of dragging him home each time he had too much to drink, at last abandoned him to his fate.

Dionisiano Barrios was just the opposite: a timid, impaired man, an enemy of brawls and abstemious by nature. He never had problems with anyone until Plinio Balmaceda began to provoke him with vile jokes about his impairment. He did what he could to avoid him, until the day Balmaceda crossed paths with him and cut his face with the whip because he felt like it. Then Dionisiano overcame his timidity, his hump, and his bad luck, and he confronted the aggressor with a gun. It was an instantaneous duel in which both men received serious wounds, but only Dionisiano died.

The historic duel in the town, however, caused the twin deaths of this same Plinio Balmaceda and Tasio Ananías, a police sergeant famous for his ethical behavior, the exemplary son of Mauricio Ananías, who played drums in the same band in which Joaquín Vega played the saxhorn. It was a formal duel in the middle of the street, each man's wounds were grave, and each endured a long death agony in his house. Plinio regained consciousness almost at once, and his immediate concern was with Ananías's fate. Tasio, in turn, was struck by the concern with which Plinio asked about him. Each began to pray that the other not die, and their families kept them informed as long as their souls were in their bodies. The entire town lived in suspense while all kinds of efforts were made to prolong both their lives.

After forty-eight hours of their death agony, the church bells tolled for a woman who had just died. The dying men heard the bells, and each in his bed believed they were tolling for the death of the other. Ananías died of grief almost at once, weeping over the death of Plinio. Plinio learned this and died two days later, weeping copious tears for Sergeant Ananías.

In a town of peaceable friends like this one, violence during those years had a less fatal but no less harmful expression: *pasquines*. Terror lived in the houses of the great families, who waited for the next morning as if it were a fateful lottery. Where least expected a punitive sheet of paper would appear, which was a relief for what it did not say about you, and at times a secret fiesta for what it did say about others. My father, perhaps the most peaceable man I have ever known, oiled the venerable revolver he had never fired and loosened his tongue in the billiard hall.

"Whoever even thinks about touching any of my daughters," he shouted, "will taste the lead of an angry man."

Several families began an exodus for fear the *pasquines* were a prelude to the police violence that was devastating entire towns in the interior of the country in order to intimidate the opposition.

Tension was transformed into another kind of daily bread. At first furtive patrols were organized, not so much to discover the authors of the *pasquines* as to learn what the sheets said before they were destroyed at dawn. A group of us who were out late found a city official at three in the morning, enjoying the cool air in the doorway of his house but in reality watching to see who put up the *pasquines*. My brother said to him, half as a joke and half in a serious way, that some told the truth. The official took out his revolver and pointed it at him, the hammer cocked.

"Repeat that!"

Then we learned that on the previous night they had put up a truthful *pasquín* aimed at his unmarried daughter. But the facts were common knowledge, even in her own house, and the only person who did not know them was her father.

At first it was evident that the *pasquines* had been written by the same person, with the same brush, on the same paper, but in a business district as small as the one on the square, only one store could sell these items, and the owner hastened to prove his innocence. Then I knew that one day I was going to write a novel about them, not because of what they said, which almost always were fantasies in the public domain, and with little wit, but because of the unbearable tension they managed to create inside the houses.

In my third novel, *In Evil Hour*, written twenty years later, it seemed an act of simple decency not to use concrete or identifiable cases, even though some of the real ones were better than those invented by me. Besides, there was no need to, because I was always more interested in the social phenomenon than in the private lives of the victims. I learned only after it had been published that in the poor districts, where those of us who lived on the main square were disliked, many *pasquines* were reasons for celebration.

The truth is that the *pasquines* served only as a point of departure for me in a plot I never managed to make real, because what I was writing demonstrated that the fundamental problem was political and not moral, as people believed. I always thought that Nigromanta's husband was a good model for the military magistrate in *In Evil Hour*, but while I was developing him as a character he was seducing me as a human being, and I had no reason to kill him, for I discovered that a serious writer cannot kill a character without a persuasive reason, and I did not have one.

Today I realize that the novel itself could be another novel. I wrote it in a student hotel on the Rue Cujas, in the Latin Quarter in Paris, a hundred meters from the Boulevard Saint Michel, while the days passed without mercy as I waited for a check that never arrived. When I thought it was finished, I rolled up the pages, tied them with one of the three neckties I had worn in better days, and buried it at the back of the closet.

Two years later, in Mexico City, I did not even know where it was when I was asked to enter it in a novel competition sponsored by Esso Colombiana, with a prize of three thousand dollars in those times of famine. The emissary was the photographer Guillermo Angulo, my old Colombian friend, who knew about the existence of the first draft that I had been writing in Paris, and he took it just as it was, still tied with the necktie, and there was not even time to smooth out the wrinkles with steam because of the pressures of the deadline. I submitted it without any hope for a prize that would have been enough money to buy a house. But just as I had submitted it, it was declared the winner by a distinguished panel of judges on April 16, 1962, almost at the exact moment that our second son, Gonzalo, was born, his loaf of bread under his arm.*

We had not even had time to think about it when I received a letter from Father Félix Restrepo, the president of the Colombian Academy of the Language, an upright man who had presided over the panel for the prize but did not know the title of the novel. Only then did I realize that in our last-minute rush I had forgotten to write the title on the first page: *This Shit-eating Town.*

Father Restrepo was scandalized when he heard it, and through Germán Vargas he asked me in the most amiable way to change it for one less brutal and more in line with the atmosphere of the book. After many exchanges with him, I decided on a title that perhaps would not say much about the drama but would serve as a banner for navigating the seas of sanctimony: *In Evil Hour.*

One week later, Dr. Carlos Arango Vélez, Colombia's ambassador to Mexico and a recent candidate for the presidency of the Republic, made an appointment to see me in his office in

---

*An allusion to the traditional saying that every child is born with a loaf of bread—that is, each child is provided for.

order to inform me that Father Restrepo was pleading that I change two words that seemed inadmissible in the text that had won the prize: *condom* and *masturbation*. The ambassador and I could not hide our astonishment, but we agreed that we ought to satisfy Father Restrepo and bring the interminable competition to a happy conclusion with an even-tempered solution.

"Very well, Señor Ambassador," I said. "I'll eliminate one of the two words, but you'll please choose which one."

With a sigh of relief the ambassador eliminated the word *masturbation*. And so the conflict was resolved, and the book was published by Editorial Iberoamericana in Madrid, with a large printing and a stellar launching. It was bound in leather, with impeccable print on excellent paper. But it was an ephemeral honeymoon, because I could not resist the temptation of doing an exploratory reading, and I discovered that the book written in my Indian language had been dubbed—like the movies in those days—into the purest Madrid dialect.

I had written: *"Así como ustedes viven ahora, no sólo están en una situación insegura sino que constituyen un mal ejemplo para el pueblo."* The transcription by the Spanish editor made my skin crawl: *"Así como vivís ahora, no sólo estáis en una situación insegura, sino que constituís un mal ejemplo para el pueblo."** Even more serious: since this sentence was said by a priest, the Colombian reader might think it was the author's sly way of indicating that the cleric was Spanish, which would complicate his behavior and altogether change an essential aspect of the drama. Not content with touching up the grammar in the dialogues, the proofreader permitted himself to change the style with a heavy hand, and the book was filled with Madrilenian patches that had nothing to do with the original. As a consequence, I had no recourse but to withdraw my permission from

---

*The grammatical person and verb form used to express the equivalent of plural "you" differ in Spain and Latin America. The passage translates: "The way you are living now, you not only are in an uncertain situation but are also setting a bad example for the town."

the edition because I considered it adulterated, and to retrieve and burn the copies that had not yet been sold. The reply of those responsible was absolute silence.

From that moment on I considered the novel unpublished, and I devoted myself to the difficult task of translating it back into my Caribbean dialect, because the only original version was the one I had submitted to the competition, which had then been sent to Spain for the Iberoamericana edition. Once the original text had been reestablished, and corrected, in passing, one more time by me, Editorial Era in Mexico brought it out with the express printed notice that this was the first edition.

I have never known why *In Evil Hour* is the only one of my books that transports me to its time and its place on a night with a full moon and spring breezes. It was Saturday, the clouds had gone, and there were too many stars for the sky. It had just struck eleven when I heard my mother in the dining room crooning a love *fado* to put the baby she was carrying to sleep. I asked her where the music came from and she answered in a manner that was typical of her:

"From the houses of the bandit women."

She gave me five pesos without my asking because she saw me dressing to go to the fiesta. Before I left she told me with her infallible foresight to leave the door to the courtyard unbarred so I could come back at any time without waking my father. I never got as far as the houses of the bandit women because there was a musicians' rehearsal in the carpentry shop of Maestro Valdés, whose group Luis Enrique had joined as soon as he returned home.

That year I joined them to play the *tiple* and sing with their six anonymous maestros until dawn. I always thought my brother was a good guitarist, but on my first night I learned that even his most bitter rivals considered him a virtuoso. There was no better group, and they were so sure of themselves that when someone hired them for a serenade of reconciliation or apology, Maestro Valdés would reassure him ahead of time:

"Don't worry, we'll leave her biting her pillow."

A vacation without him was not the same. He lit up the party when he arrived, and Luis Enrique and he, along with Filadelfo Velilla, played together like professionals. That was when I discovered the loyalty of alcohol and learned to live in the proper way, sleeping by day and singing at night. As my mother said: I had let the dogs loose.

People said all kinds of things about me, and there was a rumor that my mail was delivered not to my parents' address but to the houses of the bandit women. I became the most dependable client for their epic stews as strong-tasting as tiger bile and iguana fricassees that gave you enough drive for three whole nights. I did not read again or join the routine of the family table. This corresponded to the idea expressed so often by my mother that in my own way I did whatever I wanted, but poor Luis Enrique was the one with the bad reputation. He, without knowing what my mother said, told me during this time: "The only thing they need to say now is that I'm corrupting you and then they'll send me back to the house of correction."

At Christmas I decided to escape the annual float competition and fled with two complicit friends to the neighboring town of Majagual. I announced at home that I was going for three days but stayed for ten. The fault lay with María Alejandrina Cervantes, an unbelievable woman I met the first night, with whom I lost my head in the most uproarious carousing of my life. Until the Sunday morning when she did not wake up in my bed, and disappeared forever. Years later I rescued her from my memories, not so much for her charms as for the resonance of her name, and I revived her, to protect another woman in one of my novels, as the owner and madam of a house of pleasure that never existed.

When I went home I found my mother boiling the coffee in the kitchen at five in the morning. In a conspiratorial whisper she told me to stay with her, because my father had just awakened and was prepared to show me that not even on vacation was I as free as I thought. She served me a large cup of unsweetened coffee, even though she knew I did not like it, and had me sit next to the stove. My father came in wearing his pajamas, still in a mood of sleep, and he was surprised to see me with the steaming cup but asked me an oblique question:

"Didn't you say you didn't drink coffee?"

Not knowing how to answer him, I invented the first thing that passed through my head:

"I'm always thirsty at this time of day."

"Like all drunkards," he replied.

He did not look at me or mention the subject again. But my mother informed me that my father, depressed after that day, had begun to consider me a lost cause though he never let me know it.

My expenses increased so much that I resolved to sack my mother's reserves. Luis Enrique absolved me with his logical argument that money stolen from your parents, if it is used for the movies and not for whores, is legitimate. I suffered because of the awkwardness of my mother's complicity in keeping my father from knowing I was on the wrong path. She was right because it was all too obvious at home that at times I was still asleep for no reason at lunchtime, and had the voice of a hoarse rooster, and was so distracted that one day I did not hear two of Papá's questions, and he assailed me with his harshest diagnosis:

"You have liver trouble."

In spite of everything, I managed to preserve social appearances. I was well dressed and better behaved at the gala dances and occasional lunches organized by the families on the main square, whose houses were kept closed the whole year and were opened for the Christmas holidays when the students came home.

That was the year of Cayetano Gentile, who celebrated his vacation with three splendid dances. For me they were lucky dates, because at all three I danced with the same partner. I asked her to dance on the first night without bothering to ask who she was, or whose daughter, or who she had come with. She seemed so enigmatic that during the second number I proposed in all seriousness that she marry me, and her response was even more mysterious:

"My papá says that the prince who's going to marry me hasn't been born yet."

Days later I saw her crossing the promenade in the square under the fierce twelve o'clock sun, wearing a radiant organza dress and holding by the hand a boy and a girl about six or seven years old. "They're mine," she said, weak with laughter, without my even asking. And she said it with so much perversity that I began to suspect that my proposal of marriage had not been carried away on the wind.

From the time I was an infant in the house in Aracataca I had learned to sleep in a hammock, but only in Sucre did I make it a part of my nature. There is nothing better for taking a siesta, for experiencing the hour of stars, for thinking without haste, for making love without prejudices. The day I came back from my week of dissipation I hung it between two trees in the courtyard, as Papá used to do in other times, and slept with a clear conscience. But my mother, always tormented by her terror that her children would die in their sleep, woke me at the end of the afternoon to find out if I was alive. Then she lay down beside me and with no preambles approached the matter that made it difficult for her to live.

"Your papá and I would like to know what's happening to you."

The sentence could not have been better aimed. I had known for some time that my parents shared their uneasiness regarding the changes in my behavior, and that she would improvise trivial explanations to reassure him. Nothing happened in the house that my mother did not know about, and her rages were legendary. But the cup overflowed when for a week I did not get home until broad daylight. My reasonable position would have been to avoid her questions or put them off for a more opportune moment, but she knew that so serious a matter allowed only immediate replies.

All her arguments were legitimate: I would disappear at dusk dressed for a wedding and not come home to sleep, but the next day I dozed in the hammock until after lunch. I had stopped reading, and for the first time since my birth I dared come home not knowing with certainty where I was. "You don't even look at your brothers and sisters, you mix up their names and ages, and the other day you kissed a grandson of Clemencia Morales thinking he was one of them," said my mother. But then she became aware of her exaggerations and compensated for them with a simple truth:

"In short, you've become a stranger in this house."

"All of that is true," I said, "but the reason is very easy: I'm fed up with the whole business."

"With us?"

My answer could have been affirmative, but it would not have been fair:

"With everything," I said.

And then I told her about my situation at the *liceo*. They judged me by my grades, year after year my parents were proud of the results, they believed I was not only an irreproachable student but also an exemplary friend, the most intelligent and brightest boy, and the one most famous for his congeniality. Or, as my grandmother would say: "The perfect kid."

But to make a long story short, the truth was just the opposite. I seemed to be that way because I did not have the courage and sense of independence of my brother Luis Enrique, who did only what he wanted to do. And who without a doubt would achieve a happiness that is not what one desires for one's children but is what allows them to survive the immoderate affections, the irrational fears, and the joyful expectations of their parents.

My mother was crushed by this portrait so contrary to the one they had forged in their solitary dreams.

"Well, I don't know what we're going to do," she said after a lethal silence, "because if we tell all this to your father he'll die a sudden death. Don't you realize you're the pride of the family?"

For them it was simple: since there was no possibility I would be the eminent physician my father could not be because he did not have the money, they dreamed I would at least be a professional in something else.

"Well, I won't be anything at all," I concluded. "I refuse to let you force me into being what I don't want to be or what you would like me to be, much less what the government wants me to be."

The dispute, at cross-purposes and somewhat rambling, went on for the rest of the week. I believe my mother wanted to take the time to talk it over with Papá, and that idea filled me with new courage. One day, as if by chance, she made a surprising proposal:

"They say that if you put your mind to it you could be a good writer."

I had never heard anything like it in the family. Since I was a child my inclinations had allowed me to suppose that I would draw, be a musician, sing in church, or even be a Sunday poet. I had discovered in myself a tendency, known to everyone, toward writing that was rather convoluted and ethereal, but this time my reaction was one of surprise.

"If you're going to be a writer you have to be one of the great ones, and they don't make them anymore," I told my mother. "After all, there are better ways to starve to death."

On one of those afternoons, instead of talking to me she wept without tears. Today I would have become alarmed, because I esteem repressed crying as an infallible device used by great women to impose their purposes. But at the age of eighteen I did not know what to say to my mother, and my silence frustrated her tears.

"All right," she said, "promise me at least that you'll finish the baccalaureate the best you can, and I'll be responsible for arranging the rest with your papá."

At the same time we both felt the relief of winning. I agreed, as much for her sake as for my father's, because I feared they would die if we did not come to an understanding soon. This was how we found the easy solution of my studying law and political science, which was not only a good cultural foundation for any kind of occupation, but also a course of study humanized by classes in the morning and free time for working in the afternoon. Concerned as well by the emotional burden my mother had endured during this time, I asked her to prepare the ground for me so I could speak face-to-face with Papá. She objected, certain we would end up in a quarrel.

"There are no two men in this world more similar than you and him," she told me. "And that's the worst thing for having a conversation."

I always believed the opposite. Only now, when I have already gone past all the ages my father was in his long life, have I begun to see myself in the mirror looking much more like him than me.

My mother must have considered that night her crowning achievement, because Papá gathered the whole family around the table and announced with a casual air: "We'll have a lawyer in the house." Perhaps fearing that my father would attempt to reopen the debate for the entire family, my mother intervened with her best innocence.

"In our situation, and with this army of children," she explained to me, "we thought the best solution is the only career you can pay for yourself."

It was not anywhere near as simple as she said, but for us it might be the lesser evil and its devastation the least bloody. To go on with the game, I asked my father's opinion, and his answer was immediate and of heartbreaking sincerity:

"What do you want me to say? You've broken my heart in two, but at least I still can be proud of helping you be whatever you want to be."

The height of luxury in that January of 1946 was my first trip in a plane, thanks to José Palencia, who reappeared with a major problem. He had waltzed through five years of the baccalaureate in Cartagena but had just failed the sixth. I committed myself to getting him a place at the *liceo* so that he would receive his diploma at last, and he invited me to go there with him.

The flight to Bogotá took off twice a week in a DC-3 belonging to LANSA, and the greatest danger was not the plane but the cows that wandered onto the clay runway improvised in a pasture. Sometimes the plane had to fly around in circles until they had finally been shooed away. It was the initial experience in my legendary fear of airplanes, at a time when the Church prohibited them from carrying consecrated Hosts to keep them safe from catastrophes. The flight lasted almost four hours, with no stops, at a speed of three hundred twenty kilometers an hour. Those of us who had made the prodigious river voyage were guided in the sky by the living map of the Great Magdalena River. We recognized the miniature towns, the windup boats, the happy little dolls waving at us from the courtyards of the schools. The flesh-and-blood flight attendants spent their time reassuring the passengers who prayed as they traveled, helping those who were airsick, and convincing a good number that there was no danger of running into the flocks of turkey buzzards that kept an eye on the death down below in the river. Experienced travelers, for their part, recounted historic flights over and over again as feats of courage. The ascent to the altiplano of Bogotá, without a pressurized cabin or oxygen masks, felt like a bass drum in your heart, and the jolts and the hammering of the wings increased the joy of landing. But the greatest surprise was having arrived before our telegrams of the night before.

Passing through Bogotá, José Palencia bought instruments for an entire orchestra, and I do not know if he did it by premeditation or premonition, but from the moment Rector Espitia saw him stride in with guitars, drums, maracas, and harmonicas, I knew he was admitted. For my part, I too felt the weight of my new circumstances as I crossed the threshold: I was a sixth-year student. Until then I had not been aware of bearing on my forehead the star that everyone dreamed of, which could be seen without fail in the way they approached us, in the tone of voice they used to speak to us, even in a certain reverential awe. It was also a year of fiesta. Although the dormitory was only for scholarship students, José Palencia installed himself in the best hotel on the square, one of the women who owned it played the piano, and life was transformed into an entire year of Sundays.

It was another of the leaps in my life. While I was an adolescent my mother would buy me used clothing, which she altered for my younger brothers when I could no longer wear it. The most problematic years were the first two, because wool clothing for the cold climate was expensive and difficult to find. Even though my body did not grow with much enthusiasm, it did not allow time for altering a suit to fit two successive heights in the same year. To make matters worse, the original custom of the boarders, which was to trade clothing, could not be imposed because the items were so well known that the mockery at the expense of the new owners became unbearable. This was resolved in part when Espitia imposed a uniform of a blue jacket and gray trousers, which unified our appearance and hid the secondhand items.

In the third and fourth years I could wear the only suit that the tailor in Sucre altered for me, but in the fifth I had to buy one in very good condition, and by the sixth I could no longer wear it. My father, however, was so enthusiastic about my intention to change that he gave me money to buy a new suit made to measure, and José Palencia gave me one of his from the previous year, a three-piece camel's hair that was almost brand new. I soon realized how true it was that the habit does not make the monk. In my new suit, interchangeable with the new uniform, I attended the dances where the boys from the coast reigned, and I only managed to get a girlfriend who lasted less time than a flower.

Espitia welcomed me with unusual enthusiasm. He seemed to teach the two chemistry classes a week only for me, with rapid-fire questions and answers. My obligatory attention was a good starting point for keeping the promise to my parents that I would have an honorable ending. The rest was accomplished by Martina Fonseca's unique and simple method: pay attention in class in order to avoid staying up all night in fear of the terrifying final exam. It was a wise lesson. When I decided to use it in my last year at the *liceo*, my anguish subsided. I could answer the teachers' questions with ease, and they began to be more familiar, and I realized how easy it was to keep the promise I had made to my parents.

My only disturbing problem continued to be the howls of my nightmares. The prefect of discipline, who had very good relations with his students, was Professor Gonzalo Ocampo, and one night during the second semester he tiptoed into the dormitory in the dark to ask me for some keys of his that I had forgotten to return. As soon as he placed his hand on my shoulder, I gave a savage howl that woke up everyone. The next day they moved me to a dormitory for six that had been improvised on the second floor.

It was a solution for my nocturnal fears, but one that was too tempting because it was over the dispensary, and four students from the improvised dormitory slipped down to the kitchens and ransacked them for a midnight supper. Sergio Castro, who was above suspicion, and I, the least daring, stayed in our beds to serve as negotiators in case of emergency. After an hour they returned with half the dispensary ready for us to eat. It was the great feast of our long years as boarders, but it was followed by the indigestion of their finding us out within twenty-four hours. I thought it would all end there, and only the negotiating talent of Espitia saved us from expulsion.

It was a good period for the *liceo*, and the least promising one for the country. Lleras's impartiality, without intending to, increased the tension that was beginning to be felt for the first time at the school. Today, however, I realize that it was already inside me, but only then did I begin to be aware of the country in which I lived. Some teachers who had tried to remain impartial for the past year could not manage it in their classes, and they would let loose with indigestible outbursts about their political preferences. In particular when the hard campaign for the presidential succession began.

Each day it was more evident that with Gaitán and Turbay running at the same time, the Liberal Party would lose the presidency of the Republic after twenty-five years of absolute governments. They were two candidates as inimical as if they were from two different parties, not only for their own sins but because of the bloody determination of the Conservatives, who had seen the situation with clarity since the first day: instead of Laureano Gómez, they imposed the candidacy of Ospina Pérez, a millionaire engineer with a well-deserved reputation as a patriarch. With Liberalism divided and Conservatism united and armed, there was no alternative: Ospina Pérez was elected.

Then Laureano Gómez began to prepare to succeed him by using official forces with all-out violence. It was a return to the historic reality of the nineteenth century, when we had no peace but only ephemeral truces between eight general civil wars and fourteen local ones, three military coups, and then the War of a Thousand Days, which left some eighty thousand dead on both sides in a population of four million people. It was so simple: it was all a common plan for regressing a hundred years.

Professor Giraldo, at the end of the year, made a flagrant exception for me that I am still ashamed of. He prepared a simple set of questions for me so I could make up the algebra I had failed since my fourth year, and he left me alone in the faculty office with all the opportunities for cheating within reach. He returned an hour later filled with hope, saw the catastrophic result, and canceled out each page with a cross from top to bottom and a ferocious growl: "That brain is rotted." However, for the final grades, I passed algebra but had the decency not to thank the teacher for having gone against his principles and obligations for my sake.

The night before the last final exam of the year, Guillermo López Guerra and I had an unfortunate incident with Professor Gonzalo Ocampo because of a drunken fight. José Palencia had invited us to study in his hotel room, which was a colonial jewel with an idyllic view of the park in flower and the cathedral in the background. Since we had only one last exam, we stayed there until dark and returned to school by way of our poor men's taverns. Professor Ocampo, on duty as prefect of discipline, reprimanded us on account of the hour and the state we were in, and the two of us in chorus crowned him with curses. His furious reaction and our shouts disturbed the dormitory.

The decision of the faculty was that López Guerra and I could not sit for the only final examination we still had to take. In other words: that year, at least, we would not hold baccalaureate degrees. We never could find out about the secret negotiations among the teachers, because they closed ranks with insurmountable solidarity. Rector Espitia must have assumed responsibility for the problem, and he arranged for us to take the exam at the Ministry of Education in Bogotá. Which we did. Espitia himself accompanied us, and stayed with us while we answered the written examination, which was graded on the spot. We did very well.

It must have been a very complicated internal situation, because Ocampo did not attend the final ceremony, perhaps because of Espitia's easy solution and our excellent grades. And, in the end, because of my personal successes, for as a special prize I was awarded an unforgettable book: Diógenes Laercio's *Lives of Famous Philosophers.* It not only was more than my parents expected, but I was also the first in that year's class, though my classmates—and I more than anyone—knew I was not the best.

5

I NEVER IMAGINED that nine months after receiving the baccalaureate I would have my first story published in *Fin de Semana*, the literary supplement of *El Espectador* in Bogotá, and the most interesting and demanding of the time. Forty-two days later the second story was published. The most surprising thing for me, however, was a dedicatory note by the deputy editor of the paper and the editor of the supplement, Eduardo Zalamea Borda (Ulises), the most lucid Colombian critic at the time, and the one most alert to the appearance of new values.

The process was so unexpected that it is not easy to recount. At the beginning of the year I had matriculated in the faculty of law at the Universidad Nacional of Bogotá, as my parents and I had agreed. I lived in the very center of the city, in a *pensión* on Calle Florián, occupied for the most part by students from the Atlantic coast. On free afternoons, instead of working to support myself, I stayed in my room to read or went to the cafés that permitted it. They were books I obtained by chance and luck, and they depended more on chance than on any luck of mine, because the friends who could buy them lent them to me for such limited periods that I stayed awake for nights on end in order to return them on time. But unlike the ones I read at the *liceo* in Zipaquirá, which deserved to be in a mausoleum of consecrated authors, we read these like bread warm from the oven, printed in Buenos Aires in new translations after the long hiatus in publishing because of the Second World War. In this way I discovered, to my good fortune, the already very-much-discovered Jorge Luis Borges, D. H. Lawrence and Aldous Huxley, Graham Greene and Gilbert Chesterton, William Irish and Katherine Mansfield, and many others.

These new works were displayed in the unreachable windows of bookstores, but some copies circulated in the student cafés, which were active centers of cultural dissemination for university students from the provinces. Many of them had their places reserved year after year and received mail and even postal money orders there. Some favors from the owners, or their trusted employees, were decisive in saving a good many university careers. Numerous professionals in the country may owe more to them than to their invisible tutors.

I preferred El Molino, the café frequented by older poets, only some two hundred meters from my *pensión* and on the crucial corner of Avenida Jiménez de Quesada and Carrera Séptima. They did not allow students a fixed table, but you could be sure of learning more and learning it better than in textbooks from the literary conversations we listened to as we huddled at nearby tables. It was an enormous café, well turned out in the Spanish style, and its walls had been decorated by the painter Santiago Martínez Delgado with episodes from the battle of Don Quixote against the windmills. Although I did not have a reserved place, I always arranged for the waiters to put me as close as possible to the great master León de Greiff—bearded, gruff, charming—who would begin his *tertulia** at dusk with some of the most famous writers of the day, and end it with his chess students at midnight, awash in cheap liquor. Very few of the great names in the country's arts and letters did not sit at that table, and we played dead at ours in order not to miss a single word. Although they tended to talk

---

*An institution in the Hispanic world, a *tertulia* is a regular informal gathering for conversation; it can take place in a café or in someone's home.

more about women or political intrigues than about their art or work, they always said something new for us to learn. The most attentive of us were from the Atlantic coast, united less by Caribbean conspiracies against the Cachacos than by the vice of books. One day Jorge Álvaro Espinosa, a law student who had taught me to navigate the Bible and made me learn by heart the complete names of Job's companions, placed an awesome tome on the table in front of me and declared with his bishop's authority:

"This is the other Bible."

It was, of course, James Joyce's *Ulysses*, which I read in bits and pieces and fits and starts until I lost all patience. It was premature brashness. Years later, as a docile adult, I set myself the task of reading it again in a serious way, and it not only was the discovery of a genuine world that I never suspected inside me, but it also provided invaluable technical help to me in freeing language and in handling time and structures in my books.

One of my roommates was Domingo Manuel Vega, a medical student who had been my friend ever since Sucre and who shared my voracity in reading. Another was my cousin Nicolás Ricardo, the oldest son of my uncle Juan de Dios, who kept alive for me the virtues of the family. One night Vega came in with three books he had just bought, and he lent me one chosen at random, as he often did to help me sleep. But this time the effect was just the opposite: I never again slept with my former serenity. The book was Franz Kafka's *The Metamorphosis*, in the false translation by Borges published by Losada in Buenos Aires, that determined a new direction for my life from its first line, which today is one of the great devices in world literature: "As Gregor Samsa awoke one morning from uneasy dreams he found himself transformed in his bed into a gigantic insect." These were mysterious books whose dangerous precipices were not only different from but often contrary to everything I had known until then. It was not necessary to demonstrate facts: it was enough for the author to have written something for it to be true, with no proof other than the power of his talent and the authority of his voice. It was Scheherazade all over again, not in her millenary world where everything was possible but in another irreparable world where everything had already been lost.

When I finished reading *The Metamorphosis* I felt an irresistible longing to live in that alien paradise. The new day found me at the portable typewriter that Domingo Manuel Vega had lent me, attempting to write something that would resemble Kafka's poor bureaucrat changed into an enormous cockroach. In the days that followed, I did not go to the university for fear the spell would be broken, and I continued sweating drops of envy until Eduardo Zalamea Borda published in his pages a disconsolate commentary lamenting the fact that the new generation of Colombian writers lacked memorable names, and that nothing could be detected in the future that might remedy the situation. I do not know with what right I felt challenged, in the name of my generation, by the provocation in that commentary, but I took up the abandoned story again in an attempt at rectification. I elaborated the plot idea of the conscious corpse in *The Metamorphosis* but relieved it of its false mysteries and ontological prejudices.

In any event, I felt so uncertain I did not dare talk it over with any of my tablemates. Not even with Gonzalo Mallarino, my fellow student at the faculty of law, who was the only reader of the lyrical prose pieces that I wrote to endure the tedium of my classes. I reread and corrected my story until I was exhausted, and at last I wrote a personal note to Eduardo Zalamea—whom I had never seen—of which I cannot recall even a single letter. I put everything in an envelope and brought it in person to reception at *El Espectador*. The concierge authorized me to go up to the second floor to hand the letter to Zalamea himself, but the mere idea paralyzed me. I left the envelope on the concierge's desk and fled.

This happened on a Tuesday, and I was not troubled by any presentiments regarding the fate of my story, but I was certain that in the event it was published, it would not happen very soon. In the meantime, for two weeks I rambled and roamed from café to café to allay my Saturday-afternoon apprehension until September 13, when I went into El Molino and collided with the title of my story printed across the full width of *El Espectador*, which had just come out: "The Third Resignation."

My first reaction was the devastating certainty that I did not have the five centavos to buy the paper. This was the most explicit symbol of my poverty, because many basic things in daily life, in addition to the newspaper, cost five centavos: the trolley, the public telephone, a cup of coffee, a shoeshine. I rushed out to the street with no protection against the imperturbable drizzle, but in the nearby cafés there was no one I knew to give me a charitable coin. And I did not find anyone in the *pensión* at that dead hour on Saturday except the landlady, which was the same as not finding anyone because I owed her seven hundred twenty times five centavos for two months of room and board. When I went out again, prepared for anything, I encountered a man who came from Divine Providence and was getting out of a cab, holding *El Espectador* in his hand, and I asked him straight out if he would give it to me.

And so I could read my first story in print, with an illustration by Hernán Merino, the official sketch artist for the paper. I read it hiding in my room, my heart pounding, in a single breath. In each line I was discovering the crushing power of print, for what I had constructed with so much love and pain as a humble parody of a universal genius was revealed to me as an obscure and weak monologue barely sustained by three or four consolatory sentences. Almost twenty years had to go by before I dared read it a second time, and my judgment then—not tempered by compassion—was much less indulgent.

The most difficult thing was the avalanche of glowing friends who invaded my room with copies of the newspaper and unrestrained praises for a story I was certain they had not understood. Among my fellow students at the university, some appreciated it, others had less understanding, still others with more reason did not go past the fourth line, but Gonzalo Mallarino, whose literary judgment it was not easy for me to place in doubt, approved it without reservation.

My greatest uneasiness had to do with the verdict of Jorge Álvaro Espinosa, whose critical blade was the most dangerous even beyond our immediate circle. I had contradictory feelings: I wanted to see him right away to resolve my uncertainty once and for all, but at the same time the idea of facing him terrified me. He disappeared until Tuesday, which was not strange in an insatiable reader, and when he reappeared in El Molino he began talking to me not about the story but about my audacity.

"I suppose you realize the trouble you've gotten into," he said to me, fixing his green king-cobra eyes on mine. "Now you're in the showcase of recognized writers, and there's a lot you have to do to deserve it."

I was petrified by the only opinion that could affect me as much as that of Ulises. But before he finished, I had decided to move ahead of him with what I considered then, and always considered since, to be the truth:

"That story is a piece of shit."

He replied with immutable control that he could not say anything yet because he had only had time to glance at it. But he explained that even if it was as bad as I said, it was not bad enough to sacrifice the golden opportunity that life was offering me.

"In any case, that story already belongs to the past," he concluded. "What matters now is the next one."

He left me flabbergasted. I was foolish enough to look for contrary arguments until I became convinced I was not going to hear advice more intelligent than his. He expounded on his fixed idea that you first had to conceive of the story and then the style, but one depended on the other in a mutual servitude that was the magic wand of the classics. He spent some time on his opinion, repeated so often, that I needed to read the Greeks in a profound, unbiased way, and not only Homer, the only one I had read for the baccalaureate because I was obliged to. I promised I would, and I wanted to hear other names, but he changed the subject and began to talk about André Gide's *The Counterfeiters*, which he had read that weekend. I never found the courage to tell him that perhaps our conversation had determined my life. I stayed up all night making notes for the next story, which would not have the meanders of the first one.

I suspected that those who talked to me about it were impressed not so much by the story—which perhaps they had not read and certainly had not understood—as by its being published in an unusual display on so important a page. To begin with, I realized that my two great defects were the two greatest defects: the clumsiness of my writing and my ignorance of the human heart. And they were more than evident in my first story, which was a confused, abstract meditation made worse by my abuse of invented emotions.

Searching my memory for situations from real life for the second story, I remembered that one of the most beautiful women I had known as a child told me that she wished she could be inside the very handsome cat that she was caressing on her lap. I asked her why, and she answered: "Because it is more beautiful than I am." Then I had a point of departure for the second story, and an attractive title: "Eva Is Inside Her Cat." The rest, as in the previous story, was invented out of nothing, and for the same reason—as we liked to say in those days— both carried within them the seeds of their own destruction.

This story was published with the same display as the first, on Saturday, October 25, 1947, and illustrated by a rising star in the Caribbean sky, the painter Enrique Grau. I was struck that my friends accepted this as something routine for a renowned writer. I, on the other hand, suffered over the errors, doubted the successes, but managed to keep my hope alive. The high point came a few days later with a note published by Eduardo Zalamea employing his usual pseudonym, Ulises, in his daily column in *El Espectador*. It came straight to the point: "Readers of 'Fin de Semana,' the literary supplement of this newspaper, will have noted the appearance of a new and original talent with a vigorous personality." And further on: "In the imagination everything can happen, but knowing how to show with naturalness, simplicity, and without fuss the pearl produced there is not something that all twenty-year-old boys just beginning their relationship with letters can accomplish." And he concluded without hesitation: "With García Márquez a new and notable writer has been born."

The note—how could it not!—brought a shock of happiness, but at the same time it disturbed me that Zalamea had not left himself any way out. Now everything was complete, and I had to interpret his generosity as a call to my conscience that would last the rest of my life. The note also revealed that Ulises had discovered my identity through one of his colleagues in the newsroom. That night I learned it had been through Gonzalo González, a close cousin to my closest cousins, who sat five meters from Eduardo Zalamea's desk and for fifteen years had written for the same paper, with the pseudonym Gog and with sustained passion, a column that answered questions from readers. To my good fortune Zalamea did not search me out, and I did not search him out. I saw him once at the table of the poet De Greiff and recognized his voice and the harsh cough of an irredeemable smoker, and I was close to him at various cultural events, but no one introduced us. Some because they did not know us and others because they did not think it possible we did not know each other.

It is difficult to imagine the degree to which people lived then in the shadow of poetry. It was a frenzied passion, another way of being, a fireball that went everywhere on its own. We would open the paper, even the business section or the legal page, or we would read the coffee grounds at the bottom of the cup, and there was poetry waiting to take over our dreams. So that for us aborigines from every province, Bogotá was the capital of the country and the seat of government, but above all it was the city where poets lived. We not only believed in poetry, and would have died for it, but we also knew with certainty—as Luis Cardoza y Aragón wrote—that "poetry is the only concrete proof of the existence of man."

The world belonged to the poets. Their new works were more important for my generation than the political news that was more and more depressing. Colombian poetry had emerged from the nineteenth century illuminated by the solitary star of José Asunción Silva, the sublime romantic who at the age of thirty-one shot himself with a pistol through the circle that his doctor had painted for him with a swab of iodine over his heart. I was not born in time to know Rafael Pombo or Eduardo Castillo—the great lyric poet—whose friends described him as a ghost escaped from his tomb at dusk, with his long cape, a skin turned green by morphine, and the profile of a turkey buzzard: the physical representation of the *poètes maudits*. One afternoon I was in a streetcar that passed a large mansion on Carrera Séptima, and in the entrance I saw the most memorable man I had ever seen in my life, wearing an impeccable suit, an English hat, dark glasses for his lightless eyes, and a cattleman's poncho. He was the poet Alberto Ángel Montoya, a rather ostentatious romantic who published some of the good poems of his time. For my generation they were ghosts from the past, except for Maestro León de Greiff, on whom I spied for years at the Café El Molino.

None of them succeeded in even touching the glory of Guillermo Valencia, an aristocrat from Popayán who, before he was thirty, established himself as the supreme pontiff of the Generation of the Centenario, so called for having come upon the scene in 1910, the hundredth anniversary of national independence. His contemporaries Eduardo Castillo and Porfirio Barba Jacob, two great poets in the romantic tradition, did not receive the critical justice they more than deserved in a country dazzled by the marble rhetoric of Valencia, whose mythic shadow barred the way for three generations. The generation just before ours, which emerged in 1925 with the name and drive of The New Ones, had magnificent models like Rafael Maya and, once again, León de Greiff, who were not recognized in all their greatness as long as Valencia sat on his throne. Until that time he had enjoyed a peculiar glory that carried him to the very doors of the presidency of the Republic.

The only ones who dared oppose him were the poets from the group Stone and Sky with their juvenile chapbooks, who in the final analysis only had in common the virtue of not being Valencistas: Eduardo Carranza, Arturo Camacho Ramírez, Aurelio Arturo, and Jorge Rojas, who had financed the publication of their poems. They were not all the same in form or inspiration, but as a group they made the archaeological ruins of the Parnassians tremble and brought to life a new poetry of the heart, with multiple resonances of Juan Ramón Jiménez, Rubén Darío, García Lorca, Pablo Neruda, or Vicente Huidobro. Public acceptance was not immediate, and they themselves did not seem aware that they were viewed as being sent by Divine Providence to clean poetry's house. But Don Baldomero Sanín Cano, the most respected essayist and critic of those years, hastened to write a categorical essay to thwart any attempt against Valencia. His proverbial moderation went astray. Among many definitive judgments, he wrote that Valencia had "come into possession of ancient knowledge in order to know the soul of times distant in the past, and he ponders contemporary texts in order to discover, by analogy, the entire soul of man." He consecrated Valencia once again as a timeless poet with no frontiers and placed him among those who, "like Lucretius, Dante, Goethe, preserved his body in order to save his soul." More than one person must have thought then that with friends like this, Valencia did not need enemies.

Eduardo Carranza replied to Sanín Cano with an article that said it all, beginning with the title: "A Case of Bardolatry." It was the first well-aimed assault to situate Valencia within his proper limits and bring his pedestal down to its correct place and size. Carranza accused Valencia of having lit not a flame of the spirit in Colombia but rather an orthopedics of words, and he defined his verses as those of an artist who was precious, frigid, accomplished, and a painstaking carver. His conclusion was a question to himself that in essence was like one of his good poems: "If poetry does not make my blood run faster, open sudden windows for me onto the mysterious, help me discover the world, accompany this desolate heart in solitude and in love, in joy and in enmity, what good is poetry to me?" And he concluded: "For me—blasphemer that I am!—Valencia is barely a good poet."

The publication of "A Case of Bardolatry" in the "Lecturas Dominicales" section of *El Tiempo*, which had a wide circulation at the time, caused a social upheaval. It also had the prodigious result of producing a thorough examination of poetry in Colombia from its origins, which perhaps had not been done with any seriousness since Don Juan de Castellanos wrote the 150,000 hendecasyllables of his *Elegies to Illustrious Men of the Indies*.

From then on the sky was the limit for poetry. Not only for The New Ones, who became fashionable, but for others who emerged later and jostled and shoved for their place. Poetry became so popular that today it is not possible to understand to what extent you lived for each issue of "Lecturas Dominicales," published by Carranza, or *Sábado*, published at the time by Carlos Martín, our former rector at the *liceo*. In addition to his poetry, with his glory Carranza established a way of being a poet at six in the afternoon on the Carrera Séptima in Bogotá, which was like walking in a shop window ten blocks long holding a book in the hand that rested on your heart. He was a model for his generation, which created a school in the next, each in its own way.

In the middle of the year Pablo Neruda came to Bogotá, convinced that poetry had to be a political weapon. In his Bogotán *tertulias* he learned what kind of reactionary Laureano Gómez was, and as a farewell he composed, almost as fast as his pen could write, three punitive sonnets in his honor, the first quatrain setting the tone for all of them:

> *Farewell, Laureano unwreathed in laurel,*
> *melancholy satrap and upstart king.*
> *Farewell, O emperor of the fourth floor,*
> *paid in advance, without end, forever more.*

In spite of his right-wing sympathies and personal friendship with Laureano Gómez, Carranza highlighted the sonnets in his literary pages, more as a journalistic scoop than a political proclamation. But the negative response was almost unanimous. Above all because of the illogicality of publishing them in the paper of a dyed-in-the-wool liberal like the former president Eduardo Santos, who was as opposed to the retrograde thought of Laureano Gómez as he was to Pablo Neruda's revolutionary ideas. The noisiest reaction came from those who could not tolerate a foreigner permitting himself that kind of abuse. The mere fact that three casuistic sonnets, more ingenious than poetic, could set off such a storm was a heartening symptom of the power of poetry during those years. In any event, Laureano Gómez himself, who was then president of the Republic, later prohibited Neruda from entering Colombia, as did General Gustavo Rojas Pinilla in his day, but he was in

Cartagena and Buenaventura, ports of call for the steamships between Chile and Europe, on several occasions. For the Colombian friends to whom he announced his visit, each stopover on the round trip was a reason for stupendous celebration.

When I enrolled in the faculty of law in February 1947, my identification with the Stone and Sky group remained unshaken. Although I had met its most notable members in Carlos Martín's house in Zipaquirá, I did not have the audacity to remind even Carranza of that, and he was the most approachable. On one occasion I happened to see him in the Librería Grancolombia, so close to me and so accessible that I greeted him as an admirer. His response was very cordial but he did not recognize me. On the other hand, on another occasion, Maestro León de Greiff got up from his table at El Molino and greeted me at mine when someone told him I had published stories in *El Espectador*, and he promised to read them. Sad to say, a few weeks later the popular uprising of April 9 took place, and I had to leave the still-smoking city. When I returned after four years, El Molino had disappeared under its ashes, and the maestro had moved with all his household goods and his court of friends to the café El Automático, where we became friends of books and *aguardiente*, and he taught me to move chessmen without art or good fortune.

My friends from an earlier time found it incomprehensible that I would persist in writing stories, and even I could not explain it in a country where the greatest art was poetry. I learned this when I was very young through the success of "Miseria humana," a popular poem sold in folded sheets of coarse wrapping paper or recited for two centavos in the markets and cemeteries of Caribbean towns. The novel, on the other hand, was limited. After *María*, by Jorge Isaacs, many had been written with no great resonance. José María Vargas Vila had been an unusual phenomenon with his fifty-two novels aimed at the heart of the poor. A tireless traveler, his excessive baggage consisted of his own books that were displayed and bought up by passionate readers in the entrances to the hotels of Latin America and Spain. *Aura, or The Violets*, his stellar novel, broke more hearts than many better ones by his contemporaries.

The only novels that survived their own time were *The Ram*, written between 1600 and 1638 during the colonial period by the Spaniard Juan Rodríguez Freyle, a tale so unrestrained and free about the history of Nueva Granada* that it became a masterpiece of fiction; *María*, by Jorge Isaacs, in 1867; *The Vortex*, by José Eustasio Rivera, in 1924, *The Marquise of Yolombó*, by Tomás Carrasquilla, in 1926, and *Four Years Aboard Myself*, by Eduardo Zalamea, in 1934. None of them had even glimpsed the glory possessed, deservedly or not, by so many poets. On the other hand, the short story—with an antecedent as distinguished as Carrasquilla himself, the great writer of Antioquia—had come to grief on a craggy and soulless rhetoric.

The proof that my vocation was to be only a narrator was the stream of verses I left behind at the *liceo*, unsigned or signed with pseudonyms, because I never had the intention of dying on their account. Even more: when I published my first stories in *El Espectador*, many people who had no right to were challenging the genre. Today I think this is understandable because from many points of view, life in Colombia was still in the nineteenth century. Above all in the lugubrious Bogotá of the 1940s, still nostalgic for the colonial period, when I matriculated without vocation or desire in the faculty of law at the Universidad Nacional.

To confirm this it was enough to sink into the nerve center of Carrera Séptima and Avenida Jiménez de Quesada, baptized by Bogotán excess as the best corner in the world. When the public clock in the tower of the Church of San Francisco struck twelve noon, men stopped on the street or interrupted their conversation in the café to set their watches by the official hour of the church. Around that intersection, and on the adjacent streets, were the crowded places where businessmen, politicians, journalists—and poets, of course—met twice a day, all of them dressed in black down to the soles of their feet, like our lord King Don Felipe IV.

*Nueva Granada, or New Granada, was the name of Colombia when it was a Spanish colony.

In my time as a student, you could still read a newspaper in that spot that perhaps had few predecessors in the world. It was a blackboard, like the ones used in schools, displayed on the balcony of *El Espectador* at twelve and at five in the afternoon, with the latest news written in chalk. At those hours the passage of streetcars became difficult, if not impossible, for they were obstructed by the waiting, impatient crowds. Those street readers also had the opportunity to deliver a unanimous ovation when they thought the news was good and jeer or throw stones at the blackboard when they did not. It was a form of instantaneous democratic participation that gave *El Espectador* a thermometer more efficient than any other for taking the temperature of public opinion.

Television did not yet exist, and there were radio newscasts that were very complete but aired at fixed times, and so before you went to have lunch or dinner, you stood and waited for the blackboard to appear so you could go home with a more complete version of the world. That was where the solo flight of Captain Concha Venegas between Lima and Bogotá was announced and followed with exemplary and unforgettable rigor. When the news was like that, the blackboard was changed several times outside its scheduled hours in order to feed special bulletins to a voracious public. None of the street readers of that unique newspaper knew that the inventor and faithful follower of the idea was named José Salgar, a twenty-year-old novice reporter at *El Espectador* who became one of the great journalists without having gone beyond primary school.

Bogotá's distinctive institution were the cafés in the center of the city, where sooner or later the life of the entire country would converge. In its time, each one enjoyed a specialty—political, literary, financial—so that a large part of Colombia's history during those years had some connection to the cafés. Each person had his favorite as an infallible sign of his identity.

Writers and politicians in the first half of the century—including an occasional president of the Republic—had studied in the cafés along Calle Catorce, across from the Colegio del Rosario. The Windsor, which made history with its famous politicians, was one of the longest lasting and a refuge for the great caricaturist Ricardo Rendón, who did his major work there, and years later used a revolver to put a bullet through his inspired head in the back room of the Gran Vía.

In contrast to my many afternoons of tedium was the accidental discovery of a music room open to the public at the Biblioteca Nacional. I made it my favorite refuge for reading in the shelter of great composers whose works we requested in writing from a charming clerk. Those of us who were habitual visitors discovered all kinds of affinities with one another according to the type of music we preferred. In this way I became acquainted with most of my favorite authors through other people's tastes, which were abundant and varied, and I despised Chopin for many years because of an implacable melomaniac who requested him without mercy almost every day.

One afternoon I found the room deserted because the sound system was out of order, but the woman in charge of the room permitted me to sit and read in the silence. At first I felt that I was in a peaceful oasis, but after almost two hours I had not been able to concentrate because of flashes of uneasiness that interfered with my reading and made me feel uncomfortable in my own skin. It took me several days to realize that the remedy for my uneasiness was not the silence in the room but the ambience of music, which from then on became an almost secret and permanent passion for me.

On Sunday afternoons, when the music room was closed, my most fruitful diversion was riding on the streetcars with blue windows that for five centavos traveled without stopping from La Plaza de Bolívar to Avenida Chile, and where I spent those adolescent afternoons that seemed to trail behind them an endless train of many other lost Sundays. The only thing I did during that journey in vicious circles was to read books of poetry, perhaps a city block for each block of verses, until the first lights were turned on in the perpetual rain. Then I made the rounds of the taciturn cafés in the old neighborhoods in search of someone who would have the charity to talk to me about the poems I had just read. At times I found him—it was always a man—and we would stay until after midnight in some dismal hole, finishing the butts of the cigarettes that we ourselves had smoked and talking about poetry while in the rest of the world all of humanity was making love.

At that time everyone was young, but we were always meeting others who were younger than we. The generations shoved one another, above all the poets and the criminals, and no sooner had you done something than someone else appeared who threatened to do it better. At times I find among old papers a few of the photos taken of us by street photographers in the atrium of the Church of San Francisco, and I cannot repress a roar of compassion, because they do not seem like pictures of us but of our children, in a city of closed doors where nothing was easy, least of all surviving Sunday afternoons without love. That was where I happened to make the acquaintance of my uncle, José María Valdeblánquez, when I thought I saw my grandfather making his way with his umbrella through the Sunday crowd coming out of Mass. His attire could not in any way disguise his identity: a three-piece suit of black wool, a white shirt with a celluloid collar, a tie with diagonal stripes, a vest with a watch chain, a bowler hat, gold-rimmed glasses. The impression was so strong that I blocked his way without realizing it. He raised his menacing umbrella and held it a hand span away from my eyes:

"Can I pass?"

"Pardon me," I said in embarrassment. "I mistook you for my grandfather."

He continued scrutinizing me with his astronomer's gaze and asked with a roguish irony:

"And can one know who this famous grandfather is?"

Confused by my own insolence, I said his complete name. Then he lowered the umbrella and smiled with very good humor.

"Well, there's a reason we look alike," he said. "I'm his oldest son."

Daily life was more bearable at the Universidad Nacional. But I cannot find the reality of that time in my memory because I do not think I was a law student even for a single day, though my grades for the first year—the only one I completed in Bogotá—might lead one to believe the opposite. There was no time or opportunity to establish the kind of personal relationships we had at the *liceo*, and my fellow students scattered throughout the city when classes were over. My most pleasant surprise was finding that the general secretary of the faculty of law was the writer Pedro Gómez Valderrama, whom I knew about because of his early contributions to literary pages, and who was one of my great friends until his premature death.

My most assiduous fellow student beginning with the first year was Gonzalo Mallarino Botero, the only one accustomed to believing in certain wonders in life that were true even though they were not factual. It was he who showed me that the faculty of law was not as sterile as I thought, because after the first day he took me out of the class on statistics and demography, at seven in the morning, and challenged me to a personal poetic duel in the café on the university campus. In the wasted hours of the morning he would recite from memory the poems of the Spanish classics, and I responded with poems by the young Colombians who had opened fire on the rhetorical remnants of the previous century.

One Sunday he invited me to his house, where he lived with his mother and sisters and brothers in an atmosphere of fraternal tensions like those in my father's household. Víctor, the oldest, was already dedicated to the theater and recognized in the Spanish-speaking world for his recitations. I had escaped the tutelage of my parents but had not felt at home again until I met Pepa Botero, the mother of the Mallarinos, an untamed Antioquian woman in the hermetic heart of the Bogotán aristocracy. With her natural intelligence and prodigious talk she had a peerless faculty for knowing the precise spot where curse words recover their Cervantine ancestry. They were unforgettable afternoons, watching dusk fall on the boundless emerald of the savanna, in the hospitable warmth of perfumed chocolate and warm crullers. What I learned from Pepa Botero, with her untrammeled slang and the manner in which she said the things of ordinary life, was invaluable to me for a new rhetoric of real life.

Other kindred fellow students were Guillermo López Guerra and Álvaro Vidales Barón, who had been my accomplices at the *liceo* in Zipaquirá. But at the university I was closer to Luis Villar Borda and Camilo Torres Restrepo, who struggled, with bare hands and for love of the art, to put out the literary supplement of *La Razón*, an almost secret paper published by the poet and journalist Juan Lozano y Lozano. On the days the paper went to press I would go with them to the news-room and give them a hand in last-minute emergencies. Some-times I was there at the same time as the publisher, whose sonnets I admired, and even more so his biographical sketches of national figures, which he published in the magazine *Sábado*. He recalled with a certain vagueness Ulises's note about me but had not read any of my stories, and I evaded the subject because I was sure he would not like them. Beginning on the first day, he would say as he left that the pages of his newspaper were open to me, but I took this only as Bogotán correctness.

In the Café Asturias, Torres Restrepo and Villar Borda, my fellow students, introduced me to Plinio Apuleyo Mendoza, who at the age of sixteen had published a series of lyrical prose pieces, the fashionable genre imposed on the country by Eduardo Carranza from the literary pages of *El Tiempo*. He had tanned skin and straight, deep-black hair, which accentuated his Indian appearance. In spite of his age he had succeeded in acquiring a reputation for his articles in the weekly magazine *Sábado*, founded by his father, Plinio Mendoza Neira, a former minis-ter of war and a great born journalist who may not have written a complete line in his whole life. But he taught many others to write their own at newspapers that he established with great fanfare and then abandoned for high political posts or in order to found other enormous and catastrophic enterprises. I did not see his son more than two or three times during that period, and always with fellow students of mine. I was surprised that at his age he talked like an old man, but it never would have occurred to me to think that years later we would share so many days of reckless journalism, for the lure of journalism as an occupation had not yet occurred to me, and as a science it interested me even less than the law.

In reality I never had thought it would ever interest me until one day when Elvira Mendoza, Plinio's sister, held an emergency interview with the Argentine dramatic performer Berta Singerman, which altogether transformed my prejudices against the profession and revealed a vocation I did not know I had. More than a traditional interview of questions and answers— about which I had so many misgivings, and still do—it was one of the most original ever published in Colombia. Years later, when Elvira Mendoza was a renowned international journalist and one of my good friends, she told me it had been a desperate measure to salvage a disaster.

The arrival of Berta Singerman had been the news event of the day. Elvira—who edited the women's section in *Sábado*— asked for authorization to interview her, which she received with some hesitation on her father's part because of her lack of experience in the genre. The editorial offices at *Sábado* were a meeting place for the best-known intellectuals in those years, and Elvira asked them for some questions to use in the interview, but she was on the verge of panic when she had to face the scorn with which Singerman received her in the presidential suite of the Hotel Granada.

From the beginning, Singerman took pleasure in rejecting the questions as foolish or imbecilic, not suspecting that behind each one was a good writer, one of the many she knew and admired from her various visits to Colombia. Elvira, who always had a lively temperament, was obliged to swallow her tears and endure the rebuff. The unexpected entrance of Berta Singerman's husband saved the interview, for he managed the situation with exquisite tact and a good sense of humor just when it was about to turn into a serious incident.

Elvira did not write the dialogue she had foreseen, based on the diva's responses, but instead wrote an article about her difficulties with Berta Singerman. She took advantage of the providential intervention of the husband and turned him into the real protagonist of the meeting. Singerman went into one of her historic rages when she read the interview. But *Sábado* was already the most popular weekly magazine, and its circulation sped upward to a hundred thousand copies in a city of six hundred thousand inhabitants.

The sangfroid and ingenuity with which Elvira Mendoza

used Berta Singerman's foolishness to reveal her true personality set me to thinking for the first time about the possibilities of journalism, not as a primary source of information but as much more: a literary genre. Before many years passed I would prove this in my own flesh, until I came to believe, as I believe today more than ever, that the novel and journalism are children of the same mother.

Until then I had risked only poetry: satiric verses in the magazine of the Colegio San José and lyrical prose or sonnets of imaginary love in the manner of Stone and Sky in the single issue of the paper at the Liceo Nacional. A short while before, Cecilia González, my accomplice from Zipaquirá, had persuaded the poet and essayist Daniel Arango to publish a little ballad I had written, using a pseudonym and seven-point type, in the most obscure corner of *El Tiempo*'s Sunday supplement. Its publication did not move me or make me feel like more of a poet than I already was. On the other hand, Elvira's article made me aware of the reporter I carried sleeping in my heart, and I resolved to wake him. I began to read newspapers in a different way. Camilo Torres and Luis Villar Borda, who agreed with me, repeated Don Juan Lozano's offer of his pages in *La Razón*, but I dared submit only a couple of technical poems that I never considered mine. They suggested I speak to Plinio Apuleyo Mendoza about *Sábado*, but my tutelary shyness warned me that I still had far to go before I could risk a new occupation about which I had no more than a dim understanding. Yet my discovery had an immediate usefulness, because at the time I was entangled in the unhappy awareness that everything I wrote in prose or in verse, and even my assignments at the *liceo*, were shameless imitations of Stone and Sky, and I proposed a thorough change beginning with my next story. In the end experience convinced me that adverbs of means that end in *-mente** are a bankrupt habit. I began to correct them whenever I ran across them, and each time I became more convinced that this obsession was obliging me to find richer and more expressive forms. For a long time there have not been any

---

*The English equivalent is the *-ly* adverbial ending.

in my books except for an occasional quotation. I do not know, of course, if my translators have detected and also acquired, for occupational reasons, this stylistic paranoia.

My friendship with Torres Restrepo and Villar Borda soon overflowed the limits of classrooms and newsrooms, and we spent more time together on the street than at the university. Both of them were simmering over a slow fire in a stubborn lack of conformity with the political and social situation of the country. Enthralled by the mysteries of literature, I did not even try to understand their circular analyses and gloomy premonitions, but the memory of their friendship is among the most gratifying and useful of those years.

In the classes at the university, on the other hand, I foundered. I always regretted my lack of devotion to the merits of the teachers with great names who endured our boredom. Among them was Alfonso López Michelsen, the son of the only Colombian president in the twentieth century to be reelected, and I believe this gave rise to the general impression that he too was predestined by birth to be president, as in fact he was. He came to his introductory class on the law with an irritating punctuality and some splendid cashmere jackets made in London. He lectured without looking at anyone, with that celestial air of intelligent myopics who always seem to be walking through someone else's dreams. His classes seemed like monologues on a single note, which is what any class not about poetry was for me, but the tedium of his voice had the hypnotic power of a snake charmer. His vast literary knowledge had a reliable foundation, and he knew how to use it in his writing and speaking, but I began to appreciate it only when we met again years later and became friends far from the lethargy of the classroom. His prestige as an inveterate politician was nourished by his almost magical personal charm and a dangerous lucidity in discovering the hidden intentions of people. Above all those he liked least. But his most outstanding virtue as a public man was his astonishing ability to create historic situations with a single phrase.

In time we achieved a close friendship, but at the university I was not the most assiduous and diligent student, and my irremediable shyness kept me at a hopeless distance, in particular with people I admired. For all these reasons I was surprised to be called to the first-year final examination despite the absences that had earned me a reputation as an invisible student. I turned to my old stratagem of deviating from the subject with rhetorical devices. I realized that the teacher was aware of my trick, but perhaps he appreciated it as a literary diversion. The only stumbling block was that in the agony of the exam I used the word *prescription* and he hastened to ask that I define it to be sure I knew what I was talking about.

"To prescribe is to acquire a property over the course of time," I said.

He asked without hesitation:

"To acquire it or to lose it?"

It was the same thing, but I did not argue with him because of my congenital insecurity, and I believe it was one of his celebrated after-dinner jokes, because in the grading he did not penalize me for my indecision. Years later I mentioned the incident to him and he did not remember it, of course, but by then neither he nor I was even sure the episode was true.

We both found in literature a retreat where we could forget about politics and the mysteries of prescription, and we would discover surprising books and forgotten writers in infinite conversations that would sometimes ruin visits and exasperate our wives. My mother had convinced me that we were related, and it was true. But more than any kind of lost relationship, our shared passion for *vallenatos* connected us.

Another fortuitous relative, on my father's side, was Carlos H. Pareja, a professor of political economy and the owner of the Librería Grancolombia, a favorite of students because of its admirable custom of displaying new books by great authors on open, unguarded tables. Even his own students would invade the shop during the negligent moments at twilight, and we would make the books disappear by sleight of hand, following the students' code that says that stealing books is a crime but not a sin. Not because of virtue but physical fear, my role in these raids was limited to watching the backs of the more dexterous, on the condition that in addition to books for themselves, they would take a few that I had indicated. One afternoon, one of my accomplices had just stolen *The City Without Laura*, by Francisco Luis Bernárdez, when I felt a fierce claw on my shoulder and heard a sergeant's voice:

"At last, damn it!"

I turned around in terror and confronted Maestro Carlos H. Pareja while three of my accomplices escaped in a stampede. It was my good luck that before I could beg his pardon, I realized that he had not caught me for a thief but because he had not seen me in his class for more than a month. After a more or less conventional reprimand, he asked:

"Is it true that you're Gabriel Eligio's son?"

It was true, but I told him it was not, because I knew that his father and mine were in fact estranged because of a personal incident I never understood. But later he learned the truth, and from that day on he pointed me out in the bookstore and in classes as his nephew, and we maintained a relationship more civil than literary in spite of the fact that he had written and published several books of uneven verse under the pseudonym Simón Latino. The awareness of our relationship, however, was helpful to him only because I no longer offered my services as a screen for stealing his books.

Another excellent teacher, Diego Montaña Cuéllar, was the opposite of López Michelsen, with whom he seemed to have a secret rivalry, López as a straying Liberal and Montaña Cuéllar as a left-wing radical. I maintained good relations with him outside the classroom, and it always seemed to me that López Michelsen viewed me as a poetic dove, while Montaña Cuéllar saw me as a good prospect for his revolutionary proselytizing.

My fondness for Montaña Cuéllar began because of a difficulty he encountered with three young officers from the military school who attended his classes in parade uniform. They had the punctuality of the barracks, sat together on the same seats apart from the rest, took implacable notes, and obtained well-deserved grades on rigorous examinations. After the first few days Diego Montaña Cuéllar advised them in private not to come to class in battle uniforms. They replied with their best manners that they were obeying the orders of their superiors, and they lost no opportunity to let him feel the weight of that. In any case, aside from their peculiarities, it was always clear to students and teachers that the three officers were outstanding students.

They arrived in their identical uniforms, impeccable, always together, and punctual. They sat to one side and were the most serious and methodical students, but it always seemed to me that they were in a world different from ours. If you spoke to them, they were attentive and polite, but their formality was invincible: they said no more than answers to what they had been asked. When we had exams, we civilians would divide into groups of four to study in cafés, we would meet at the Saturday dances, at the student stone-throwing fights, in the tame taverns and dreary brothels of the period, but we never ran into our military fellow students.

I almost never exchanged greetings with them during the long year when we were all at the university. Besides, there was no opportunity, because they came to classes right on time and left at the teacher's last word, not mixing with anyone except other young soldiers in the second year, whom they would join during rest periods. I never learned their names or heard anything else about them. Today I realize that the reticence was not so much theirs as mine, for I never could overcome the bitterness with which my grandparents had evoked their frustrated wars and the atrocious slaughters of the banana companies.

Jorge Soto del Corral, the teacher of constitutional law, was famous for knowing by heart all the constitutions of the world, and in class he kept us dazzled by the brilliance of his intelligence and legal erudition, marred only by a limited sense of humor. I believe he was one of the teachers who did everything possible to keep their political opinions from cropping up in class, but they were more evident than they themselves believed, even in the gestures of their hands and the emphasis placed on their ideas, for it was in the university where one felt with greatest clarity the profound pulse of a country that was on the verge of a new civil war after some forty years of armed peace.

In spite of my chronic absenteeism and judicial negligence, I passed the easy first-year law courses with overheated last-minute cramming, and the more difficult ones by using my old trick of eluding the subject with clever devices. The truth is I was not comfortable in my own skin and did not know how to continue groping my way along that dead-end street. I understood the law less and had much less interest in it than any of the subjects at the *liceo*, and I felt I was enough of an adult to make my own decisions. In short, after sixteen months of miraculous survival, all I had was a group of good friends for the rest of my life.

My scant interest in my studies was even scantier after the note by Ulises, above all at the university, where some of the other students began to call me Maestro and introduced me as a writer. This coincided with my resolve to learn how to build a structure that was credible and fantastic at the same time but had no cracks. With perfect distant models, like Sophocles' *Oedipus the King*, whose protagonist investigates the murder of his father and ends up discovering that he himself is the murderer; like "The Monkey's Paw," by W. W. Jacob, the perfect story in which everything that happens is accidental; like Maupassant's *Boule de suif* and so many other great sinners, may God keep them in His holy kingdom. I was involved in this one Sunday night when at last something happened to me that deserved to be recounted. I had spent almost the entire day venting my frustrations as a writer with Gonzalo Mallarino in his house on the Avenida Chile, and when I was returning to the *pensión* on the last streetcar a flesh-and-blood faun got on at the Chapinero station. No mistake: I said a faun. I noticed that none of the few passengers at midnight seemed surprised to see him, and this made me think he was just another of the men in costume who sold a variety of things on Sundays in the children's parks. But reality convinced me I could have no doubts, because his horns and beard were as wild as those of a goat, and when he passed I could smell the stink of his pelt. Before Calle 26, the street where the cemetery was located, he got off with the manners of a good paterfamilias and disappeared among the trees in the park.

After half a night of being awakened by my tossing and turning in bed, Domingo Manuel Vega asked me what was wrong.

"It's just that a faun got on the streetcar," I told him, half asleep. He was wide awake when he replied that if it was a nightmare, it must be due to Sunday's poor digestion, but if it was the subject for my next story, he thought it was fantastic. The next morning I did not know if in reality I had seen a faun on the streetcar or if it had been a Sunday hallucination. I began by admitting I had fallen asleep, tired at the end of the day, and had a dream that was so clear I could not separate it from reality. But in the end, the essential thing for me was not if the faun was real but that I had lived the experience as if he were. And for the same reason—real or dreamed—it was not legitimate to consider this as a bewitchment of the imagination but as a marvelous experience in my life.

And so I wrote it the next day in one sitting, put it under my pillow, and read it and reread it for several nights before I went to sleep and in the mornings when I woke up. It was a bare, literal transcription of the episode on the streetcar, just as it occurred and in a style as innocent as the announcement of a baptism on the society page. At last, hounded by new doubts, I decided to submit it to the infallible test of print, not in *El Espectador* but in the literary supplement of *El Tiempo*. Perhaps it was a way to encounter a judgment different from that of Eduardo Zalamea, and to not involve him in an adventure he had no reason to share. I sent the story with a friend from the *pensión*, along with a letter for Don Jaime Posada, the new and very young editor of the "Suplemento Literario" of *El Tiempo*. But the story was not published and my letter was not answered.

My stories of that period, in the order in which they were written and published in *Fin de Semana*, disappeared from the archives of *El Espectador* in the assault on and burning of that newspaper by government mobs on September 6, 1952. I had no copies, nor did my most conscientious friends, so I thought with a certain sense of relief that they had been burned by oblivion. But some provincial literary supplements had reproduced them at the time without authorization, and others were published in a variety of magazines, until they were collected in a single volume by Ediciones Alfil of Montevideo in 1972, with the title of one of the stories: *Nabo, the Black Man Who Made the Angels Wait.*

One was missing that has never been included in a book, perhaps for lack of a reliable version: "Tubal Caín Forges a Star," published by *El Espectador* on January 17, 1948. The name of the protagonist, as not everyone knows, is that of a biblical blacksmith who invented music. There were three stories. Read in the order in which they were written and published, they seemed to me inconsequential and abstract, some absurd, and none based on real feelings. I never could establish the judgment with which a critic as severe as Eduardo Zalamea read them. Yet for me they have an importance they do not have for anyone else, for in each one there is something that corresponds to the rapid evolution of my life during this time.

Many of the novels I was reading then, and which I admired, interested me only because of their technical lessons. That is: their secret carpentry. From the metaphysical abstractions of the first three stories to the last three of that period, I have found precise and very useful clues to the elementary formation of a writer. The idea of exploring other forms had not even passed through my mind. I thought that the story and the novel not only were different literary genres but two organisms with natures so diverse it would be fatal to confuse them. Today I still believe that, and I am convinced more than ever of the supremacy of the short story over the novel.

The publications in *El Espectador*, on the margins of literary success, created other more terrestrial and amusing problems for me. Misguided friends would stop me in the street to ask for the loans that would save them, since they could not believe that a writer displayed with so much prominence had not received enormous sums for his stories. Very few believed the truth when I told them I had never been paid a centavo for their publication nor had I expected it, because that was not the custom in the country's press. Even more serious was my papá's disappointment when he became convinced I could not take over my own expenses when three of the eleven children who had already been born were in school. The family sent me thirty pesos a month. The *pensión* alone cost me eighteen with no right to eggs at breakfast, and I always found myself obliged to dip into that money for unforeseen expenses. I do not know where I had acquired the habit of making unconscious sketches in the margins of newspapers, on the napkins in restaurants, on the marble tables in cafés. I dare to believe that those drawings were direct descendants of the ones I had painted as a child on the walls of my grandfather's workshop, and that perhaps they were easy outlets for my feelings. A casual acquaintance from El Molino with enough influence at a ministry to be placed as a draftsman without having the slightest idea about drawing proposed that I do the work for him and we divide the salary. Never again in my life was I so close to being corrupted, but not so close that I repented.

My interest in music also grew at this time, when the popular songs of the Caribbean—which I had taken in with my mother's milk—were making their way into Bogotá. The radio program with the largest audience was *The Coastal Hour*, animated by Don Pascual Delvecchio, a kind of musical consul of the Atlantic coast in the capital. It had become so popular on Sunday mornings that we students from the Caribbean would go to dance in the offices of the radio station until late in the afternoon. That was the origin of the immense popularity of our music in the interior of the country, and then even in its most remote corners, and of social advancement in Bogotá for students from the coast.

The only disadvantage was the phantom of obligatory marriage. I do not know what wicked precedents had advanced the coastal belief that the girls in Bogotá were loose with boys from the coast and set traps for us in bed so that we would be obliged to marry them. And not for love but because they hoped to live with a window facing the sea. I never believed it. On the contrary, the most disagreeable memories of my life are the sinister brothels on the outskirts of Bogotá where we would go to drain away our gloomy bouts of drunkenness. In the most sordid of them, I almost left behind the little life I had inside me when a woman I had just been with appeared naked in the corridor, shouting that I had stolen twelve pesos from a drawer in her dressing table. Two thugs from the house knocked me down, and not satisfied with emptying my pockets of the two pesos I had left after a ruinous lovemaking, they stripped me of everything including my shoes to search every inch for the stolen money. In any event, they had decided not to kill me but to turn me over to the police when the woman remembered that the day before she had changed the hiding place for her money, and she found it intact.

Among the friendships I still had from the university, that of Camilo Torres not only was the least forgettable but also the most dramatic of our youth. One day, for the first time, he did not attend classes. The reason spread like wildfire. He had arranged his things and decided to leave home for the seminary at Chiquinquirá, some one hundred kilometers from Bogotá. His mother overtook him at the railroad station and locked him in the library. I visited him there, and he was paler than usual and wearing a white poncho, and he had a serenity that for the first time made me think of a state of grace. He decided to enter the seminary because of a vocation he had hidden very well but was resolved to obey to the end.

"The most difficult part is over," he said.

It was his way of telling me that he had said goodbye to his girlfriend, and that she approved of his decision. After a resplendent afternoon he gave me an indecipherable gift: Darwin's *On the Origin of Species*. I said goodbye to him with the strange certainty I would not see him again.

I lost touch with him while he was in the seminary. I heard vague reports that he had gone to Lovaina for three years of theological training, that his devotion had not changed his student's spirit and lay manners, and that the girls who sighed for him treated him like a movie star who had been disarmed by a cassock.

Ten years later, when he returned to Bogotá, he had assumed in body and soul the character of his investiture but preserved the best virtues of an adolescent. By then I was a writer and a journalist without a byline, married and with a son, Rodrigo, who had been born on August 24, 1959, in the Palermo Hospital in Bogotá. At home we decided that Camilo should baptize him. His godfather would be Plinio Apuleyo Mendoza, with whom my wife and I had long ago established a friendship of *compadres*. His godmother would be Susana Linares, the wife of Germán Vargas, who had transmitted to me his skills as a good reporter and a better friend. Camilo was closer to Plinio than we were and had been his friend for a much longer time, but he did not want to accept him as the godfather because of his kinship at the time with the Communists, and perhaps, too, because of his mocking spirit that might well destroy the solemnity of the sacrament. Susana agreed to be responsible for the spiritual formation of the child, and Camilo did not find, or did not wish to find, other arguments that would block the godfather's way.

The baptism took place in the chapel of the Palermo Hospital, in the icy gloom of six in the evening, with no one present except the godparents and I, and a campesino in a poncho and sandals who approached as if he were levitating in order to attend the ceremony without being noticed. When Susana arrived with the newborn, his incorrigible godfather let fly as a joke his first provocation:

"We're going to make this boy into a great guerrilla fighter."

Camilo, preparing the articles for the sacrament, counterattacked in the same tone: "Yes, but a guerrilla fighter for God." And he began the ceremony with the highest-caliber decisiveness, not at all usual in those years:

"I am going to baptize him in Spanish so that unbelievers can understand what this sacrament signifies."

His voice resonated in a high-sounding Castilian that I followed through the Latin of my early years as an altar boy in Aracataca. At the moment of the ablution, without looking at anyone, Camilo invented another provocative formula:

"Those who believe that at this moment the Holy Spirit has descended on this infant, let them kneel."

The godparents and I remained standing, perhaps somewhat discomfited by the glibness of our friend the priest, while the baby bellowed under the inflexible stream of water. The only one who kneeled was the campesino in sandals. The impact of this episode remained with me as one of the harsh reprimands in my life, because I have always believed that it was Camilo who brought in the campesino with complete premeditation in order to punish us with a lesson in humility. Or, at least, in good manners.

I saw him only a few times after that, and always for some valid and pressing reason, most of the time having to do with his charitable work to benefit those who suffered political persecution. One morning he appeared at my house soon after I had married, accompanied by a thief who had served his sentence, yet the police would not leave him in peace: they stole everything he had. Once I gave him a pair of hiking boots with a special design on the sole for greater safety. A few days later, the maid recognized the soles in the photograph of a street criminal who had been found dead in a ditch. It was our friend the thief.

I do not pretend that this episode had anything to do with Camilo's ultimate destiny, but months later he entered the military hospital to visit a sick friend, and nothing more was known about him until the government announced that he had reappeared as an ordinary guerrilla fighter in the Army of National Liberation. He died on February 5, 1966, at the age of thirty-seven, in open combat with a military patrol.

Camilo's entering the seminary coincided with my own decision not to go on wasting time in the faculty of law, but I did not have the courage to confront my parents once and for all. Through my brother Luis Enrique—who had come to Bogotá with a good job in February 1948—I knew they were so satisfied with the results of my baccalaureate and my first year as a law student that they sent me the most lightweight and modern typewriter on the market as a surprise gift. The first one I ever had in this life, and also the most unfortunate, because that same day we pawned it for twelve pesos in order to continue the welcoming party with my brother and my friends from the *pensión*. The next day, crazed with headaches, we went to the pawnshop to make certain the typewriter was still there with its seals intact, and to be sure it would remain in good condition until the money to redeem it rained down on us from heaven. We had a good opportunity with what my friend the false draftsman paid me, but at the last minute we decided to put off redeeming it. Each time my brother and I passed the pawnshop, together or alone, we would confirm from the street that the typewriter was still in its place, wrapped like a jewel in cellophane paper and an organdy bow, among rows of well-protected household appliances. After a month, the joyous calculations we had made in the euphoria of our drunkenness were still unfulfilled, but the typewriter was intact in its place and could remain there as long as we paid the quarterly interest.

I believe we were not yet aware of the terrible political tensions that were beginning to disturb the country. Despite the prestige as a moderate Conservative with which Ospina Pérez came to power, most members of his party knew his victory had been possible only because of the division among the Liberals. And they, stunned by the blow, reproached Alberto Lleras for his suicidal impartiality that had made defeat possible. Dr. Gabriel Turbay, more overwhelmed by his depressive nature than by adverse votes, left for Europe without purpose or direction on the pretext of completing an advanced specialization in cardiology, and after a year and a half he died alone, struck down by the asthma of defeat among the paper flowers and faded tapestries of the Hotel Plaza Athénée in Paris. Jorge Eliécer Gaitán, on the other hand, did not interrupt for a single day his election campaign for the next term, but radicalized it in a fundamental way with a program of moral renewal of the Republic that went beyond the historic division of the country into Liberals and Conservatives, making it more profound with a horizontal and more realistic distinction between the exploiters and the exploited: the political country and the national country. With his historic slogan—"*¡A la carga!*"*—and his supernatural energy, he sowed the seed of resistance even in the most remote places with a gigantic campaign of agitation that continued gaining ground until, in less than a year, it was on the verge of being an authentic social revolution.

Only in this way did we become aware that the country was beginning to slide into the abyss of the same civil war we had

*"Let's get them!"

been fighting since our independence from Spain and that now was overtaking the great-grandchildren of its original protagonists. The Conservative Party, which had recovered the presidency because of Liberal divisions after four consecutive terms, was determined to use any means not to lose it again. To achieve this, the government of Ospina Pérez pushed forward a scorched-earth policy that bloodied the country and affected even daily life in people's homes.

Given my political unawareness and the height of my literary clouds, I had not even suspected this clear reality until one night when I was returning to the *pensión* and encountered the phantom of my conscience. The deserted city, whipped by the glacial wind that blew along the openings in the hills, was swept by the metallic voice and intentional rough emphasis of Jorge Eliécer Gaitán in his obligatory Friday speech at the Teatro Municipal. Its capacity was no more than a thousand crowded people, but the speech was broadcast in concentric waves, first by the loudspeakers in adjacent streets and then by radios played at top volume that resounded like the lashes of a whip over the astonished city, and for three and even four hours overflowed onto a national audience.

That night I had the impression I was the only person on the streets, except at the crucial corner of the newspaper *El Tiempo*, protected as it was every Friday by a crowd of police armed as if for war. To me it was a revelation, for I had allowed myself the arrogance of not believing in Gaitán, and that night I understood all at once that he had gone beyond the Spanish country and was inventing a lingua franca for everyone, not so much because of what his words said as for the passion and shrewdness in his voice. In his epic speeches he himself would advise his listeners in a guileful paternal tone to return in peace to their houses, and they would translate that in the correct fashion as a coded order to express their repudiation of everything that represented social inequalities and the power of a brutal government. Even the police who had to maintain order were stirred by a warning that they interpreted in reverse.

The subject of that night's speech was an unadorned recounting of the devastation caused by official violence in its scorched-earth policy meant to destroy the Liberal opposition, with a still-incalculable number of killings by government forces in the rural areas, and entire populations of homeless, starving refugees in the cities. After a terrifying enumeration of murders and assaults, Gaitán began to raise his voice, to take delight word by word, sentence by sentence, in a marvel of sensationalist, well-aimed rhetoric. The tension in the audience increased to the rhythm of his voice, until a final outburst exploded within the confines of the city and reverberated on the radio into the most remote corners of the country.

The inflamed crowd poured into the street in a bloodless pitched battle, faced with the secret tolerance of the police. I believe that was the night when I understood at last the frustrations of my grandfather and the lucid analyses of Camilo Torres Restrepo. It surprised me that at the Universidad Nacional the students continued to be Liberals and Goths with knots of Communists, but the breach Gaitán was excavating in the country was not felt there. I reached the *pensión* dazed by the turmoil of the night and found my roommate reading Ortega y Gasset in the peace of his bed.

"I'm a new man, Dr. Vega," I said. "Now I know how and why the wars of Colonel Nicolás Márquez began."

A few days later—on February 7, 1948—Gaitán held the first political ceremony I ever attended in my life: a procession for the countless victims of official violence in the country, with more than sixty thousand women and men in strict mourning, carrying the red flags of the party and the black flags of Liberal grief. There was only one rallying cry: absolute silence. And it was maintained with inconceivable dramatic effect, even on the balconies of residences and offices where people watched us walk along the eleven crowded blocks of the main avenue. Beside me a woman murmured a prayer to herself. A man nearby looked at her in surprise:

"Señora, please!"

She moaned an apology and sank into an ocean of phantoms. What brought me to the verge of tears, however, was the crowd's careful steps and breathing in the supernatural silence. I had come without political conviction, drawn by the curiosity of the silence, and the sudden knot of tears in my throat took me by surprise. Gaitán's speech on the Plaza de Bolívar, from the balcony of the municipal comptroller's office, was a funeral oration with an overwhelming emotional charge. Against the sinister predictions of his own party, he ended with the most hazardous circumstance of his rallying cry: there was no applause at all.

That was the "march of silence," the most moving of all the marches ever held in Colombia. The impression left after that historic afternoon, among his partisans and his enemies, was that Gaitán's election was unstoppable. The Conservatives knew it as well, because of the degree of depravity that the violence had reached all over the country, the ferocity shown by the regime's police against unarmed Liberalism, and its scorched-earth policy. The darkest manifestation of the country's state of mind was experienced that weekend by those who attended the bullfight in the Bogotá arena, when the people in the bleachers invaded the bullring, indignant at the tameness of the bull and the inability of the bullfighter to kill it once and for all. The enraged crowd quartered the bull while it was still alive. Numerous reporters and writers who experienced the horror, or heard about it, interpreted this as the most frightening symptom of the brutal rage afflicting the country. In that climate of high tension the Ninth Pan-American Conference in Bogotá opened on March 30, at four-thirty in the afternoon. The city had been renovated at enormous cost, following the pompous esthetic of Minister of State Laureano Gómez, who by virtue of his position was president of the conference. The ministers of state of all the countries in Latin America attended, as well as important personages of the time. The most eminent Colombian politicians were invited as guests of honor, with the unique exception of Jorge Eliécer Gaitán, excluded no doubt by the very significant veto of Laureano Gómez, and perhaps by that of some Liberal leaders who despised him for his attacks on the oligarchy common to both parties. The polestar of the conference was General George Marshall, the delegate from the United States and the great hero of the recent war, who had the dazzling brilliance of a film star because he was directing the reconstruction of a Europe annihilated by the conflict.

But on Friday, April 9, Jorge Eliécer Gaitán was the man of the day in the news because he had obtained the pardon of Lieutenant Jesús María Cortés Poveda, accused of killing the journalist Eudoro Galarza Ossa. Gaitán had been euphoric when he came to his law offices at the crowded intersection of Carrera Séptima and Avenida Jiménez de Quesada, a little before eight in the morning, in spite of having been at court until the small hours. He had various appointments for the next few hours, but he accepted without hesitation when Plinio Mendoza Neira invited him to have lunch, a little before one o'clock, with six personal and political friends who had gone to his office to congratulate him for the legal victory that the newspapers had not published yet. Among them was his personal physician, Pedro Eliseo Cruz, who was also a member of his political inner circle.

In that intense atmosphere, I sat down to have lunch in the dining room of the *pensión* where I lived, less than three blocks away. They had not yet served the soup when Wilfrido Mathieu came and stood in horror at my table.

"The country's fucked," he told me. "They just killed Gaitán in front of El Gato Negro."

Mathieu was an exemplary student of medicine and surgery, a native of Sucre like other residents in the *pensión*, who suffered from sinister premonitions. Less than a week before he had announced that the most imminent and terrible one, because of its devastating consequences, might be the assassination of Jorge Eliécer Gaitán. But this did not impress anyone because you did not need premonitions to suppose that would happen.

I almost did not have the heart to race across the Avenida Jiménez de Quesada and arrive breathless at the café El Gato Negro, almost at the corner of Carrera Séptima. They had just taken the wounded man, still alive but without hope of surviving, to the Clínica Central, some four blocks away. A group of men were dipping their handkerchiefs into the pool of warm blood to keep as historical relics. A woman in a black shawl and espadrilles, one of the many who sold trinkets in the area, held a bloody handkerchief and growled:

"Sons of bitches, they went and killed him."

Bands of bootblacks armed with their wooden boxes tried to knock down the metal gates of the Granada drug store, where the few police on duty had locked away the attacker to protect him from the angry mob. A tall man, very much in control of himself and wearing an irreproachable gray suit as if he were going to a wedding, urged them on with well-calculated shouts that were so effective the owner of the pharmacy had raised the metal gates for fear they would burn the store. The attacker, clutching a police officer, succumbed to panic at the sight of the maddened crowds rushing toward him.

"Officer," he pleaded, almost without a voice, "don't let them kill me."

I will never be able to forget him. He had disheveled hair, a two-day beard, a dead man's gray color, and eyes that bulged with terror. He had a very worn brown suit with vertical stripes, its lapels ripped by the first tugs of the mob. It was an instantaneous and eternal apparition, because the bootblacks tore him away from the police with blows of their boxes and then kicked him to death. The first time he went down he had lost a shoe.

"To the Palacio!" shouted the man in gray, who has never been identified. "To the Palacio!"

The most hotheaded obeyed. They seized the bloody corpse by the ankles and dragged it along Carrera Séptima toward Plaza de Bolívar past the last electric streetcars stopped by the news, shouting warlike insults against the government. From sidewalks and balconies they were urged on with shouts and applause, while the corpse disfigured by blows was leaving shreds of his clothing and his body on the paving stones. Many joined the march, which in less than six blocks had reached the size and expansive power of an outbreak of war. All that was left on the macerated corpse were undershorts and a shoe.

The Plaza de Bolívar, which had just been refurbished, did not have the majesty of other historic Fridays, with its graceless trees and the rudimentary statues of the new official esthetic.

At the Capitolio Nacional, where the Pan-American Conference had opened ten days earlier, the delegates had left for lunch. And so the mob continued on to the Palacio Presidencial, which had also been abandoned. There they left what remained of the corpse, clothed only in the shreds of his undershorts, his left shoe, and two inexplicable ties knotted around his neck. Minutes later the president of the Republic, Mariano Ospina Pérez, and his wife arrived for lunch after having opened a cattle fair in the town of Engativá. Until that moment they had not known about the assassination because the radio in the presidential automobile had been turned off.

I remained at the scene of the crime for ten more minutes, surprised by the speed with which the accounts of witnesses were changing in form and substance until they lost all resemblance to reality. We were at the intersection of Avenida Jiménez and Carrera Séptima, at the time of day it was most crowded, and fifty steps from *El Tiempo*. By then we knew that those accompanying Gaitán when he left his office were Pedro Eliseo Cruz, Alejandro Vallejo, Jorge Padilla, and Plinio Mendoza Neira, minister of war in the recent government of Alfonso López Pumarejo. It was he who had invited them all to lunch. Gaitán had left the building where he had his office without bodyguards of any kind, surrounded by a compact group of friends. As soon as they reached the sidewalk, Mendoza took his arm, led him a step ahead of the others, and said:

"What I wanted to tell you is something really stupid."

He could not say more. Gaitán covered his face with his arm and Mendoza heard the first shot before he saw, standing in front of them, the man who with the coldness of a professional aimed the revolver and shot three bullets into the head of the leader. An instant later there was already talk of a fourth shot that missed, and perhaps a fifth.

Plinio Apuleyo Mendoza, who had come with his father and his sisters, Elvira and Rosa Inés, saw Gaitán sprawled faceup on the sidewalk a minute before he was taken to the hospital. "He didn't seem dead," he told me years later. "He was like an imposing statue lying on the sidewalk beside a meager bloodstain and with a great sadness in his open, staring eyes." In the confusion of the moment his sisters thought their father had been killed too, and they were so dazed that Plinio Apuleyo took them onto the first streetcar that passed to get them away from the scene. But the conductor had full knowledge of what had happened, and he threw his cap to the floor and left the trolley in the middle of the street in order to join in the first shouts of the rebellion. Minutes later it was the first streetcar overturned by the crazed mob.

The discrepancies regarding the number and role of the protagonists were unresolvable because one witness declared there had been three who took turns firing, and another said that the real shooter had slipped into the unruly crowd and without haste had climbed onto a moving streetcar. What Mendoza Neira wanted to ask Gaitán when he took his arm was none of the many things that have been speculated on since then, only that he authorize the creation of an institute to educate union leaders. Or, as his father-in-law had joked a few days earlier: "A school to teach philosophy to the chauffeur." Before he could mention it the first shot had been fired in front of them.

Fifty years later, my memory is still fixed on the image of the man who seemed to incite the crowd outside the pharmacy, and I have not found him in any of the countless testimonies I have read about that day. I had seen him up close, with his expensive suit, his alabaster skin, and a millimetric control of his actions. He attracted my attention so much that I kept an eye on him until he was picked up by too new a car as soon as the assassin's corpse was dragged away, and from then on he seemed to be erased from historical memory. Even mine, until many years later, in my days as a reporter, when it occurred to me that the man had managed to have a false assassin killed in order to protect the identity of the real one.

The Cuban student leader Fidel Castro was in that uncontrollable tumult, twenty years old and a delegate from the University of Havana to the student congress convened as a democratic replica of the Pan-American Conference. He had arrived some six days earlier, in the company of Alfredo Guevara, Enrique Ovares, and Rafael del Pino—Cuban university students like him—and one of his first acts was to request an appointment with Jorge Eliécer Gaitán, whom he admired. Two days later Castro saw Gaitán, who scheduled an appointment with him for the following Friday. Gaitán himself made a note of the meeting in his desk diary, on the page corresponding to April 9: "Fidel Castro, 2pm."

According to what he has recounted in various media and on different occasions, and in the endless accounts we have made together in the course of a long friendship, Fidel first heard of the crime while walking around the area so that he would be on time for his two o'clock appointment. All of a sudden he was surprised by the first crowds running wild and the general shout:

"They killed Gaitán!"

Fidel Castro did not realize until later that the meeting could not in any way take place before four or five o'clock, because of Mendoza Neira's unexpected invitation to Gaitán to have lunch.

There was no room for anyone else at the crime scene. Traffic had stopped and streetcars were overturned, and so I headed for the *pensión* to finish lunch, when my teacher, Carlos H. Pareja, blocked my way at the door to his office and asked me where I was going.

"I'm going to eat lunch," I said.

"Don't fuck around," he said in his unrepentant Caribbean slang. "How can you think about eating lunch when they just killed Gaitán?"

Without giving me time to do anything else, he ordered me to go to the university and put myself at the head of the student protest. The strange thing was that contrary to my nature, I paid attention to him. I continued north along Carrera Séptima, in the opposite direction from the mob that was curious, grief-stricken, and enraged as it rushed toward the crime corner. Buses from the Universidad Nacional, driven by angry students, were at the head of the march. In the Parque Santander, a hundred meters from the crime corner, employees were hurrying to close the entrances to the Hotel Granada—the most luxurious in the city—where some ministers and notable guests of the Pan-American Conference were staying at the time.

A new throng of poor people in an open attitude of combat surged forward from every corner. Many were armed with machetes they had just stolen in the first assaults on stores, and they seemed eager to use them. I did not have a clear perspective on the possible consequences of the assassination, and I was more interested in lunch than in the protest, and so I retraced my steps to the *pensión*. I ran up the stairs, convinced that my politicized friends were ready for war. But no: the dining room was empty, and my brother and José Palencia—who shared the adjoining room—were singing with other friends in their bedroom.

"They killed Gaitán!" I shouted.

They signaled that they already knew, but everyone's state of mind was more recreational than funereal, and they did not interrupt the song. Then we sat down to eat lunch in the deserted dining room, convinced the matter would go no further, until someone turned up the volume of the radio so that we indifferent ones could hear. Carlos H. Pareja, honoring the way he had incited me an hour earlier, announced the formation of the Junta Revolucionaria de Gobierno composed of the most notable Liberals on the left, among them the very well-known writer and politician Jorge Zalamea. Their first resolution was the establishment of the executive committee, the command of the National Police, and all the organisms for a revolutionary state. Then the other members of the junta spoke with rallying cries that grew more and more extravagant.

In the solemnity of the act, the first thing that occurred to me was what my father would think when he learned that his cousin, the hard-nosed Goth, was the principal leader of an extreme left-wing revolution. The landlady at the *pensión*, considering the importance of the names connected to universities, was surprised that they were behaving not like professors but like rowdy students. It was enough to go past two stations on the dial to find a different country. On Radio Nacional, the pro-government Liberals were calling for calm, on other stations they were clamoring against Communists loyal to Moscow, while the highest leaders of official Liberalism defied the dangers of the warring streets as they tried to reach the Palacio

Presidencial to negotiate a pledge of unity with the Conservative government.

We continued to be dazed by that demented confusion until one of the landlady's sons shouted that the house was on fire. In fact, a crack had opened in the rear masonry wall and thick black smoke was beginning to rarefy the air in the bedrooms. It came, no doubt, from the Departmental Office of the Interior adjacent to the *pensión*, which had been set on fire by the rioters, but the wall seemed strong enough to keep standing. And so we raced down the stairs and confronted a city at war. The tumultuous attackers were throwing everything they could find in the offices of the Gobernación out the windows. The smoke from the fires had darkened the air, and the clouded sky was a sinister blanket. Maddened hordes, armed with machetes and all kinds of tools stolen from the hardware stores, attacked and set fire to the businesses along Carrera Séptima and the adjacent streets with the help of mutinous police officers. An instantaneous glance was enough for us to realize that the situation was out of control. My brother anticipated my thought with a shout:

"Shit, the typewriter!"

We ran to the pawnshop, which was still intact with its metal grates locked, but the typewriter was not where it had always been. We were not concerned, thinking that in the days that followed we could recover it, still not realizing that this colossal disaster would have no days that followed.

The military garrison in Bogotá limited itself to protecting government centers and banks, and public order was left to no one's responsibility. After the first few hours many high-ranking officials of the police had entrenched themselves in the Quinta División, and numerous patrolmen followed them with loads of weapons they had picked up on the streets. Several of them, wearing the red armband of the rebels, fired a rifle so close to us that it resonated in my chest. Since then I have been convinced that just the report of a rifle can kill.

When we returned to the pawnshop we saw the businesses along Carrera Octava, the richest in the city, laid to waste in minutes. The exquisite jewels, English woolens, and Bond Street hats that we students from the coast had admired in unreachable shopwindows were now within reach of everyone under the gaze of impassive soldiers guarding foreign banks. The very refined Café San Marino, which we never could enter, was open and dismantled, for once without the waiters in tuxedos hurrying to stop Caribbean students from going in.

Some of those who came out loaded down with fine clothing and great bolts of woolen cloth on their shoulders left them abandoned in the middle of the street. I picked one up, not thinking it would weigh so much, and much to my sorrow I had to leave it behind. Wherever we went we stumbled across household appliances thrown into the street, and it was not easy to walk through the bottles of expensive brands of whiskey and all kinds of exotic drinks that the mobs beheaded with blows of their machetes. My brother Luis Enrique and José Palencia found remnants of the looting in a good clothing store, including a sky-blue suit of very good wool in my father's exact size, which he wore for years on important occasions. My only providential trophy was the calfskin briefcase from the most expensive tearoom in the city, which allowed me to carry my originals under my arm on the many nights during the years that followed when I had no place to sleep.

I was with a group making its way along Carrera Octava toward the Capitolio, when machine-gun fire swept over the first ones to approach Plaza de Bolívar. The instantaneous dead and wounded piled up in the middle of the street stopped us cold. A dying man bathed in blood who dragged himself out of that promontory clutched at my trouser cuff and shouted a heartrending plea:

"Boy, for the love of God, don't let me die!"

I fled in terror. Since then I have learned to forget horrors, my own and other people's, but I never forgot the hopelessness of those eyes in the brilliant glow of the fires. Yet it still surprises me not to have thought, even for an instant, that my brother and I might die in that pitiless hell.

At three in the afternoon it began to rain in great gusts, but after five o'clock a biblical deluge put out many smaller fires and lessened the impetus of the uprising. The small Bogotá garrison, incapable of confronting it, managed to separate the fury in the streets into smaller groups. It was not reinforced until after midnight by emergency troops from neighboring departments, in particular Boyacá, infamous for being the school of official violence. Until then the radio incited but did not inform, so that no news report had a source and the truth was impossible to determine. In the small hours the replacement troops took control of the business center devastated by the mobs and with no light other than the fires, but politicized resistance still continued for several days, with snipers stationed in towers and on roofs. By then, the dead in the streets were uncountable.

When we returned to the *pensión* most of the city's center was in flames, with overturned streetcars and ruined automobiles serving as improvised barricades. We put the few things worth saving in a suitcase, and only later did I realize that I left behind the first drafts of two or three unpublishable stories, my grandfather's dictionary, which I never recovered, and the book by Diógenes Laercio that I received as a prize in the first year of my baccalaureate.

The only thing my brother and I could think of was to ask for shelter in Uncle Juanito's house, only four blocks from the *pensión*. It was a second-floor apartment with a living room, dining room, and two bedrooms, and my uncle lived there with his wife and children, Eduardo, Margarita, and Nicolás, the oldest, who had been in the *pensión* with me for a while. We almost did not fit, but the Márquez Caballeros had the good heart to improvise spaces where there were none, even in the dining room, and not only for us but for other friends and companions of ours from the *pensión*: José Palencia, Domingo Manuel Vega, Carmelo Martínez—all of them from Sucre—and others whom we did not know.

A little before midnight, when it stopped raining, we went up to the roof to see the infernal landscape of the city illuminated by the embers of the fires. In the background the hills of Monserrate and La Guadalupe were two immense masses of shadow against the sky darkened by smoke, but the only thing I kept seeing in the desolate fog was the enormous face of the dying man who dragged himself toward me to beg for impossible help. The hunt in the streets had subsided, and in the awful silence you could hear only the scattered shooting by countless snipers posted all around the center, and the clamor of troops who little by little were exterminating all traces of armed or unarmed resistance in order to control the city. Overwhelmed by the landscape of death, Uncle Juanito expressed in a single sigh the feelings of all of us:

"My God, it's like a dream!"

Back in the semidarkness of the living room I collapsed onto the sofa. The official bulletins from the radio stations occupied by the government depicted a panorama of gradual tranquility. There were no more speeches, but you could not distinguish with precision between the official stations and those still controlled by the rebellion, and even these were impossible to differentiate from the uncontrollable avalanche of ill-intentioned rumors. It was said that all the embassies were overflowing with refugees, and that General Marshall was staying in the embassy of the United States, protected by an honor guard from the military school. Laureano Gómez had also taken refuge there in the first few hours and had held telephone conversations with his president, trying to stop him from negotiating with the Liberals in a situation that he considered directed by the Communists. The former president Alberto Lleras, who was then secretary general of the Pan-American Union, had saved his life by a miracle when he was recognized in his unarmored car as he was leaving the Capitolio, and the mob had tried to make him pay for the legal transfer of power to the Conservatives. By midnight most of the delegates to the Pan-American Conference were safe.

Among so many contradictory news reports, it was announced that Guillermo León Valencia, the son of the poet of the same name, had been stoned to death and his body hanged in the Plaza de Bolívar. But the idea that the government was controlling the situation began to take shape as soon as the army recovered the radio stations that were in the hands of the rebels. Instead of proclamations of war, the news reports attempted to calm the country with the consoling thought that the government was master of the situation, while high-ranking Liberals were negotiating with the president of the Republic for half the power.

In reality, the only ones who seemed to act with any political sense were the Communists, a minority of zealots, who could be seen in the midst of the disorder in the streets directing the crowd—like traffic police—toward the centers of power. Liberalism, on the other hand, showed itself to be divided into the two halves denounced by Gaitán in his campaign: the leaders who tried to negotiate a portion of power in the Palacio Presidencial, and their voters who resisted however they could and as far as they could from towers and roofs.

The first doubt that arose in connection with the death of Gaitán concerned the identity of his assassin. Even today there is no unanimous belief that it was Juan Roa Sierra, the solitary shooter who fired at him from the crowd on Carrera Séptima. What is not easy to understand is that he would have acted alone, since he did not seem to have the kind of background of autonomy that would allow him to decide by himself on that devastating death, on that day, at that time, in that place, in that manner. His mother, Encarnación Sierra, the Widow Roa, who was fifty-two years old, had learned on the radio about the assassination of Gaitán, her political hero, and was dyeing her best dress black in order to mourn him. She had not finished when she heard that the assassin was Juan Roa Sierra, the thirteenth of her fourteen children. None of them had gone past primary school, and four of them—two boys and two girls—had died.

She stated that for some eight months she had noticed strange changes in Juan's behavior. He talked to himself and laughed for no reason, and at one point he confessed to the family that he believed he was the incarnation of General Francisco de Paula Santander, the hero of our independence, but they thought it was a bad drunken joke. Her son was never known to do harm to anyone, and he had succeeded in having people of a certain importance give him letters of recommendation for obtaining work. He was carrying one of them in his wallet when he killed Gaitán. Six months earlier he had written in his own hand to President Ospina Pérez requesting an interview in order to ask him for a job.

His mother told investigators that her son had also outlined his problem in person to Gaitán, who had not offered him any hope. It was not known if he had ever fired a weapon in his life, but the manner in which he handled the one used in the crime was very far from being a novice's. The revolver was a long .38, so battered it was astonishing that it had not misfired.

Some employees of the building believed they had seen him on the floor where Gaitán's offices were located on the night before the assassination. The porter stated without any doubt that on the morning of April 9 he had seen him go up the stairs and come down afterward in the elevator with an unknown man. It seemed to him that both men waited for several hours near the entrance to the building, but Roa was by himself next to the door when Gaitán went up to his office.

Gabriel Restrepo, a reporter on *Jornada*—the newspaper of Gaitán's campaign—inventoried the identity papers Roa Sierra was carrying with him when he committed the crime. They left no doubt regarding his identity and social status but gave no clue regarding his intentions. In his trouser pockets he had eighty-two centavos in mixed coins, when several important things in daily life cost only five. In an inner pocket of his jacket he carried a black leather wallet with a one-peso bill. He also had a certificate that guaranteed his honesty, another from the police according to which he had no criminal record, and a third with his address in a poor district: Calle Octava, number 30-73. According to the record of military service as a reservist second class that he carried in the same pocket, he was the son of Rafael Roa and Encarnación Sierra, born twenty-one years earlier on November 4, 1927.

Everything seemed in order, except for a man of such humble background and with no criminal record to have with him so many proofs of good conduct. But the only thing that left me with doubts I have never been able to overcome was the elegant, well-dressed man who had thrown him to the enraged hordes and then disappeared forever in a luxury automobile.

In the midst of the uproar over the tragedy, as they were

embalming the corpse of the murdered apostle, the members of the Liberal leadership met in the dining room of the Clínica Central to decide on emergency measures. The most urgent was to go to the Palacio Presidencial without a prior appointment to discuss with the chief of state an emergency measure that would avert the cataclysm threatening the country. A little before nine that night the rain tapered off, and the first delegates made their difficult way along the streets wrecked by the popular uprising and past the corpses riddled by the blind bullets of snipers on balconies and roofs.

In the waiting room of the presidential office they met some Conservative functionaries and politicians, and the wife of the president, Doña Bertha Hernández de Ospina, very much in control of herself. She still had on the dress she wore when she accompanied her husband to the exposition in Engativá, and a regulation revolver was at her waist.

At the end of the afternoon the president had lost contact with the most critical sites, and behind closed doors he was trying to evaluate the state of the nation with military men and his ministers. The visit of the Liberal leaders a short while before ten at night took him by surprise, and he did not want to receive them all at once but two by two, but they decided that under those circumstances none of them would enter the office. The president gave in, but the Liberals still took this as a reason to be discouraged.

They found him seated at the head of a long conference table, in a faultless suit and showing no sign at all of uneasiness. The only thing that betrayed a certain tension was the constant, avid way he smoked, at times putting out a cigarette when it was half smoked and then lighting another one. One of the visitors told me years later how much he had been struck by the light from the fires on the silver head of the impassive president. Through the large windows of the presidential office, the embers in the debris under the burning sky could be seen all the way to the horizon.

What is known about that meeting we owe to the little recounted by the protagonists themselves, the rare breaches of faith of some and the many fantasies of others, and the reconstruction of those ominous days put together piecemeal by the poet and historian Arturo Alape, who to a large extent made it possible to sustain these memoirs.

The visitors were Don Luis Cano, publisher of the Liberal evening paper *El Espectador*, Plinio Mendoza Neira, who had encouraged the meeting, and three of the youngest and most active Liberal leaders: Carlos Lleras Restrepo, Darío Echandía, and Alfonso Araujo. In the course of the discussion, other prominent Liberals went in or came out.

According to the lucid recollections I heard years later from Plinio Mendoza Neira in his impatient exile in Caracas, none of them had prepared a plan. He was the only witness to the assassination of Gaitán, and he recounted it step by step with the artfulness of a born narrator and a chronic journalist. The president listened with solemn attention and then asked the visitors to express their ideas for a just and patriotic solution to the colossal emergency.

Mendoza, famous among friends and enemies for his unadorned frankness, replied that the most appropriate action would be for the government to delegate power to the Armed Forces because of the confidence the people had in them just then. He had been minister of war in the Liberal government of Alfonso López Pumarejo, he knew the military well from the inside, and he thought that only they could reopen the channels of normalcy. But the president did not agree with the realism of the plan, and the Liberals themselves did not support it.

The next intervention was from Don Luis Cano, well known for his brilliant prudence. He had almost paternal feelings for the president, and he would offer himself only for any rapid and just decision that Ospina decided with the backing of the majority. Ospina gave him assurances that he would find the indispensable means for a return to normalcy, but always adhering to the constitution. And pointing through the windows at the hell that was devouring the city, he reminded them with barely repressed irony that it was not the government that had caused the situation.

He was famous for his moderation and good breeding, in contrast to the obstreperousness of Laureano Gómez and the arrogance of other members of his party who were experts in arranged elections, but on that historic night he demonstrated that he was not prepared to be any less recalcitrant than they. And so the discussion went on until midnight, without any agreement, and with interruptions by Doña Bertha de Ospina bringing news that grew more and more frightening.

By this time the number of dead in the streets, of snipers in unassailable positions, of mobs crazed by grief, rage, and the expensive brands of alcohol looted from luxury stores, was incalculable. For the center of the city was devastated and still in flames, and exclusive shops, the Palacio de Justicia, the Gobernación, and many other historic buildings had been destroyed or set on fire. This was the reality that was narrowing without mercy the paths to a peaceful agreement by several men against one on the desert island of the presidential office.

Darío Echandía, who perhaps had the greatest authority, was the least expressive. He made two or three ironic comments about the president and again took refuge in his impassivity. He seemed to be the indispensable candidate to replace Ospina Pérez in the presidency, but that night he did nothing to deserve or to avoid it. The president, considered a moderate Conservative, seemed to resemble one less and less. He was the grandson and nephew of two presidents in one century, a paterfamilias, a retired engineer, a lifetime millionaire, and several other things that he engaged in without any noise at all, to the point where it was said, with no foundation, that the one who in fact gave the orders, at home and in the palace, was his resolute and aggressive wife. And even so—he concluded with acid sarcasm— he would not mind accepting the proposition, but he felt very comfortable heading the government from the chair where he was sitting by the will of the people.

As he spoke he was no doubt fortified by information the Liberals did not have: a certain and complete knowledge of the security forces in the country. He kept it up-to-date, for he had left his office several times to have thorough briefings. The garrison in Bogotá had fewer than a thousand men, and in every department the news was more or less grave, but in all of them the Armed Forces were loyal and had matters under control. In the neighboring department of Boyacá, famous for its historic Liberalism and its harsh Conservatism, the governor José María Villarreal—a hard-nosed Goth—not only had repressed local disturbances at the start but was dispatching better-armed troops to subdue the capital. So that all the president needed to do was to put off the Liberals with his well-measured moderation, speaking little and smoking without haste. At no moment did he look at his watch, but he must have calculated with care the hour when the city would be well supplied with fresh troops more than proven in official repression.

After a long exchange of tentative plans, Carlos Lleras Restrepo suggested what the Liberal leadership had agreed on at the Clínica Central and held in reserve as a last resort: proposing to the president that he delegate power to Darío Echandía for the sake of political harmony and social tranquility. The plan, no doubt, would be accepted without reservation by Eduardo Santos and Alfonso López Pumarejo, former presidents and men of high political standing, but on that day they were out of the country.

The president's reply, spoken with the same circumspection he used when he smoked, was not what one might have expected. He did not miss the opportunity to display his true disposition, which few people had known until then. He said that for him and his family, the most comfortable thing would be to withdraw from power and live abroad with his personal fortune and no political worries, but he was troubled by what it could mean for the country if an elected president were to flee office. Civil war would be inevitable. And when Lleras Restrepo insisted again on his retirement, he allowed himself to recall his obligation to defend the constitution and the laws, which was a commitment not only to his country but to his conscience and God as well. That was when they say he said the historic sentence that it seems he never said, though it was regarded as his forever after: "A dead president is worth more to Colombian democracy than a fugitive one."

None of the witnesses recalled hearing it from his lips or from anyone else's. Over time it was attributed to a variety of talents, and people even discussed its political merits and historical validity, but never its literary splendor. From that time on it became the motto of the government of Ospina Pérez, and one of the pillars of his glory. It has even been said that it was invented by various Conservative journalists, and with more reason by the noted writer, politician, and current minister of mines and petroleum, Joaquín Estrada Monsalve, who in fact was in the Palacio Presidencial but not inside the conference room. So the sentence remained in history as having been said by the one who should have said it, in a devastated city where the ashes were beginning to cool, and in a country that would never be the same again.

In the long run, the real merit of the president was not inventing historic sentences but putting off the Liberals with soporific candies until after midnight, when fresh troops arrived to put down the rebellion of the lower classes and impose a Conservative peace. Only then, at eight in the morning on April 10, did he wake Darío Echandía with a nightmarish eleven rings of the telephone and name him minister of the interior for a regime of consolatory bipartisanship. Laureano Gómez, displeased with the solution and uneasy about his personal safety, traveled to New York with his family while conditions were beginning to favor his eternal longing to be president.

Every dream of fundamental social change for which Gaitán had died vanished in the smoking rubble of the city. The dead in the streets of Bogotá and the deaths caused by official repression in the years that followed must have amounted to more than a million, not to mention the wretched poverty and exile of so many others. Long before the Liberal leaders placed high in the government began to realize they had assumed the risk of passing into history as accomplices.

Among the many historic witnesses to that day in Bogotá, there were two who did not know each other at the time and years later would be two of my great friends. One was Luis Cardoza y Aragón, a political and literary poet and essayist from Guatemala who was attending the Pan-American Conference as the foreign minister of his country and the head of its delegation. The other was Fidel Castro. Both were also accused at one time or another of being implicated in the disturbances.

The specific accusation against Cardoza y Aragón was that he had been one of the instigators, cloaked by his credentials as a special delegate of the progressive government of Jacobo Arbenz in Guatemala. It must be understood that Cardoza y Aragón was the delegate of a historic government and a great poet of our language who never would have lent support to an insane adventure. The most painful evocation in his beautiful book of memoirs was the accusation by Enrique Santos Montejo (Calibán), who claimed in his popular column in *El Tiempo*, "The Dance of the Hours," that his official mission was to assassinate General George Marshall. Numerous delegates to the conference took steps to have the paper rectify that lunatic rumor, but it was not possible. *El Siglo*, the official organ of Conservatism in power, proclaimed to the four winds that Cardoza y Aragón had instigated the riots.

I met him and his wife, Lya Kostakowsky, many years later in Mexico City at their house in Coyoacán, sanctified by memories and made even more beautiful by the original works of great painters of the time. Their friends would gather there on Sunday nights for intimate evenings of an unpretentious importance. He considered himself a survivor, first because his car was machine-gunned by snipers just hours after the crime. And days later, when the rebellion had been put down, a drunkard stopped him in the street and fired into his face with a revolver that jammed twice. April 9 was a recurrent subject of our conversations, in which rage mixed with nostalgia for the years that were gone.

Fidel Castro, in turn, was the victim of all kinds of absurd charges because of actions connected to his position as a student activist. On the black night, after an awful day among the rampaging mobs, he ended up in the Quinta División of the Policía Nacional, looking for a useful way to help end the slaughter in the streets. One would have to know him to imagine his desperation in the fortress in revolt, where it seemed impossible to reach a consensus.

He met with the leaders of the garrison and other rebelling officers and tried to convince them, without success, that any force that stays in its barracks is lost. He proposed that they

take their men out to struggle in the streets for the mainte-
nance of order and a more equitable system. He presented all
kinds of historical precedents but was not heard, while official
troops and tanks were riddling the fortress with bullets. In the
end, he decided to throw in his lot with the others.

In the small hours Plinio Mendoza Neira arrived at the Quinta
División with instructions from the Liberal leadership to obtain
the peaceful surrender not only of the officers and men in revolt,
but of numerous Liberals who were adrift as they waited for
orders to act. In the long hours needed to negotiate an agreement, the image remained fixed in Mendoza Neira's memory
of the stocky, argumentative Cuban student who intervened
several times in the controversies between the Liberal leaders
and the rebellious officers with a lucidity that surpassed everyone else's. He learned who he was only years later in Caracas,
when Fidel Castro was already in the Sierra Maestra, because
he happened to see him in a photograph of that terrible night.

I met him eleven years later, when I was present as a reporter
for his triumphant entry into Havana, and in time we achieved
a personal friendship that has endured countless difficulties
over the years. In my long conversations with him about everything divine and human, April 9 has been a recurrent subject
that Fidel Castro would always evoke as one of the decisive
dramas in his formation. Above all the night in the Quinta
División, where he realized that most of the rebels who were
coming in and going out were wasting their time looting instead
of persisting in the urgent effort to find a political solution.

While those two friends were witnesses to the events that
divided the history of Colombia in two, my brother and I survived in the darkness with the other refugees in Uncle Juanito's
house. At no moment did I realize that I was already an apprentice writer who would try one day to reconstruct from memory
the testimony of the hideous days we were living through. My
only concern at the time was the most mundane of all: to inform
our family that we were alive—at least so far—and find out at
the same time about our parents and brothers and sisters, and
above all about Margot and Aida, the two oldest girls, who
were students at boarding schools in distant cities.

Uncle Juanito's refuge had been a miracle. The first days were difficult because of the constant shooting and the lack of reliable news. But little by little we began exploring the nearby businesses and were able to buy things to eat. The streets were occupied by assault troops with absolute orders to shoot. In order to circulate with no restrictions, the incorrigible José Palencia disguised himself as a soldier with an explorer's hat and gaiters he found in a box of trash, and by a miracle he escaped the first patrol that discovered him.

The commercial radio stations, silenced before midnight, remained under the control of the army. The telegraph and telephones, primitive and scarce, were reserved for security forces, and no other means of communication existed. The lines for sending telegrams were endless outside the packed offices, but the radio stations inaugurated a service for sending messages on the air for those lucky enough to hear them. This seemed the easiest and most reliable method, and we turned to it without much hope.

My brother and I went outside after three days of confinement. It was a horrific sight. The city was in ruins, cloudy and dark because of the constant rain that had dampened the fires but delayed recovery. Many streets in the center were closed because of nests of snipers on the roofs, and you had to make senseless detours by order of patrols armed as if for a world war. The stink of death in the streets was unbearable. The army trucks had not yet picked up the promontories of bodies on the sidewalks, and the soldiers had to confront groups of people desperate to identify their relatives.

In the ruins of what had been the business center, the stench was so unbreathable that many families had to give up their search. On one of the great pyramids of corpses one body stood out, barefoot and trouserless but wearing an impeccable frock coat. Three days later, the ashes still exhaled the stench of unclaimed bodies rotting in the rubble or piled up on the sidewalks.

When we least expected it, my brother and I were stopped cold by the unmistakable sound of a rifle bolt at our backs, and a categorical order:

"Hands up!"

I raised them without even thinking about it, petrified with terror, until I was brought back to life by the laugh of our friend Ángel Casij, who had responded to the Armed Forces call-up as a reservist first class. Thanks to him, the refugees in Uncle Juanito's house were able to send a message over the air after waiting for a day in front of Radio Nacional. My father heard it in Sucre among the countless messages that were read day and night for two weeks. My brother and I, irredeemable victims of the family's conjectural mania, were afraid our mother might interpret the news as an act of charity by friends while they prepared her for the worst. We were not far from wrong: beginning on the first night, our mother had dreamed that her two oldest children had drowned in a sea of blood during the disturbances. It must have been so convincing a nightmare that when the truth reached her by other means, she decided that neither of us would ever return to Bogotá, even if we had to stay at home and die of hunger. Her decision must have been final because the only order our parents gave us in their first telegram was that we should travel to Sucre as soon as possible to determine our futures.

In the tense period of waiting, various fellow students had painted the golden possibilities of continuing my studies in Cartagena de Indias, thinking that Bogotá would recover from its rubble but the Bogotáns would never recover from the terror and horror of the slaughter. Cartagena had a centenarian university as prestigious as its historical relics, and a faculty of law on a human scale where they would accept as valid my poor grades from the Universidad Nacional.

I did not want to reject the idea without first letting it cook over a high flame, or mention it to my parents until I had tested it myself. All I told them was that I would fly to Sucre by way of Cartagena, since the Magdalena River during that shooting war might be a suicidal route. Luis Enrique, for his part, said he would look for work in Barranquilla as soon as he could settle accounts with his employers in Bogotá.

In any case, I knew I would not be a lawyer anywhere. I just wanted to gain a little more time in order to distract my parents, and Cartagena might be a good technical stopping place to think. What never occurred to me is that this reasonable calculation would lead me to resolve, my heart in my hand, that it was the place where I wanted to continue my life.

Obtaining five seats in the same plane for any place along the coast during that time was a feat of my brother's. After standing in interminable and dangerous lines and spending an entire day running around an emergency airport, he found the five seats in three separate planes, at improbable times and in the midst of invisible shots and explosions. Two seats were confirmed for my brother and me in the same plane to Barranquilla, but at the last minute we left on different flights. The drizzle and fog that had persisted in Bogotá since the previous Friday stank of gunpowder and rotting bodies. On the way from the house to the airport we were questioned at two successive military checkpoints where the soldiers were dazed with terror. At the second checkpoint they threw themselves to the ground and made us go down too because of an explosion followed by the firing of heavy weapons that turned out to have been caused by a leak of industrial gas. Other passengers heard him when a soldier told us that his drama was standing guard there for three days with no relief, but also with no ammunition since there was none left in the city. We almost did not dare to speak after they stopped us, and the terror of the soldiers was the finishing touch. But after the formal procedures involving identification and destination, it comforted us to know we had to remain there and do nothing else until we were taken on board. The only thing I smoked while I was waiting were two of the three cigarettes that someone had given me out of charity, and I saved one for the terror of the flight.

Since there were no telephones, the announcements of flights and other changes were learned at the different checkpoints by means of military orderlies on motorcycles. At eight in the morning they called a group of passengers to board without delay a plane for Barranquilla that was not mine. Later I learned that the other three people in our group embarked with my brother at another checkpoint. My solitary wait was an asinine cure for my congenital fear of flying, because when it was time to board the plane the sky was overcast and there was stony thunder. And since the stairs to our plane had been taken for another, two soldiers had to help me board on a bricklayer's ladder. It was in the same airport and at the same time that Fidel Castro boarded another plane that left for Havana with a cargo of fighting bulls—as he told me years later.

To my good or bad fortune, I was on a DC-3 smelling of fresh paint and recent grease, without individual lights or ventilation regulated from the passenger cabin. It was outfitted to transport troops, and instead of separate seats in rows of three, as on tourist flights, there were two long benches made of ordinary planks well anchored to the floor. My luggage consisted of a canvas suitcase with two or three changes of dirty clothing, books of poetry, and clippings from literary supplements that my brother Luis Enrique had managed to save. The passengers sat facing one another from the cockpit to the tail. Instead of safety belts there were two hemp cables for tying up ships, which were like two long collective safety belts for each side. The hardest thing for me was that as soon as I lit the only cigarette I had saved in order to survive the flight, the pilot in overalls announced from the cockpit that smoking was prohibited because the plane's gasoline tanks were at our feet under the wooden floor. Those were three interminable hours of flying.

When we arrived in Barranquilla it had just rained as it rains only in April, with houses torn up by the roots and carried away by the current in the streets, and solitary patients drowned in their beds. I had to wait for the weather to clear, in the airport thrown into confusion because of the flood, and I just managed to learn that the plane taken by my brother and his two companions had arrived on time, but they had rushed to leave the terminal before the initial thunderclaps of the first downpour.

I needed another three hours to reach the travel agency, and I missed the last bus that left for Cartagena on a schedule that had been moved up in anticipation of the storm. I did not worry because I believed my brother had gone there, but I was frightened for myself at the idea of spending the night in Barranquilla with no money. At last, thanks to José Palencia, I obtained emergency shelter in the house of the beautiful sisters Ilse and Lila Albarracín, and three days later I traveled to Cartagena in the broken-down vehicle of the Postal Agency. My brother Luis Enrique would stay in Barranquilla hoping for a job. I had no more than eight pesos left, but José Palencia promised to bring me a little more on the night bus. There was no room, not even standing room, but the driver agreed to carry three passengers on the roof, sitting on the freight and suitcases, for a quarter of the regular price. In so strange a situation, and in the full sunlight, I believe I had become aware that on April 9, 1948, the twentieth century began in Colombia.

6

AT THE END OF A JOURNEY of lethal jolting along the hairpin curves of the highway, the Postal Agency truck breathed its last just where it deserved to: mired in a mangrove swamp that reeked of rotting fish half a league from Cartagena de Indias. "The man who travels in a truck doesn't know where he's going to die," I recalled, along with the memory of my grandfather. The passengers, stupefied by six hours of naked sun and the stink of the salt marshes, did not wait for the ladder to be lowered in order to disembark but hurried to throw over the side the crates of chickens, bundles of plantains, and all kinds of things for selling or for killing that they had used as seats on the roof of the truck. The driver jumped down from the cab and announced in a caustic shout:

"La Heroica!"

It is the emblematic name by which Cartagena de Indias is known because of its past glories, and that is where it should have been. But I did not see it because I almost could not breathe inside the black wool suit I had been wearing since April 9. The other two in my wardrobe had met the same fate as the typewriter in the pawnshop, but the honorable version for my parents was that the typewriter and other personal trifles had disappeared along with my clothes in the confusion of the fire. The brash driver, who had made fun of my bandit's appearance during the trip, was about to burst with amusement as I kept turning in circles without finding the city.

"It's up your ass!" he shouted at me for all to hear. "And be careful, they give medals to assholes there."

Cartagena de Indias, in fact, had been at my back for four hundred years, but it was not easy for me to imagine it half a league from the mangrove swamps, concealed by the legendary wall that had kept it safe from heathens and pirates during its great years, and disappearing in the end under a thicket of branches growing wild and long trails of yellow bellflowers. And so I joined the confusion of passengers and dragged my suitcase through brambles carpeted with live crabs whose shells popped like firecrackers under the soles of our shoes. Then it was impossible for me not to remember the *petate* that my companions tossed into the Magdalena River on my first trip, or the funereal trunk I dragged across half the country crying with rage during my early years at the *liceo*, and that I at last threw over a precipice in the Andes in honor of my bachelor's degree. It always seemed to me there was something of another person's destiny in those undeserved extra loads, and my years have not been long enough to disprove that.

We had just begun to glimpse the outline of the domes of some churches and convents in the late-afternoon mists when a windstorm of bats came out to meet us, flying at the level of our heads, and it was only because of their knowledge that they did not knock us to the ground. Their wings whirred like a rush of thunderclaps and left in their wake a stench of death. Overwhelmed by panic, I dropped the suitcase and crouched on the ground with my arms over my head, until an older woman who was walking beside me shouted:

"Say *La Magnífica*!"

That is: the secret prayer for conjuring attacks by the devil, repudiated by the Church but sanctified by great atheists when they ran out of blasphemies. The woman realized I did not know how to pray, and she seized my suitcase by the other strap to help me carry it.

"Pray with me," she said. "But remember: with a lot of faith."

She recited *La Magnífica* for me line by line and I repeated them all with a devotion I have never felt again. The wind-storm of bats, though I find it hard to believe today, disappeared from the sky before we finished praying. All that was left then was the immense crashing of the ocean against the cliffs.

We had reached the great gate of El Reloj. For a hundred years there had been a drawbridge that connected the old city to the outlying district of Getsemaní and the dense slums of the poor from the mangrove swamps, but it was raised from nine at night until dawn. The population was left isolated not only from the rest of the world but also from history. It was said that the Spanish colonists had built that bridge because of their terror that the poverty-stricken from the outskirts would sneak across at midnight and cut their throats as they slept. But something of its divine grace must have remained in the city, because it was enough for me to take a step inside the wall to see it in all its grandeur in the mauve light of six in the evening, and I could not repress the feeling of having been born again.

And with reason. At the beginning of the week I had left Bogotá, splashing through a swamp of blood and mud, with promontories of unclaimed corpses abandoned among smoking ruins. Then the world changed in Cartagena. There were no traces of the war that was laying waste to the country, and it was hard for me to believe that this solitude without sorrow, this incessant ocean, this immense sensation of having arrived was happening to me less than a week later in the same life.

Because I had heard it talked about so much from the time I was born, I identified without hesitation the little square where the horse-drawn carriages parked, and the freight carts that were pulled by donkeys, and in the background the arcaded galleries where popular commerce became denser and noisier. Although it was not recognized as such in official consciousness, that was the last active heart of the city since its origins. During the colonial period it was called the Portal de los Mercaderes. From there the invisible threads of the slave trade were controlled and spirits heated up against Spanish domination. Close by was the Portal de los Escribanos, its name derived from the taciturn calligraphers in woolen vests and false half sleeves who wrote love letters and all kinds of documents there for the illiterate poor. Many sold inexpensive books under the table, in particular works condemned by the Holy Office, and it is believed they were oracles of the American-born conspiracy against the Spaniards. At the beginning of the twentieth century, my father would relieve his poet's impulses with the art of writing love letters in the Portal. The truth is he did not prosper as either poet or scribe because some clients who were shrewd, or in reality destitute, asked not only that he write their letters out of charity but give them the five reales for postage.

For several years it had been called the Portal de los Dulces, with rotted canvas awnings and beggars who came to eat the leavings of the market, and the oracular shouts of Indians who charged a good deal of money not to sing out to the client the day and hour of his death. The schooners of the Caribbean would stop at the port to buy sweets with names invented by the same *comadres* who made them, and versified in their vendors' cries: "Sugar cream for my dream, chocolate drops for pops, coconut candies for dandies, brown sugar cakes, no mistakes."* For in good times and bad the Portal continued to be the vital center of the city where matters of state were aired behind the government's back, the only place in the world where the women who peddled fried food knew who the next governor would be before the president of the Republic in Bogotá had even thought about him.

Fascinated on the spot by the clamor, and dragging my suitcase behind me, I made my way by fits and starts through the six o'clock crowd. From the bootblacks' stand a ragged old man, nothing but skin and bones, watched me, not blinking, with the icy eyes of a hawk. He stopped me cold. As soon as he realized that I had seen him he offered to carry the suitcase for me. I thanked him, until he specified in his mother tongue:

*The rhymes in English, of course, do not correspond to the ones in Spanish, but they are essentially nonsense verses: *Los piononos para los monos, los diabolines para los mamines, las de coco para los locos, las de panela para Manuela.*

"For thirty pieces."

Impossible. Thirty centavos for carrying a suitcase was a huge bite out of the four pesos I had left until I received reinforcements from my parents the following week.

"That's worth the suitcase and everything inside it," I told him.

Besides, the *pensión* where the group from Bogotá must have already gone was not very far. The old man resigned himself to three pieces, hung the sandals he was wearing around his neck, loaded the suitcase on his shoulder with a strength that was unbelievable for his bones, and ran like an athlete barefooted along a rough terrain of colonial houses crumbling after centuries of abandonment. I was twenty-one and my heart almost burst out of my mouth as I tried not to lose sight of the Olympic old man who could not have had many hours of life left in him. After five blocks he went through the large door of the hotel and climbed the stairs two at a time. With his breath intact he placed the suitcase on the floor and held out his palm:

"Thirty pieces."

I reminded him that I had already paid him, but he insisted that the three centavos at the Portal did not include the staircase. The landlady, who came out to greet us, said he was right: the staircase was a separate charge. And she made a prediction that was valid for the rest of my life:

"You'll see, in Cartagena everything's different."

I also had to face the bad news that none of my companions from the *pensión* in Bogotá had arrived yet, even though they had confirmed reservations for four, including me. The plan I had made with them was to meet at the hotel before six that day. The change from the regular bus to the risky vehicle from the Postal Agency had delayed me three hours, but I was there before everyone else and unable to do anything with four pesos less thirty-three centavos. The landlady was a charming mother but a slave to her own norms, as I would confirm in the two long months I lived in her hotel. And so she refused to register me unless I paid the first month in advance: eighteen pesos for three meals and a room that slept six.

I did not expect help from my parents for another week,

which meant that my suitcase would not move from the landing until the friends who could help me arrived. I sat down to
wait in an archbishop's easy chair with large flowers printed on
it that was like a gift from heaven after an entire day in the full
sun on the truck of my misfortune. The truth was that no one
was sure of anything during that time. Our agreeing to meet
there on an exact day and at an exact hour lacked a sense of
reality, because we did not dare say, even to ourselves, that half
the country was involved in a bloody war that had been hidden
in the provinces for several years, and open and lethal in the
cities for the past week.

Eight hours later, stranded in the hotel in Cartagena, I did
not understand what could have happened to José Palencia and
his friends. After another hour of waiting with no word from
them, I went out to wander the deserted streets. In April it gets
dark early. The streetlights were already on, so dim they could
be confused with stars through the trees. It was enough for me
to take that first fifteen-minute aimless walk along the cobbled
twists and turns of the colonial district to discover, with great
relief in my chest, that this strange city had nothing to do with
the canned fossil they described to us in school.

There was not a soul on the streets. The crowds who came in
from the outskirts at dawn to work or sell returned in a rush to
their neighborhoods at five in the afternoon, and the inhabitants of the walled enclosure shut themselves in their houses to
eat supper and play dominoes until midnight. The custom of
owning private cars had not yet been established, and the few
for hire remained outside the wall. Even the haughtiest functionaries still arrived at the Plaza de los Coches in buses made
by local artisans, and from there they made their way to their
offices, jumping over the stores of trinkets displayed on the
public sidewalks. One of the most affected governors during
those tragic years boasted that he still traveled from his elite
quarter to the Plaza de los Coches on the same buses he had
taken to school.

The curbing of automobiles had been unavoidable because
they were contrary to historical reality: they did not fit in the
narrow, twisting streets of the city where the unshod hooves of

rachitic horses resounded in the night. When it was very hot, when balconies were opened to let in the cool air from the parks, you could hear, with a spectral resonance, sudden bursts of the most intimate conversations. Dozing grandfathers heard furtive steps on the stone streets, paid attention to them without opening their eyes until they recognized them, and said in disappointment: "There goes José Antonio to see Chabela." The only thing that in reality drove the wakeful out of their minds were the dry knocks of the pieces on the domino table that echoed all through the walled district.

It was a historic night for me. I almost did not recognize in their reality the academic fictions from books, which had already been defeated by life. It moved me to tears that the old palaces of the marquises were the ones I saw in front of me, chipped and peeling, with beggars sleeping in the entrances. I saw the cathedral without the bells that had been carried off by the pirate Francis Drake to make cannons. The few that were saved from the assault were exorcised after the archbishop's sorcerers sentenced them to burn because of their malignant resonances meant to summon the devil. I saw the faded trees and the statues of illustrious heroes that did not seem like sculptures in perishable marble but living dead men. For in Cartagena they were not preserved from the rust of time; on the contrary, time was preserved for things that continued to be their original age while the centuries grew old. That was how, on the night of my arrival, the city revealed its own life to me with every step, not as the papier-mâché fossil of the historians but as a flesh-and-blood city, no longer sustained by its martial glories but by the dignity of its ruins.

With that new spirit I returned to the *pensión* as it was striking ten in the tower of El Reloj. The watchman, who was half asleep, told me that none of my friends had arrived, but that my suitcase was safe in the hotel's storeroom. I realized only then that I had not had anything to eat or drink since my meager breakfast in Barranquilla. My legs were giving way because of hunger, but I would have been content if the landlady had taken my suitcase and allowed me to sleep in the hotel that one night, even if it was on the armchair in the sitting room. The watchman laughed at my innocence.

"Don't be an asshole!" he said in raw Caribbean. "With the piles of money that madam has, she goes to sleep at seven and gets up the next day at eleven."

The argument seemed so legitimate to me that I sat on a bench in the Parque de Bolívar, on the other side of the street, and waited for my friends to arrive, not bothering anyone. The faded trees were almost invisible in the light from the street, because the lamps in the park were lit only on Sundays and important holidays. The marble benches had traces of legends often erased and rewritten by brazen poets. In the Palacio de la Inquisición, behind its viceregal facade carved in virgin stone and its entrance of a sham basilica, you could hear the inconsolable lament of an ailing bird that could not be of this world. Then my longing to smoke attacked at the same time as my longing to read, two habits that I confused in my youth because of their intrusiveness and their tenacity. *Point Counter Point*, the novel by Aldous Huxley that physical fear had not allowed me to read on the plane, was sleeping under lock and key in my suitcase. And so I lit my last cigarette with a strange sensation of relief and terror, and I put it out half smoked to keep it on reserve for a night with no morning.

My mind was already prepared to sleep on the bench where I was sitting when it seemed to me that something was hidden in the deepest shadows of the trees. It was the equestrian statue of Simón Bolívar. No one else: General Simón José Antonio de la Santísima Trinidad Bolívar y Palacios, my hero since my grandfather had commanded me to idolize him, with his radiant dress uniform and his head of a Roman emperor, shat upon by pigeons.

He had continued to be my unforgettable protagonist despite his irredeemable inconsistencies, or perhaps because of them. After all, they were not comparable to those with which my grandfather won his colonel's rank and risked his life so many times in the war the Liberals fought against the same Conservative Party that Bolívar founded and sustained. I was lost in those mists when a peremptory voice behind me brought me down to earth:

"Hands up!"

I raised them in relief, certain my friends were there at last, and I encountered two police officers, rustic and somewhat ragged, who aimed their new rifles at me. They wanted to know why I had violated the curfew that had been in effect for the past two hours. I did not even know one had been imposed the previous Sunday, as they informed me, and I had not heard a bugle call or bells ring or any other sign that would have allowed me to understand why there was no one on the streets. The officers were more lazy than understanding when they saw my identity papers as I was explaining why I was there. They returned them without looking at them. They asked how much money I had and I said less than four pesos. Then the more resolute of the two asked for a cigarette and I showed them the butt I was planning to smoke before I went to sleep. He took it and smoked it down to his nails. After a while they led me by the arm along the street, more because of their desire to smoke than any stipulation of the law, looking for a place that was open where they could buy loose cigarettes for a centavo each. The night had become clear and cool under the full moon, and the silence seemed an invisible substance that could be breathed like air. Then I understood what Papá had told us so many times without our believing him—that he had practiced his late-night violin in the silence of the cemetery in order to feel that his waltzes of love could be heard all around the Caribbean.

Tired of the useless search for loose cigarettes, we went outside the wall toward a coastal shipping dock with its own life behind the public market, where the schooners from Curaçao and Aruba and other Lesser Antilles dropped anchor. It was the all-night haunt for the most amusing and useful people in the city, who had the right to a safe-conduct pass in the curfew because of the kind of work they did. They ate until dawn at an open-air stand with good prices and better company, because not only night workers went there but also everybody who wanted to eat when there was no other place open. It did not have an official name and it was known by the one that suited it least: La Cueva—the Cave.

The police walked in as if it were their house. It was evident that the patrons already seated at the table had always known one another and were happy to be together. It was impossible to detect any last names because they all called everyone by their school nicknames and talked at the top of their voices, all at the same time, without understanding or looking at anybody. They were in work clothes, except for an Adonis-like man in his sixties with a snow-white head, wearing a tuxedo from another day, with a mature and still very beautiful woman in a worn sequinned dress and too many real jewels. Her presence might have been a vivid fact of her status in life, because there were very few women whose husbands would permit them to appear in those places with bad reputations. One might have thought they were tourists if it had not been for their ease and their local accent and their familiarity with everyone. Later I learned that they were nothing like what they seemed but an old married couple, Cartagenians gone astray who dressed in formal clothes on any pretext in order to eat out, and that night they had found the headwaiters asleep and the restaurants closed because of the curfew.

They were the ones who invited us to supper. The others made room for us at the long table, and the three of us sat down, somewhat crowded and intimidated. They also treated the police officers with the familiarity used with servants. One was serious and confident and showed vestiges of a good upbringing at the table. The other seemed distracted except in eating and smoking. I, more because of timidity than courtesy, ordered fewer dishes than they did, and when I realized I would be left with more than half my hunger, the others had already finished.

The proprietor and only server in La Cueva was named José Dolores, an almost adolescent black of discomfiting beauty who was wrapped in the immaculate sheets of a Muslim and always wore a live carnation behind his ear. But the most notable thing about him was his excessive intelligence, which he used without qualms to be happy and to make other people happy. It was clear that he lacked very little to be a woman, and his reputation for going to bed only with his husband was well founded. No one ever made a joke about his circumstances, because his wit and rapid responses gave thanks for every favor and retaliation for every affront. He did everything himself, from cooking with exactitude what he knew each patron liked to frying the slices of green plantain with one hand and adding up the bills with the other, his only help the little he received from a boy of about six who called him mamá. When we said goodbye I was excited by our discovery but never imagined that this spot for wayward night owls would be one of the unforgettable places in my life.

After the meal I accompanied the policemen while they completed their delayed rounds. The moon was a gold plate in the sky. A breeze was beginning to blow, and it brought from a great distance fragments of music and the remote shouts of uninhibited carousing. But the officers knew that in the poor districts nobody went to bed on account of the curfew; they organized subscription dances instead, in a different house each night, and did not go outside until dawn.

When the clocks struck two we stopped at my hotel, not doubting for a moment that my friends had arrived, but this time the watchman told us to go straight to hell for waking him up for no reason. Then they realized I had no place to sleep, and they decided to take me to their barracks. I thought the joke so shameless that I lost my temper and said something disrespectful. One of them, surprised by my childish reaction, put me in my place, pressing the barrel of his rifle against my stomach.

"Stop being an asshole," he said, weak with laughter. "Remember you're still under arrest for violating curfew."

And so I slept—in a cell for six and on a straw mat fermented by other people's sweat—on my first joyful night in Cartagena.

Reaching the soul of the city was much easier than surviving my first day. In less than two weeks I had resolved relations with my parents, who approved without reservation my decision to live in a city where there was no war. The landlady of the hotel, repentant for having condemned me to a night in jail, found a place for me with twenty other students in a shed she had constructed not long before on the roof of her beautiful colonial house. I had no reason to complain, because it was a Caribbean copy of the dormitory in the Liceo Nacional, and with everything included it cost less than the *pensión* in Bogotá.

Enrolling in the faculty of law was taken care of in an hour with an admission examination held before the secretary, Ignacio Vélez Martínez, and a teacher of political economy whose name I have not managed to find in my memory. As was the custom, the ceremony was conducted in the presence of the entire second year. Beginning with the preamble, I was struck by the clear judgment and precise language of the two teachers, in a region famous in the interior of the country for its verbal disorder. The first subject, chosen by lot, was the Civil War in the United States, about which I knew a little less than nothing. It was a shame I had not yet read the new North American novelists, who had just begun to reach us, but it was my good luck that Dr. Vélez Martínez began with a casual reference to *Uncle Tom's Cabin*, which I had known very well since my baccalaureate. I caught it on the wing. The two teachers must have suffered an attack of nostalgia, because the sixty minutes we had reserved for the examination were used in their entirety for an emotional analysis of the ignominy of the slaveholding regime in the southern United States. And that was as far as we got. So that what I had foreseen as a game of Russian roulette was a diverting conversation that received a good grade and some cordial applause.

I enrolled in the university to complete the second year of law, on the condition, which was never met, that I sit for makeup exams in one or two subjects still outstanding from my first year in Bogotá. Some of my fellow students became enthusiastic about my way of domesticating subjects, because there existed among them a certain militancy in favor of creative freedom in a university mired in academic rigor. This had been my solitary dream every since the *liceo*, not because of gratuitous nonconformity but as my only hope for passing examinations without studying. But the same students who proclaimed independent thinking in the classrooms could not help but surrender to fate as they climbed the gallows of examinations, having memorized atavistic tomes of colonial texts. To our good fortune, in real life they were masters in the art of keeping alive the Friday subscription dances despite the dangers of a repression that grew more and more blatant in the shadow of the state of siege. The dances continued to be held while the curfew was in effect with the sub-rosa permission of the police authorities, and when it was canceled they came back to life with more spirit than ever. Above all in Torices, Getsemaní, or the foot of La Popa, the most pleasure-loving districts during those gloomy years. All we had to do was look in the windows and choose the party we liked best, and for fifty centavos we danced until dawn to the hottest music in the Caribbean, amplified by clamoring loudspeakers. The girls invited as a courtesy were the same students we saw during the week as they came out of school, except that they wore their uniforms for Sunday Mass and danced like guileless women under the watchful eye of chaperoning aunts or liberated mothers. On one of those nights of big-game hunting, I was making my way through Getsemaní, which had been the slave quarter in colonial times, when I recognized a strong slap on my back and a booming voice as if they were a password:

"Bandit!"

It was Manuel Zapata Olivella, an inveterate resident of the Calle de la Mala Crianza where the family of the grandparents of his African great-great-grandparents had lived. We had seen each other in Bogotá, in the midst of the turmoil of April 9, and our first shock in Cartagena was finding the other alive. Manuel, in addition to being a charity doctor, was a novelist, a political activist, and a promoter of Caribbean music, but his principal calling was trying to resolve everyone else's problems. As soon as we had exchanged our experiences on that fateful Friday, as well as our plans for the future, he proposed that I try my luck in journalism. One month earlier the Liberal leader Domingo López Escauriaza had founded the newspaper *El Universal*, whose editor-in-chief was Clemente Manuel Zabala. I had heard about him, not as a journalist but as a scholar of all kinds of music, and as a Communist at rest. Zapata Olivella insisted we go to see him, because he knew he was looking for new people in order to provoke by example a creative journalism in opposition to the routine and submissive reporting that prevailed in the country, above all in Cartagena, which at that time was one of the most backward cities.

It was very clear to me that journalism was not my profession. I wanted to be a distinctive writer, but I was trying to achieve that through the imitation of other authors who had nothing to do with me. So that those days were an interval of reflection for me, because after the publication of my first three stories in Bogotá and the high praise received from Eduardo Zalamea and other critics, and good and bad friends, I felt I had reached a dead end. Zapata Olivella insisted, despite my arguments, that journalism and literature were the same thing in the short run, and a connection with *El Universal* could assure me of three outcomes at the same time: it would resolve my life in a dignified and useful manner, place me in the environment of a profession that in and of itself was important, and allow me to work with Clemente Manuel Zabala, the best journalism teacher anyone could imagine. The constraints of shyness produced in me by this simple argument could have saved me from a misfortune. But Zapata Olivella did not know how to endure failure and he made an appointment with me for the following day at five in the afternoon at 381 Calle de San Juan de Dios, where the paper was located.

My sleep was restless that night. The next day at breakfast I asked the landlady of the hotel where Calle de San Juan de Dios was, and she pointed it out to me through the window.

"It's right there," she said, "two blocks away."

The offices of *El Universal* were across from the immense wall of golden stone of the Church of San Pedro Claver, the first saint from the Americas, whose uncorrupted body has been displayed for more than a hundred years beneath the main altar. It was an old colonial building embroidered with republican patches, and two large doors, and windows through which you could see everything that the newspaper was. But my real terror sat behind an unpolished wooden railing some three meters from the window: a mature, solitary man dressed in white drill, with a jacket and tie, a swarthy complexion, and the coarse black hair of an Indian, who was writing with a pencil at an old desk that had stacks of papers needing attention. I passed by again in the opposite direction, feeling an urgent fascination, and then two more times, and the fourth time, as on the first, I did not have the slightest doubt that the man was Clemente Manuel Zabala, just as I had supposed him to be, but more frightening. Terrified, I made the simple decision not to keep that afternoon's appointment with a man you only had to see through a window to discover that he knew too much about life and its professions. I returned to the hotel and presented myself with another of my typical days without regret, lying on my back on the bed with Gide's *The Counterfeiters*, and smoking without letup. At five in the afternoon, the door to the dormitory was shaken by an open palm delivering a blow as dry as a rifle shot.

"Let's go, damn it!" Zapata Olivella shouted at me from the entrance. "Zabala's waiting for you, and nobody in this country can allow himself the luxury of standing him up."

The beginning was more difficult than I could have imagined in a nightmare. Zabala received me not knowing what to do, smoking without pause, his uneasiness made worse by the heat. He showed us everything. On one side, the offices of the publisher and the manager, on the other the newsroom and typesetting shop with three empty desks at that early hour, and in the rear a rotary printing press that had survived a riot, and their only two linotypes.

My great surprise was that Zabala had read my three stories, and Zalamea's note had seemed fair to him.

"Not to me," I said. "I don't like the stories. I wrote them on somewhat unconscious impulses, and after I read them in print I didn't know how to continue."

Zabala inhaled the smoke deep into his lungs and said to Zapata Olivella:

"That's a good sign."

Manuel seized the opportunity and said I could be useful at the paper in the time I had free from the university. Zabala said he had thought the same thing when Manuel asked him to make an appointment with me. He introduced me to Dr. López Escauriaza, the publisher, as the possible contributor about whom he had spoken the night before.

"That would be wonderful," said the publisher with his eternal smile of an old-fashioned gentleman.

We did not arrange anything but Maestro Zabala asked me to come back the next day to meet Héctor Rojas Heraza, a fine poet and painter and his star columnist. Because of a timidity that today I find inexplicable, I did not tell him he had been my drawing teacher at the Colegio San José. When we left, Manuel gave a great leap on the Plaza de la Aduana, across from the imposing facade of San Pedro Claver, and exclaimed with premature jubilation:

"You see, tiger, the whole thing's taken care of!"

I responded with a cordial hug so as not to disillusion him, but I had serious doubts about my future. Then Manuel asked me what I had thought of Zabala, and I told him the truth. He seemed like a fisher of souls to me. Perhaps that was a determining reason for the groups of young people who were nourished by his reason and circumspection. I concluded, no doubt with the false estimation of a premature old man, that perhaps this disposition of his had prevented him from playing a decisive role in the public life of the country.

Manuel called me that night weak with laughter because of a conversation he had with Zabala, who spoke of me with great enthusiasm, reiterated his certainty that I would be an important acquisition for the editorial page, and said the publisher was of the same opinion. But the real reason for his call was to tell me that the only thing that disturbed Maestro Zabala was that my unhealthy timidity might be a great obstacle to me in my life.

If at the last minute I decided to go back to the paper, it was because the next morning one of my roommates opened the door to the shower and held the editorial page of *El Universal* up to my eyes. There was a terrifying note about my arrival in the city, which committed me as a writer before I was one and as an imminent journalist less than twenty-four hours after I had seen the inside of a newspaper for the first time. I reproached Manuel, who called me without delay to congratulate me, and I did not hide my anger at his writing something so irresponsible without speaking to me first. But something changed in me, perhaps forever, when I learned that it was Maestro Zabala who had written the note in his own hand. And so I fastened my trousers and went back to the newsroom to thank him. He paid little attention. He introduced me to Héctor Rojas Herazo, with his khaki pants and shirt with Amazonian flowers and enormous words fired off in a voice of thunder, who did not yield in a conversation until he had trapped his prey. He, of course, did not recognize me as one more of his students at the Colegio San José in Barranquilla.

Maestro Zabala—as everyone called him—put us in his orbit with memories of two or three mutual friends, and some others whom I ought to know. Then he left us alone and returned to the fierce battle of his blood-red pencil and his urgent papers, as if he had never had anything to do with us. Héctor continued talking to me in the light drizzling noise of the linotypes as if he had never had anything to do with Zabala either. He was an infinite conversationalist with a dazzling verbal intelligence, an adventurer of the imagination who invented improbable realities that he himself came to believe. We talked for hours about other friends living and dead, about books that never should have been written, about women who forgot us and whom we could not forget, about the idyllic beaches in the Caribbean paradise of Tolú—where he had been born—and about the infallible wizards and biblical misfortunes of Aracataca. About everything that had been and should be, not drinking, almost not taking a breath, and smoking without pause for fear that life would not last long enough for everything we still had to talk about.

At ten o'clock that night, when the paper went to press, Maestro Zabala put on his jacket, tightened his tie, and with a ballet dancer's step that had little youth left in it, he invited us to eat. At La Cueva, of course, where to their surprise José Dolores and several of his late-night diners recognized me as an old patron. Their surprise increased when one of the policemen from my first visit passed by, made an equivocal joke about the bad night I had spent at the barracks, and confiscated a pack of cigarettes I had just opened. Héctor, in turn, started a tourney of double entendres with José Dolores that had the other patrons bursting with laughter while Maestro Zabala maintained a contented silence. I dared interject a reply without wit that at least allowed me to be recognized as one of the few clients José Dolores favored by serving them on credit up to four times a month.

After the meal, Héctor and I continued the afternoon's conversation on the Paseo de los Mártires, which faced the bay polluted by republican garbage from the public market. It was a splendid night at the center of the world, and the first schooners from Curaçao were dropping anchor in secret. That night Héctor gave me my first insights into the underground history of Cartagena, concealed by sympathetic friends, which perhaps resembled the truth more than the amiable fiction of the academics. He told me about the lives of the ten martyrs whose marble busts were on both sides of the promenade as a memorial to their heroism. The popular version—which seemed to be his—was that when they were set in their original places, the sculptors had not carved the names and dates on the busts but on the pedestals. When they were dismantled to be cleaned for their centenary, no one knew which busts corresponded to which names and dates, and they had to be put back on the pedestals at random because no one knew who they were. The story had circulated as a joke for many years, but I, on the contrary, thought it had been an act of historical justice to erect a monument to heroes who were nameless not so much because of the lives they had lived as because of the destiny they had shared.

Those nights without sleep were repeated almost on a daily basis during my years in Cartagena, but after the first two or three I realized that Héctor had the power of immediate seduction, with a sense of friendship so complex that only those of us who loved him a good deal could understand it without reservation. For his tenderheartedness was unqualified, but at the same time he was capable of deafening and at times catastrophic rages, which he celebrated afterward with the innocence of the Holy Infant. One understood then how he was, and why Maestro Zabala did everything possible to have us love him as much as he did. On that first night, as on so many others, we stayed on the Paseo de los Mártires until dawn, protected from the curfew because of our status as reporters. Héctor's voice and memory were intact when he saw the radiance of the new day on the sea's horizon, and he said:

"If only tonight would end like *Casablanca*."

He did not say anything else, but his voice brought back to me in all its splendor the image of Humphrey Bogart and Claude Rains walking shoulder to shoulder through the fog at dawn toward the radiant light on the horizon, and the now legendary sentence of that tragic happy ending: "I think this is the beginning of a beautiful friendship."

Three hours later Maestro Zabala woke me by telephone with a less happy phrase:

"How's that masterpiece coming along?"

I needed a few minutes to understand that he was referring to my piece for the next day's paper. I do not remember our having closed any deal or my having said either yes or no when he asked me to write my first contribution, but that morning I felt capable of anything after the verbal Olympiad of the previous night. Zabala must have understood matters in this way, because he already had indicated some current topics and I proposed another that seemed more immediate: the curfew.

He gave me no orientation. My intention was to recount the adventure of my first night in Cartagena, which is what I did, in my own hand, because I could not manage the prehistoric typewriters in the newsroom. It took almost four hours to produce, and the maestro revised it in front of me without any expression that would reveal his thinking, until he found the least bitter way to tell me:

"It's not bad, but publishing it is impossible."

I was not surprised. On the contrary, I had foreseen it, and for a few minutes I was relieved of the unpleasant burden of being a journalist. But his real reasons, which I did not know, were conclusive: since April 9, in every newspaper in the country, beginning at six in the evening, a government censor installed himself at a desk in the newsroom as if he were in his own house, with the intention and the power not to authorize a single letter that might interfere with public order.

Zabala's motives weighed on me much more than the government's, because I had written not a press commentary but a subjective recounting of a personal incident with no pretensions to editorial journalism. Further, I had treated the curfew not as a legitimate instrument of the state but as the pretext for ignorant police officers to obtain cigarettes for a centavo each. It was my good fortune that before condemning me to death, Maestro Zabala returned the article, which I had to rewrite from top to bottom, not for him but for the censor, and he had the charity to pronounce a two-edged verdict.

"It has literary merit, there's no question," he said. "But we'll talk about that later."

That is how he was. From my first day at the paper, when Zabala conversed with me and with Zapata Olivella, I was struck by his unusual habit of talking to one while looking in the face of the other as his nails were singed by the burning end of his cigarette. At first this caused an uncomfortable insecurity in me. The least foolish thing that occurred to me, out of sheer timidity, was to listen to him with real attention and enormous interest, and not look at him but at Manuel in order to draw my own conclusions from both of them. Afterward, when we spoke with Rojas Herazo, and then with the publisher López Escauriaza, and with so many others, I realized it was Zabala's own method for conversing in a group. I understood it in this way, and in this way he and I could exchange ideas and feelings through unwary accomplices and innocent intermediaries. With the confidence of many years I dared to tell him about this impression of mine, and he explained with no surprise that he looked at the other person almost in profile so as not to blow cigarette smoke in his face. That is how he was: I never met anyone with so peaceable and reserved a nature, with a temperament as civil as his, because he always knew how to be what he wanted to be: a wise man in the shadows.

In reality, I had written speeches, premature verses at the *liceo* in Zipaquirá, patriotic proclamations, petitions to protest the bad food, and very little else, not counting the letters to my family that my mother would send back with the spelling corrected even when I had been recognized as a writer. The piece that at last was published on the editorial page had nothing to do with the one I had written. Between the emendations of Maestro Zabala and those of the censor, what remained of mine were some scraps of lyrical prose lacking discernment or style and finished off by the grammatical sectarianism of the proofreader. At the last minute we agreed on a daily column, perhaps to delimit responsibilities, with my complete name and a permanent title: "Period. New Paragraph."

Zabala and Rojas Herazo, already accustomed to the daily grind, managed to console me for my disheartening first article, and so I dared to follow it with a second and a third, which were no better. I stayed in the newsroom for almost two years, publishing as many as two daily articles that I managed to get past the censorship, signed and unsigned, until I was ready to marry the censor's niece.

I still ask myself what my life would have been without the pencil of Maestro Zabala and the tourniquet of censorship, whose mere existence was a creative challenge. But the censor was more on his guard than we were because of his delusions of persecution. Citations from great authors seemed like suspicious ambushes to him, which in fact they often were. He saw phantoms. He was a second-rate student of Cervantes who inferred imaginary meanings. One night, under his unlucky star, he had to go to the toilet every quarter of an hour until he dared to tell us he was going crazy because of the shocks we caused him.

"Damn it!" he shouted. "With these runs I won't have an asshole left!"

The police had been militarized as another demonstration of the government's severity in the political violence that was bleeding the country, though there was a certain degree of moderation on the Atlantic coast. But at the beginning of May, without reasons either good or bad, the police harassed a procession on the streets of Carmen de Bolívar, about twenty leagues from Cartagena. I had a sentimental weakness for the town, where my Aunt Mama had grown up and where my grandfather Nicolás had invented his celebrated little fish of gold. With unusual determination Maestro Zabala, who had been born in the neighboring town of San Jacinto, gave me editorial management of the news item without regard for censorship and with all its consequences. My first unsigned article on the editorial page demanded that the government hold a thorough investigation of the aggression and punish those responsible. And it ended with a question: "What happened in Carmen de Bolívar?" Faced with official scorn, and now in open warfare with censorship, we continued repeating the question with growing energy in a daily article on the same page, prepared to make the government much more irascible than it already was. After three days, the publisher of the paper verified with Zabala that he had consulted the entire editorial staff and agreed that we ought to continue with the subject. And so we continued asking the question. In the meantime, the only thing we heard from the government reached us through a leak: they had given orders to leave us alone with our lunatics-at-large subject until we ran out of steam. It was not easy, because the question we asked every day was already on the street as a popular greeting: "Hey, brother, what happened in Carmen de Bolívar?"

One night when we least expected it, without any announcement, an army patrol closed Calle de San Juan de Dios with a huge clamor of voices and weapons, and Colonel Jaime Polanía Puyo, commander of the militarized police, strode into the building of *El Universal*. He wore the meringue-white uniform used on important occasions, and patent leather gaiters, and his sword was tied with a silken cord, and his buttons and insignias were so brilliant they looked like gold. In no way was he unworthy of his reputation for elegance and charm, though we knew he was a hard man in peace and in war, as he demonstrated years later at the head of the Colombia battalion in the Korean War. No one moved in the two intense hours he spoke behind closed doors to the publisher. They drank twenty-two cups of black coffee, without cigarettes or alcohol because both men were free of vices. When he left, the colonel seemed even larger as he said goodbye to us one by one. He took a little longer with me, looked straight into my eyes with his lynx's eyes, and said:

"You'll go far."

My heart skipped a beat, thinking that perhaps he already knew all about me and that for him the farthest I could go might be death. In the confidential report that the publisher made to Zabala about his conversation with the colonel, he revealed that Polanía Puyo knew the given and family names of the person who wrote each daily article. The publisher, in a gesture very typical of his nature, told him that they were written on his orders, and that on newspapers, as in barracks, orders were obeyed. In any event, the colonel advised the publisher to have us moderate the campaign in case some barbarian caveman wanted to impose justice in the name of his government. The publisher understood, and we all understood even what he left unsaid. What most surprised the publisher were the colonel's boasts that he knew the internal life of the paper as if he lived there. No one doubted that his secret agent was the censor, who swore on his dead mother that he was not. The only thing the colonel did not try to answer on his visit was our daily question. The publisher, who had a reputation for wisdom, advised us to believe everything we had been told, because the truth might be worse.

After I became involved in the war against censorship, I had nothing to do with the university or with writing stories. It was just as well that most of the teachers did not take attendance, which encouraged missing class. Besides, the liberal teachers who knew about my evasions of censorship suffered more than I did as they looked for a way to help me on examinations. Today, trying to recount those days, I do not find them in my recollection, and I have come to believe more in forgetting than in memory.

My parents rested easy after I let them know that at the paper I earned enough to live on. It was not true. The monthly salary for an apprentice did not last a week. Before three months had passed I left the hotel with an unpayable debt that the landlady later traded for a note on the society page about her granddaughter's fifteenth birthday. But she agreed to the exchange only once.

The most crowded and coolest bedroom in the city continued to be the Paseo de los Mártires, even with the curfew. I would stay there and doze sitting up when the late-night *tertulias* had ended. At other times I slept in the newspaper storeroom on rolls of paper, or appeared with my circus hammock under my arm in the rooms of other judicious students and stayed for as long as they could stand my nightmares and my bad habit of talking in my sleep. In this way I survived by luck and chance, eating whatever there happened to be and sleeping wherever God willed, until the humanitarian tribe of the Franco Múnera family proposed giving me two meals a day for a compassionate price. The father of the tribe—Bolívar Franco—was a historic primary-school teacher, with a joyful, fanatical family of artists and writers who obliged me to eat more than I had paid them for so my brains would not dry up. Often I had no money, but they took consolation in recitations after the meal. I paid frequent installments in that inspiring transaction with the stanzas of variable long and short lines written by Don Jorge Manrique on the death of his father, and the *Gypsy Ballads* of García Lorca.

The open-air brothels on the broad beaches of Tesca, far from the disturbing silence behind the wall, were more hospitable than the tourist hotels along the shore. Half a dozen of us, students at the university, settled down at El Cisne in the early evening to prepare for final exams under the blinding lights of the courtyard for dancing. The ocean breeze and the bellow of the ships at dawn consoled us for the blare of Caribbean brass and the provocations of the girls who danced without panties in very wide skirts so that the ocean breeze would blow them up above their waists. From time to time some little bird nostalgic for her papá would invite us to sleep with the little bit of love she had left at dawn. One of them, whose name and measurements I remember very well, let herself be seduced by the fantasies I recounted while I was asleep. Thanks to her I passed Roman law without any trickery, and escaped several roundups when the police prohibited sleeping in the parks. We got along like a serviceable married couple, not only in bed but in domestic chores, which I did for her at dawn so that she could sleep a few hours longer.

By then I was beginning to adjust very well to editorial work, which I always considered more a form of literature than of journalism. Bogotá was a nightmare of the past, two hundred leagues away and more than two thousand meters above sea level, about which I remembered only the stench of the ashes on April 9. I still had the fever of arts and letters, above all in midnight *tertulias*, but I was beginning to lose my enthusiasm for being a writer. This was so true that I did not write another story after the three published in *El Espectador* until Eduardo Zalamea found me early in July and asked me, with the mediation of Maestro Zabala, to send him another one for his paper after six months of silence. Because the request came from the person it came from, I picked up in haphazard fashion ideas that had been mislaid in my rough drafts and wrote "Death's Other Rib," which was a little more of the same thing. I remember very well that I had no plot prepared and invented it as I was writing. It was published on July 25, 1948, in the "Fin de Semana" supplement, just as the others had been, and I wrote no more stories until the following year, when my life was no longer the same. I needed only to renounce the few law classes I still attended on occasion, but they were my last alibi for maintaining my parents' dream.

I did not suspect at the time that I would soon be a better student than ever in the library of Gustavo Ibarra Merlano, a new friend introduced to me with great enthusiasm by Zabala and Rojas Herazo. He had just returned from Bogotá with a degree from Normal Superior, and without delay he joined the *tertulias* at *El Universal* and the discussions at dawn on the Paseo de los Mártires. Between the volcanic loquacity of Héctor and the creative skepticism of Zabala, Gustavo brought me the systematic rigor that my improvised and scattered ideas, and the frivolity of my heart, were in real need of. And all that with great tenderness and an iron character.

The next day he invited me to his parents' house on the Marbella beach, with the immense sea as a backyard, and a new, well-ordered library along a twelve-meter wall, where only the books you had to read in order to live without regrets were kept. He had editions of the Greek, Latin, and Spanish classics in such good condition they did not seem to have been read, but scribbled in the margins were learned notes, some of them in Latin. Gustavo also said them aloud, and when he did he blushed to the roots of his hair and tried to get around them with a corrosive humor. A friend had told me before I met him: "The guy's a priest." I soon understood why this was easy to believe, though after I knew him well it was almost impossible to believe he was not.

That first time we talked without stopping until the small hours, and I learned that his readings were long and varied but sustained by a thorough knowledge of the Catholic intellectuals of the day, whom I had never heard of. He knew everything that one should know about poetry, in particular the Greek and Latin classics, which he read in their original versions. He had well-informed opinions of our mutual friends and gave me valuable information that made me love them even more. He also confirmed the importance of my meeting the three journalists from Barranquilla—Cepeda, Vargas, and Fuenmayor—about whom Rojas Herazo and Maestro Zabala had spoken so often. I found it remarkable that in addition to having so many intellectual and civic virtues, he swam like an Olympic champion and had a body trained to be one. What concerned him most about me was my dangerous contempt for the Greek and Latin classics, which seemed boring and useless to me, except for the *Odyssey*, which I had read and reread in bits and pieces several times at the *liceo*. And so before we said goodbye, he chose a leather-bound book from the library and handed it to me with a certain solemnity. "You may become a good writer," he said, "but you'll never become very good if you don't have a good knowledge of the Greek classics." The book was the complete works of Sophocles. From that moment on Gustavo was one of the decisive beings in my life, for *Oedipus Rex* revealed itself to me on first reading as the perfect work.

It was a historic night because I had discovered Gustavo Ibarra and Sophocles at the same time, and because hours later

I could have died an awful death in the room of my secret girlfriend at El Cisne. I remember as if it had happened yesterday when a former lover of hers, whom she had thought dead for over a year, kicked down the door of her room, shouting a wild man's insults. I recognized him at once as a fellow student at the primary school in Aracataca who had come back in a rage to take possession of his bed. We had not seen each other since then, and he had the good taste to pretend not to notice when he recognized me, naked and muddied with terror, in the bed.

That year I also met Ramiro and Oscar de la Espriella, endless conversationalists, above all in houses prohibited by Christian morality. They both lived with their parents in Turbaco, an hour from Cartagena, and they showed up almost every day at the *tertulias* of writers and artists at the Americana ice cream parlor. Ramiro, a graduate of the faculty of law in Bogotá, was very close to the group at *El Universal*, where he published an occasional column. His father was a formidable lawyer and a freewheeling Liberal, and his mother was charming and outspoken. They both had the admirable custom of conversing with young people. In our long talks under the leafy ash trees of Turbaco, they offered invaluable information about the War of a Thousand Days, the literary source that had been extinguished for me with the death of my grandfather. To her I owe the view that seems most reliable to me, and the one I still have, of General Rafael Uribe Uribe, from his respectable elegance to the caliber of his wrists.

The best testimony to what Ramiro and I were like in those days was created in oils on canvas by the painter Cecilia Porras, who felt right at home at men's wild parties, in defiance of the prudery of her social milieu. It was a portrait of the two of us sitting at the table in the café where we would see her and other friends twice a day. When Ramiro and I were about to go our separate ways, we had an irreconcilable argument about who owned the painting. Cecilia resolved it with the Solomonic formula of cutting the canvas in half with pruning shears and giving each of us our part. Years later mine was left rolled up in the closet of an apartment in Caracas, and I never could get it back.

In contrast to the rest of the country, official violence had not ravaged Cartagena until the beginning of that year, when our friend Carlos Alemán was elected deputy to the Departmental Assembly by the very distinguished district of Mompox. He was an attorney fresh out of the oven, and very good-natured, but the devil played a bad joke on him in the opening session when the two rival parties opened fire on each other and a stray bullet scorched his shoulder pad. Alemán must have thought, and with reason, that a legislative power as useless as ours did not deserve the sacrifice of a life, and he preferred to spend his government salary in advance in the good company of his friends.

Oscar de la Espriella, who was a sterling carouser, agreed with William Faulkner that a brothel is the best residence for a writer, because the mornings are quiet, there is a party every night, and you are on good terms with the police. Deputy Alemán took this in a literal way and made himself our full-time host. One night, however, I repented of having believed in Faulkner's illusions when an old boyfriend of Mary Reyes, the madam of the house, knocked down the door to take away their son, a child of five, who lived with her. Her current boyfriend, who had been a police officer, came out of the bedroom in his shorts to defend the honor and goods of the house with his regulation revolver, and the other man greeted him with a burst of gunfire that resounded in the dance hall like a shot from a cannon. The frightened sergeant hid in his room. When I came out of mine, half dressed, the transient tenants were contemplating the boy from their rooms as he urinated at the end of the hallway, while his papá smoothed his hair with his left hand and held the still-smoking revolver in his right. All you could hear in the house were Mary's insults as she reproached the sergeant for not having any balls.

During this same time a gigantic man came into the offices of *El Universal* unannounced, removed his shirt with a great sense of theater, and walked around the newsroom to surprise us with the sight of his back and arms mottled with scars that seemed to be of cement. Moved by the astonishment he had inspired in us, he explained the devastation of his body in a thundering voice:

"Lions' claws!"

It was Emilio Razzore, who had just arrived in Cartagena to prepare for the performance season of his famous family circus, one of the great ones in the world. It had left Havana the week before on the steamship *Euskera*, of Spanish registry, and it was expected the following Saturday. Razzore boasted of having been in the circus since before he was born, and you did not need to see him perform to know he was a wild-animal tamer. He called the beasts by their first names as if they were members of his family, and they responded with behavior that was affectionate and brutal at the same time. He would go unarmed into the cages of tigers and lions and feed them out of his hand. His pet bear had given him a loving hug that kept him in the hospital for one entire spring. The great attraction, however, was not Razzore or the fire-eater, but the man who screwed off his head and walked around the ring holding it under his arm. The least forgettable thing about Emilio Razzore was his indomitable nature. After listening to him, fascinated, for many long hours, I published an editorial in *El Universal* in which I dared to write that he was "the most tremendously human man I have ever met." At the age of twenty-one there had not been that many, but I believe the phrase is still valid. We ate at La Cueva with the people from the paper, and he was cherished there, too, with his tales of wild animals humanized by love. On one of those nights, after thinking about it a good deal, I dared to ask him to take me into his circus, even if it was to wash out the cages when the tigers were not inside. He did not say anything but gave me his hand in silence. I understood this as a secret circus gesture, and I considered it done. The only person I told was Salvador Mesa Nicholls, a poet from Antioquia with a mad love for the circus who had just come to Cartagena as a local partner of the Razzores. He too had gone away with a circus when he was my age, and he warned me that those who see clowns cry for the first time want to go away with them but regret it the next day. Yet he not only approved of my decision but convinced the tamer, on the condition we keep it a complete secret so that it would not become news too early. Waiting for the circus, which until then had been exciting, now became irresistible.

The *Euskera* did not arrive on the anticipated date and it had been impossible to communicate with her. After a week we established from the newspaper offices a system of ham radio operators to track weather conditions in the Caribbean, but we could not prevent the beginning of speculation in the press and on the radio about the possibility of horrifying news. Mesa Nicholls and I spent those intense days with Emilio Razzore in his hotel room, not eating or sleeping. We saw him collapse, diminishing in volume and size during the interminable wait, until all our hearts confirmed that the *Euskera* would never arrive anywhere, and there would be no report on what had happened to her. The animal tamer spent another day alone in his room, and the next day he visited me at the paper to say that a hundred years of daily struggle could not disappear in a single day. And so he was going to Miami with not even a nail and without a family to rebuild piece by piece, and starting with nothing, the shipwrecked circus. I was so struck by his determination in spite of the tragedy that I accompanied him to Barranquilla to see him off on the plane to Florida. Before he boarded he thanked me for my decision to join his circus, and he promised he would send for me as soon as he had something concrete. He said goodbye with so heartbreaking an embrace that I understood with my soul the love his lions had for him. I never heard from him again.

The Miami plane took off at ten in the morning on the same day that my editorial on Razzore appeared: September 16, 1948. I was preparing to return to Cartagena that same afternoon when it occurred to me to stop by *El Nacional*, an evening paper where Germán Vargas and Álvaro Cepeda, the friends of my friends in Cartagena, were working. The newsroom was in a decayed building in the old city, a long, empty room divided by a wooden railing. At the back of the room a young blond man in shirtsleeves was typing on a machine whose keys exploded like bombs in the deserted room. I approached almost on tiptoe, intimidated by the mournful creaking of the floor, and I waited at the railing until he turned to look at me, and in a curt way, in the harmonious voice of a professional announcer, he said:

"What is it?"

He had short hair, strong cheekbones, and clear, intense eyes that seemed annoyed by the interruption. I answered the best I could, letter by letter:

"I'm García Márquez."

Only when I heard my own name spoken with so much conviction did I realize that Germán Vargas might not know who I was, though in Cartagena they had said they talked about me a good deal with their friends in Barranquilla after they read my first story. *El Nacional* had published an enthusiastic note by Germán Vargas, who was not easy to fool when it came to new literature. But the enthusiasm with which he received me confirmed that he knew very well who I was, and his affection was more real than I had been told. A few hours later I met Alfonso Fuenmayor and Álvaro Cepeda in the Librería Mundo, and we had drinks at the Café Colombia. Don Ramón Vinyes, the learned Catalan whom I longed to meet and was terrified of meeting, had not come to the six o'clock *tertulia* that afternoon. When we left the Café Colombia, with five drinks under our belts, we had been friends for years.

It was a long night of innocence. Álvaro, an inspired driver who became more certain and prudent the more he drank, followed the itinerary for memorable occasions. In Los Almendros, an open-air tavern under the flowering trees where they only admitted fans of the Deportivo Junior team, several patrons were involved in an argument that was about to come to blows. I tried to calm them down until Alfonso advised me not to intervene because in that place filled with doctors of soccer, things did not go well for pacifists. And so I spent the night in a city that was not the one it had always been for me, or the one of my parents in their early years, or the one of poverty-stricken times with my mother, or the one of Colegio San José, but my first time in Barranquilla as an adult, in the paradise of its brothels.

The red-light district was four blocks of metallic music that made the earth tremble, but they also had domestic corners that came very close to charity. There were family brothels whose owners, with their wives and children, tended to their veteran clients according to the norms of Don Manuel Antonio Carreño's Christian morality and urbanity. Some served as guarantors so that apprentices would go to bed on credit with known clients. Martina Alvarado, the oldest brothel, had a furtive door and humanitarian rates for repentant clerics. There were no hidden charges, no doctored accounts, no venereal surprises. The last French madams from the First World War, ailing and melancholy, sat in the doors of their houses under the stigma of red lightbulbs, waiting for a third generation who still believed in their aphrodisiac condoms. There were houses with cooled rooms for clandestine meetings of conspirators and sanctuaries for mayors fleeing their wives.

El Gato Negro, with a courtyard for dancing under a bower of crape myrtle, had been the paradise of the merchant fleet ever since its purchase by a bleached-blond Guajiran who sang in English and sold her hallucinogenic pomades for ladies and gentlemen under the table. On a historic night in the house's annals, Álvaro Cepeda and Quique Scopell could not endure the racism of a dozen Norwegian sailors who stood in line outside the room of the only black girl while sixteen white girls sat snoring in the courtyard, and they challenged the sailors to a fight. By dint of their fists the two forced the twelve to flee, with the help of the white girls who were happy when they woke and finished the job by hitting the sailors with their chairs. In the end, in a lunatic act of indemnification, they crowned the naked black girl queen of Norway.

Outside the red-light district there were other houses, legal or clandestine, and all on good terms with the police. One was a courtyard of large flowering almond trees in a poor district, with a dilapidated shop and a bedroom with two cots for rent. The merchandise consisted of two anemic girls from the neighborhood who earned a peso at a time with confirmed drunkards. Álvaro Cepeda discovered the place by accident one afternoon when he was caught in an October downpour and took refuge in the shop. The owner invited him to have a beer, and she offered him two girls instead of one with a right to repeat until the weather cleared. Álvaro continued inviting his friends to drink ice-cold beer under the almond trees, not to go to bed with the girls but to teach them to read. He obtained scholarships for the most diligent to study at state schools. One of them had been a nurse at the Hospital de Caridad for years. He made the owner a present of the house, and until its natural extinction, the ramshackle kindergarten had an enticing name: "The house with the little girls who go to bed because they're hungry."

For my first historic night in Barranquilla they chose the house of La Negra Eufemia that had an enormous cement courtyard for dancing surrounded by leafy tamarind trees, with cabanas for five pesos an hour and little tables and chairs painted bright colors and curlews wandering as they pleased. Eufemia in person, monumental and almost a hundred years old, greeted and selected clients at the entrance, behind an office desk whose only implement—inexplicable—was an enormous church nail. She chose the girls herself for their good manners and natural graces. Each one took whatever name she liked, and some preferred the ones that Álvaro Cepeda, with his passion for Mexican movies, gave them: Irma the Wicked, Susana the Perverse, Midnight Virgin.

It seemed impossible to have a conversation with an ecstatic Caribbean orchestra playing the new mambos of Pérez Prado at top volume, and a group that played boleros for forgetting bad memories, but we were all expert in shouting our conversations. The night's topic, brought up by Germán and Álvaro, had to do with the ingredients common to the novel and feature articles. They were enthusiastic about the one John Hersey had published about the dropping of the atomic bomb on Hiroshima, but I preferred the direct reportorial testimony of *Journal of the Plague Year,* until the others explained to me that Daniel Defoe had been no more than five or six years old during the plague in London, which served as his model.

By this path we came to the enigma of *The Count of Monte Cristo,* which the three of them had carried over from previous discussions as a riddle for novelists: how did Alexandre Dumas manage to have a sailor who was innocent, ignorant, poor, and imprisoned without cause, escape an impenetrable fortress transformed into the richest and most cultivated man of his time? The answer was that when Edmund Dantès entered the castle of If he already had constructed inside him the Abbot Faria, who transmitted to him in prison the essence of his knowledge and revealed what he needed to know for his new life: the place where a fantastic treasure was hidden, and the way to escape. That is: Dumas constructed two different characters and then switched their destinies. So that when Dantès escaped he was already one character inside another, and all that was left of himself was his good swimmer's body.

It was clear to Germán that Dumas had made his character a sailor so that he could escape from the burlap sack and swim to shore when they threw him into the sea. Álvaro, erudite and no doubt more caustic, replied that this was no guarantee of anything because sixty percent of Christopher Columbus's crews did not know how to swim. Nothing pleased him as much as sprinkling those grains of pepper to rid the stew of any aftertaste of pedantry. Carried away by the game of literary enigmas, I began to drink without moderation the cane rum with lemon that the others were drinking in slow sips. The conclusion of all three was that the talent and handling of information by Dumas in that novel, and perhaps in all his work, was more a reporter's than a novelist's.

In the end it was clear to me that my new friends read Quevedo and James Joyce with the same pleasure they derived from reading Arthur Conan Doyle. They had an inexhaustible sense of humor and were capable of spending whole nights singing boleros and *vallenatos* or reciting without hesitation the best poetry of the Golden Age. By different paths we came to agree that the summit of world poetry are the stanzas of Don Jorge Manrique on the death of his father. The night turned into a delicious entertainment that did away with any last prejudices that could have hindered my friendship with this band of learned maniacs. I felt so comfortable with them and the barbarous rum that I took off the straitjacket of my shyness. Susana the Perverse, who in March of that year had won the dance contest during Carnival, asked me to dance. They shooed the chickens and curlews away from the floor and stood in a circle around us to encourage us.

We danced the series of Dámaso Pérez Prado's *Mambo No. 5*. With the breath I had left I took over the maracas on the tropical group's platform and for more than an hour I sang without stopping boleros of Daniel Santos, Agustín Lara, and Bienvenido Granda. As I sang I felt redeemed by a wind of liberation. I never knew if the three of them were proud or ashamed of me, but when I went back to the table they greeted me as one of their own.

Álvaro had begun a topic that the others never discussed with him: the movies. For me it was a providential discovery, because I always had considered movies a subsidiary art nourished more by the theater than the novel. But Álvaro viewed film, in a sense, as I viewed music: as an art that was useful to all the others.

At dawn, when he was both sleepy and drunk, Álvaro drove the car crammed with recent books and literary supplements of the *New York Times* as if he were a master cab driver. We dropped Germán and Alfonso at their houses, and Álvaro insisted on taking me to his to see his library, which covered three walls, floor to ceiling, of his bedroom. He made a complete turn, pointing at them with his index finger, and said:

"These are the only writers in the world who know how to write."

I was in a state of excitement that made me forget what yesterday had been hunger and fatigue. The alcohol was still alive inside me like a state of grace. Álvaro showed me his favorite books, in Spanish and English, and he spoke of each one with his rusty voice, his disheveled hair, his eyes more demented than ever. He spoke of Azorín and Saroyan—two weaknesses of his—and of others whose public and private lives he knew down to their underwear. It was the first time I heard the name of Virginia Woolf, whom he called Old Lady Woolf, like Old Man Faulkner. My amazement inspired him to the point of delirium. He seized the pile of books he had shown me as his favorites and placed them in my hands.

"Don't be an asshole," he said, "take them all, and when you finish reading them we'll come get them no matter where you are."

For me they were an inconceivable treasure that I did not dare put at risk when I did not have even a miserable hole where I could keep them. At last he resigned himself to giving me the Spanish version of Virginia Woolf's *Mrs. Dalloway*, with the unappealable prediction that I would learn it by heart.

Day was breaking. I wanted to go back to Cartagena on the first bus, but Álvaro insisted that I sleep in the other twin bed.

"What the hell!" he said with his last bit of strength. "Come live here and tomorrow we'll find you a fabulous job."

I lay down in my clothes on the bed, and only then did I feel in my body the immense weight of being alive. He did the same and we slept until eleven in the morning, when his mother, the adored and feared Sara Samudio, knocked on the door with a clenched fist, believing that the only child of her life was dead.

"Don't pay attention to her, Maestro," Álvaro said to me from the depths of sleep. "Every morning she says the same thing, and the serious part is that one day it'll be true."

I went back to Cartagena with the air of someone who had discovered the world. Then the recitations after meals in the house of the Franco Múnera family were not poems of the Golden Age and Neruda's *Twenty Love Poems*, but paragraphs from *Mrs. Dalloway* and the ravings of its heartbreaking character, Septimus Warren Smith. I turned into another person, restless and difficult, to the point where Héctor and Maestro Zabala thought I had become a conscious imitator of Álvaro Cepeda. Gustavo Ibarra, with his compassionate vision of the Caribbean heart, was amused by my tale of the night in Barranquilla, while he gave me more and more rational spoonfuls of Greek poets, with the express and never-explained exception of Euripides. He introduced me to Melville: the literary feat of *Moby-Dick*, the magnificent sermon about Jonah for whalers weathered on all the oceans of the world under the immense dome constructed with the ribs of whales. He lent me Nathaniel Hawthorne's *The House of the Seven Gables*, which marked me for life. Together we attempted a theory of the fatality of nostalgia in the wanderings of Ulysses Odysseus, where we became lost and never found our way out. Half a century later I discovered it resolved in a masterful text by Milan Kundera.

During this same period I had my sole encounter with the great poet Luis Carlos López, better known as El Tuerto, or One-eye, who had invented a comfortable way of being dead without dying, and buried without a funeral, and above all without orations. He lived in the historic center in a historic house on the historic Calle del Tablón, where he was born and lived without disturbing anyone. He saw a very few old friends, while his reputation for being a great poet continued to grow in his lifetime as only posthumous glory grows.

They called him one-eyed even though he was not, because in reality he was only cross-eyed, but in an unusual way that was very difficult to characterize. His brother, Domingo López Escauriaza, the publisher of *El Universal*, always had the same answer for those who asked about him:

"He's there."

It seemed an evasion, but it was the only truth: he was there. More alive than anyone else, but also with the advantage of being alive without anyone finding out too much, aware of everything, and determined to walk to his own funeral. People spoke of him as if he were a historical relic, in particular those who had not read him. In fact, since my arrival in Cartagena I had not tried to see him, out of respect for his privileges as an invisible man. At the time he was sixty-eight years old, and no one had any doubt that he was a great poet for the ages, though there were not many of us who knew who he was or why, and it was not easy to believe because of the rare quality of his work.

Zabala, Rojas Herazo, Gustavo Ibarra: we all knew poems of his by heart and always quoted them without thinking, in a spontaneous and knowledgeable way, to illuminate our conversations. He was not unsociable but shy. Even today I do not remember having seen a portrait of him, if there was one, only some quick caricatures that were published instead. I believe that because we did not see him we had forgotten he was still alive, and one night when I was finishing my piece for the day, I heard a stifled exclamation from Zabala:

"Damn, it's El Tuerto!"

I looked up from the typewriter and saw the strangest man I would ever see. Much shorter than we had imagined, with hair so white it looked blue and so unruly it looked borrowed. His left eye was not missing, but as his nickname indicated, it was crossed.* He dressed as if he were at home, in dark drill trousers and a striped shirt, his right hand, at the height of his shoulder, holding a silver holder with a lit cigarette that he did not smoke and whose ash fell without tapping when it could no longer hold on by itself.

He walked through to his brother's office and came out two hours later, when only Zabala and I were left in the newsroom, waiting to greet him. He died two years later, and the upheaval it caused among the faithful seemed to be not because he had died but because he had been resuscitated. On view in his coffin he did not appéar as dead as when he was alive.

During the same period the Spanish writer Dámaso Alonso and his wife, the novelist Eulalia Galvarriato, gave two lectures in the main auditorium of the university. Maestro Zabala, who did not like to disturb anyone's life, for once overcame his circumspection and requested a meeting. Gustavo Ibarra, Héctor Rojas Herazo, and I accompanied him, and there was an immediate chemistry with them. We stayed some four hours in a private meeting room in the Hotel del Caribe, exchanging impressions of their first trip to Latin America and our dreams as new writers. Héctor brought them a book of poems, and I had a photocopy of a story published in *El Espectador*. What interested both of us most was the frankness of their reservations, because they used them as oblique confirmations of their praise.

In October I found a message from Gonzalo Mallarino at *El Universal* saying that he was waiting for me, with the poet Álvaro Mutis, in Villa Tulipán, an unforgettable *pensión* in the beach resort of Bocagrande, a few meters from the place where Charles Lindbergh had landed some twenty years earlier. Gonzalo, my accomplice in private recitations at the university, was

---

*In addition to "one-eyed," the word *tuerto* also means "twisted," "crooked," or "bent."

already a practicing attorney, and in his capacity as head of public relations for LANSA, a national airline founded by its own pilots, Mutis had invited him so to see the ocean.

Poems by Mutis and stories of mine had coincided at least once in "Fin de Semana," and it was enough for us to see each other to begin a conversation that is still going on, in countless places in the world, after more than half a century. First our children and then our grandchildren have often asked us what we talk about with such fierce passion, and we tell them the truth: we always talk about the same thing.

My miraculous friendships with adults in arts and letters gave me the courage to survive those years, which I still remember as the most uncertain of my life. On July 10 I had published the last "Period. New Paragraph" in *El Universal*, after three arduous months in which I could not overcome the obstacles of being a novice, and I preferred to stop writing it, the sole merit being that I would escape in time. I took refuge in the impunity of commentaries on the editorial page, unsigned except when they needed a personal touch. I kept this up through sheer routine until September 1950, with a pompous note on Edgar Allan Poe, its sole merit being that it was the worst of them.

During all that year I had persisted in asking Maestro Zabala to teach me the secrets of writing feature articles. He never decided to, given his mysterious nature, but he left me troubled by the enigma of a twelve-year-old girl, buried in the Convent of Santa Clara, whose hair grew after her death, more than twenty meters in two centuries. I never imagined I would return to this subject forty years later and recount it in a romantic novel with sinister implications. But these were not my best days for thinking. I had fits of rage for any reason at all, and would disappear from work with no explanations until Maestro Zabala sent someone to calm me down. I passed the final exams of the second year of law by a stroke of luck, with only two subjects to make up, and I was able to matriculate for the third year, but a rumor circulated that I had achieved this through political pressure from the paper. The publisher had to intervene when I was stopped coming out of the movies carrying a false record of military service, and I was on the list to be sent on punitive missions to enforce public order.

In my political obfuscation at the time, I did not even know that martial law had been reimposed in the country because of the increase in lawlessness. Press censorship was tightened a few more turns. The atmosphere rarefied as it did in the worst times, and a political police reinforced with common criminals sowed panic in the countryside. The violence obliged Liberals to abandon lands and homes. Their possible candidate, Darío Echandía, the teacher of teachers of civil law, a born skeptic and habitual reader of Greek and Latin authors, pronounced in favor of a Liberal abstention at the polls. The way was open for the election of Laureano Gómez, who seemed to direct the government from New York with invisible strings.

I did not have a clear awareness then that these misfortunes were not only the infamies of the Goths but symptoms of evil changes in our lives, until one of many nights at La Cueva, when it occurred to me to boast about my freedom to do whatever I wished. Maestro Zabala held in midair the spoonful of soup he was about to eat, looking at me over the arch of his eyeglasses, and stopped me cold:

"Just tell me one thing, Gabriel: in the midst of all the damn fool things you do, have you been able to realize that this country is coming to an end?"

The question hit its mark. I was dead drunk when I lay down at dawn to sleep on a bench on the Paseo de los Mártires, and a biblical downpour left me soaked to the skin. I spent two weeks in the hospital with a pneumonia resistant to the first known antibiotics, which had a bad reputation for causing side effects as terrifying as premature impotence. I was more skeletal and pale than I was by nature, and my parents called me back to Sucre to help me recuperate from an excess of work—as they said in their letter. *El Universal* went even further, with a farewell editorial that sanctified me as a journalist and writer of masterful talents, and another that cited me as the author of a novel that never existed and with a title that was not mine: *We've Already Cut the Hay*. Even stranger at a time when I had no intention of backsliding into fiction. The truth is that this title, so alien to me, was invented by Héctor Rojas Herazo while he was typing, as one more contribution from César Guerra Valdés, an imaginary writer of the purest Latin American stock created by him to enrich our polemics. Héctor had published news of his arrival in Cartagena in *El Universal*, and I had written him a greeting in "Period. New Paragraph" in the hope of shaking the dust from the dormant awareness of an authentic continental narrative. In any case, the imaginary novel with the beautiful title invented by Héctor was reviewed years later in an essay on my books, I do not know where or why, as a fundamental work of the new literature.

The atmosphere I found in Sucre was very favorable to my ideas at the time. I wrote to Germán Vargas and asked him to send me books, lots of books, as many as possible so that I could drown a predicted convalescence of six months in masterpieces. The town was inundated. Papá had renounced the slavery of the pharmacy, and at the entrance to town he had built a house large enough for his children, who numbered eleven after the birth of Eligio sixteen months earlier. A large house full of light, with a terrace for visitors overlooking the river of dark water, and windows opened to the January breezes. It had six well-ventilated bedrooms with a bed for each person— not shared, as before—and hooks for hanging hammocks at different levels, even in the hallways. The courtyard had no wire fence, and it extended all the way to uncut woods with fruit trees in the public domain, and animals belonging to the family and to other people strolled through the bedrooms. My mother, who missed the courtyards of her childhood in Barrancas and Aracataca, treated the new house like a farm, with uncorralled chickens and ducks and libertine pigs who got into the kitchen to eat the food for lunch. It was still possible to take advantage of the summers and sleep with open windows, with the asthmatic sound of the chickens on their perches and the odor of ripe custard apples that fell from the trees at dawn with an instantaneous, dense thud. "They sound like children," my mother would say. My papá reduced his consultations to the morning hours for a few believers in homeopathy, continued reading all the printed paper that came near him as he lay in a hammock that he hung between two trees, and contracted the idle fever of billiards to counter the melancholy of dusk. He had also abandoned his white linen suits with a tie, and he walked on the street as I had never seen him do before, wearing juvenile short-sleeved shirts.

My grandmother Tranquilina Iguarán had died two months earlier, blind and deranged, and in the lucidity of her death agony she continued preaching the family's secrets in her radiant voice and perfect diction. Her constant subject until her final breath was my grandfather's retirement. My father prepared the body with preservative aloes and covered it with lime inside the coffin for a gentle decomposition. Luisa Santiaga always marveled at her mother's passion for red roses, and she made her a garden at the back of the courtyard so there would always be enough for her grave. They bloomed with so much splendor that there was not enough time to satisfy the strangers who came from great distances, eager to know if so many magnificent roses were the work of God or the devil.

Changes in my life and temperament corresponded to changes in my house. On each visit it seemed different to me because of my parents' alterations and transformations on account of my brothers and sisters, who were born and grew up looking so much alike it was easier to confuse them than to recognize them. Jaime, who was already ten, took the longest to leave the maternal lap because he had been three months premature, and my mother was still nursing him when Hernando (Nanchi) was born. Three years later came Alfredo Ricardo (Cuqui), and a year and a half after that Eligio (Yiyo), the last one, who on that vacation was beginning to discover the miracle of crawling.

We also included my father's children before and after his marriage: Carmen Rosa, in San Marcos, and Abelardo, both of whom spent periods of time in Sucre; Germaine Hanai (Emi), whom my mother had taken in as one of her own with the approval of her other children, and, last of all, Antonio María

Claret (Toño), brought up by his mother in Sincé, who visited us often. A total of fifteen, and we ate like thirty when there was enough, and sat wherever there was room.

The stories that my sisters have told about those years give an exact idea of what it was like in a house where one child had not finished nursing when another was born. My mother herself was conscious of her negligence, and she begged her daughters to take charge of the younger ones. Margot would die of fright when she learned that my mother was pregnant again, because she knew she would not have the time to rear them all. And so before she left for boarding school in Montería, she pleaded with my mother in absolute seriousness to make the next child the last. My mother promised, as she always did, though it was only to please her, because she was certain that God, in His infinite wisdom, would resolve the problem in the best possible fashion.

Meals at the table were disastrous, because there was no way for everyone to eat together. My mother and the older girls would serve as the others came in, but it was not unusual for a stray to wander in late asking for his portion. In the course of the night the younger ones kept going to my parents' bed, unable to sleep because of the cold or the heat, because they had a toothache or were afraid of the dead, because they loved their parents or were jealous of the others, and all of them woke the next morning curled up in the double bed. If others were not born after Eligio it was thanks to Margot, who imposed her authority when she returned from boarding school, and my mother kept her promise not to have another child.

Sad to say, reality had time to interpose other plans for my two oldest sisters, who never married. Aida, as happened in sentimental novels, entered a convent on a life sentence, which she renounced after twenty-two years of meeting every obligation, when she no longer found Rafael or any other man within reach. Margot, with her stern character, lost her Rafael because of an error on both their parts. To counter precedents as sad as these, Rita married the first man she liked, and was happy with five children and nine grandchildren. The other two girls—

Ligia and Emi—married the men they wanted to when my parents had already grown tired of doing battle with real life.

The family's troubles seemed to be part of the crisis the country was going through because of economic uncertainty and the bloodshed of the political violence that had reached Sucre like an ill-fated season and entered the house, on tiptoe but with a firm step. By that time we had already eaten our scant reserves and were as poor as we had been in Barranquilla before the move to Sucre. But my mother did not worry because of her already proven certainty that each child carries his own loaf of bread under his arm. This was the state of the house when I arrived from Cartagena, convalescing from pneumonia, but the family had conspired to keep me from noticing.

The favorite subject of gossip in the town was the supposed relationship between our friend Cayetano Gentile and the schoolteacher in the nearby hamlet of Chaparral, a beautiful girl whose social status was different from his but who was very serious and came from a respectable family. It was not surprising: Cayetano always chased girls, not only in Sucre but also in Cartagena, where he had completed his baccalaureate and begun his study of medicine. But no one had known of any sweetheart in Sucre or even a favorite partner at dances.

One night we saw him coming from his farm on his best horse, the schoolteacher in the saddle holding the reins, and he sitting behind, his arms around her waist. We were surprised not only by the degree of intimacy they had achieved, but by their audacity in entering along the promenade of the main square at the time it was most crowded, and in so evil-minded a town. Cayetano explained to anyone who wished to listen that he had found her at the door of her school waiting for someone kind enough to take her into town at that time of night. I warned him as a joke that he was going to wake up any day now with a *pasquín* on his door, and he shrugged in a typical gesture of his and cracked his favorite joke:

"They don't dare to with the rich."

In fact, the *pasquines* had gone out of fashion as fast as they had come in, and people thought that perhaps they were another symptom of the bad political mood devastating the country. Serenity returned to the sleep of those who had feared them. On the other hand, a few days after my arrival, I felt that something had changed toward me in the minds of certain of my father's fellow party members, who pointed me out as the author of articles against the Conservative government that had been published in *El Universal*. It was not true. If I ever had to write political pieces, they were always unsigned and the responsibility of management after their decision to suspend the question of what had happened in Carmen de Bolívar. The ones in my signed column no doubt revealed a clear position on the sad state of the country, and the ignominy of the violence and injustice, but there were no party slogans. In fact, I was never a member of any party, not then, not ever. The accusation alarmed my parents, and my mother began to light candles to the saints, above all when I stayed out very late. For the first time I felt so oppressive an atmosphere around me that I decided to leave the house as little as possible.

It was during these ugly times that an imposing man who seemed to be the ghost of himself appeared in Papá's office, with a skin that let the color of his bones show through and an abdomen as swollen and tense as a drum. He needed only one sentence to be remembered forever:

"Doctor, they made a monkey grow in my belly and I've come to have you take it out."

After examining him, my father knew the case was beyond the reach of his science, and he sent him to a surgeon who did not find the monkey the patient thought was there but a formless monstrosity with a life of its own. What mattered to me, however, was not the beast in his abdomen but the tale the patient told about the magical world of La Sierpe, a legendary country within the town limits of Sucre that could be reached only through steaming bogs, where it was common practice to avenge an offense with a curse, like having the devil's spawn grow inside your abdomen.

The residents of La Sierpe were devout Catholics but they lived the religion in their own way, with magic prayers for each occasion. They believed in God, in the Virgin, and in the Holy

Trinity, but they worshipped them in any object that they thought revealed divine faculties. What might seem unimaginable to them was that someone who had a satanic beast growing inside his abdomen would be rational enough to have recourse to the heresy of a surgeon.

I was soon amazed to learn that everybody in Sucre knew about the existence of La Sierpe as a real fact, the only problem being getting there past all kinds of geographical and mental obstacles. I happened to discover that the expert on the subject of La Sierpe was my friend Ángel Casij, whom I had last seen when he escorted us through the pestilential rubble of April 9 so that we could communicate with our families. I found him more reasonable than he had been on that occasion, and with a dazzling account of his various trips to La Sierpe. Then I learned all that could be known about La Marquesita, lady and mistress of that vast kingdom, who knew secret prayers for doing good or evil, for raising a dying man from his bed without knowing anything more about him than his physical description and precise location, or for sending a serpent through the swamps so that in six days' time it would kill an enemy.

The only thing forbidden to her was the resurrection of the dead, a power reserved to God. She lived all the years she wished, and it is supposed she reached two hundred thirty-three, but without having aged a single day after sixty-six. Before she died she brought together her fabulous flocks and had them spin around her house for two days and two nights until the swamp of La Sierpe was formed, a limitless expanse hung with phosphorescent anemones. It is said that in the center there is a tree hung with golden gourds, and to its trunk is tied a canoe that every second of November, the Day of the Dead, goes sailing with no one in it to the other shore, guarded by white caimans and snakes wearing golden bells, where La Marquesita buried her unlimited fortune.

After Ángel Casij told me this fantastic story, I began to be plagued by a longing to visit the paradise of La Sierpe mired in reality. We prepared everything, horses immunized by contrary prayers, invisible canoes, magical guides, and everything that might be necessary for writing the chronicle of a supernatural realism.

But the mules were left saddled. My slow convalescence from pneumonia, the mockery of friends at the dances on the square, and the dire warnings of older friends obliged me to put off the trip for a later that never came. Today I recall it, however, as a fortunate misfortune, because lacking the fantastic La Marquesita, I immersed myself the next day in writing a first novel, of which only the title remains: *La casa*.

It was supposed to be a drama about the War of a Thousand Days in the Colombian Caribbean, about which I had talked to Manuel Zapata Olivella on an earlier visit to Cartagena. On that occasion, and with no relation at all to my project, he gave me a pamphlet written by his father about a veteran of that war whose portrait was printed on the cover, and who, with his *liquilique* shirt and his mustache singed by gunpowder, reminded me somehow of my grandfather. I have forgotten his first name, but his surname would stay with me forever after: Buendía. That was why I thought I would write a novel with the title *La casa*, the epic tale of a family that could have in it a good deal of our own history during the sterile wars of Colonel Nicolás Márquez.

The title was based on my intention of never having the action leave the house. I made several starts and partial outlines of characters, to whom I gave family names that I was able to use later in other books. I am very sensitive to the weakness of a sentence in which two words in proximity rhyme, even if the rhyme is assonant, and I prefer not to publish it until I solve the problem. This was why I was often on the verge of dispensing with the name Buendía because of its unavoidable rhyme with verbs in the imperfect tense.* But in the end the name imposed itself because I had achieved a convincing identity for it.

I was involved in this when a wooden crate without painted labels or any other kind of reference appeared one morning at the house in Sucre. My sister Margot accepted it, not know-

---

*In Spanish, many verbs in the imperfect tense have endings based on *-ía*, which would create a rhyme with the name Buendía.

ing from whom, certain it was some leftover from the pharmacy that had been sold. I thought the same thing and had breakfast with the family, my heart in its right place. My papá said he had not opened the crate because he thought it was the rest of my luggage, not remembering that I no longer had the rest of anything in this world. My brother Gustavo, who at the age of thirteen already had practice in nailing or unnailing anything, decided to open it without permission. Minutes later we heard his shout:

"It's books!"

My heart leaped up before I did. In fact they were books, with no clue as to the sender, packed by a master hand up to the top of the crate, and there was a letter difficult to decipher because of the hieroglyphic calligraphy and hermetic lyrics of Germán Vargas: "This thing's for you, Maestro, let's see if you learn something at last." It was also signed by Alfonso Fuenmayor, and a scrawl that I identified as belonging to Don Ramón Vinyes, whom I did not know yet. The only thing they recommended was not to commit any plagiarism that would be too obvious. Inside one of the books by Faulkner there was a note from Álvaro Cepeda, written in his difficult hand and in great haste besides, in which he said that the following week he was leaving for a year to pursue a special course of study at the School of Journalism at Columbia University in New York.

The first thing I did was to display the books on the table in the dining room while my mother finished clearing away the breakfast dishes. She had to arm herself with a broom to chase away her younger children, who wanted to cut out the illustrations with the pruning shears, and the street dogs that sniffed at the books as if they were something to eat. I smelled them too, as I always do with every new book, and I looked over all of them at random, reading paragraphs in a haphazard way. I moved from place to place that night because I was too restless, or the dim light in the corridor to the courtyard faded, and at dawn my back had cramped and I still did not have the remotest idea of the benefit I could derive from that miracle.

There were twenty-three distinguished works by contemporary authors, all of them in Spanish and selected with the evident intention that they be read for the sole purpose of learning to write. And in translations as recent as William Faulkner's *The Sound and the Fury*. Fifty years later it is impossible for me to recall the entire list, and the three eternal friends who knew it are no longer here to remember. I had read only two of them: *Mrs. Dalloway*, by Mrs. Woolf, and *Point Counter Point*, by Aldous Huxley. The ones I remember best were those by William Faulkner: *The Hamlet, The Sound and the Fury, As I Lay Dying*, and *The Wild Palms*. Also *Manhattan Transfer* and perhaps another by John Dos Passos; *Orlando*, by Virginia Woolf; John Steinbeck's *Of Mice and Men* and *The Grapes of Wrath; Portrait of Jenny*, by Robert Nathan, and *Tobacco Road*, by Erskine Caldwell. Among the titles I do not remember at a distance of half a century, there was at least one by Hemingway, perhaps a book of short stories, which was the work of his the three in Barranquilla liked best; another by Jorge Luis Borges, no doubt stories as well, and perhaps another by Felisberto Hernández, the extraordinary Uruguayan storyteller my friends had just discovered with shouts of joy. I read them all in the months that followed, some of them well and others less so, and thanks to them I managed to get out of the creative limbo where I was foundering.

Because of the pneumonia I was forbidden to smoke, but I smoked in the bathroom as if hiding from myself. The doctor knew and spoke to me with real seriousness, but I could not obey him. Already in Sucre, as I tried to read without pause the books I had received, I chain-smoked until I could not bear it, and the more I tried to quit the more I smoked. I smoked four packs a day, I would interrupt meals to smoke, and I burned the sheets because I fell asleep holding a lit cigarette. The fear of death would wake me at any hour of the night, and only by smoking could I endure it, until I decided I would rather die than stop smoking.

More than twenty years later, when I was married and had children, I was still smoking. A doctor who saw my lungs on the screen told me in horror that in two or three years I would not be able to breathe. Terrified, I reached the extreme of sitting for hours and hours without doing anything because I could not read, or listen to music, or talk to friends or enemies without smoking. One night, during a casual supper in Barcelona, a friend who was a psychiatrist explained to the others that tobacco was perhaps the most difficult addiction to break. I dared ask him what the fundamental reason was, and his reply had a chilling simplicity:

"Because for you, quitting smoking would be like killing someone you love."

It was a sudden burst of clairvoyance. I never knew why and did not want to know, but I put out the cigarette I had just lit in the ashtray, and with no anxiety or regret I never smoked another one again in my life.

My other addiction was no less persistent. One afternoon a maid from the house next door came in, and after talking to everyone she went to the terrace and with great respect asked permission to speak with me. I did not stop reading until she asked:

"Do you remember Matilde?"

I did not remember, but she did not believe me.

"Don't play the fool, Señor Gabito," she said with deliberate emphasis. "Ni-gro-man-ta."

And with reason: Nigromanta was now a free woman, with a child by the dead policeman, and she lived alone in the same house as her mother and other members of the family, but in a bedroom that was set apart, with its own door out to the back end of the cemetery. I went to see her, and our reencounter went on for more than a month. Each time I delayed my return to Cartagena and wanted to stay in Sucre forever. Until one dawn when I was caught by surprise in her house by a storm with thunder and lightning like the one on the night of Russian roulette. I tried to stay under the eaves, but when I no longer could I plunged into the middle of the street with the water up to my knees. It was my good luck that my mother was alone in the kitchen and took me to my bedroom along the garden paths so that Papá would not hear. As soon as she helped me take off my dripping wet shirt, she held it at arm's length with the tips of her thumb and index finger and tossed it into the corner with a shudder of disgust.

"You were with that woman," she said.

I turned to stone.

"How do you know that?"

"Because it's the same odor as the other time," she said, her face impassive. "It's just as well her man is dead."

I was surprised by this lack of compassion for the first time in her life. She must have noticed, because she drove the point home without thinking about it.

"It's the only death that made me glad when I heard about it."

I asked in perplexity:

"How did you know who she is?"

"Oh, son," she said with a sigh, "God tells me everything about all of you."

Then she helped me take off my dripping trousers and tossed them in the corner with the rest of the clothes. "All of you are going to be just like your papá," she said without warning, heaving a deep sigh, while she dried my back with a burlap towel. And she finished with all her heart:

"God willing, you'll also be husbands as good as he is."

The dramatic treatments to which my mother subjected me must have had the desired effect of forestalling a recurrence of pneumonia. Until I realized that she herself complicated them in order to keep me from returning to the thunder-and-lightning bed of Nigromanta, whom I never saw again.

I returned to Cartagena restored and happy, with the news that I was writing *La casa*, and I talked about it as if it were an accomplished fact after I had just begun the first chapter. Zabala and Héctor greeted me like the prodigal son. At the university, my good teachers seemed resigned to accepting me as I was. At the same time I continued to write very occasional pieces that were paid by the job at *El Universal*. My career as a short-story writer continued with the little I managed to write, almost to please Maestro Zabala: "Dialogue of the Mirror" and "Bitterness for Three Sleepwalkers," published by *El Espectador*. Although in both of them there was an evident lightening of the primary rhetoric of the first four stories, I still was not out of the swamp.

By this time Cartagena was infected by the political tension in the rest of the country, which should have been considered as an omen that something serious was going to happen. At the end of the year the Liberals declared their abstention from the entire election because of the savagery of the political persecution, but they did not renounce their underground plans to overthrow the government. The violence grew worse in the countryside and people fled to the cities, but censorship obliged the press to write about this in an oblique manner. It was common knowledge, however, that fugitive Liberals had organized guerrilla bands in different parts of the country. In the eastern Llanos—an immense ocean of green pastureland that occupies more than a quarter of the national territory—they had become legendary. Their general commander, Guadalupe Salcedo, was already viewed as a mythic figure, even by the army, and his photographs were distributed in secret and copied by the hundreds, and candles were lit to them on altars.

The De la Espriella family appeared to know more than they said, and in their walled enclosure they spoke with complete naturalness about an imminent coup against the Conservative regime. I did not know the details, but Maestro Zabala had warned me that as soon as I noticed any disturbance in the street I should go straight to the newspaper. You could touch the tension with your hands when I walked into the Americana ice cream parlor at three in the afternoon to keep an appointment. I sat down to read at a back table as someone approached, and one of my old classmates, with whom I had never talked about politics, said as he passed by without looking at me:

"Get to the paper, the thing's about to begin."

I did just the opposite: I wanted to know how things turned out right in the center of the city and not behind the closed doors of the newsroom. Minutes later a press officer in the Gobernación, whom I knew well, sat down at my table, and I did not think he had been ordered to neutralize me. I talked to him for half an hour in the purest state of innocence, and when he stood to leave I discovered that the enormous room in the ice cream parlor had emptied out without my realizing it. He followed my glance and confirmed the hour: ten past one.

"Don't worry," he said with controlled relief. "Nothing happened."

In fact, the most important group of Liberal leaders, desperate because of the official violence, had come to an agreement with democratic military men of the highest rank to end the slaughter that had been unleashed throughout the country by the Conservative regime, which was prepared to remain in power at any price. Most of them had participated in the steps taken on April 9 to achieve peace through an agreement with President Ospina Pérez, and less than twenty months later they realized too late that they had been victims of a colossal deception. The frustrated action that day had been authorized by the president of the Liberal leadership, Carlos Lleras Restrepo, through Plinio Mendoza Neira, who had excellent relations within the Armed Forces since he had been minister of war under the Liberal government. The action coordinated by Mendoza Neira, with the secret collaboration of prominent party members all over the country, was supposed to begin at dawn that day with the bombing of the Palacio Presidencial by planes from the air force. The movement was supported by the naval bases at Cartagena and Apiay, by most of the military garrisons in the country, and by trade unions determined to seize power for a civilian government of national reconciliation.

Only after the failure was it learned that two days before the anticipated date of the action, the former president Eduardo Santos had brought together the high Liberal officials and the leaders of the coup for a final review of the project in his house in Bogotá. In the midst of the debate, someone asked the ritual question:

"Will there be bloodshed?"

No one was ingenuous enough or cynical enough to say no. Other leaders explained that maximum measures had been taken to avoid it, but no magical formulas existed for preventing the unforeseen. Frightened by the extent of their own conspiracy, the Liberal leadership issued the counterorder without discussion. Many of those who were involved but did not receive the order in time were arrested or killed during the attempt. Others advised Mendoza to continue alone until the power takeover, and he did not for reasons more ethical than political, but he did not have the time or the means to warn all those involved. He managed to take refuge in the embassy of Venezuela, and he lived in exile for four years in Caracas, safe from a court-martial that sentenced him in absentia to twenty-five years in prison for sedition. Fifty-two years later my hand does not tremble when I write—without his authorization—that he repented for the rest of his life, in his exile in Caracas, because of the devastating balance left by Conservatism in power: no less than three hundred thousand dead.

For me as well, in a certain sense, this was a crucial moment. In less than two months I had failed the third year at the faculty of law and ended my commitment to *El Universal*, for I did not see my future in either one. My pretext was to free my time for the novel I had just begun, though in the depths of my soul I knew it was neither true nor a lie; instead, the project had revealed itself to me without warning as a rhetorical formula, with very little of the good that I had known how to use from Faulkner and all the bad of my inexperience. I soon learned that telling stories parallel to the ones you are writing—without revealing their essence—is a valuable part of the conception and the writing. This, however, was not the case at the time, but for lack of something to show I had invented a spoken novel to entertain my listeners and deceive myself.

That awareness obliged me to rethink, from beginning to end, the project that never had more than forty pages written in fits and starts and yet was cited in magazines and newspapers—and by me as well—and imaginative readers even published some very smart advance reviews. At bottom, the reason for this custom of recounting parallel projects deserves not reproaches but compassion: the terror of writing can be as intolerable as the terror of not writing. In my case, moreover, I am convinced that telling the real story brings bad luck. It comforts me, however, that at times the oral account might be better than the written one, and without realizing it we may be inventing a new genre that literature needs now: the fiction of fiction.

The real truth is that I did not know how to go on living. My convalescence in Sucre allowed me to realize that I did not know where I was going in life, but it gave me no clues as to the right direction or any new argument for convincing my parents that they would not die if I took the liberty of deciding that for myself. So I went to Barranquilla with two hundred pesos from her household funds that my mother had given me before I returned to Cartagena.

On December 15, 1949, I walked into the Librería Mundo at five in the afternoon to wait for the friends I had not seen since our night in May when I had left with the unforgettable Señor Razzore. I had only a small beach bag with another change of clothing, some books, and the leather briefcase with my rough drafts. Minutes after I arrived all of them came into the bookstore, one behind the other. It was a noisy welcome, without Álvaro Cepeda, who was still in New York. When the group was complete we moved on to drinks, which no longer were in the Café Colombia next to the bookstore but in a new one with closer friends across the street: Café Japy.

I had no destination, not that night and not ever in my life. The strange thing is that I never thought my destination could be Barranquilla, and if I went there it was only to talk about literature and to thank them in person for the shipment of books they had sent me in Sucre. We had more than enough of the first but nothing of the second, though I tried many times, because the group had a sacramental terror of the custom of giving or receiving thanks among ourselves.

That night Germán Vargas improvised a meal for twelve people, who ran the gamut from journalists, painters, and notaries to the governor of the department, a typical Barranquillan Conservative with his own way of perceiving and governing. Most of them left after midnight, and the rest drifted away until only Alfonso, Germán, and I were left, along with the governor, more or less in the right mind we tended to be in at the dawns of our adolescence.

In that night's long conversations I received a surprising lesson from him on the nature of those who governed the city during the blood-soaked years. He calculated that in all the destruction of that barbarous policy, the most devastating aspect was the impressive number of refugees without housing or food in the cities.

"At this rate," he concluded, "my party, with the help of weapons, will have no adversary in the next elections and will be in absolute control of power."

The only exception was Barranquilla, in accordance with a culture of political coexistence that the local Conservatives themselves took part in and that had made the city a refuge of peace in the eye of the hurricane. I tried to make an ethical observation, but he stopped me cold with a gesture of his hand.

"Excuse me," he said, "but this does not mean we are on the margins of national life. On the contrary: because of our peacefulness, the social drama of the country has come tiptoeing in through the back door, and now we have it here inside."

Then I learned that there were some five thousand refugees who had come from the interior in the worst misery, and no one knew how to rehabilitate them or where to hide them so that the problem would not become public. For the first time in the history of the city there were military patrols guarding critical locations, and everyone saw them but the government denied it and the censorship kept it from being denounced in the press.

At dawn, after almost dragging the distinguished governor home, we went to the Chop Suey, the breakfast spot for great all-nighters. At the kiosk on the corner Alfonso bought three copies of *El Heraldo*, whose editorial page had a note signed by Puck, his pseudonym for the column that appeared every other day. It was only a greeting for me, but Germán kidded him because the note said I was there on an informal vacation.

"The best thing would have been to say that he's going to live here so you wouldn't have to write a greeting and then a farewell," joked Germán. "Less expensive for a paper as cheap as *El Heraldo*."

Serious now, Alfonso thought his editorial section could use another columnist. But Germán was indomitable in the light of the dawn.

"He'll be a fifth columnist because you already have four."

Neither one consulted with me as I wanted them to so that I could say yes. The subject was not spoken of again. It was not really necessary, because that night Alfonso told me he had spoken to the management of the paper and they liked the idea of a new columnist, as long as he was good but without too many pretensions. In any case, they could not resolve anything until after the New Year holiday. And so I stayed with the pretext of the job, even though they might tell me no in February.

7

THAT WAS HOW my first piece was published on the editorial page of *El Heraldo* in Barranquilla on January 5, 1950. I did not want to sign my name so that I would have the cure ready in case things did not work out, which is what had happened at *El Universal*. I did not have to think twice about the pseudonym: Septimus, taken from Septimus Warren Smith, Virginia Woolf's deluded character in *Mrs. Dalloway*. The title of the column—"La Jirafa"—was the secret nickname I alone knew for my only partner at the dances in Sucre.

It seemed to me that the January winds blew harder than ever that year, and it was almost impossible to walk into them on the streets they castigated until dawn. The topic of conversation when you woke was the devastation caused by the mad winds during the night, when they carried away dreams and henhouses and turned sheets of zinc from the roofs into flying guillotines.

Today I think those wild winds swept away the remains of a sterile past and opened the doors to a new life for me. My relationship with the group was no longer based only on pleasure; it became a professional partnership. At first we commented on the subjects we planned to write about or exchanged observations that were not at all doctoral though they were not to be forgotten. The definitive one for me came one morning when I went into the Japy as Germán Vargas was finishing his silent reading of "La Jirafa," cut out of that day's paper. The others in the group sat around the table waiting for his verdict with a kind of reverential terror that made the smoke in the room even denser. When he finished, without even looking at me, Germán ripped it into pieces, did not say a single word, and mixed the scraps of paper into the trash of cigarette butts and burned matches in the ashtray. No one said anything, the mood at the table did not change, and the episode was never commented on. But the lesson is still useful to me when out of laziness or haste I am assaulted by the temptation to write a paragraph just to get out of a difficult situation.

At the cheap hotel where I lived for almost a year, the owners began to treat me like a member of the family. My only fortune at the time consisted of my historic sandals, two changes of clothing that I washed in the shower, and the leather briefcase I had stolen from the most exclusive tearoom in Bogotá during the disturbances of April 9. I carried it everywhere with the originals of whatever I was writing, which was the only thing I had to lose. I would not have risked leaving it under seven locks and keys in the armored vault of a bank. The only person to whom I had entrusted it during my first nights there was Lácides, the secretive hotel porter, who accepted it as security for the price of my room. He gave intense scrutiny to the strips of typewritten paper entwined in corrections and put the briefcase away in the drawer of the counter. I ransomed it the next day at the time I had promised and continued meeting my payments with so much rigor that he would accept it as a pledge for as many as three successive nights. This became so serious an understanding that sometimes I would leave it on the counter without saying anything more than good evening, and take the key down from the board myself and go up to my room.

Germán was always aware of my needs, to the point of knowing if I did not have a place to sleep, and he would slip me the peso and a half for a bed. I never knew how he knew. Thanks to my good behavior I grew close to the hotel personnel, to the point where the little whores would lend me their own soap for my shower. Presiding over life at the command post, with her sidereal breasts and calabash cranium, was the hotel's owner and mistress, Catalina la Grande. Her full-time man, the mulatto Jonás San Vicente, had been a deluxe trumpet player until his gold-filled teeth were knocked out in a mugging meant to steal everything he had. Battered and without the wind to play, he had to change professions and could find nothing better for his six-inch tool than the golden bed of Catalina la Grande. She too had an intimate treasure that in two years helped her to climb from miserable nights on the river docks to the throne of a great madam. I had the luck to become familiar with the cleverness and free hand of both in making their friends happy. But they never understood why I so often did not have the peso and a half to sleep and yet very elegant people came to pick me up in official limousines.

Another happy event of those days was that I became the only copilot of Mono Guerra, a taxi driver so blond he seemed albino, and so intelligent and good-natured he had been elected honorary councilman without running for office. His dawns in the red-light district were like movies, because he himself took charge of enriching them—and at times making them crazy— with inspired detours. He would let me know when he had a slow night, and we would spend it together in the lunatic red-light district where our fathers and the fathers of their fathers had learned how to make us.

I never could discover why, in the middle of so simple a life, I sank without warning into an unexpected apathy. My novel-in-progress—*La casa*—begun some six months earlier, seemed like an uninspired farce to me. I talked about it more than I wrote it, and in reality the small amount of coherent writing I had were fragments that I published earlier and later in "La Jirafa" and in *Crónica* when I did not have a topic. In the solitude of my weekends, when the others took refuge in their houses, I was lonelier than my left hand in the empty city. My poverty was absolute, and I had the timidity of a quail, which I tried to counteract with insufferable arrogance and brutal frankness. I felt I did not belong anywhere, and even certain acquain-

tances made me aware of this. It was most critical in the newsroom at *El Heraldo*, where I would write for as many as ten hours
straight in a remote corner without talking to anyone, enveloped
in the dense smoke from the rough cigarettes I smoked without
pause in unrelieved solitude. I wrote at top speed, often until
daybreak, on strips of newsprint that I carried everywhere in
my leather briefcase.

In one of my many acts of carelessness during those days, I
left it in a taxi, and I understood this without bitterness as one
more dirty trick played on me by my bad luck. I made no effort
to recover it, but Alfonso Fuenmayor, alarmed by my negligence, wrote and published a note at the end of my column:
"Last Saturday a briefcase was left in an automobile for hire. In
view of the fact that the owner of the briefcase and the author
of this column are, coincidentally, the same person, both of us
would be grateful if the person who has it would be kind
enough to communicate with either one of us. The briefcase
contains absolutely no objects of value: only unpublished
'jirafas.' " Two days later someone left my rough drafts at the
porter's office at *El Heraldo*, without the briefcase and with
three spelling errors corrected in green ink in a very fine hand.

My daily salary was just enough to pay for my room, but what
mattered to me least in those days was the abyss of poverty. On
the many occasions when I could not pay for the room, I would
go to read in the Café Roma as if I were what in reality I was: a
solitary man adrift in the night on the Paseo Bolívar. Anyone I
knew would receive a distant greeting from me, if I deigned to
look at him, and I would walk along to my habitual place,
where I often read until I was startled by the sun. For even then
I was still an insatiable reader without any systematic formation. A reader above all of poetry, even bad poetry, because
even in the worst of spirits I was convinced that sooner or later
bad poetry leads to good.

In my pieces for "La Jirafa" I showed a great sensitivity to
popular culture, in contrast to my stories, which seemed more
like Kafkian riddles written by someone who did not know
what country he was living in. But the truth of my soul was that
the drama of Colombia reached me like a remote echo and

moved me only when it spilled over into rivers of blood. I would light a cigarette without finishing the one before, I would breathe in the smoke with the longing for life seen in asthmatics gulping down air, and the three packs I consumed each day were evident on my nails and in an old dog's cough that disrupted my youth. In short, I was shy and sad, like a good Caribbean, and so jealous of my intimate life that I would answer any question about it with a rhetorical digression. I was convinced my bad luck was congenital and irremediable, above all with women and with money, but I did not care, because I believed I did not need good luck in order to write well. I did not care about glory, or money, or old age, because I was sure I was going to die very young, and in the street.

The trip with my mother to sell the house in Aracataca rescued me from that abyss, and the certainty of the new novel indicated to me the horizon of a different future. It was decisive among the many I have taken in my life because it showed me in my own flesh that the book I had tried to write was pure rhetorical invention with no foundation at all in poetic truth. The project, of course, shattered when it confronted reality on that revelatory journey.

The model for an epic poem like the one I dreamed about could not be anything but my own family, which was never a protagonist or even a victim of anything, but only a pointless witness and a victim of everything. I began to write it at the very moment I returned, because an elaboration by artificial means was no longer of any use to me, only the emotional weight I had carried without knowing it and that was waiting for me intact in my grandparents' house. With the first step I took onto the burning sands of the town, I had realized that my method was not the happiest for recounting that earthly paradise of desolation and nostalgia, though I devoted a good deal of time and effort to finding the correct one. The problems associated with *Crónica*, which was about to come out, were not an obstacle but just the opposite: they reined in my disquiet.

Except for Alfonso Fuenmayor—who caught me in a creative fever just hours after I began to write it—the rest of my friends believed for a long time that I was still working on the old project of *La casa*. I decided it should be this way because of a childish fear that people would discover the failure of an idea I had talked about as much as if it had been a masterpiece. But also because of the superstition I still cultivate of telling one story and writing another so that nobody knows which is which. Above all in press interviews, which in the long run are a dangerous kind of fiction for shy writers who do not want to say more than they should. Germán Vargas, however, must have found out with his mysterious shrewdness, because months after Don Ramón's trip to Barcelona he told him about it in a letter: "I believe that Gabito has abandoned the project of *La casa* and is involved in another novel." Don Ramón, of course, knew that before he left.

From the first line I was certain that the new book ought to be based on the memories of a seven-year-old boy who had survived the public massacre in the banana zone in 1928. But I rejected this very soon because it limited the narrative to the point of view of a character without sufficient poetic resources to tell it. Then I became aware that my adventure in reading *Ulysses* at the age of twenty, and later *The Sound and the Fury*, were premature audacities without a future, and I decided to reread them with a less biased eye. In effect, much of what had seemed pedantic or hermetic in Joyce and Faulkner was revealed to me then with a terrifying beauty and simplicity. I planned to diversify the monologue with voices of the entire town, like a narrative Greek chorus, in the style of *As I Lay Dying*, with the reflections of an entire family interposed around a dying man. I did not feel able to repeat his simple device of indicating the names of the characters at each speech, as in theatrical texts, but it gave me the idea of using no more than the three voices of the grandfather, the mother, and the boy, whose tones and destinies were so different they could be identified on their own. The grandfather in the novel would not be one-eyed like mine, but lame; the mother, absorbed but intelligent, like mine; the boy immobile, frightened, and pensive, as I always had been at his age. It was not in any way a creative discovery but a simple technical device.

The new book had no change in background during its writing or any version different from the original, except for excisions and corrections that went on for some two years before its first edition because of my vice of continuing the corrections until death. I had visualized the town in reality—very different from the one in the earlier project—when I returned to Aracataca with my mother, but this name—as the very wise Don Ramón had warned me—seemed as unconvincing as the name Barranquilla, because it too was lacking in the mythic air I wanted for the novel. And so I decided to call it by the name I no doubt had known as a boy but whose magical charge had not been revealed to me until then: Macondo.

I had to change the title *La casa*—so familiar by then to my friends—because it had nothing to do with the new project, but I made the mistake of noting in a school copybook the titles that occurred to me as I was writing, and I came up with more than eighty. At last I found it without looking for it in the first version that was almost finished when I succumbed to the temptation of writing an author's prologue. The title sprang to my eye, as the disdainful and at the same time compassionate name with which my grandmother, in the fragments of her aristocratic self, baptized the desolation left behind by the United Fruit Company: *Leaf Storm*.

The authors who stimulated me most in the writing of it were North American novelists, in particular those whose books my friends from Barranquilla had sent to me in Sucre. Above all because of the affinities of all kinds that I found between the cultures of the Deep South and the Caribbean, with which I have an absolute, essential, and irreplaceable identification in my formation as a human being and as a writer. After I became aware of this, I began to read like a real working novelist, not only for pleasure but out of an insatiable curiosity to discover how books by wise people were written. I read them forward first, then backward, and subjected them to a kind of surgical disemboweling until I reached the most recondite mysteries of their structure. In the same way, my library has never been much more than a working tool, where without delay I can consult a chapter by Dostoevsky, or verify a fact about Julius Caesar's epilepsy or the mechanism of an automobile carburetor. I even have a manual on how to commit perfect murders in the event one of my defenseless characters should ever need it. The rest of it was created by friends who guided me in my reading and at the right moment lent me the books I had to read, and by those who have made pitiless readings of my originals before they are published.

Examples like these produced a new self-awareness in me, and the *Crónica* project gave me wings. Our morale was so high that in spite of insurmountable obstacles we even had our own offices on the third floor of a building without an elevator, surrounded by the shouts of the women peddling food, and the lawless buses on Calle San Blas, which was a tumultuous fair from daybreak until seven at night. There was almost no room for us. The telephone had not yet been installed, and an air conditioner was a fantasy that could cost us more than publishing the weekly, but Fuenmayor had already had time to fill the office with his ragged encyclopedias, his press cuttings in any language, and his celebrated manuals of strange trades. On his publisher's desk was the historic Underwood he had rescued at grave risk to his own life from a burning embassy, which today is a jewel in the Museo Romántico in Barranquilla. I occupied the only other desk, with a typewriter lent to us by *El Heraldo*, in my brand-new capacity as editor-in-chief. There was a drawing table for Alejandro Obregón, Orlando Guerra, and Alfonso Melo, three famous painters who had agreed in their right minds to illustrate the contributions, and they did, at first because of their congenital generosity, and in the end because we did not have a *céntimo* to spare even for ourselves. The dedicated and self-sacrificing photographer was Quique Scopell.

Aside from the editorial work that corresponded to my title, it was also my job to supervise the typesetting and help the proofreader in spite of my Dutchman's spelling. Since my commitment to *El Heraldo* to continue "La Jirafa" was still in effect, I did not have much time for regular contributions to *Crónica*. I did, however, have time to write my stories in the idle small hours of the morning.

Alfonso, a specialist in every genre, placed the weight of his faith in detective stories, for which he had a burning passion.

He translated or selected them, and I subjected them to a process of formal simplification that would help me in my own work. It consisted of saving space through the elimination not only of useless words but also of superfluous actions, until the stories were reduced to their pure essence without affecting their ability to convince. That is, deleting everything unnecessary in a forceful genre in which each word ought to be responsible for the entire structure. This was one of the most useful exercises in my oblique research into learning the technique for telling a story.

Some of the best ones by José Félix Fuenmayor saved us on several Saturdays, but circulation was immovable. The perpetual life raft, however, was the temperament of Alfonso Fuenmayor, who had never been recognized for his talents as a man of business, and with a tenacity superior to his strength he persisted in ours, which he himself tried to wreck at every step with his terrible sense of humor. He did everything, writing the most lucid editorials or the most trivial notes with the same perseverance he brought to obtaining advertisements, unthinkable amounts of credit, and exclusive pieces from difficult contributors. But they were sterile miracles. When the newsboys came back with the same number of copies they had taken out to sell, we attempted personal distribution in our favorite taverns, from El Tercer Hombre to the taciturn bars in the river port, where we had to collect our scant profits in ethylic kind.

One of the most reliable contributors, and no doubt the one who was read the most, turned out to be El Vate Osío. Beginning with the first issue of *Crónica* he was unfailing, and in his "Diary of a Typist," written under the pseudonym Dolly Melo, he succeeded in conquering readers' hearts. No one could believe that so many different kinds of jobs were performed with so much flair by the same man.

Bob Prieto could prevent the shipwreck of *Crónica* with some medical or artistic find from the Middle Ages. But in questions of work he had a transparent standard: if you do not pay there is no product. Very soon, of course, and with sorrow in our hearts, there was none.

We managed to publish four enigmatic stories by Julio Mario

Santodomingo, written in English, which Alfonso translated with the eagerness of a dragonfly hunter in the foliage of his strange dictionaries, and Alejandro Obregón illustrated with the refinement of a great artist. But Julio Mario traveled so much, and with so many contrary destinations, that he became an invisible partner. Only Alfonso Fuenmayor knew where to find him, and he revealed it to us in an unsettling phrase:

"Every time I see a plane fly over I think Julio Mario Santodomingo is on it."

The rest were occasional contributors who in the last minutes before going to press—or before payment—kept us in suspense.

Bogotá approached us as equals, but none of those useful friends made any kind of effort to keep the weekly afloat. Except Jorge Zalamea, who understood the affinities between his magazine and ours and proposed an agreement for exchanging material, which had good results. But I believe that in reality no one appreciated what *Crónica* already had of the miraculous. The editorial board consisted of sixteen members chosen by us according to each one's recognized merits, and all of them were flesh-and-blood creatures but so powerful and busy that it was easy to doubt their existence.

For me, *Crónica* had the lateral importance of obliging me to improvise emergency stories to fill unexpected spaces in the anguish of going to press. I would sit at the typewriters while linotypists and typesetters did their work, and out of nothing I would invent a tale the size of the space. This was how I wrote "How Natanael Pays a Visit," which solved an urgent problem for me at dawn, and "A Blue Dog's Eyes" five weeks later.

The first of these two stories was the origin of a series with the same character, whose name I took without permission from André Gide. Later I wrote "The End of Natanael" in order to resolve another last-minute drama. Both formed part of a sequence of six, which I filed away without sorrow when I realized they had nothing to do with me. Of those I remember in part, I recall one but do not have the slightest idea of its plot: "How Natanael Dresses Like a Bride." Today the character does not resemble anyone I have known, and it was not based on my own or other people's experiences, and I cannot even imagine how it could be a story of mine with so equivocal a subject. No question, then, that Natanael was a literary risk with no human interest. It is good to remember these disasters in order not to forget that a character is not invented from zero, as I tried to do with Natanael. It was my good luck that I did not have enough imagination to go too far away from myself, and my bad luck that I was also convinced that literary work had to be paid as well as laying bricks, and if we paid typographers good salaries, and on time, with even more reason we had to pay writers.

The greatest resonance we had from our work on *Crónica* came to us in Don Ramón's letters to Germán Vargas. He was interested in the most unexpected news, and in events and his friends in Colombia, and Germán would send him newspaper clippings and tell him in endless letters the news prohibited by the censors. That is, for him there were two *Crónicas*: the one we produced and the one Germán summarized for him on weekends. Our most rapacious desire was for Don Ramón's enthusiastic or harsh comments on our articles.

People proposed several causes to explain *Crónica*'s difficulties, and even the uncertainties of the group, and I found out by accident that some attributed these to my congenital and contagious bad luck. As lethal proof they would cite my article on Berascochea, the Brazilian soccer player, with which we had wanted to reconcile sport and literature in a new genre, and which was a categorical disaster. When I learned about my infamous reputation it was already widespread among the patrons at Japy. Demoralized down to the marrow of my bones, I mentioned it to Germán Vargas, who already knew about it, as did the rest of the group.

"Take it easy, Maestro," he said without the slightest doubt. "Writing the way you write can be explained only by a kind of good luck that no one can defeat."

Not all nights were bad. July 27, 1950, in the sporting house of La Negra Eufemia, had a certain historical value in my life as a writer. I do not know for what good reason the madam had ordered an epic stew with four kinds of meat, and the curlews, excited by the untamed aromas, shrieked without restraint around the fire. A frenetic patron grabbed a curlew by the neck and threw it alive into the boiling pot. The animal just managed a howl of pain and a final flap of its wings, and then it sank into the depths of hell. The savage killer tried to grab another one, but La Negra Eufemia had already risen from her throne with all her power.

"Be still, damn it," she shouted, "or the curlews will peck out your eyes!"

It mattered only to me, because I was the only one who did not have the heart to taste the sacrilegious stew. Instead of going to sleep, I hurried to the *Crónica* office and wrote in a single sitting the story about three patrons in a bordello whose eyes were pecked out by curlews and nobody believed it. It had only four office-size pages, double spaced, and it was told in the first person plural by a nameless voice. Its realism is evident and yet it is the most enigmatic of my stories, and it also turned me onto a path I was about to abandon because I could not follow it. I had begun writing at four in the morning on Friday and finished at eight, tormented by a prophet's blinding light. With the infallible complicity of Porfirio Mendoza, the historic typesetter at *El Heraldo*, I altered the layout for the edition of *Crónica* that would circulate the next day. At the last minute, desperate because of the guillotine of going to press, I dictated to Porfirio the definitive title I had found at last, and he wrote it straight into molten lead: "The Night of the Curlews."

For me it was the beginning of a new era, after nine stories that were still in metaphysical limbo and when I had no plans to continue with a genre I could not manage to grasp. The following month, Jorge Zalamea reproduced it in *Crítica*, an excellent journal of important poetry. I reread it fifty years later, before I wrote this paragraph, and I believe I would not change even a comma. In the midst of the disorder without a compass in which I was living, that was the beginning of spring.

The country, on the other hand, was going into a tailspin. Laureano Gómez had returned from New York to be proclaimed the Conservative candidate for the presidency of the Republic. Liberalism abstained in the face of the empire of violence, and Gómez was elected as the lone candidate on August 7, 1950. Since Congress was in adjournment, he took office before the Supreme Court.

He almost had no chance to govern in person, for after fifteen months he retired from the presidency for real reasons of health. He was replaced by the Conservative jurist and parliamentarian Roberto Urdaneta Arbeláez, in his capacity as first deputy of the Republic. Shrewd observers interpreted this as a formula, very typical of Laureano Gómez, to leave power in other hands but not lose it, and to continue governing from his house by means of an intermediary. And in urgent cases, by means of the telephone.

I think that the return of Álvaro Cepeda with his degree from Columbia University a month before the sacrifice of the curlew was decisive for enduring the grim prospects of those days. He came back with more disheveled hair and without his brush mustache, and wilder than when he left. Germán Vargas and I, who had been expecting him for several months fearful that he had been tamed in New York, died laughing when we saw him leave the plane in a jacket and tie, waving at us from the steps with Hemingway's latest: *Across the River and into the Trees*. I tore it out of his hands, caressed it on both sides, and when I tried to ask him something, Álvaro anticipated me:

"It's a piece of shit!"

Germán Vargas, weak with laughter, whispered into my ear: "He's just the same." But Álvaro clarified for us later that his opinion of the book was a joke, because he had just started to read it on the flight from Miami. In any case, what raised our spirits was that he brought back with him, more virulent than ever, the measles rash of journalism, movies, and literature. In the months that followed, as he reacclimated, he kept our fever at 104 degrees.

The contagion was immediate. "La Jirafa," which for months had been circling around itself tapping a blind man's stick, began to breathe with two fragments plundered from the rough draft of *La casa*. One was "The Colonel's Son," never born, and the other was "Ny," a fugitive girl at whose door I knocked very often looking for different paths, and she never answered. I also recovered my adult interest in comic strips, not as a Sunday pastime but as a new literary genre condemned without reason to the nursery. My hero, one of many, was Dick Tracy. And, of course, I also recovered the cult of the movies that my grandfather had inculcated in me, that had been nourished by Don Antonio Daconte in Aracataca, and that Álvaro Cepeda converted into an evangelical passion for a country where the best movies were known through the tales of pilgrims. It was fortunate that his return coincided with the opening of two masterpieces: *Intruder in the Dust*, directed by Clarence Brown and based on the novel by William Faulkner, and *Portrait of Jenny*, directed by William Dieterle and based on the novel by Robert Nathan. I commented on both of them in "La Jirafa" after long discussions with Álvaro Cepeda. I became so interested that I began to look at films with a different eye. Before I knew him I did not realize that the most important thing was the name of the director, which is the last one that appears in the credits. For me it was a simple question of writing scripts and managing actors, since the rest was done by the countless members of the crew. When Álvaro returned he gave me a complete course based on shouts and white rum until dawn at tables in the worst taverns, in order to teach me by force what they had taught him about movies in the United States, and we would stay up all night with the waking dream of doing the same thing in Colombia.

Aside from those luminous explosions, the impression of the friends who followed Álvaro at his cruising speed was that he did not have the serenity to sit down to write. Those of us who lived close to him could not conceive of him sitting for more than an hour at any desk. But two or three months after his return, Tita Manotas—his sweetheart of many years and his lifelong wife—called us in terror to say that Álvaro had sold his historic station wagon and left behind in the glove compartment the originals, that had no copies, of his unpublished stories. He made no effort to find them, using an argument typical of him that they were "six or seven pieces of shit." Those of us who were his friends and correspondents helped Tita in her search for the station wagon, which had been sold several more times, all along the Caribbean coast and inland as far as Medellín. At last we found it in a shop in Sincelejo, some two hundred kilometers away. We entrusted the originals, on ragged and incomplete strips of newsprint, to Tita, for fear Álvaro would misplace them again through negligence or on purpose.

Two of those stories were published in *Crónica*, and Germán Vargas kept the rest for some two years until a publishing solution was found. The painter Cecilia Porras, always faithful to the group, illustrated them with inspired drawings that were an X ray of Álvaro dressed as everything he could be at the same time: truck driver, carnival clown, mad poet, Columbia student, or any other occupation except being a common, ordinary man. The book was published by Librería Mundo with the title *We Were All Waiting*, and it was a publishing event that went unnoticed only by academic critics. For me—and this is what I wrote at the time—it was the best book of stories that had been published in Colombia.

Alfonso Fuenmayor, for his part, wrote comments as a critic and teacher of letters in newspapers and magazines, but he was very shy about collecting them in books. He was a reader of extraordinary voracity, comparable perhaps to that of Álvaro Mutis or Eduardo Zalamea. Germán Vargas and he were powerful critics, more so with their own stories than with those of others, but their mania for finding youthful values never failed them. That was the creative spring when the insistent rumor circulated that Germán was staying up all night writing masterful stories, but nothing was known about them until many years later when he locked himself in his bedroom in his father's house and burned them just hours before marrying my *comadre* Susana Linares, so that he could be certain they would not be read, not even by her. It was assumed that they were stories and essays, perhaps the first draft of a novel, but Germán never said a word about them either before or after, and only on the eve of his wedding did he take drastic precautions so that no one, including the woman who would be his wife the next day, would ever find out. Susana knew what he was doing but did not go into the room to stop him because her mother-in-law would not have permitted it. "In those days," Susi told me years later with her trenchant humor, "a girl could not go into her fiancé's bedroom before they were married."

Less than a year had gone by when the letters from Don Ramón began to be less explicit and more and more melancholy and sketchy. I went into the Librería Mundo on May 7, 1952, at twelve noon, and Germán did not have to say anything for me to know that Don Ramón had died, two days earlier, in the Barcelona of his dreams. The only comment, as we walked to the midday café, was the same for everyone:

"I can't believe it!"

I was not conscious at the time that this was a different kind of year in my life, but today I have no doubt that it was decisive. Until then I had been content with my dissolute appearance. I was loved and respected by many, and admired by some, in a city where people lived in their own way and manner. I had an intense social life, I took part in artistic and social debates wearing my pilgrim's sandals that looked as if they had been bought to imitate Álvaro Cepeda, with one pair of linen trousers and two twill shirts that I washed in the shower.

From one day to the next, for a variety of reasons—some of them too frivolous—I began to improve my clothing, cut my hair like a recruit, trimmed my mustache, and learned to wear a pair of senator's shoes given to me unworn by Dr. Rafael Marriaga, an itinerant member of the group and a historian of the city, because they were too big for him. Through the unconscious dynamic of social climbing, I began to feel that I was suffocating from the heat in the room at The Skyscraper, as if Aracataca had been in Siberia, and to suffer on account of transient guests who spoke in loud voices when they woke up, and to never weary of grumbling because the little birds of the night continued to flood their rooms with entire crews of freshwater sailors.

Today I realize that my beggar's appearance was not because I was poor or a poet but because my energies were concentrated in a profound way on the stubborn difficulties of learning to write. As soon as I could see the right path I left The Skyscraper and moved to the tranquil El Prado district, its urban and social opposite, two blocks from the house of Meira Delmar and five from the historic hotel where the sons of the rich danced with their virgin sweethearts after Sunday Mass. Or as Germán said: I began to improve for the worse.

I lived in the house of the Ávila sisters—Esther, Mayito, and Toña—whom I had known in Sucre, and who for some time had been bent on saving me from perdition. Instead of a cardboard cubicle where I shed so many of the scales I had accumulated as a spoiled grandson, I had my own bedroom with a private bath and a window overlooking the garden, and three meals a day for very little more than my carter's salary. I bought a pair of trousers and half a dozen tropical shirts printed with flowers and birds, which for a time won me secret fame as a shipboard faggot. Old friends whom I had not run into again I now found everywhere I went. I discovered to my delight that they quoted from memory the nonsense from "La Jirafa," were devoted fans of *Crónica* because of what they called its sportsmanlike integrity, and even read my stories without really understanding them. I ran into Ricardo González Ripoll, my dormitory neighbor at the Liceo Nacional, who had settled in Barranquilla with his architect's degree and in less than a year had resolved his life with a tail-finned Chevrolet of uncertain age into which he could pack up to eight passengers at dawn. Three times a week he would pick me up at home early in the evening to go carousing with new friends obsessed with setting the country to rights, some with formulas of political magic and others by fighting with the police.

When she learned of these developments, my mother sent me a message very typical of her: "Money calls to money." I did not tell the members of the group anything about the change until one night when I met them at the table in the Café Japy, and I seized on the brilliant formula of Lope de Vega: "I took orders, and so it suited me to order my life in line with my disorder." I do not remember comparable catcalls even in a soccer stadium. Germán wagered I would not have a single idea away from The Skyscraper. According to Álvaro, I would not survive the cramps that come with three meals a day at regular hours. Alfonso, on the other hand, protested the abusiveness of intervening in my private life and buried the subject with a discussion regarding the urgency of making radical decisions about the future of *Crónica*. I think at bottom they felt guilty about my disorder but were too decent not to give thanks for my decision with a sigh of relief.

Contrary to expectations, my health and morale improved. I was reading less because of lack of time, but I raised the tone of "La Jirafa" and forced myself to continue writing *Leaf Storm* in my new room, on the prehistoric typewriter that Alfonso Fuenmayor lent me, during the small hours I had wasted earlier with Mono Guerra. On a normal afternoon in the newsroom at the paper I could write "La Jirafa," an editorial, some of my many unsigned articles, the condensation of a detective story, and last-minute pieces before *Crónica* went to press. It was fortunate that instead of becoming easier as the days passed, the novel-in-progress began to impose its own criteria in opposition to mine, and I was ingenuous enough to understand this as a symptom of favorable winds.

My mood was so resolute that in an emergency I improvised my tenth story—"Someone Is Messing Up These Roses," because the political commentator for whom we had reserved three pages in *Crónica* for a last-minute article had suffered a serious heart attack. I discovered only when I corrected the printed proof of my story that it was another static drama of the kind I wrote without thinking. This reversal intensified my remorse for having awakened a friend a little before midnight so that he would write the article in less than three hours. In this penitential spirit I wrote the story in the same amount of time, and on Monday I again brought up to the editorial board the urgency of our going out on the street to pull the magazine out of its doldrums with hard-hitting articles. But the idea—which was everyone's—was rejected once again with an argument favorable to my happiness: given the idyllic notion we had about reporting, if we went out on the street the magazine would never again come out on time—if it came out at all. I should have understood this as a compliment, but I never could overcome the disagreeable idea that the real reason was their unpleasant memory of my article on Berascochea.

A good consolation at that time was the telephone call from Rafael Escalona, the composer of the songs that were sung and are still being sung on this side of the world. Barranquilla was a vital center because of frequent visits from the troubadours of the accordion whom we had met at the fiestas in Aracataca, and because of their intense exposure on the radio stations along the Caribbean coast. A very well-known singer at the time was Guillermo Buitrago, who boasted of keeping new songs from the Province up-to-date. Another who was very popular was Crescencio Salcedo, a barefoot Indian who would stand on the corner of the Americana to sing without ceremony songs of his own and other people's creation, in a voice that had some tin in it, but with a very personal art that imposed itself on the daily crowd on Calle San Blas. I had spent a good part of my early youth standing near him, not even greeting him, not letting myself be seen, until I learned by heart his vast repertoire of everybody's songs.

The culmination of that passion reached its climax one torpid afternoon when the telephone interrupted me as I was writing "La Jirafa." A voice like those of so many people I knew in my childhood greeted me with no preliminary formulas:

"What's doing, brother? I'm Rafael Escalona."

Five minutes later we met at a reserved table in the Café Roma to begin a lifelong friendship. As soon as we exchanged greetings I began to press Escalona to sing his latest songs. Isolated lines, in a voice that was very low and well modulated, which he accompanied by drumming his fingers on the table. In each stanza the popular poetry of our lands strolled by wearing a new dress. "I'll give you a bouquet of forget-me-nots so you'll do what their meaning says," he sang. For my part, I showed him that I knew by heart the best songs of his home, which I had pulled since I was very young from the tumultuous river of the oral tradition. But what surprised him most was that I talked to him about the Province as if I knew it.

Days earlier, Escalona had traveled by bus from Villanueva to Valledupar while he composed in his mind the music and lyrics of a new song for Carnival on the following Sunday. It was his primary method because he did not know how to write music or play any instrument. In one of the towns along the way, a wandering troubadour with sandals and an accordion got on the bus, one of the countless men who traveled the region from fair to fair to sing. Escalona had him sit beside him and sang into his ear the two completed stanzas of his new song.

The happy troubadour got off in the middle of the road, and Escalona stayed on the bus until Valledupar, where he had to go to bed to sweat out the 104-degree fever of a common cold. Three days later was the Sunday of Carnival, and the unfinished song that Escalona had sung in secret to his passing friend swept away all the music, old and new, from Valledupar to Cabo de la Vela. Only he knew who had divulged it while he was sweating out his Carnival fever, and gave it the name "La vieja Sara."

The story is true but not strange in a region and in a guild where the most natural thing is what is astonishing. The accordion, not a native or widespread instrument in Colombia, is popular in the province of Valledupar and may have been imported from Aruba and Curaçao. During the Second World War its importation from Germany was interrupted, and those that were already in the Province survived because of the care given them by their native owners. One was Leandro Díaz, a carpenter who not only was an inspired composer and master of the accordion, but the only man during the war who knew how to repair them even though he was blind from birth. The way of life of these genuine troubadours is to go from town to town and sing the amusing and simple facts of ordinary history, at religious or pagan celebrations, and above all in the wild confusion of Carnival. Rafael Escalona's case was different. The son of Colonel Clemente Escalona, the nephew of the celebrated Bishop Celedón, and the holder of a baccalaureate from the *liceo* in Santa Marta that bears his name, he began to compose when he was very young, scandalizing his family who considered singing with an accordion something that day laborers did. Not only was he the only troubadour with a baccalaureate degree, he was one of the few in those days who knew how to read and write, and the haughtiest, most amorous

man who ever existed. But he is not and will not be the last:
now there are hundreds of them, younger and younger each
day. Bill Clinton understood it this way in the final days of his
presidency, when he listened to a group of primary-school children who traveled from the Province to sing for him at the
White House.

During those days of good fortune I happened to run into
Mercedes Barcha, the daughter of the pharmacist in Sucre to
whom I had been proposing marriage since she was thirteen. In
contrast to those other times, at last she accepted an invitation
to go dancing the following Sunday at the hotel in El Prado.
Only then did I learn that she had moved to Barranquilla with
her family because of a political situation that was growing
more and more oppressive. Demetrio, her father, was a hard-
core Liberal who was not intimidated by the early threats
against him when the persecution and social ignominy of the
pasquines worsened. But under pressure from his family, he sold
off the few things he had left in Sucre and set up his pharmacy
in Barranquilla, close to the hotel in El Prado. Although he was
the age of my papá, he always maintained a youthful friendship
with me that we would heat up at the tavern across the street,
and more than once we ended up in a galley slave's drunken
carousing with the entire group at El Tercer Hombre. At that
time Mercedes was studying in Medellín and spent time with
her family only during Christmas vacation. She always was
amusing and amiable with me, but she had an illusionist's talent
for evading questions and answers and not allowing herself to
be explicit about anything. I had to accept this as a more compassionate stratagem than indifference or rejection, and I
resigned myself to her seeing me with her father and his friends
in the tavern across the street. If he did not suspect my interest
during that vacation of longing, it was because it was the best-
kept secret of the first twenty centuries of Christianity. On
various occasions he boasted in El Tercer Hombre about the
sentence she had quoted to me in Sucre at our first dance: "My
papá says that the prince who will marry me hasn't been born
yet." I also did not know if she believed him, but she behaved as
if she did, until that Christmas holiday when she agreed that

we would meet the following Sunday at the morning dance at the hotel in El Prado. I am so superstitious that I attributed her decision to the artist's hairstyle and mustache that the barber had made for me, and the unbleached linen suit and silk tie bought for the occasion at an auction run by Turks. Certain that she would go there with her father, as she did wherever she went, I also invited my sister Aida Rosa, who was spending her vacation with me. But Mercedes showed up very much alone, and she danced with so much naturalness and so much irony that any serious proposal would have seemed ridiculous to her. That day was the beginning of the unforgettable season of my *compadre* Pacho Galán, the glorious creator of the *merecumbé* that was danced for years and gave rise to new Caribbean airs that are still alive. She danced very well to popular music, and she used her mastery to elude with magical subtlety the proposals that pursued her. It seems to me her tactic was to make me believe she did not think I was serious, but with so much skill that I always found the way to move ahead.

At twelve sharp she became alarmed about the time and left me standing while the music was still playing, but she did not want me to accompany her even to the door. This seemed so strange to my sister that in some way she felt responsible, and I still wonder if that sad example did not have something to do with her sudden decision to enter the Salesian convent in Medellín. In time, after that day, Mercedes and I invented a personal code with which we understood each other without saying anything, and even without seeing each other.

I heard from her again after a month, on January 22 of the following year, with an unadorned message that she left for me at *El Heraldo:* "They killed Cayetano." For us it could be only one person: Cayetano Gentile, our friend in Sucre, a soon-to-be doctor, an organizer of dances, and a lover by trade. The immediate version was that he had been knifed by two brothers of the young teacher at the school in Chaparral: we had seen him ride with her on his horse. In the course of the day, from one telegram to the next, I learned the complete story.

It was still not the time of easy telephones, and personal long-distance calls were arranged first by telegram. My immediate reaction was a reporter's. I decided to travel to Sucre to write the story, but at the paper they interpreted this as a sentimental impulse. And today I understand, because even back then we Colombians killed one another for any reason at all, and at times we invented one, but crimes of passion were reserved as luxuries for the rich in the cities. It seemed to me that the subject was eternal and I began to take statements from witnesses, until my mother discovered my hidden intentions and begged me not to write the article. At least while Cayetano's mother, Doña Julieta Chimento, was alive, the most important of the reasons being that she was my mother's *comadre* because she had been godmother at the baptism of Hernando, my brother number eight. Her statement—indispensable in a good article—was of great significance. Two of the teacher's brothers had pursued Cayetano when he tried to take refuge in his house, but Doña Julieta had hurried to lock the street door because she believed that her son was already in his bedroom. And so he was the one who could not come in, and they stabbed him to death against the locked door.

My immediate reaction was to sit down to write the report of the crime but I found all kinds of impediments. What interested me was no longer the crime itself but the literary theme of collective responsibility. No argument convinced my mother, however, and it seemed a lack of respect to write it without her permission. But after that not a day went by that I was not hounded by the desire to write the story. I was beginning to become resigned, and then, many years later, I was waiting for a plane to take off at the airport in Algiers. The door to the first-class lounge opened, and an Arab prince came in wearing the immaculate tunic of his lineage, and carrying on his fist a splendid female peregrine falcon that instead of the leather hood of classic falconry wore one of gold encrusted with diamonds. Of course I thought of Cayetano Gentile, who had learned from his father the fine arts of falconry, at first with local sparrow hawks and then with magnificent examples transplanted from Arabia Felix. At the moment of his death he had a professional falcon coop on his farm, with two female cousins and a male trained to hunt partridges, and a Scottish kite skilled in personal defense. I knew about the historic interview of Ernest Hemingway by George Plimpton in *The Paris Review* regarding the process of transforming a character from real life into a character in a novel. Hemingway said: "If I explained how that is sometimes done, it would be a handbook for libel lawyers." But after that providential morning in Algiers, my situation was just the opposite: I had no desire to continue living in peace if I did not write the story of the death of Cayetano.

My mother remained firm in her determination to prevent this despite every argument, until thirty years after the drama, when she herself called me in Barcelona to give me the sad news that Julieta Chimento, Cayetano's mother, had died without ever getting over the loss of her son. But this time, with her strong moral sense, my mother found no reasons to interfere with the article.

"I ask only one thing as a mother," she said. "Treat Cayetano as if he were a son of mine."

The story, with the title *Chronicle of a Death Foretold*, was published two years later. My mother did not read it for a reason that I keep as another of her gems in my personal museum: "Something that turned out so awful in life can't turn out well in a book."

A week after the death of Cayetano, the telephone on my desk rang at five in the afternoon as I was beginning to write my daily assignment at *El Heraldo*. The call was from my papá, who had just arrived in Barranquilla unannounced and was waiting for me with some urgency at the Café Roma. The tension in his voice frightened me, but I was more alarmed at seeing him as I never had seen him before, disheveled and unshaven, wearing the April 9 sky-blue suit dusty with the suffocating heat of the road, sustained only by the strange placidity of the defeated.

I was so overwhelmed that I do not feel capable of transmitting the anguish and lucidity with which Papá informed me of the family disaster. Sucre, paradise of the easy life and beautiful girls, had succumbed to the seismic onrush of political violence. The death of Cayetano was no more than a symptom.

"You don't realize what that hell is like because you live in this oasis of peace," he said. "But if we're still alive there it's because God knows us."

He was one of the few members of the Conservative Party who had not needed to hide from raging Liberals after April 9, and now the same Conservatives who had taken refuge in his shadow were repudiating him for his half-heartedness. He painted a picture for me that was so terrifying—and so real— that it more than justified his rash decision to leave everything behind and take the family to Cartagena. I had no rational or emotional counterargument, but I thought I could slow him down with a solution less radical than an immediate move.

We needed time to think. We had two soft drinks in silence, each of us lost in his own thoughts, and he recovered his feverish idealism before we finished and left me speechless. "The only thing that consoles me in all of this," he said with a tremulous sigh, "is my joy that at last you can finish your studies." I never told him how much I was affected by that illusive happiness for so trivial a reason. I felt an icy gust in my belly, set off by the perverse idea that the family's exodus was nothing more than a trick of his to oblige me to be a lawyer. I looked straight into his eyes and they were two astonished pools. I realized he was so defenseless and worried that he would not oblige me to do anything, and would not deny me anything, but he had enough faith in his Divine Providence to believe he could make me surrender through sheer exhaustion. Even more: with the same captive spirit he revealed that he had found me a position in Cartagena and had everything ready for me to begin the following Monday. A wonderful position, he explained, and I would only have to show up every two weeks to collect my salary.

It was much more than I could digest. With clenched teeth I put forward a few misgivings to prepare him for my final refusal. I told him about the long conversation with my mother on the trip to Aracataca about which I had never received any comments from him, but I had understood that his indifference toward the subject was the best response. The saddest part was that I was playing with loaded dice, since I knew I would not be accepted into the university because I had failed two subjects in the second year, which I never made up, and another three in the third year that were unsalvageable. I had hidden this from the family to spare them unnecessary grief, and I did not even want to imagine what Papá's reaction would be if I told him that afternoon. At the beginning of our conversation I had resolved not to give in to any sentimental weakness, because it hurt me that so kind a man had to let himself be seen by his children in such a state of defeat. But it seemed to me that this meant placing too much confidence in life. In the end I surrendered to the easy formula of asking him for a night to think about it.

"Agreed," he said, "as long as you don't lose sight of the fact that you hold the fate of the family in your hands."

The condition was unnecessary. I was so aware of my weakness that when I saw him off on the last bus, at seven in the evening, I had to suborn my heart not to sit in the seat beside him. For me it was clear that we had gone full circle, and the family was so poor again that it could survive only with the assistance of all its members.

It was not a good night for deciding anything. The police had removed by force several families of refugees fleeing the rural violence in the interior who had camped in the Parque San Nicolás. But the peace in Café Roma was impregnable. The Spanish refugees always asked me what I had heard from Don Ramón Vinyes, and I always told them as a joke that his letters did not carry news from Spain but worried questions about the news from Barranquilla. After he died they did not mention him again, but they kept his chair empty at the table. A member of his *tertulia* congratulated me for the previous day's "La Jirafa," which had reminded him somehow of the heartrending romanticism of Mariano José de Larra, and I never knew why. Professor Pérez Domenech saved me from an awkward situation with one of his opportune remarks: "I hope you don't also follow his bad example and shoot yourself." I believe he would not have said it if he had known to what extent it might have been true that night.

Half an hour later I led Germán Vargas by the arm to the

back of Café Japy. As soon as we had been served I said that I had to have an urgent consultation with him. He froze, the cup halfway to his lips—identical to Don Ramón—and asked in alarm:

"Where are you going?"

His clairvoyance impressed me.

"How the hell do you know!" I said.

He did not know but had foreseen it, and he thought my resignation would be the end of *Crónica*, a grave lack of responsibility that would weigh on me for the rest of my life. He made it clear that this was little less than treason, and no one had more right than he to tell me so. No one knew what to do with *Crónica*, but we were all aware that Alfonso had supported it at a crucial moment, including investments beyond his means, so that I could never shake Germán free of the bad idea that my irremediable move was a death sentence for the magazine. I am certain that he, who understood everything, knew that my reasons were inescapable, but he fulfilled his moral duty to tell me what he thought.

The next day, as he was driving me to the *Crónica* office, Álvaro Cepeda gave a moving demonstration of the turmoil that his friends' inner storms caused him. No doubt he already knew from Germán about my decision to leave, and his exemplary timidity saved both of us from any salon argument.

"What the hell," he said. "Going to Cartagena isn't going anywhere. The fucked-up thing would be if you went to New York, like I had to do, but here I am again, in the flesh."

It was the kind of parabolic response that helped him in cases like mine to leap past his desire to cry. By the same token I was not surprised that he chose to talk for the first time about the project of making films in Colombia, a conversation that we would continue without results for the rest of our lives. He brought it up in passing as an oblique way of leaving me with some hope, and he stopped short in the midst of the surging crowd and the little shops that sold trinkets on Calle San Blas.

"I already told Alfonso," he shouted at me through the window, "to hell with the magazine: let's do one like *Time*!"

My conversation with Alfonso was not easy for me or him

because we had been postponing a clarification for six months, and we both suffered from a kind of mental stammer on difficult occasions. During one of my puerile tantrums in the typesetting room I had removed my name and title from the masthead of *Crónica* as a metaphor of my formal resignation, and when the storm had passed I forgot to replace them. No one noticed it except Germán Vargas, two weeks later, and he talked about it with Alfonso. It was a surprise for him as well. Porfirio, the head typesetter, told them about my tantrum, and they agreed to leave things as they were until I gave them my reasons. To my misfortune, I forgot about it altogether until the day Alfonso and I agreed I would leave *Crónica*. When we finished, he said goodbye to me weak with laughter at a joke that was typical of him, strong but irresistible.

"The lucky thing is," he said, "that we don't even have to take your name off the masthead."

Only then did I relive the incident as if it were a knife wound, and I felt the earth sinking beneath my feet, not because of what Alfonso had said in so opportune a way but because I had forgotten to clarify the matter. Alfonso, as was to be expected, gave me an adult interpretation. If it was the only injustice we had not aired, it was not decent to leave it pending without an explanation. Alfonso would take care of the rest with Álvaro and Germán, and if all of us were needed to save the boat, I could get back in two hours. As a last resort we were counting on the editorial board, a kind of Divine Providence that we never had managed to seat at the long walnut table of major decisions.

The comments of Germán and Álvaro filled me with the courage I needed to leave. Alfonso understood my reasons and accepted them with a kind of relief, but in no way did he suggest that *Crónica* would come to an end with my resignation. On the contrary, he advised me to take the crisis with serenity, calmed me down with the idea of constructing a firm base with the editorial board, and said he would let me know when something could be done that in reality would be worthwhile.

It was the first clue I had that Alfonso could conceive of the unimaginable possibility that *Crónica* would end. And it did, without grief or glory, on June 28, after fifty-eight issues in fourteen months. But half a century later, I have the impression that the magazine was an important event in the nation's journalism. No complete collection remained, only the first six issues and some clippings in the Catalan library of Don Ramón Vinyes.

A fortunate coincidence was that they wanted to change the living-room furniture in the house where I was living, and they offered it to me at a very reduced price. The night before I left, as I was settling accounts at *El Heraldo*, the paper agreed to pay me in advance for six months of "La Jirafa." With part of that money I bought Mayito's furniture for our house in Cartagena, because I knew the family was not taking what they had in Sucre and had no way to buy new furniture. I cannot omit that after fifty years it is in good condition and still in use, because my grateful mother never allowed it to be sold.

A week after my father's visit I moved to Cartagena, taking only the furniture and little more than what I was wearing. In contrast to the first time, I knew how to do everything necessary, I was familiar with everything that might be needed in Cartagena, and I hoped with all my heart that things would go well for the family but not for me, as a punishment for my lack of character.

The house was in a good location in the district of La Popa, in the shadow of the historic convent that always has seemed on the verge of falling over a precipice. The four bedrooms and two bathrooms on the ground floor were reserved for the parents and their eleven children, ranging from me, the oldest, almost twenty-six years old, to Eligio, the youngest, who was five. All of them well brought up in the Caribbean culture of hammocks and straw mats on the floor and beds for as many as could fit in.

On the upper floor lived Uncle Hermógenes Sol, my father's brother, and Carlos Martínez Simahan, his son. The entire house was not large enough for so many people, but the rent was lowered because of my uncle's business dealings with the owner, about whom we knew only that she was very rich and was called La Pepa. The family, with its implacable gift for making jokes, did not take long to find the perfect address in the style of a popular tune: "The house of La Pepa at the foot of La Popa."

The arrival of the offspring is a mysterious recollection for me. The electricity had gone out in half the city, and we were trying to prepare the house in the dark so that the children could go to sleep. We older children recognized one another by our voices, but the younger ones had changed so much since my last visit that their enormous sad eyes frightened me in the light of the candles. I endured the disorder of trunks, bundles, and hammocks hanging in the dark as a domestic April 9. But what made the deepest impression on me was trying to move a shapeless sack that kept slipping out of my hands. It contained the remains of my grandmother Tranquilina, which my mother had disinterred and taken along in order to place them in the ossuary of San Pedro Claver; the remains of my father and my aunt, Elvira Carrillo, are in the same crypt.

My uncle Hermógenes Sol was the providential man in that emergency. He had been appointed general secretary of the Departmental Police in Cartagena, and his first radical action was to open a bureaucratic breach to save the family. Including me, with my misguided politics and a reputation for being a Communist that I had earned not for my ideology but because of how I dressed. There were jobs for everyone. They gave an administrative position without political responsibility to Papá. My brother Luis Enrique was named a detective, and they gave me a sinecure in the offices of the National Census, which the Conservative government insisted on carrying out, perhaps in order to have some idea of how many of its adversaries were still alive. The moral cost of the job was more dangerous for me than the political cost, because I collected my salary every two weeks and could not let myself be seen in the area for the rest of the month in order to avoid questions. The official explanation, not only for me but for more than a hundred other employees, was that I was on assignment outside the city.

The Café Moka, across the street from the census offices, was always crowded with false bureaucrats from neighboring towns who came only to collect their money. There was not a *céntimo* for my personal use during the time I signed for my wages, because my salary was substantial but all of it went for household expenses. In the meantime, Papá had tried to matriculate me in the faculty of law and collided with the truth I had hidden from him. The mere fact that he knew it made me as happy as if I had received my diploma. My happiness was even more warranted because in the midst of so many setbacks and difficulties, I at last had found the time and space to finish my novel.

When I walked into *El Universal* they made me feel as if I were coming home. It was six in the evening, the busiest time, and the abrupt silence that my entrance caused at the linotypes and typewriters brought a lump to my throat. Not a minute had gone by for the Indian hair of Maestro Zabala. As if I had never left, he asked me to please write an editorial piece for him that had been delayed. An adolescent novice was using my typewriter, and he fell in his reckless haste to give up his seat to me. The first thing that surprised me was how difficult it was to write an anonymous note with editorial circumspection after some two years of the excesses of "La Jirafa." I had a page of copy when the publisher López Escauriaza came over to say hello. His British impassivity was a commonplace in *tertulias* with friends and political caricatures, and I was touched by his flush of joy when he greeted me with a hug. When I finished the editorial, Zabala was waiting with a slip of paper on which the publisher had offered me a salary of one hundred twenty pesos a month for writing editorials. I was so impressed by the sum, unusual for that time and place, that I did not even give an answer or say thank you but sat down to write two more, intoxicated by the sensation that in reality the Earth did revolve around the Sun.

It was as if I had come back to my origins. The same topics corrected in liberal red by Maestro Zabala, then abbreviated by the same censorship of a censor already defeated by the impious tricks of the newsroom, the same midnights with steak topped by a fried egg and fried plantains at La Cueva, and the same topic of changing the world that went on until dawn on the Paseo de los Mártires. Rojas Herazo had spent a year selling paintings so that he could move anywhere else, until he married Rosa Isabel, la Grande, and moved to Bogotá. At the end of the night I sat down to write "La Jirafa," which I sent to *El Heraldo*, by the only modern means available at the time, which was ordinary mail, and I missed very few times, always through force majeure, until the debt was paid.

Life with my entire family, in difficult circumstances, lies in the domain not of memory but imagination. My parents slept in a bedroom on the ground floor with some of the younger children. My four sisters felt they had the right to a bedroom of their own. Hernando and Alfredo Ricardo slept in the third, under the care of Jaime, who kept them in a state of alert with his philosophical and mathematical preaching. Rita, who was fourteen, studied until midnight at the street door, in the light of the streetlamp, in order to save electricity in the house. She memorized her lessons by singing them aloud with the grace and good diction that she still has. Many strange moments in my books come from her reading exercises, with the mule that goes to the mill, and the child who chases the chocolate chicken, and the seer who sees the seesaw.* The house was livelier and above all more human after midnight, between going to the kitchen for a drink of water, or to the toilet for liquid or solid emergencies, or hanging crisscrossed hammocks at different levels in the hallways. I slept on the second floor with Gustavo and Luis Enrique—when my uncle and his son moved into their family house—and later with Jaime, who was subjected to the penance of not pontificating about anything after nine o'clock. One night we were kept awake for several hours by the cyclical bleating of an orphaned lamb. Gustavo said in exasperation:

"It sounds like a lighthouse."

I never forgot it, because at the time it was the kind of simile I caught on the fly in real life for the imminent novel.

---

*The content of the phrases in English is different from Spanish in order to preserve the repetition of sounds typical of these exercises. The Spanish reads: . . . *la mula que va al molino y el chocolate del chico de la cachucha chica y el adivino que se dedica a la bebida.*

It was the liveliest of several houses in Cartagena, which became more and more humble as the family's resources diminished. Looking for cheaper neighborhoods, we came down in class until we reached the house in Toril, where the ghost of a woman would appear at night. I was lucky enough not to have been there, but the accounts of my parents and brothers and sisters caused me as much terror as if I had. On the first night my parents were dozing on the sofa in the living room, and they saw the apparition as she passed from one bedroom to another, not looking at them, wearing a dress with little red flowers, her short hair fastened behind her ears with red ribbons. My mother described her down to the print on her dress and the style of her shoes. Papá denied having seen her in order not to further upset his wife or frighten the children, but the familiarity with which the apparition moved through the house starting at dusk did not permit anyone to ignore her. My sister Margot once woke before dawn and saw her on the rail of her bed, scrutinizing her with an intense gaze. But what affected her most was the terror of being seen from the next life.

On Sunday, coming out of Mass, a neighbor confirmed for my mother that no one had lived in that house for many years because of the boldness of the phantom, who once appeared in the dining room in the middle of the day while the family was eating lunch. The next day my mother went out with two of the youngest children to look for a house to move into, and she found one in four hours. But it was difficult for most of my brothers and sisters to exorcise the idea that the ghost of the dead woman had moved along with them.

In the house at the foot of La Popa, in spite of all the time I had at my disposal, I took so much joy in writing that the days seemed too short. Ramiro de la Espriella reappeared with his degree of doctor of laws, more political than ever and enthusiastic about his readings of recent novels. Above all *Skin*, by Curzio Malaparte, which that year had become a key book for my generation. The effectiveness of its prose, the vigor of its intelligence, and the truculent conception of contemporary history kept us trapped until dawn. But time showed us that Malaparte was destined to be a useful example of virtues other than the ones I desired, and in the end they overthrew his image. Just the opposite of what happened to us almost at the same time with Albert Camus.

The De la Espriellas lived close to us at the time, and they had a family wine cellar that they looted in innocent bottles and brought to our house. Disregarding the advice of Don Ramón Vinyes, I would read long selections from my rough drafts to them and my brothers and sisters, just as they were, with the rubbish still not cleared away, and on the same strips of newsprint where I wrote everything during my sleepless nights at *El Universal.*

At this time Álvaro Mutis and Gonzalo Mallarino returned, but I had the fortunate modesty not to ask them to read the unfinished rough draft that still had no title. I wanted to lock myself away and without interruption make the first copy on standard paper before the final correction. I had some forty pages more than the version I had anticipated, but I still did not know that this could be a serious obstacle. I soon learned that it was: I am slave to a perfectionist exactitude that forces me to make a preliminary calculation of the length of a book, with the exact number of pages in each chapter and in the book as a whole. A single notable mistake in these calculations would oblige me to reconsider everything, because even a typing error disturbs me as much as a creative one. I thought this absolutist method was due to a heightened sense of responsibility, but today I know it was simple terror, pure and physical.

On the other hand, once again not heeding Don Ramón Vinyes, I sent the complete first draft to Gustavo Ibarra when I considered it finished, though it still did not have a title. Two days later he invited me to his house. I found him in a reed rocking chair on the terrace facing the sea, tanned and relaxed in beach attire, and I was moved by the tenderness with which he caressed my pages as he talked to me. A true teacher, who did not deliver a lecture on the book or tell me if he thought it was good or bad, but who made me aware of his ethical values. When he finished he observed me with satisfaction and concluded with his everyday simplicity:

"This is the myth of Antigone."

From my expression he realized that I did not understand, and he took the book by Sophocles down from his shelves and read to me what he meant. The dramatic situation in my novel was in essence the same as Antigone's, condemned to leaving the body of her brother Polynices unburied by order of King Creon, their uncle. I had read *Oedipus in Colonus* in the volume that Gustavo himself had given to me in the days when we first met, but I did not recall the myth of Antigone well enough to reconstruct it from memory within the drama of the banana zone, and I had not noticed their emotional affinities until then. I felt my soul stirred by happiness and disillusionment. That night I read the work again, with a strange mixture of pride at having coincided in good faith with so great a writer, and sorrow at the public embarrassment of plagiarism. After a week of dark crisis I decided to make some fundamental changes that would rescue my good faith, still not realizing the superhuman vanity of modifying a book of mine so that it would not resemble one by Sophocles. At last—resigned—I felt I had the moral right to use a sentence of his as a reverential epigraph, which I did.

The move to Cartagena saved us in time from the serious and dangerous deterioration in Sucre, but most of our calculations were illusory, as much for the meagerness of our income as for the size of the family. My mother used to say that the children of the poor eat more and grow faster than those of the rich, and the example of her own house was sufficient proof of this. All of our salaries would not have been enough for us to live without sudden alarms.

Time took care of the rest. Jaime, by means of another family scheme, became a civil engineer, the only one in a family that valued a degree as if it were an aristocratic title. Luis Enrique was a teacher of accounting, and Gustavo graduated as a topographer, and both continued to be the same guitarists and singers of other people's serenades. Yiyo surprised us from a very early age with a well-defined literary vocation and a strong character, of which he had given us an early demonstration at the age of five when he was caught trying to set fire to a closet full of clothes in the hope of seeing firefighters putting out the blaze inside the house. Later, when he and his brother Cuqui were invited by older fellow students to smoke marijuana, Yiyo was frightened and refused. Cuqui, on the other hand, who was always curious and reckless, inhaled the smoke deep into his lungs. Years later, shipwrecked in the quicksand of drugs, he told me that after that first trip he had said to himself: "Shit! I don't want to do anything else in my life but this." For the next forty years, with a passion that had no future, he did nothing but keep the promise to die of his convictions. At the age of fifty-two he fell from his artificial paradise and was struck down by a massive heart attack.

Nanchi—the most peaceable man in the world—stayed on in the army after his obligatory military service, excelled in all kinds of modern weaponry, participated in numerous war games, but never took part in any of our many chronic wars. He settled for being a firefighter when he left the army, but there too he never had occasion to put out a single fire in more than five years. But he did not feel frustrated, because of a sense of humor that made him famous in the family as a master of the instant joke, and allowed him to be happy because of the mere fact of being alive.

Yiyo, in the most difficult years of poverty, became a writer and journalist by sheer hard work, without ever having smoked or taken a drink too many in his life. His irresistible literary vocation and concealed creativity stood firm against adversity. He died at the age of fifty-four, almost not enough time to publish a book of more than six hundred pages of masterful research into the secret life of *One Hundred Years of Solitude*, which he had worked on for years without my knowing about it and without ever making a direct inquiry of me.

Rita, early in her adolescence, knew how to learn from other people's experience. When I returned to my parents' house after a long absence, I found her suffering the same purgatory that all the girls had suffered because of her love for a good-looking, serious, and decent dark-skinned man whose only incompatibility with her was a height of some fifty centimeters. That same night I found my father listening to the news on his hammock in the bedroom. I turned down the volume, sat on the bed facing him, and asked him with my right of primo-geniture what was going on with Rita's boyfriend. He fired the answer at me that he no doubt had always anticipated.

"The only thing going on is that the guy's a thief."

Just what I expected.

"What kind of thief?" I asked him.

"A thief thief," he said, still not looking at me.

"But what has he stolen?" I asked him without mercy.

He still did not look at me.

"Well," he said at last with a sigh. "Not him, but he has a brother who's in jail for stealing."

"Then there's no problem," I said with easy imbecility, "because Rita doesn't want to marry him but the one who's not in jail."

He did not reply. His well-proven honesty had gone astray beginning with the first answer, because he also knew that the rumor about the imprisoned brother was not true. With no further arguments, he tried to cling to the myth of dignity.

"All right, but they should marry right away, because I don't want long engagements in this house."

My reply was immediate and had a lack of charity that I have never forgiven myself for:

"Tomorrow, first thing."

"Man! There's no need to exaggerate!" Papá replied, startled but smiling his earlier smile. "That girl doesn't even have anything to wear yet."

The last time I saw Aunt Pa, when she was almost ninety years old, was on an afternoon when the heat was hideous and she arrived unannounced in Cartagena. She had traveled from Riohacha in an express taxi, carrying a student's schoolbag and wearing strict mourning and a black cloth turban. She entered the house happy, her arms spread wide, and shouted to everyone:

"I've come to say goodbye because I'm going to die now."

We took her in not only because she was who she was, but because we knew to what extent she understood her dealings with death. She stayed in the house, waiting for her time in the little maid's room, the only one she would agree to sleep in, and

there she died in the odor of chastity at an age that we calculated to be a hundred and one years old.

That period was the most intense at *El Universal*. Zabala
guided me with his political knowledge so that my pieces
would say what they had to and not collide with the censor's
pencil, and for the first time he was interested in my old idea of
writing feature articles for the paper. A dreadful subject soon
arose when tourists were attacked by sharks on the beaches of
Marbella. But the most original idea that occurred to the
municipality was to offer fifty pesos for each dead shark, and on
the following day there were not enough branches on the almond
trees to display the ones captured during the night.
Héctor Rojas Herazo, collapsing with laughter, wrote from
Bogotá in his new column in *El Tiempo* a mocking note about
the blunder of applying to the shark hunt the timeworn
method of barking up the wrong tree. This gave me the idea of
writing an article about the nocturnal hunt. Zabala supported
me with enthusiasm, but my failure began from the moment I
set foot on the boat and they asked me if I got seasick and
I answered no; if I was afraid of the ocean and the truth was
yes but again I said no; and the last question was if I knew
how to swim—it should have been the first—and I did not
dare tell the lie that I did. In any event, on solid ground and in
a conversation with sailors, I learned that the hunters went to
Bocas de Ceniza, eighty-nine nautical miles from Cartagena,
and returned loaded down with innocent sharks to sell as criminals at fifty pesos each. The big news ended that same day, and
my hope for the article ended too. In its place I published story
number eight: "Nabo, the Black Man Who Made the Angels
Wait." At least two serious critics and my uncompromising
friends in Barranquilla judged it a good change of direction.

I do not believe I had enough political maturity to be
affected, but the truth is that I suffered a relapse similar to the
previous one. I felt so bogged down that my only diversion was
to stay up all night singing with the drunks in Las Bóvedas, the
vaults at the walls, which had been soldiers' brothels during the
colonial period and then a sinister political prison. General
Francisco de Paula Santander had served an eight-month sen-

tence there before he was exiled to Europe by his comrades in cause and in arms.

The custodian of those historical relics was a retired linotypist whose active colleagues met there with him after the papers went to press to celebrate the new day every day with a demijohn of clandestine white rum made by the arts of horse thieves. They were educated typographers by family tradition, dramatic grammarians, and great Saturday drinkers. I joined their brotherhood.

The youngest was named Guillermo Dávila, and he had accomplished the feat of working on the coast in spite of the intransigence of some regional leaders who resisted admitting Cachacos into the brotherhood. Perhaps he accomplished this by means of the art of his art, because in addition to his good trade and personal charm he was a marvelous illusionist. He kept us dazzled with the magical mischief of making live birds come out of desk drawers or leaving the paper blank on which the editorial was written that we had just turned in as the edition was about to close. Maestro Zabala, so uncompromising in his duty, forgot for an instant about Paderewski and the proletarian revolution, and requested applause for the magician with the warning, always repeated and always disobeyed, that this was the last time. For me, sharing the daily routine with a magician was like discovering reality at last.

On one of those dawns in Las Bóvedas, Dávila told me his idea of putting out a newspaper measuring twenty-four by twenty-four—half a standard sheet of paper—that would be distributed free of charge at the busy time in the afternoons when businesses closed. It would be the smallest newspaper in the world, meant to be read in ten minutes. And it was. It was called *Comprimido (Condensed)*, I wrote it in an hour at eleven in the morning, Dávila typeset and printed it in two hours, and a daring newsboy who did not even have enough breath to shout its name more than once handed it out.

It came out on Tuesday, September 18, 1951, and it is impossible to conceive of a more overwhelming or short-lived success: three editions in three days. Dávila confessed to me that not even with an act of black magic would he have been able to conceive of so great an idea at so little cost, that would fit into so small a space, be executed in so short a time, and disappear with such great speed. The strangest thing was that for an instant on the second day, intoxicated by the scramble of takers on the street and the fervor of fans, I came to think that the solution to my life might be this simple. The dream lasted until Thursday, when the manager showed us that one more edition would leave us bankrupt even if we decided to publish advertisements, for they would have to be so small and so expensive there was no rational solution. The very concept of the paper, based on its size, brought with it the mathematical seed of its own destruction: the more it sold the more unaffordable it was.

I was left in a difficult position. The move to Cartagena had been opportune and useful after my experience on *Crónica*, and it also provided a very favorable environment for continuing to write *Leaf Storm*, above all because of the creative fever with which we lived in our house, where the most unusual things always seemed possible. It would be enough for me to recall a lunch when we were talking to my papá about the difficulty many writers had in writing their memoirs when they no longer could remember anything. Cuqui, just six years old, drew the conclusion with masterful simplicity:

"Then," he said, "the first thing a writer ought to write is his memoirs, when he can still remember everything."

I did not dare confess that the same thing that had happened to me with *La casa* was happening with *Leaf Storm*: I was becoming more interested in the technique than in the subject. After a year of working with so much euphoria, the novel revealed itself to me as a circular labyrinth without an entrance or an exit. Today I believe I know why. The *costumbrismo** that offered such good examples of renovation in its origins had, in the end, fossilized the great national themes that were trying to open emergency exits. The fact is I could not bear another minute of uncertainty. I only needed to verify some information and make some stylistic decisions before putting in the final period, and still I could not feel it breathing. But I was so

*A literary genre that focuses on typical or picturesque regional customs.

bogged down after so much time working in the dark that I saw the book foundering and did not know where the cracks were. The worst thing was that at this point in the writing no one could help me, because the fissures were not in the text but inside me, and only I had the eyes to see them and the heart to endure them. Perhaps for this same reason I suspended "La Jirafa" without thinking too much about it when I finished paying *El Heraldo* the advance I had used to buy the furniture.

Sad to say, neither ingenuity, resistance, nor love were enough to defeat poverty. Everything seemed to favor it. The census had ended after a year, and my salary at *El Universal* was not enough to compensate. I did not return to the faculty of law in spite of the stratagems of certain teachers who had conspired to move me ahead despite my disinterest in their interest and erudition. At home everyone's money was not enough, but the hole was so large that my contribution was never enough and the lack of hope affected me more than the lack of money.

"If we're all going to drown," I said at lunch on a decisive day, "let me save myself so I can at least try to send you a lifeboat."

And so the first week in December I moved back to Barranquilla, with everyone resigned, certain the boat would come. Alfonso Fuenmayor must have imagined it at first glance when he saw me walk unannounced into our old office at *El Heraldo*, for the *Crónica* office had been left without funds. He looked up at me from his typewriter as if I were a ghost and exclaimed in alarm:

"What the hell are you doing here without letting anyone know!"

Few times in my life have I given an answer so close to the truth:

"It's all a pain in my balls, Maestro."

Alfonso calmed down.

"Ah, good!" he replied in his usual way, citing the most Colombian line from the national anthem. "It's our good fortune: that's how all of humankind is, moaning in their chains."

He did not show the slightest curiosity about the reason for my trip. It seemed like a kind of telepathy to him, because he had told everyone who had asked about me in recent months that at any moment I would be coming back to stay. He was happy as he got up from his desk and put on his jacket, because I had arrived like a gift from heaven. He was half an hour late for an appointment, he had not finished the next day's editorial, and he asked me to finish it for him. I just had time to ask him what the subject was, and as he ran down the hallway he answered in an offhand manner that was typical of the way we were friends:

"Read it and you'll find out."

The next day there were two typewriters facing each other again in the office of *El Heraldo,* and I was writing "La Jirafa" again for the same page. And—of course!—at the same price. And with the same close association between Alfonso and me, in which many editorials had paragraphs by one or the other and it was impossible to distinguish them. Some students of journalism or of literature have tried to differentiate them in the archives and have not been able to, except in the case of specific subjects, not because of the style but because of the cultural information.

At El Tercer Hombre I was saddened by the bad news that they had killed our friend the thief. On a night like every other he had gone out to ply his trade, and the only thing anyone knew, with no further details, was that he had been shot through the heart in the house that he was robbing. The body was claimed by an older sister, his sole relative, and only we and the owner of the tavern attended his charity funeral.

I returned to the house of the Ávila sisters. Meira Delmar, my neighbor once again, continued purifying my bad nights at El Gato Negro with her tranquil evenings. She and her sister Alicia seemed like twins because of their natures, and because they made time circular for us when we were with them. In some very special way they were still in the group. At least once a year they invited us to a meal of Arab delicacies that nourished our soul, and in their house there were unexpected evenings with illustrious visitors, from great artists in any genre to mad poets. I think they and Maestro Pedro Biava were the ones who imposed order on my misguided melomania and enrolled me in the happy crowd at the arts center.

Today it seems to me that Barranquilla gave me a better perspective on *Leaf Storm*, for as soon as I had a desk and typewriter, I began correcting it with renewed energy. At this time I dared to show the group the first legible copy, knowing it was not finished. We had talked so much about it that there was no need for any kind of warning. Alfonso spent two days writing across from me without even mentioning it. By the third day, when we had finished our assignments late in the afternoon, he put the rough draft on his desk and read the pages he had marked with slips of paper. More than a critic, he seemed like a tracker of the inconsequential and a purifier of style. His observations were so unerring that I used them all, except one that seemed farfetched to him even after I proved that it was a real episode from my childhood.

"Even reality is mistaken when the literature is bad," he said, weak with laughter.

Germán Vargas's method was that if the text was all right he made no immediate comments but gave a soothing opinion and ended with an exclamation point:

"Damn fine!"

But in the days that followed he kept throwing out strings of scattered ideas about the book, which would culminate on some night of drinking with a well-aimed opinion. If he did not like the rough draft, he met with the author alone and told him so with so much frankness and elegance that the apprentice could only thank him with all his heart even though he wanted to cry. That was not the case with me. On a day when I did not anticipate it, Germán made a half-joking, half-serious comment about my rough draft that returned my soul to my body.

Álvaro had disappeared from the Japy without any signs of life. Almost a week later, when I least expected it, he blocked my way with his car on the Paseo Bolívar, and shouted in his best manner:

"Get in, Maestro, I'm going to fuck you over for being an idiot!"

It was his anesthetic sentence. We drove without a destination around the business center, burning in the summer heat, while Álvaro shouted a somewhat emotional but impressive analysis of his reading. He interrupted it each time he saw someone he knew on the sidewalk in order to yell a cordial or mocking absurdity at him, and then resumed his impassioned harangue, with his voice cracking with the strain, his hair disheveled, and those bulging eyes that seemed to look at me through the bars of a panopticon. We ended up drinking cold beer on the terrace of Los Almendros, overwhelmed by the shrieking fans of Junior and Sporting across the street, and then overrun by the avalanche of maniacs who escaped from the stadium deflated by a contemptible score of 2–2. At the last minute Álvaro called his only definitive opinion about the rough draft of my book through the car window:

"In any case, Maestro, you still have a lot of *costumbrismo!*"

Grateful, I managed to shout back:

"But it's the good Faulkner kind!"

And he put an end to everything not said or thought with a phenomenal guffaw:

"Don't be a sonuvabitch!"

Fifty years later, whenever I remember that afternoon, I can hear his explosive outburst of laughter again, resonating like a shower of stones on the burning street.

It was clear to me that the three of them had liked the novel, with their personal and perhaps correct reservations, but they did not say it in so many words, perhaps because that seemed like an easy tactic to them. No one talked about publishing it, which was also very typical of them, for whom the important thing was writing well. The rest was a matter for publishers.

Which is to say: I was back again in our same old Barranquilla, but my misfortune was my awareness that this time I would not have the heart to go on with "La Jirafa." In reality it had fulfilled its mission of imposing on me a daily job of carpentry so I could learn how to write, starting from zero, with tenacity and the fierce aspiration to be a distinctive writer. On many occasions I could not handle the subject, and I would change it for another when I realized it was still too big for me. In any case, it was essential gymnastics for my formation as a writer, with the comfortable certainty that it was no more than a source of nourishment without any historical commitment.

The simple search for a daily subject had made my first few months bitter. It did not leave me time for anything else: I lost hours scrutinizing other newspapers, I took notes on private conversations, I became lost in fantasies that disturbed my sleep until real life came out to meet me. In that sense, my happiest experience occurred one afternoon when I saw from a passing bus a simple sign on the door of a house: "Funeral palms for sale."

My first impulse was to knock at the door in order to ascertain the facts of that discovery, but shyness vanquished me. And so life itself taught me that one of the most useful secrets for writing is to learn to read the hieroglyphs of reality without knocking or asking anything. In recent years this became much clearer to me when I reread the more than four hundred published "jirafas" and compared them to some of the literary texts they had given rise to.

At Christmas the staff of *El Espectador* arrived on vacation, beginning with the publisher Don Gabriel Cano, with all his children: Luis Gabriel, the manager; Guillermo, who was then deputy editor; Alfonso, the assistant manager, and Fidel, the youngest, an apprentice in everything. With them was Eduardo Zalamea, Ulises, who had a special value for me because of the publication of my stories and his introductory note. It was their custom to enjoy as a group the first week of the new year at Pradomar, a resort ten leagues from Barranquilla, where they took over the bar by storm. The only thing I recall with any precision in that tumult is that Ulises in person was one of the great surprises of my life. I had often seen him in Bogotá, at first in El Molino and years later in El Automático, and sometimes at Maestro de Greiff's *tertulia*. I remembered his unsociable appearance and his metal voice, and on that basis I concluded that he was bad-tempered, which no doubt was the reputation he had among the good readers at the university. As a consequence I had avoided him on various occasions in order not to contaminate the image I had invented for my own personal use. I was mistaken. He was one of the most affectionate and obliging people I can remember, though I understand he needed a special reason of the mind or heart.

His temperament was nothing like that of Don Ramón Vinyes, Álvaro Mutis, or León de Greiff, but he shared with them an innate aptitude for teaching at any hour, and the uncommon luck of having read all the books that had to be read.

I became more than a friend of the younger Canos—Luis Gabriel, Guillermo, Alfonso, and Fidel—when I worked as a reporter at *El Espectador*. It would be reckless to try to recall any dialogue from those free-for-all conversations during the nights in Pradomar, but it would also be impossible to forget their unbearable insistence on the mortal sickness of journalism and literature. They made me another member of the family and their personal storyteller, discovered and adopted by them and for them. But I do not remember—as has been said so often—anybody even suggesting that I go to work with them. I did not regret it, because at that bad moment I did not have the slightest idea what my destiny would be or if I would be allowed to choose it.

Álvaro Mutis, enthusiastic about the enthusiasm of the Canos, returned to Barranquilla when he was named head of public relations for Colombian Esso and tried to persuade me to work with him in Bogotá. His real mission, however, was much more dramatic: through a terrifying error by some local concessionaire, the tanks at the airport had been filled with gasoline for cars instead of planes, and it was unthinkable that an aircraft filled with that mistaken fuel could go anywhere. Mutis's job was to correct the mistake in absolute secrecy before dawn without the airport officials finding out, much less the press. And he did. The fuel was changed to the correct kind in four hours of conversation and whiskey at the storage tanks of the local airport. We had more than enough time to talk about everything, but the unimaginable subject for me was that Editorial Losada of Buenos Aires would publish the novel I was about to finish. Álvaro Mutis knew this from direct communication with the new manager of Losada in Bogotá, Julio César Villegas, a former minister of the government of Peru who had taken refuge not long before in Colombia.

I do not remember a more intense emotion. Editorial Losada was one of the best in Buenos Aires, filling the publishing vacuum created by the Spanish Civil War. Its editors nourished us on a daily basis with new books that were so interesting and unusual we almost had no time to read them. Its salespeople were punctual in bringing us the books we had ordered, and we welcomed them as messengers of joy. The mere idea that one of them might publish *Leaf Storm* almost drove me mad. As soon as I said goodbye to Mutis in a plane filled with the correct fuel, I ran to the paper to do a thorough revision of the original.

In the days that followed I dedicated all my time to the frantic examination of a text that very well might have gotten away from me. There were no more than one hundred twenty double-spaced pages, but I made so many adjustments, changes, and inventions that I never knew if I left it better or worse. Germán and Alfonso reread the most critical parts and had the kindness not to make irredeemable observations. In that state of apprehension I revised the final version, my heart in my hand, and made the serene decision not to publish it. In the future, this would become a mania. Once I felt satisfied with a completed book, I was left with the devastating impression that I would not be able to write another one that was better.

It was my good fortune that Álvaro Mutis suspected the reason for my delay, and he flew to Barranquilla to take the only clean copy and have it sent to Buenos Aires, not giving me time for a final reading. Commercial photocopiers did not exist yet, and the only thing I had was the first rough draft corrected in the margins and between the lines with inks in different colors to avoid confusion. I threw it in the trash and did not recover my tranquility for the two long months it took to receive their answer.

One day I was handed a letter at *El Heraldo* that had been mislaid on the desk of the editor-in-chief. The imprint of Editorial Losada of Buenos Aires froze my heart, but I was too shy to open it there and I went to my private cubicle. And so I faced without witnesses the unadorned notification that *Leaf Storm* had been rejected. I did not have to read the entire verdict to feel its brutal impact and know I was going to die then and there.

The letter was the supreme judgment of Don Guillermo de Torre, president of the editorial board, and it was supported by a series of simple arguments resonant with the diction, emphasis, and smugness of white men from Castilla. The only consolation was the surprising final concession: "One must recognize in the author his excellent gifts as an observer and a poet." Even today, however, it surprises me that beyond my own consternation and shame, even the most acidic objections seemed relevant.

I never made a copy of the letter or knew what happened to it after it circulated for several months among my friends in Barranquilla, who summoned all kinds of soothing reasons to try to console me. Of course, fifty years later, when I tried to obtain a copy in order to document these memoirs, not a trace of it was to be found in the publishing house in Buenos Aires. I do not remember if it was published as a news item, though I never intended it to be, but I do know that I needed a long time to recover my spirits after losing my temper and writing a furious letter that was published without my authorization. This breach of trust caused me even greater sorrow, because my final reaction had been to take advantage of what was useful to me in the verdict, correct everything that in my judgment was correctable, and move ahead.

The opinions of Germán Vargas, Alfonso Fuenmayor, and Álvaro Cepeda gave me the greatest encouragement. I found Alfonso at a food stand in the public market, where he had discovered an oasis for reading in the bustle of trade. I asked him if I should leave my novel as it was or try to rewrite it with a different structure, because it seemed to me that the second half lost the tension of the first. Alfonso listened with a certain impatience, and gave me his verdict.

"Look, Maestro," he said at last, like a complete teacher, "Guillermo de Torre is as respectable as he believes himself to be, but I don't think he's very up-to-date on the modern novel."

In other conversations that I had at the time, I was comforted by the precedent of Guillermo de Torre rejecting the original of Pablo Neruda's *Residence on Earth*, in 1927. Fuenmayor thought my novel might have met a different fate if the reader had been Jorge Luis Borges, but then the devastation would have been worse if he had rejected it too.

"So don't fuck around anymore," Alfonso concluded. "Your novel is as good as we thought it was, and the only thing you have to do, starting right now, is to go on writing."

Germán—faithful to his prudent ways—did me the favor of not exaggerating. He thought the novel was not so bad that it should not be published on a continent where the genre was in crisis, and not so good that it was worth provoking an international scandal in which the only loser would be an unknown novice writer. Álvaro Cepeda summarized the opinion of Guillermo de Torre with another of his florid memorials:

"It's just that Spaniards are very stupid."

When I realized I did not have a clean copy of my novel, Editorial Losada let me know by a third or fourth party that it was their practice not to return originals. It was a stroke of luck that Julio César Villegas had made a copy before forwarding mine to Buenos Aires, and he sent it to me. Then I began another correction based on my friends' conclusions. I eliminated a long episode in which the female protagonist contemplated a three-day rainstorm from the hallway of the begonias, which I later turned into the "Monologue of Isabel Watching It Rain in Macondo." I dropped a superfluous dialogue between the grandfather and Colonel Aureliano Buendía a short time before the slaughter of the banana workers, and some thirty pages that interfered in form and substance with the unified structure of the novel. Almost twenty years later, when I believed they were forgotten, parts of those fragments helped me sustain nostalgic memories throughout the length and breadth of *One Hundred Years of Solitude*.

I had almost overcome the blow when the news was published that the Colombian novel selected instead of mine for publication by Editorial Losada was *Christ with His Back Turned*, by Eduardo Caballero Calderón. It was an error, or a truth falsified in bad faith, because it was not a question of a contest but rather a scheme of Editorial Losada to enter the Colombian market with Colombian authors, and my novel was not rejected in competition with any other but because Don Guillermo de Torre did not consider it publishable.

My consternation was greater than I recognized at the time, and I did not have the courage to endure it if I did not convince myself. And so I dropped in unannounced to see my childhood friend, Luis Carmelo Correa, on the Sevilla banana plantation—a few leagues from Cataca—where he worked as a part-time comptroller and fiscal auditor. We spent two days recapitulating once again our shared childhood, as we always did. His memory, his intuition, and his frankness were so revelatory that they caused a certain terror in me. As we spoke, he used his toolbox to make repairs on the house, and I listened to him from a hammock rocked by the tenuous breeze of the plantations. Nena Sánchez, his wife, weak with laughter in the kitchen, corrected our wild ideas and lapses of memory. At last, in a stroll of reconciliation through the deserted streets of Aracataca, I understood to what extent I had recovered my good spirits, and I had no doubt at all that *Leaf Storm*—rejected or not—was the book I had intended to write after the trip with my mother.

Encouraged by that experience, I went to find Rafael Escalona in his paradise in Valledupar, trying to dig into my world down to the roots. It did not surprise me, because it was as if I had already lived everything I found, everything that happened, all the people I encountered, not in another life but in the one that I was living. Later, on one of my countless trips, I met Colonel Clemente Escalona, Rafael's father, who impressed me from the first with his dignity and old-fashioned patriarch's bearing. He was as slim and straight as a reed, with weather-beaten skin, prominent bones, and perfect dignity. From the time I was very young I had been pursued by the subject of the anguish and decorum with which my grandparents waited until the end of their long lives for the veteran's pension. But four years later, when at last I was writing the book in an old hotel in Paris, the image I always had in mind was not my grandfather but Don Clemente Escalona as the physical replica of the colonel who had nobody to write to him.

I learned from Rafael Escalona that Manuel Zapata Olivella

had set up practice as a doctor to the poor in the town of La Paz, a few kilometers from Valledupar, and that was where we went. We arrived at dusk, and there was something in the air that made it difficult to breathe. Zapata and Escalona reminded me that only twenty days earlier the town had been the victim of an assault by the police who were sowing terror in the region in order to impose the will of the government. It was a night of horror. They killed at random and set fire to fifteen houses.

Because of the iron censorship we had not learned the truth. But at the time I did not even have the opportunity to imagine it. Juan López, the best musician in the region, had left never to return after that black night. In his house we asked Pablo, his younger brother, to play for us, and with intrepid simplicity he said:

"I'll never sing again in my life."

Then we learned that not only he but all the musicians in the town had put away their accordions, their bass drums, their *guacharacas*,* and had not sung again out of grief for their dead. It was understandable, and Escalona himself, who was the teacher of many of them, and Zapata Olivella, who was beginning to be the physician to all of them, could not persuade anyone to sing.

Faced with our insistence, the neighbors came to give their reasons, but at the bottom of their hearts they felt that the mourning could not go on any longer. "It's like having died along with the dead," said a woman who wore a red rose behind her ear. People supported her. Then Pablo López must have felt authorized to wring the neck of his grief, for without saying a word he went into his house and came out with his accordion. He sang as never before, and as he sang other musicians began to arrive. Someone opened the store across the way and offered drinks on the house. The other stores started to open after a month of mourning, and the lights were turned on, and we all sang. Half an hour later the entire town was singing. On

---

*A rasping percussion instrument, also known as a *güiro*, usually made of wood or a gourd, and sometimes metal, which is played by rubbing a stick up and down along the ridges cut into the instrument.

the empty square the first drunk in a month came out, and at the top of his lungs he sang one of Escalona's songs, dedicated to Escalona himself in homage to the miracle of his having resuscitated the town.

It was fortunate that life went on in the rest of the world. Two months after the rejection of the manuscript I met Julio César Villegas, who had broken with Editorial Losada and been named the representative in Colombia of Editorial González Porto, which sold encyclopedias and scientific and technical books on the installment plan. Villegas was the tallest and strongest man, the most resourceful when faced with the worst dangers of real life, an immoderate consumer of the most expensive whiskeys, an ineluctable conversationalist, and a salon fabulist. On the night of our first meeting in the presidential suite of the hotel in El Prado, I staggered out carrying a traveling salesman's case filled with advertising brochures and samples of illustrated encyclopedias and books on medicine, law, and engineering from Editorial González Porto. After the second whiskey I had agreed to transform myself into a seller of books on the installment plan in the province of Padilla, from Valledupar to La Guajira. My earnings were an advance in cash on a twenty-percent commission, which I had to earn in order to live without difficulties after paying my expenses, including the hotel.

This is the trip that I myself made legendary because of the incorrigible defect of not weighing my adjectives in time. The legend is that it was planned as a mythic expedition in search of my roots in the land of my elders, following the same romantic itinerary as my mother when her mother took her away to save her from the telegraph operator in Aracataca. The truth is that mine was not one trip but two, which were very brief and bewildering.

On the second trip I returned only to the towns around Valledupar. Once there, of course, I anticipated continuing on to Cabo de la Vela on the same route as my enamored mother, but I only got as far as Manaure de la Sierra, La Paz, and Villanueva, a few leagues from Valledupar. At that time I did not know San Juan del César, or Barrancas, where my grandparents married and my mother was born, and where Colonel Nicolás Márquez killed Medardo Pacheco; I did not even visit Rio-hacha, which is the embryo of my tribe, until 1984, when President Belisario Betancur sent a group of invited friends from Bogotá to inaugurate the coal mines in Cerrejón. It was my first trip to my imaginary Guajira, which seemed as mythic as the one I had so often described without knowing it, though I do not think it was on account of my false recollections but because of the memory of the Indians my grandfather had pur-chased for a hundred pesos each for the house in Aracataca. My greatest surprise, of course, was my first glimpse of Riohacha, the city of sand and salt where my people had been born since my great-great-grandparents, where my grandmother saw the Virgen de los Remedios put out the flame in the oven with an icy breath when the bread was about to burn, where my grand-father fought his wars and suffered prison for a crime of love, and where I was conceived on my parents' honeymoon.

In Valledupar I did not have much time at my disposal for selling books. I was staying at the Hotel Wellcome, a stupen-dous, well-preserved colonial mansion on the main square, which had a long bower of palm in the courtyard with rustic tables at the bar and hammocks hanging from hooks. Víctor Cohen, the proprietor, was as vigilant as Cerberus about the order of his house, as well as his moral reputation when it was threatened by dissipated strangers. He was also a purist con-cerning the language, and he would declaim Cervantes from memory with a lisping Castilian accent, and place García Lorca's morality in dispute. I got along well with him because of his knowledge of Don Andrés Bello and his rigorous recita-tions of Colombian romantics, and did not get on with him because of his obsession with stopping infractions of the moral codes within the pure environs of his hotel. All this began in a very simple way because he was an old friend of my uncle Juan de Dios, and took pleasure in evoking his memories.

For me that shed in the courtyard was a stroke of luck, because the many hours I had to spare I spent reading in a hammock in the suffocating heat of midday. In times of famine I even read treatises on surgery and accounting manuals, not thinking they would be of use to me in my adventures as a writer. The work was almost spontaneous, because most of my clients were connected somehow to the Iguarán and Cotes clans, and one visit that would last until lunch, evoking family secrets, was enough. Some signed the contract without reading it so as to be on time since the rest of the tribe was waiting for us to have lunch in the shade of the accordions. Between Valledupar and La Paz I reaped my great harvest in less than a week and returned to Barranquilla with the feeling that I had been in the only place in the world I really understood.

Very early on June 13, I was going somewhere on the bus when I learned that the Armed Forces had taken power in light of the disorder that reigned in the government and throughout the country. The year before, on September 6, a mob of Conservative thugs and uniformed police in Bogotá had set fire to the buildings of *El Tiempo* and *El Espectador*, the two most important daily papers in the country, and used guns in their attacks on the residences of former president Alfonso López Pumarejo, and Carlos Lleras Restrepo, president of the Liberal leadership. The latter, known as a politician with a hard character, managed to exchange shots with his attackers, but in the end he found himself obliged to escape over the walls of a nearby house. The situation of official violence that the country had endured since April 9 had become untenable.

Until dawn of that June 13, when the division general Gustavo Rojas Pinilla removed the acting president, Roberto Urdaneta Arbeláez. Laureano Gómez, the titular president who had resigned on the advice of his doctors, then reassumed power in a wheelchair and tried to effect a coup against himself and govern for the fifteen months remaining in his constitutional term. But Rojas Pinilla and his staff had come to stay.

National backing was immediate and unanimous for the decision of the Constituent Assembly that legitimized the military coup. Rojas Pinilla was invested with powers until the end of the presidential term, in August of the following year, and Laureano Gómez traveled with his family to Benidorm, on the east coast of Spain, leaving behind the illusory impression that his times of raging fury had come to an end. The Liberal patriarchs proclaimed their support of national reconciliation with a call to their fellow party members fighting throughout the country. The most significant photograph that the newspapers printed in the days that followed was of an advance party of Liberals singing a lovers' serenade under the balcony of the presidential bedroom. The homage was led by Don Roberto García Peña, publisher of *El Tiempo* and one of the fiercest opponents of the deposed regime.

In any case, the most moving photograph from those days showed the interminable line of Liberal guerrillas turning in their weapons on the eastern Llanos, commanded by Guadalupe Salcedo, whose image as a romantic bandit had touched in a profound way the hearts of Colombians punished by official violence. It was a new generation of guerrilla fighters against the Conservative regime, who were identified somehow as left over from the War of a Thousand Days and who maintained relations that were in no way clandestine with the legal heads of the Liberal Party.

At their head, Guadalupe Salcedo had disseminated a new mythic image to all levels in the country, those in favor of him and those opposed. Perhaps that was why—four years after his surrender—he was riddled with bullets by the police somewhere in Bogotá, in a place that has never been specified, under circumstances that have not been established with certainty.

The official date is June 6, 1957, and in a solemn ceremony his body was placed in a numbered crypt of the central cemetery in Bogotá, with well-known politicians in attendance. For Guadalupe Salcedo, from his fighting headquarters, maintained not only political but social relations with the leaders of a Liberalism in disgrace. But there are at least eight different versions of his death, and no lack of skeptics from that time and this who still wonder if the body was his and if in fact it is in the crypt where it was buried.

In that state of mind I set out on my second business trip to the Province, after confirming with Villegas that everything was in order. As I had the first time, I made very rapid sales in Valledupar to a clientele convinced ahead of time. I went with Rafael Escalona and Poncho Cotes to Villanueva, La Paz,

Patillal, and Manaure de la Sierra to visit veterinarians and agronomists. Some had spoken with buyers from my previous trip and were waiting for me with special orders. Any time of day was fine for organizing a fiesta with these same clients and their good-natured *compadres,* and we would stay up all night singing with the great accordion players, not interfering with commitments or the payment of urgent bills because ordinary life continued its natural rhythm in the uproar of our carousing. In Villanueva we were with an accordion player and two drummers who appeared to be the grandchildren of someone we had listened to as children in Aracataca. So that what had been a childhood enthusiasm was revealed to me on that trip as an inspired craft that would accompany me for the rest of my life.

This time I got to know Manaure, in the heart of the sierra, a beautiful and tranquil town, historic in my family because that was where they took my mother for a change of climate when she was a girl and had a tertian fever that resisted all kinds of potions. I had heard so much about Manaure, about its May afternoons and medicinal breakfasts, that when I was there for the first time I realized I remembered it as if I had known it in a former life.

We were having a cold beer in the only tavern in town when a man approached our table who looked like a tree, wore riding gaiters, and had a military revolver in his belt. Rafael Escalona introduced us, and he stood looking into my eyes, still holding my hand.

"Do you have anything to do with Colonel Nicolás Márquez?" he asked.

"I'm his grandson," I told him.

"Then," he said, "your grandfather killed my grandfather."

That is to say, he was the grandson of Medardo Pacheco, the man my grandfather had killed in a duel. He did not give me time to be frightened because he said it in a very warm manner, as if this too was a way of being kin. We caroused with him for three days and three nights in his double-bottomed truck, drinking warm brandy and eating stewed goat in memory of our dead grandfathers. Several days went by before he confessed the truth: he had arranged with Escalona to frighten me, but he did not have the heart to go on with the jokes about our dead grandfathers. In reality his name was José Prudencio Aguilar, and he was a smuggler by trade, an upright and goodhearted man. In homage to him, and to even the score, in *One Hundred Years of Solitude* I gave his name to the rival killed with a lance by José Arcadio Buendía in the cockfighting pit.

The bad thing was that at the end of that nostalgic trip the books I had sold had not yet arrived, and without them I could not collect my advance. I was left without a *céntimo* and the hotel metronome was moving faster than my nights of fiesta. Víctor Cohen began to lose the little patience remaining to him because of the lie that I was squandering the money for his bill with low-class drunks and cheap sluts. The only thing that gave me back my peace of mind was the thwarted love affair in *The Right to Be Born*, the radio soap opera by Don Félix B. Caignet, whose popular impact revived my old illusions about sentimental literature. The unexpected reading of Hemingway's *The Old Man and the Sea*, which came as a surprise in the magazine *Life en Español*, completed my recovery from my sorrows.

In the same mail delivery the shipment of books arrived, which I had to distribute to their owners in order to collect my advance. Everyone paid on time, but by now I owed the hotel more than twice what I had earned, and Villegas warned me that I would not get anything else for another three weeks. Then I had a serious conversation with Víctor Cohen, and he accepted an IOU with a guarantor. Since Escalona and his crew were not available, a providential friend did that favor for me with no obligations, just because he had liked a story of mine published in *Crónica*. But at the moment of truth I could not pay anyone.

The IOU became historic years later when Víctor Cohen would show it to his friends and visitors, not as an accusatory document but as a trophy. The last time I saw him he was almost one hundred years old, tall, slim, and lucid, and with his sense of humor intact. Almost fifty years later, at the baptism of the son of my *comadre* Consuelo Araujonoguera, for whom I was godfather, I saw the unpaid IOU. Víctor Cohen showed it to anyone who wanted to see it, with his usual grace and courtesy. I was surprised by the neatness of the document he had written and the enormous will to pay that could be seen in the boldness of my signature. Víctor celebrated it that night by dancing a *vallenato* promenade with the kind of colonial elegance no one had brought to that dance since the days of Francisco el Hombre. When it was over, many friends thanked me for not having paid the IOU that had given rise to that priceless night.

The seductive magic of Dr. Villegas would produce even more, but not with books. It is not possible to forget the majestic skill with which he sidestepped creditors and the joy with which they understood his reasons for not paying on time. The most tempting of his subjects at the time had to do with the novel *The Roads Have Been Closed*, by the Barranquillan writer Olga Salcedo de Medina, which had provoked an uproar more social than literary, with few regional precedents. Inspired by the success of *The Right to Be Born*, which I had followed with growing interest for the entire month, I thought we were in the presence of a popular phenomenon we writers could not ignore. Without even referring to my debt, I had mentioned this to Villegas on my return from Valledupar, and he proposed that I write the adaptation with enough wickedness to triple the vast audience already caught up in the radio drama of Félix B. Caignet.

I made the adaptation for radio broadcast in two weeks of seclusion that seemed much more revelatory than I had anticipated, with measured dialogues, degrees of intensity, and situations and quick tempos that in no way resembled anything I had written before. With my inexperience in dialogue—which still is not my forte—the effort was valuable and I was more grateful for what I learned than for what I earned. But I had no complaints about that either, because Villegas advanced me half the amount in cash and agreed to cancel my earlier debt with the first income from the soap opera.

It was recorded at the Atlántico station, with the best possible regional distribution, and directed without experience or inspiration by Villegas himself. For the narrator, Germán Vargas had been recommended as a speaker who would be distinctive because of the contrast between his sobriety and the stridency of local radio. The first great surprise was that Germán agreed, and the second was that after the first rehearsal he concluded he was not the right person. Then Villegas in person assumed responsibility for the narration with his Andean cadence and hisses, which in the end denatured that bold adventure.

The entire soap opera was recorded with more grief than glory, and it was a brilliant classroom for my insatiable ambitions as a narrator in any genre. I attended the recordings, which were made directly onto the blank disc with a needle like a plow that left tufts of black, luminous, almost invisible filaments, like angel hair. Each night I took home a large handful that I distributed to my friends as an unusual trophy. With untold difficulties and shoddy work, the soap opera was aired at the same time as a colossal party very typical of the promoter.

No one could invent even a pro forma argument to make me believe that anyone liked it, but it had a good audience and enough of a publicity campaign to save face. It was my good fortune that it infused me with new energy in a genre that seemed to be racing toward unimaginable horizons. My gratitude to and admiration for Don Félix B. Caignet reached the point where I asked him for a private interview some ten years later, when I lived for a few months in Havana as a reporter at the Cuban agency Prensa Latina. But despite all kinds of arguments and pretexts, he never would see me, and all I had from him was a brilliant lesson that I read in one of his interviews: "People always want to cry: the only thing I do is give them an excuse." And Villegas's magic spells produced nothing else. There were complications with Editorial González Porto—as there had been earlier with Losada—and there was no way to settle our final accounts because he abandoned his dreams of greatness and returned to his country.

Álvaro Cepeda Samudio took me out of purgatory with his old idea of transforming *El Nacional* into the modern newspaper he had learned how to make in the United States. Until then, aside from his occasional contributions to *Crónica*, which always were literary, he had only had the opportunity to use his degree from Columbia University in the condensed pieces he would send to *The Sporting News*, in St. Louis, Missouri. At last, in 1953, our friend Julián Davis Echandía, who had been Álvaro's first employer, called to ask him to take charge of the general management of his evening paper, *El Nacional*. Álvaro himself had disturbed him with the astronomical project he presented to him on his return from New York, but once the mastodon had been captured he called to ask me to help him carry it, with no titles or specified duties, but with an advance on my first paycheck that was enough for me to live on even without collecting my entire salary.

It was a fatal adventure. Álvaro had formulated the entire plan with models from the United States. Davis Echandía was like God on high, a precursor from the heroic days of local sensationalist journalism and the least decipherable man I ever knew, good by birth and more sentimental than compassionate. The rest of the staff were a boisterous crop of great hard-hitting reporters, all of them friends and colleagues of many years' standing. In theory each one had his well-defined orbit, but beyond that no one ever knew who did what, so that the enormous technical mastodon never managed to even take its first step. The few issues that were put out were the result of a heroic act, but no one ever knew whose. When it was time to go to press, the plates were out of order. Urgent material would disappear, and we would go mad with rage. I do not recall the paper ever coming out on time and without corrections, on account of the crouching devils we had in the printing facilities. No one ever knew what happened. The prevailing explanation was perhaps the least perverse: some aging veterans could not tolerate the renovatory regime and conspired with their soulmates until they succeeded in destroying the enterprise.

Álvaro left, the door slamming behind him. I had a contract that would have been a guarantee under normal conditions, but under the worst it was a straitjacket. Eager to derive some benefit from the time that had been lost, I attempted to assemble as fast as I could type any valid pieces with loose ends that were left over from earlier efforts: fragments of *La casa*, parodies of the truculent Faulkner of *Light in August*, of Nathaniel Hawthorne's dead birds raining down, of the detective stories I had grown tired of because they were repetitive, and some bruises I still had left from the trip to Aracataca with my mother. I was letting them flow as they pleased in my sterile office, where nothing was left but the chipped, peeling desk and the typewriter breathing its last, until in one sitting I came to the final title: "One Day After Saturday." One of my few stories that left me satisfied after the first version.

At *El Nacional* I was approached by a salesman peddling wristwatches. I had never had one, for obvious reasons at that time, and the one he was offering was showy and expensive. Then the salesman himself confessed that he was a member of the Communist Party whose job was to sell watches as bait for catching contributors.

"It's like buying the revolution on the installment plan," he said.

I answered in a good-natured way:

"The difference is that I get the watch right away but not the revolution."

The salesman did not take the bad joke very well, and I ended up buying the cheapest watch just to make him happy, with a schedule of payments that he would come by to collect every month. It was the first watch I ever owned, and so accurate and durable that I still keep it as a relic of those days.

At this time Álvaro Mutis returned with the news of a vast cultural budget from his company and the imminent appearance of the magazine *Lámpara*, its literary publication. When he invited me to contribute I proposed an emergency project: the legend of La Sierpe. I thought that if I wanted to tell it one day, it should not be through any rhetorical prism but recovered from the collective imagination as what it was: a geographical and historical truth. That is—at last—a great feature article.

"You do whatever you want and however you want to do it," Mutis told me. "But do it, because it has the atmosphere and tone we're looking for in the magazine."

I promised he would have it in two weeks. Before he left for the airport he called his office in Bogotá and ordered payment in advance. The check that came in the mail a week later left me breathless. Even more so when I went to cash it and the bank teller was troubled by my appearance. I was obliged to go to a higher office, where a far too amiable manager asked me where I worked. I answered, as was my habit, that I wrote for *El Heraldo*, although by then it was no longer true. That was all. The manager examined the check on his desk, observed it with an air of professional suspicion, and at last passed judgment:

"This is a perfect document."

That same afternoon, as I was beginning to write "La Sierpe," they told me I had a call from the bank. I began to think that the check was not reliable for any of the countless reasons possible in Colombia. I almost could not swallow the lump in my throat when the bank official, with the dissolute cadence of the Andeans, apologized for not having known at the time that the beggar who cashed the check was the author of "La Jirafa."

Mutis returned again at the end of the year. He ate little of his lunch as he helped me think of some stable and permanent way to earn more money without wearing myself out. In the end, what seemed best to him was to let the Cano family know I would be available for *El Espectador*, though the mere idea of returning to Bogotá still put my nerves on edge. But Álvaro never let up when it was a matter of helping a friend.

"Let's do this," he said, "I'm going to send you the fare so you can go whenever you want and however you want, and we'll see what we can come up with."

It was too much for me to say no, but I was sure that the last plane in my life had been the one that took me out of Bogotá after April 9. Besides, the scant rights from the soap opera and the projected publication of the first chapter of "La Sierpe" in the magazine *Lámpara* had gotten me some advertising copy that paid enough for me to send a relief ship to my family in Cartagena. And so once again I resisted the temptation to move to Bogotá.

Álvaro Cepeda, Germán and Alfonso, and most of my friends from the Japy and the Café Roma, spoke to me in good terms about "La Sierpe" when the first chapter was published in *Lámpara*. They agreed that the direct journalistic solution had been the one best suited to a theme that was on the dangerous frontier of what could not be believed. Alfonso, with his half-joking, half-serious style, told me something I never forgot: "The fact is that credibility, my dear Maestro, depends a good deal on the face you put on when you tell the story." I was about to reveal to them Álvaro Mutis's proposals for a job, but I did not dare to, and today I know it was because of my fear that they would approve. He had pressed me again, even after he made a reservation for me on the plane and I canceled it at the last minute. He gave me his word that he was not delivering a message secondhand for *El Espectador* or any other written or spoken medium. His only purpose—he insisted until the end—was his desire to talk about a series of fixed contributions to the magazine and to examine some technical details regarding the complete series of "La Sierpe," whose second chapter was to appear in the upcoming issue. Álvaro Mutis seemed certain that this kind of reporting could be a good kick at trite *costumbrismo* on its own terrain. Of all the reasons he had suggested so far, this was the only one that left me thinking.

One Tuesday filled with melancholy drizzle, I realized I could not go even if I wanted to because the only clothes I had were my dancer's shirts. At six in the evening I did not find anyone in the Librería Mundo, and I stood waiting in the doorway, with a knot of tears for the melancholy twilight that was beginning to fall. On the sidewalk across the street was a store window with formal clothing that I had never seen although it had always been there, and without thinking about what I was doing I crossed Calle San Blas under the ashes of the rain, and walked with a firm step into the most expensive store in the city. I bought a clerical suit of midnight-blue wool, perfect for the spirit of Bogotá at that time, two white shirts with stiff collars, a tie with diagonal stripes, and a pair of shoes of the kind that the actor José Mojica made fashionable before he became a saint. The only people whom I told that I was leaving were Germán, Álvaro, and Alfonso, and they approved the decision as a sensible one as long as I did not come back a Cachaco.

We celebrated at El Tercer Hombre with the entire group until dawn, as an advance party for my next birthday, for Germán Vargas, who was the guardian of the saints' calendar, let it be known that on March 6 I would be twenty-seven years old. In the midst of the good wishes of my great friends, I felt ready to devour raw the seventy-three I still had left before I celebrated the first hundred.

8

THE PUBLISHER OF *El Espectador*, Guillermo Cano,
called me on the phone when he learned I was in
Álvaro Mutis's office, four floors above his in a building that had just opened, about five blocks from his former
location. I had arrived the night before and was getting ready
to have lunch with a group of Mutis's friends, but Guillermo
insisted I stop by first to say hello. I did. After the effusive hugs
in the style of the capital of fine speech, and a comment or two
on the news of the day, he seized me by the arm and moved me
away from his colleagues in the newsroom. "Listen to me for a
minute, Gabriel," he said with an innocence that was beyond
suspicion, "why don't you do me a huge favor and write just a
short editorial that I need before we send the paper to press?"
With his thumb and index finger he showed me the size of half
a glass of water and concluded:

"This long."

More amused than he was, I asked him where I could sit, and
he pointed to an empty desk with a typewriter from another
day. I sat down with no further questions, thinking about a
good subject, and I remained seated there in the same chair, at
the same desk, and with the same typewriter for the next eighteen months.

Minutes after my arrival Eduardo Zalamea Borda, the

deputy editor, came out of the next office, absorbed in a bundle of papers. He was startled when he recognized me.

"Man! Don Gabo!" he almost shouted, using the name he had invented for me in Barranquilla as a shortened form of Gabito, and which only he used. But this time it spread around the newsroom and they continued using it even in print: Gabo.

I do not remember the subject of the editorial that Guillermo Cano had me write, but since my days at the Universidad Nacional, I had been very familiar with the dynastic style of *El Espectador*. And in particular the one used in the section "Day by Day" on the editorial page, which enjoyed a well-deserved prestige, and I decided to imitate it with the sangfroid of Luisa Santiaga confronting the demons of adversity. I finished it in half an hour, made some corrections by hand, and turned it in to Guillermo Cano, who stood as he read it over the arc of his glasses for myopia. His concentration seemed to belong not only to him but to an entire dynasty of white-haired forebears, begun by Don Fidel Cano, the founder of the paper in 1887, continued by his son Don Luis, consolidated by his brother Don Gabriel, and taken into his bloodstream when it was already mature by his grandson Guillermo, who had just assumed the general management of the paper at the age of twenty-three. Just as his forebears would have done, he made a few minor revisions and finished with the first practical and simplified use of my new name:

"Very nice, Gabo."

On the night of my return I had realized that Bogotá would not be the same for me again as long as my memories survived. Like many great catastrophes in the country, April 9 had produced more forgetting than history. The Hotel Granada had been razed in its centenarian park and the far too new building of the Banco de la República was beginning to rise in its place. The old streets from our time did not seem to belong to anyone but the well-lit streetcars, and the corner of the historic crime had lost its grandeur in the spaces vanquished by fires. "Now it really looks like a big city," someone who was with us said in astonishment. And finished breaking my heart with the ritual phrase:

"We have to be grateful for April 9."

On the other hand, I had never been more comfortable than in the nameless *pensión* where Álvaro Mutis had put me. A house beautified by misfortune, on the side of the Parque Nacional, where on the first night I could not endure the envy I felt toward my neighbors in the next room who were making love as if engaged in joyous battle. The next day, when I saw them leave, I could not believe they were the same people: a skinny little girl in a dress from a public orphanage and a very old gentleman with silver hair, who was two meters tall and could have been her grandfather. I thought I had been mistaken, but they themselves made sure to confirm it for me every night thereafter, shouting their deaths until dawn.

El Espectador published my piece in a prominent position on the editorial page. I spent the morning in large stores buying clothing that Mutis imposed on me in the booming English accent he invented to amuse the salesclerks. We had lunch with Gonzalo Mallarino and other young writers who had been invited so that I could be presented to society. I heard nothing further from Guillermo Cano until three days later, when he called while I was in Mutis's office.

"Listen, Gabo, what happened to you?" he said with a poor imitation of the severity of a publisher. "Yesterday we went to press late waiting for your article."

I went down to the newsroom to talk to him, and I still do not know how I continued writing unsigned editorials every afternoon for more than a week without anybody talking to me about a job or a salary. In our conversations during breaks the reporters treated me as if I were one of them, and in fact I was without imagining to what extent.

The section "Day by Day" was never signed, and as a rule Guillermo Cano led off with a political editorial. In an order established by management, next came a piece on any subject by Gonzalo González, who also wrote the most intelligent and popular section in the paper—"Questions and Answers"— where he dispensed with readers' doubts under the pseudonym Gog, not on account of Giovanni Papini but because of his own name. After that they published my editorials, and on very rare occasions something special by Eduardo Zalamea, who occupied the best space every day on the editorial page—"The City and the World"—using the pseudonym Ulises, not Homer's—as he would always explain—but James Joyce's.

Álvaro Mutis had to make a business trip to Port-au-Prince early in the new year, and he invited me to go with him. Haiti became the country of my dreams after I read Alejo Carpentier's *The Kingdom of This World*. I still had not given him my answer on February 18, when I wrote a piece about the queen mother of England lost in the solitude of an immense Buckingham Palace. It surprised me that it was published in the lead position of "Day by Day" and had been well received in our offices. That night, at a small gathering at the house of José Salgar, the editor-in-chief, Eduardo Zalamea's comments were even more enthusiastic. Some benevolent traitor later told me that this opinion had dissipated any remaining reluctance on the part of management to make me a formal offer of a permanent job.

Very early the next day Álvaro Mutis called me to his office to give me the sad news that the trip to Haiti had been canceled. What he did not tell me was that this had been decided after a casual conversation with Guillermo Cano, who had asked in all sincerity that he not take me to Port-au-Prince. Álvaro, who did not know Haiti either, wanted to know why. "Well, when you see it," Guillermo told him, "you'll understand that it's the place Gabo may like most in the world." And he put the finishing touch on the afternoon with a masterful bullfighter's pass:

"If Gabo goes to Haiti he'll never come back."

Álvaro understood, canceled the trip, and made it seem a decision by his company. And so I never visited Port-au-Prince, but I did not know the real reasons until a few years ago, when Álvaro told them to me in yet another of our endless evocations worthy of grandfathers. Guillermo, for his part, once he had me tied down with a contract at the paper, repeated to me for years that I should think about a great feature article on Haiti, but I never could go and I never told him why.

The thought of being a staff reporter for *El Espectador* had never crossed my mind. I understood that they would publish my stories because of the scarcity and poor quality of the genre in Colombia, but writing every day for an evening paper was quite a different challenge for someone with little experience in hard-hitting journalism. Half a century old, brought up in a rented house on surplus machines from *El Tiempo*—a rich, powerful, and influential paper—*El Espectador* was a modest evening newspaper of sixteen crowded pages, but its five thousand copies, counted in a lax way, were snatched from the newsboys almost at the doors of the printing plant and read in half an hour in the taciturn cafés of the old city. Eduardo Zalamea Borda had stated on the BBC in London that it was the best newspaper in the world. What was most compelling was not the statement itself, but the fact that almost everyone who worked on the paper, and many of those who read it, were convinced that this was true.

I must confess that my heart skipped a beat on the day following the cancellation of the trip to Haiti, when Luis Gabriel Cano, the general manager, made an appointment with me in his office. The interview, with all its formality, lasted less than five minutes. Luis Gabriel had a reputation for being a gruff man, generous as a friend and the kind of miser a good manager should be, but then, and always, he seemed to me very concrete and cordial. His proposal in solemn terms was that I stay on the paper as a staff reporter to write articles on general topics, as well as opinion pieces and whatever else might be needed in the tribulations of the last minute, at a salary of nine hundred pesos a month. I could not breathe. When I recovered I asked him again how much, and he repeated it for me, letter by letter: nine hundred. This made so great an impression on me that some months later, talking about it at a party, my dear Luis Gabriel revealed to me that he had interpreted my surprise as an expression of rejection. Don Gabriel had expressed the final doubt, based on a well-founded fear: "He's so skinny and pale, he might die in the office." This was how I became a staff reporter at *El Espectador*, where I used the greatest amount of paper in my life in less than two years.

It was a fortunate coincidence. The most frightening institution at the paper was Don Gabriel Cano, the patriarch, who by his own decision established himself as the implacable inquisitor of the newsroom. With his millimetric magnifying glass he would read even the most unexpected comma in the daily edition, mark in red the mistakes in each article, and display on a bulletin board the clippings punished by his devastating comments. The bulletin board was known from the first day as the "Wall of Infamy," and I do not recall a single reporter who escaped his bloodthirsty pen.

The spectacular advancement of Guillermo Cano to publisher of *El Espectador* at the age of twenty-three did not seem to be the early fruit of his personal merits but the fulfillment of a destiny written before he was born. For that reason my first surprise was learning that he really was the publisher, when many of us on the outside thought he was no more than an obedient son. What struck me most was the speed with which he could recognize what was news.

At times he had to confront everyone, even without many arguments, until he succeeded in convincing them of the truth. It was a time when the profession was not taught at universities but learned on the job, breathing in the printer's ink, and *El Espectador* had the best teachers, with good hearts but firm hands. Guillermo Cano had begun there as soon as he could write, with articles on the bulls so severe and erudite that his principal calling did not seem to be journalism but bullfighting. And so the most difficult experience of his life must have been seeing himself advanced from one day to the next, with no intermediate steps, from beginning student to senior teacher. No one who did not know him well could have imagined the awful determination of his character behind a gentle and somewhat evasive manner. He engaged in vast and dangerous battles with the same passion, not ever stopping when faced with the certainty that behind even the most noble causes death could be lying in ambush.

I have never known anyone more unwilling to engage in public life, more reluctant to accept personal honors, more disdainful of the blandishments of power. He was a man with few friends, but those few were very close, and I felt that I was one of them from the first day. Perhaps the fact that I was one of the youngest in a newsroom of battle-scarred veterans contributed to this, for it created between the two of us a sense of complicity that never weakened. What was exemplary about that friendship was its ability to prevail over opposing opinions. Our political disagreements were very deep and became even deeper as the world around us fell apart, but we always knew how to find a common ground where we could continue fighting together for the causes we thought were just.

The newsroom was enormous, with desks on both sides, and an atmosphere dominated by good humor and crude jokes. There was Darío Bautista, a strange kind of counterminister of finance, who from first cockcrow devoted himself to making the dawn bitter for the highest functionaries, with cabalistic divinations of a sinister future that were almost always correct. There was the legal reporter, Felipe González Toledo, a born journalist who often was far ahead of any official investigation in the art of stopping an injustice and solving a crime. Guillermo Lanao, who took care of several ministries, preserved the secret of being a child until his tenderest old age. Rogelio Echaverría, one of the great poets, was responsible for the morning edition and we never saw him in the light of day. My cousin Gonzalo González, his leg in a cast because of a soccer injury, had to study in order to answer questions about anything, and in the end he became a specialist in anything. In spite of having been a front-rank soccer player at the university, he had endless faith in theoretical study over and above experience. He gave us a stellar demonstration of this in the reporters' bowling championship, when he devoted himself to studying the physical laws of the game in a manual instead of practicing until dawn at the alleys, like the rest of us, and he was that year's champion.

With a staff like this the newsroom was an eternal entertainment, always subject to the motto of Darío Bautista or Felipe González Toledo: "If you lose your temper you're fucking yourself." We all knew everybody else's subjects and helped as much as we could and to the extent that we were asked. Sharing was so great that you could almost say we worked out loud. But when things became difficult you could not hear anyone breathing. From the only desk set on an angle, at the back of the room, José Salgar was in command, and he would walk around the room, informing and becoming informed about everything, while he vented his soul's passion with his conjurer's therapy.

I believe that the afternoon when Guillermo Cano took me from desk to desk, walking the length of the room in order to introduce me into society, was the trial by fire for my invincible timidity. I could not speak and my knees were shaking when, without looking at anyone, Darío Bautista bellowed in his fearsome thundering voice:

"The genius has arrived!"

The only thing I could think of was to make a theatrical half-turn with my arm extended toward everyone and say the least witty thing that came from my soul:

"Your humble servant."

I still suffer from the impact of everyone's jeers, but I also feel the consolation of the embraces and kind words with which each of them welcomed me. From then on I was one more member of that community of charitable tigers whose friendship and esprit de corps never weakened. Any information I needed for an article, no matter how small, I would request from the corresponding reporter, who never failed to get it to me on time.

I received my first great lesson as a reporter from Guillermo Cano, and the entire newsroom experienced it one afternoon when a downpour fell on Bogotá that kept it in a state of universal flood for three hours on end. The torrent of churning water on the Avenida Jiménez de Quesada swept everything in its path down the slope of the hills and left a wake of catastrophe on the streets. Cars of every description and public transport were paralyzed in the place where the emergency had caught them, and thousands of pedestrians struggled to find shelter in the flooded buildings until there was no room left for more. We reporters, surprised by the disaster at the moment the paper was going to press, contemplated the sad spectacle from the windows, not knowing what to do, standing like punished children with our hands in our pockets. All of a sudden

Guillermo Cano seemed to wake from a bottomless sleep, and he turned toward the paralyzed staff and shouted:

"This storm is news!"

It was an unissued order that was obeyed without delay. We ran to our combat posts to obtain by phone the hasty facts indicated by José Salgar so that all of us could write in bits and pieces the story of the rainstorm of the century. Ambulances and emergency radio patrol cars were immobilized by vehicles stalled in the middle of the streets. Domestic drains were blocked by the water and the entire corps of firefighters was not enough to conjure away the emergency. Whole neighborhoods had to be evacuated because an urban dam broke. In other districts the sewers erupted. The sidewalks were occupied by ancient invalids, the sick, and asphyxiated children. In the middle of the chaos, five owners of motorboats used for fishing on weekends organized a championship race on the Avenida Caracas, the busiest street in the city. José Salgar distributed these facts, which had been collected on the spot, to the reporters, and we elaborated on them for the special edition that was improvised on the fly. The photographers, soaked to the skin through their raincoats, processed their photographs at once. A little before five, Guillermo Cano wrote the masterful synthesis of one of the most dramatic storms in the memory of the city. When the weather cleared at last, the improvised edition of *El Espectador* circulated as it did every day, no more than an hour late.

My initial relationship with José Salgar was the most difficult, but it was always more creative than any other. I believe he had the opposite problem to mine: he was always trying to get his staff reporters to make a supreme effort, while I longed for him to put me on that wavelength. But my other commitments to the paper tied me down, and the only hours I had free were on Sunday. It seems to me that Salgar had his eye on me to be a reporter, while the others had relegated me to films, editorials, and cultural matters because I always had been designated a short-story writer. But my dream was to be a reporter ever since my first steps on the coast, and I knew that Salgar was the best teacher, but he closed doors to me, perhaps in the hope that I would knock them down and force my way in. We worked very well in a cordial and dynamic way, and each time I handed him material written according to Guillermo Cano and even Eduardo Zalamea, he approved it without hesitation but did not forgo the ritual. He made the strenuous gesture of forcing a cork out of a bottle and said with more seriousness than he himself seemed to believe:

"Wring the neck of the swan."*

But he was never aggressive. Just the opposite: a cordial man, forged in fire, who had climbed the ladder of good service, from distributing coffee in the printing plant when he was fourteen to becoming the editor in chief with the greatest professional authority in Colombia. I believe he could not forgive me for wasting my time on lyrical sleight-of-hand in a country where so many hard-hitting reporters were needed. On the other hand, I thought that no journalism was better than feature articles for expressing daily life. But today I know that the obstinacy with which we both tried to do this was the greatest incentive I had for realizing the distant dream of becoming a reporter.

The opportunity waylaid me at twenty past eleven on the morning of June 9, 1954, as I was coming back from visiting a friend in the Modelo Prison in Bogotá. Army troops armed for war kept a crowd of students at bay on Carrera Séptima, two blocks from the corner where Jorge Eliécer Gaitán had been assassinated six years earlier. It was a demonstration protesting the killing of a student the day before by members of the Colombia Battalion who had been trained for the Korean War, and the first street clash between civilians and the government of the Armed Forces. From where I stood you could hear only the shouts of the argument between the students who were trying to proceed to the Palacio Presidencial and the soldiers who were stopping them. In the middle of the crowd we could not understand what they were shouting, but you could sense the

*This comment is based on a well-known admonition to Latin American poets, early in the twentieth century, to abandon the symbolist and Parnassian school of Modernism for a more local and relevant style of writing.

tension in the air. Then, with no warning at all, we heard a burst of machine-gun fire followed by two more, one right after the other. Several students and some passersby were killed on the spot. The survivors who tried to take the wounded to the hospital were dissuaded with blows from rifle butts. The troops evacuated the area and closed off the streets. In the stampeding crowd I lived again in a few seconds all the horror of April 9, at the same hour and in the same place.

I almost raced the three steep blocks to the building of *El Espectador* and found the newsroom cleared for action. With a knot in my throat I recounted what I had been able to see at the site of the massacre, but someone who knew even less was already writing at top speed the first article about the identity of the nine dead students and the condition of the wounded in the hospitals. I was sure they would order me to recount the outrage because I was the only one who had seen it, but Guillermo Cano and José Salgar had already agreed that it ought to be a collective report in which each person would contribute something. The reporter in charge, Felipe González Toledo, would give it its final unity.

"Take it easy," said Felipe, concerned about my disappointment. "People know that everybody here works on everything even if it's unsigned."

For his part, Ulises consoled me with the idea that the editorial I had to write could be the most important element because it would deal with a very serious problem of public order. He was right, but it was so delicate a piece, and so compromising to the paper's politics, that it was written by several hands at the highest levels. I believe it was an important lesson for everyone, but to me it seemed disheartening. That was the end of the honeymoon between the government of the Armed Forces and the Liberal press. It had begun a year earlier with General Rojas Pinilla's assumption of power, which allowed the country a sigh of relief after the bloodbath of two successive Conservative governments, and it lasted until that day. For me it was also a trial by fire in my dream of being an ordinary reporter.

A short while later a photograph was published of the body of an unclaimed child whom they had not been able to identify in the amphitheater of Forensic Medicine, and to me it looked the same as one published a few days earlier of another child who had disappeared. I showed them to the head of the judicial section, Felipe González Toledo, and he called the mother of the first boy, who still had not been found. It was a lesson for the rest of my life. The mother of the child who had disappeared was waiting for Felipe and me in the vestibule of the amphitheater. She seemed so poor and diminished that I made a supreme effort, wishing with all my heart that the corpse was not her son. In the long glacial basement, under intense lighting, there were some twenty tables arranged in a row with bodies like stone burial mounds under dull sheets. The three of us followed the solemn guard to the next-to-the-last table in the rear. Under the bottom edge of the sheet the soles of some sad little boots could be seen, the heels very worn down by use. The woman recognized them, turned livid, but controlled herself with her last breath until the guard removed the sheet with a bullfighter's flourish. It was the body of a boy about nine years old, his eyes open and astonished, and wearing the same wretched clothes in which he had been found, dead for several days, in a ditch beside the road. The mother let out a howl and fell to the floor, screaming. Felipe picked her up and calmed her with murmurs of consolation, while I asked myself if that ought to be the profession I dreamed about. Eduardo Zalamea confirmed for me that it was not. He also thought that crime reporting, so well established among readers, was a difficult specialization that required a certain kind of character and an impregnable heart. I never attempted it again.

A very different kind of reality forced me to be a movie critic. It had never occurred to me that I could be one, but in Don Antonio Daconte's Olympia Theater in Aracataca, and then in the traveling school of Álvaro Cepeda, I had glimpsed the basic elements for writing a guide to films using a more helpful criterion than the one known until then in Colombia. Ernesto Volkening, a great German writer and literary critic who had lived in Bogotá since the war, broadcast a commentary on new films on Radio Nacional, but it was limited to an audience of specialists. There were other excellent but occasional commentators associated with the Catalan bookseller Luis Vicens, a resident of Bogotá since the Spanish Civil War. It was he who founded the first cinema club with the painter Enrique Grau, the critic Hernando Salcedo, and the hard work of the journalist Gloria Valencia de Castaño Castillo, who had first-class credentials. There was an immense public in the country for big action movies and tearful melodramas, but good cinema was limited to well-educated aficionados, and exhibitors were willing to risk less and less on films that ran for three days on posters. Finding a new public in that faceless crowd required a difficult but possible pedagogy that would foster an audience open to good films and help exhibitors who wanted to show them but could not finance them. The greatest difficulty was that exhibitors could hold over the press the threat of canceling movie advertisements—which provided substantial income to the papers—in reprisal for negative reviews. *El Espectador* was the first to face the risk, and I was assigned the task of commenting on the movie openings of the week, more as an elementary primer for fans than as pontificating criticism. One precaution taken by common consent was that I would always carry my complimentary pass intact as proof that I had bought my ticket at the box office.

The first reviews soothed the exhibitors because they were about films in a good sampling of foreign cinema. Among them, *Puccini*, an extensive recapitulation of the life of the great musician; *So This Is Love*, which was the well-told story of the singer Grace Moore; and *La Fête à Henriette*, a peaceable comedy by Julien Duvivier. The owners we met as we left the theater indicated their satisfaction with our critical comments. Álvaro Cepeda, on the other hand, woke me at six in the morning with a call from Barranquilla when he learned of my audacity.

"How could you even think of being a movie critic without my permission, damn it!" he shouted into the telephone, convulsed with laughter. "You're an imbecile about films!"

He became my constant assistant, of course, though he never agreed with the idea that it was not a question of teaching but of orienting an elementary public without academic training. And the honeymoon with the owners was not as sweet as we thought at the beginning. When we faced commercial cinema pure and simple, even the most understanding complained of the harshness of our comments. Eduardo Zalamea and Guillermo Cano were able to deflect them on the phone until the end of April, when an exhibitor who presumed to be a leader accused us in an open letter of intimidating the public in order to prejudice his interests. It seemed to me that the heart of the problem was that the author of the letter did not know the meaning of the word intimidate, but I felt on the verge of defeat because I did not believe it possible that in the paper's crisis of expansion, Don Gabriel Cano would renounce movie advertisements for the sake of pure esthetic pleasure. On the day he received the letter, he summoned his sons and Ulises to an urgent meeting, and I considered it a given that the section would be dead and buried. But as he passed my desk after the meeting, Don Gabriel said to me without specifying the subject and with a grandfather's mischievousness:

"Don't worry, my little namesake."

The next day the response to the producer appeared in "Day by Day," written by Guillermo Cano in a deliberate academic style, and its conclusion said it all: "The public is not intimidated and certainly no one's interests are prejudiced if the press publishes serious and responsible cinematic criticism, which resembles that of other countries and breaks the old and prejudicial patterns of immoderate praise for what is good as well as what is bad." It was not the only letter or our only response. Functionaries from the movie theaters attacked with bitter complaints, and we received contradictory letters from confused readers. But it was all in vain: the column survived until movie criticism stopped being occasional in the country and became routine in the press and on the radio.

After that, in a little less than two years, I published seventy-five critical reviews, to which should be added the hours spent seeing the films. In addition to some six hundred editorials, a signed or unsigned article every three days, and at least eighty feature articles, some signed, some anonymous. My literary contributions were published in the *Magazine Dominical* of the same paper, including several stories and the complete series on "La Sierpe," which had been interrupted in the magazine *Lámpara* because of internal disagreements.

It was the first prosperity in my life, but I had no time to enjoy it. The apartment that I rented furnished, with laundry service, was no more than a bedroom with a bath, telephone, breakfast in bed, and a large window looking out on the eternal drizzle of the saddest city in the world. I used it only for sleeping from three in the morning, after I had read for an hour, until the morning newscasts on the radio would orient me to the actuality of the new day.

I did not stop thinking with a certain disquiet that it was the first time I had my own fixed place to live but had no time even to think about it. I was so busy dealing with my new life that my only notable expense was the lifeboat I sent without fail at the end of the month to my family. I realize only today that I almost had no time to think about my private life. Perhaps because there survived inside me the idea of Caribbean mothers that women from Bogotá gave themselves without love to men from the coast only to fulfill their dream of living by the ocean. But in my first bachelor apartment in Bogotá, I accomplished this without risk when I asked the porter if visits from female friends at midnight were permitted, and he gave me this wise reply:

"It's prohibited, Señor, but I don't see what I shouldn't."

At the end of July, without prior warning, José Salgar stopped in front of my desk as I was writing an editorial and looked at me in a long silence. I stopped in the middle of a sentence and said to him, intrigued:

"What's going on!"

He did not even blink, playing an invisible bolero with his red pencil, wearing a diabolical smile whose purpose was far too noticeable. He explained without being asked that he had not authorized me to write the article on the massacre of the students on Carrera Séptima because it was a difficult assignment for a beginner. On the other hand, he would offer me, on his own responsibility, the reporter's diploma, in a direct way but without the slightest spirit of a challenge, if I was capable of accepting a mortal proposition from him:

"Why don't you go to Medellín and tell us what the hell it was that happened there?"

It was not easy to understand, because he was talking about something that had occurred more than two weeks earlier, which allowed the suspicion that the news was stale beyond recovery. It was known that on the morning of July 12 there had been a landslide in La Media Luna, a steep, craggy place in the east of Medellín, but the outrage in the press, the disorder among the authorities, and the panic of those injured had caused administrative and humanitarian confusions that obscured the reality. Salgar did not ask me to try to establish as far as possible what had happened, he ordered me flat out to reconstruct the whole truth and nothing but the truth on the site, and in a minimum amount of time. But something in the way he said it made me think that at last he had loosened the rein.

Until then the only thing everyone knew about Medellín was that Carlos Gardel had died there, burned to a crisp in an aerial catastrophe. I knew it was a land of great writers and poets, and that the Colegio de la Presentación, where Mercedes Barcha had begun to study that year, was located there. Faced with so delirious a mission, it no longer seemed unattainable to reconstruct, piece by piece, the calamity of a mountain. And so I landed in Medellín at eleven in the morning, in a rainstorm so frightening I deceived myself into thinking I would be the final victim of the landslide.

I left my suitcase in the Hotel Nutibara, with clothing for two days and an emergency tie, and went out to the street in an idyllic city still clouded over with the remnants of the storm. Álvaro Mutis had made the trip to help me endure my fear of planes, and he put me on the track of well-placed people in the life of the city. But the chilling truth was that I did not have the slightest idea of where to begin. I wandered streets radiant under the golden dust of a splendid sun following the storm, and after an hour I had to take shelter in the first store I came to because it started raining again while the sun was shining. Then I began to feel the first flutterings of panic in my chest. I tried to repress them with my grandfather's magic formula in the middle of combat, but in the end my fear of fear overcame my morale. I realized I would never be able to do what I had been assigned to do, and I had not had the courage to say so. Then I understood that the only sensible thing would be to write a letter of thanks to Guillermo Cano and go back to Barranquilla and the state of grace in which I had found myself six months earlier.

With the immense relief of having come out of hell, I took a taxi to go back to the hotel. The midday newscaster made a long commentary at the top of his voice, as if the landslides had happened yesterday. The driver almost shouted as he gave vent to his feelings about the negligence of the government and the poor handling of relief for the injured, and somehow I felt responsible for his righteous anger. But then it cleared again, and the air became diaphanous and fragrant because of the explosion of flowers in Parque Berrío. All of a sudden, I do not know why, I felt the onset of madness.

"Let's do this," I said to the driver. "Before we go to the hotel, take me to the place where the landslides happened."

"But there's nothing to see there," he said. "Just lit candles and little crosses for the dead they haven't been able to get out."

This was how I learned that victims as well as survivors came from different parts of the city, and the survivors had walked across town en masse to recover the bodies of those killed in the first slide. The great tragedy occurred when curious on-lookers overran the site, and another part of the mountain slid down in a devastating avalanche. So that the only people who could tell the story were the few who had escaped successive slides and were alive at the other end of the city.

"I understand," I told the driver, trying to control the tremor in my voice. "Take me to where the living are."

He made a U-turn in the middle of the street and raced off in the opposite direction. His silence must have been the result not only of his current speed but also his hope of convincing me with his explanations.

The thread of the story began with two boys, eight and eleven years old, who had left their house to cut wood on Tuesday, July 12, at seven in the morning. They had gone about a hundred meters when they heard the crash of the avalanche of earth and rocks rushing toward them down the side of the hill. They just managed to escape. Their three younger sisters were trapped in the house along with their mother and their new-born baby brother. The only survivors in the family were the two boys who had just gone out, and the father, who had left early for his work as a sand vendor ten kilometers from the house.

The place was an inhospitable wasteland along the highway from Medellín to Rionegro, which at eight in the morning had no inhabitants to become further victims. The radio stations had broadcast the exaggerated news item with so many bloody details and urgent appeals that the first volunteers arrived before the firefighters. At noon two more victimless slides had taken place, which increased the general anxiety, and a local radio station set itself up for direct transmission from the site where the disaster had occurred. At that time almost all the inhabitants of nearby towns and neighborhoods were there, in addition to the curious from all over the city drawn by the appeals on the radio, and the passengers who got off intercity buses more to interfere than to help. In addition to the few bodies from the morning, there were another three hundred in the successive slides. But late in the afternoon, more than two thousand unprepared volunteers were still offering confused assistance to the survivors. By sunset there was almost no room to breathe. The crowd was dense and chaotic at six o'clock, when another devastating avalanche of six hundred thousand cubic meters came down with a colossal din, causing as many victims as if it had happened in Parque Berrío in Medellín. A catastrophe so rapid that Dr. Javier Mora, the city's secretary of public works, found in the rubble the body of a rabbit that did not have time to escape.

Two weeks later, when I visited the site, only seventy-four corpses had been recovered, and numerous survivors were out of danger. Most were victims not of the slides but of impru-dence and unruly solidarity. As happens in earthquakes, it was not possible to calculate the number of people with problems who took advantage of the opportunity to disappear without a trace in order to escape their debts or change their wife. But good fortune also had a part to play, because a subsequent investigation showed that after the first day, while recoveries were still being attempted, a mass of rock capable of generating an avalanche of fifty thousand cubic meters had been about to dislodge. More than fifteen days later, with the help of survivors who now were calm, I was able to reconstruct the story, which would not have been possible at the moment it happened because of the awkwardness and unwieldiness of reality.

My job was reduced to rescuing the truth that had been lost in a tangle of contrary suppositions and reconstructing the human drama in the order in which it had occurred, and apart from all political and sentimental calculation. Álvaro Mutis had set me on the right track when he sent me to the publicist Cecilia Warren, who organized the data I brought back from the site of the disaster. The feature article was published in three parts, and it at least had the merit of awakening interest in a forgotten news item two weeks after the event and bringing order to the chaos of the tragedy.

But my best memory of those days is not what I did but what I almost did thanks to the delirious imagination of my old pal from Barranquilla, Orlando Rivera (Figurita), whom I happened to run into on one of my few breaks from the investigation. He had been living in Medellín for the past few months, and was the happy new husband of Sol Santamaría, a charming, free-spirited nun whom he had helped to leave a cloistered convent after seven years of poverty, obedience, and chastity. During one of our memorable drinking bouts, Figurita revealed that he had prepared, with his wife and on his own account, a masterful plan to get Mercedes Barcha out of her boarding school. A priest who was a friend of his, and famous for his arts as a matchmaker, would be ready at any hour to marry us. The only condition, of course, was that Mercedes agree, but we found no way to talk it over with her inside the four walls of her captivity. Today more than ever I feel fierce regret at not having the temerity to live that newspaper-serial drama. Mercedes, for her part, did not learn of the plan until more than fifty years later, when she read about it in the rough draft of this book.

It was one of the last times I saw Figurita. During Carnival in 1960, disguised as a Cuban tiger, he slipped from the float that was taking him back to his house in Baranoa after the final parade and broke his neck on the pavement covered with debris and trash.

On the second night of my work on the landslides in Medellín, two reporters from *El Colombiano*—so young they were even younger than me—were waiting at the hotel, determined to interview me about the stories of mine that had been published up to that time. It was hard for them to persuade me, because I had, and still have, a prejudice that may be unfair against interviews understood as a session of questions and answers in which both parties make an effort to maintain a revelatory conversation. I suffered from this prejudice at the two papers where I had worked, and above all at *Crónica*, where I tried to infect the contributors with my reluctance. But I granted that first interview for *El Colombiano*, and its sincerity was suicidal.

Today I have been the victim of countless interviews over the course of fifty years and in half the world, and I still have not convinced myself of the efficacy of the genre, either asking the questions or answering them. An immense majority of the ones I have not been able to avoid on any subject ought to be considered as an important part of my works of fiction, because they are no more than that: fantasies about my life. On the other hand, I consider them invaluable, not for publication but as raw material for feature articles, which I value as the stellar genre of the best profession in the world.

In any case, it was not the time for festivals. The government of General Rojas Pinilla, now in open conflict with the press and a large part of public opinion, had ended the month of September with the decision to divide the remote and forgotten department of El Chocó among its three prosperous neighbors: Antioquia, Caldas, and Valle. Quibdó, the capital, could be reached from Medellín only on a one-lane road in such bad condition that more than twenty hours were needed to travel one hundred seventy kilometers. The situation is no better today.

In the newsroom of the paper we regarded it as certain that there was not much we could do to stop the dismemberment decreed by a government on bad terms with the Liberal press. Primo Guerrero, *El Espectador*'s veteran correspondent in Quibdó, reported on the third day that a popular demonstration of entire families, including the children, had occupied the main square, determined to stay there day and night until the government abandoned its plan. The first photographs of the rebellious mothers holding their children in their arms were languishing as the days passed because of the ravages of the vigil on a population living outdoors. Every day we reinforced these reports in the newsroom with editorials or statements by Chocoan politicians and intellectuals residing in Bogotá, but the government seemed resolved to win through indifference. After several days, however, José Salgar approached my desk with his puppeteer's pencil and suggested that I go to investigate what was really happening in El Chocó. I tried to resist with the small authority I had gained with my report on Medellín, but it was not enough. Guillermo Cano, who was writing with his back to us, shouted without turning around:

"Go on, Gabo, the women in El Chocó are better than the ones you wanted to see in Haiti!"

And so I left without even asking myself how you could write an article on a protest demonstration that rejected violence. I was accompanied by the photographer Guillermo Sánchez, who for months had been pestering me about our doing war stories together. Tired of hearing him, I had shouted at him:

"What war, damn it!"

"Don't be a damn fool, Gabo," he delivered the truth with a single stroke, "I always hear you saying that this country has been at war since Independence."

At dawn on Tuesday, September 21, he appeared in the newsroom ready to cover a muzzled war, dressed more like a guerrilla fighter than a photojournalist, with cameras and bags hanging all over his body. The first surprise before you even left Bogotá was that you went to El Chocó from a secondary airport without services of any kind, surrounded by the wreckage of dead trucks and rusted airplanes. Ours, still alive through the arts of magic, was one of the legendary Catalinas from the Second World War operated as a cargo plane by a civilian company. It had no seats. The interior was unadorned and gloomy, with small clouded windows and a cargo of bales of fibers for making brooms. We were the only passengers. The copilot in shirtsleeves, young and good-looking like the aviators in movies, told us to sit on the bales because they seemed more comfortable. He did not recognize me, but I knew he had been a notable baseball player in the La Matuna leagues in Cartagena.

The takeoff was terrifying, even for a passenger as experienced as Guillermo Sánchez, because of the thundering roar of the engines and the scrap-metal clanging of the fuselage, but once stabilized in the translucent sky of the savanna, the plane glided along with the courage of a war veteran. But past Medellín we were surprised by a diluvian rainstorm over a tangled forest between two cordilleras, and we had to fly right into it. Then we experienced something that perhaps very few mortals have experienced: it rained into the airplane through the leaks in the fuselage. Our friend the copilot, leaping over bales of brooms, brought us the day's papers to use as umbrellas. I covered even my face with mine, not so much to protect myself from the rain as to keep the others from seeing me weep with terror.

After two hours of luck and chance, the plane leaned to its left, descended in attack position over a dense forest, and gave two exploratory turns above the main square of Quibdó. Guillermo Sánchez, prepared to capture from the air the protest exhausted by its erosive vigils, found nothing but the empty square. The dilapidated amphibian gave one last turn to confirm that there were no obstacles living or dead in the peaceful Atrato River, and completed its felicitous landing on water in the suffocating heat of midday.

The church patched with boards, the cement benches plastered by birds, and an ownerless mule crunching on the branches of a gigantic tree were the only signs of human existence in the dusty, solitary square that looked like nothing so much as an African capital. Our original intention had been to take urgent photographs of the crowd standing in protest and send them to Bogotá on the return plane, while we obtained enough first-hand information for tomorrow's edition, which we could send by telegraph. None of that was possible, because nothing had happened.

There were no witnesses as we walked the very long street parallel to the river, lined with shops that were closed for lunch and residences with wooden balconies and rusted roofs. It was the perfect stage but there was no play. Our good colleague Primo Guerrero, correspondent for *El Espectador*, was taking a siesta without a care in the world in a springlike hammock under the arbor in his house, as if the silence that surrounded him was the peace of the grave. The frankness with which he explained his indolence could not have been more objective. After the demonstrations of the first few days, the tension had eased for lack of topics. Then a mobilization of the entire town was organized with theatrical techniques, some pictures were taken that were not published because they were not very credible, and patriotic speeches were given that in fact had shaken the country, but the government remained imperturbable. Primo Guerrero, with an ethical flexibility that perhaps even God has forgiven him for, kept the protest alive in the press by dint of telegrams.

Our professional problem was simple: we had not undertaken that Tarzanic expedition in order to report that the news did not exist. On the other hand, we had access to the means to make it true and achieve its purpose. Primo Guerrero proposed organizing the portable demonstration one more time, and nobody could think of a better idea. Our most enthusiastic collaborator was Captain Luis A. Cano, the new governor appointed after the angry resignation of the previous one, and he had the fortitude to delay the plane so that the paper would receive Guillermo Sánchez's red-hot photographs in time. That was how the news item invented by necessity became the only one that was true, magnified by the press and radio throughout the country and caught on the fly by the military government in order to save face. That same night a general mobilization of Chocoan politicians began—some of them very influential in certain sectors of the country—and two days later General Rojas Pinilla declared the cancellation of his own decision to distribute pieces of El Chocó to its neighbors.

Guillermo Sánchez and I did not return to Bogotá right away because we persuaded the paper to allow us to travel through the interior of El Chocó in order to gain profound knowledge of the reality of that fantastic world. After ten days of silence, when we walked into the newsroom tanned by the sun and dropping with fatigue, José Salgar received us, happy but with his usual firmness of character.

"Do you know," he asked us with his unconquerable certainty, "how long the news about El Chocó has been over?"

The question confronted me for the first time with the mortal condition of journalism. No one, in fact, had taken interest again in El Chocó once the presidential decision not to dismember it had been published. But José Salgar supported me in the risky undertaking of cooking up what I could out of that dead fish.

What we tried to convey in four long installments was the discovery inside Colombia of another inconceivable country that we had not been aware of. A magical homeland of flowering jungles and eternal downpours, where everything seemed like an unimaginable version of ordinary life. The great difficulty in constructing overland routes was the enormous number of indomitable rivers, but there was no more than one bridge in the entire territory. We found a highway seventy-five kilometers long through the virgin forest, built at enormous cost to connect the towns of Itsmina and Yuto, though it did not pass through either one: an act of retaliation by the builder because of his disputes with the two mayors.

In one of the villages in the interior the postal agent asked us to take six months' worth of mail to his colleague in Itsmina. A pack of domestic cigarettes cost thirty centavos there, as it did in the rest of the country, but when the small weekly supply plane was late the cigarettes increased in price for each day of delay, until the inhabitants found themselves forced to smoke foreign cigarettes that ended up cheaper than domestic ones. A sack of rice cost fifteen pesos more than at the site of cultivation because it was carried through eighty kilometers of virgin jungle on the backs of mules that clung like cats to the mountainsides. The women in the poorest towns panned for gold and platinum in the rivers while the men fished, and on Saturdays they would sell commercial travelers a dozen fish and four grams of platinum for only three pesos.

All this took place in a society famous for its desire to study. But schools were few and far between, and students had to travel several leagues every day, on foot and by canoe, to get to school and come home again. Some were so crowded that the same school was used Mondays, Wednesdays, and Fridays for boys, and Tuesdays, Thursdays, and Saturdays for girls. Circumstances made them the most democratic in the country, because the child of the laundress who did not have enough to eat attended the same school as the child of the mayor.

Very few Colombians at the time knew that in the very heart of the Chocoan jungle was one of the most modern cities in the country. Its name was Andagoya, located at the juncture of the San Juan and Condoto Rivers, and it had a perfect telephone system, and docks for the boats and launches that belonged to the city of beautiful tree-lined avenues. The small, clean houses, with large fenced-in spaces and picturesque wooden steps at the door, seemed planted on the lawns. In the center was a casino with a cabaret-restaurant and a bar where imported liquors cost less than in the rest of the country. It was a city inhabited by men from all over the world who had forgotten nostalgia and lived there better than in their own lands under the all-embracing authority of the local manager of the Chocó Pacífico. For Andagoya, in real life, was a foreign nation of private property, whose dredgers plundered gold and platinum from prehistoric rivers and carried them away in its own boats that went out into the world under no one's control through the mouths of the San Juan River.

This was the Chocó that we wanted to reveal to Colombians, but with no result at all, because once the news was over everything fell back into place and it continued to be the most forgotten region in the country. I believe that the reason is evident: Colombia had always been a country with a Caribbean identity that opened to the world by means of the umbilical cord of Panama. Its forced amputation condemned us to be what we are today: a nation with an Andean mentality whose circumstances favor the canal between two oceans belonging not to us but to the United States.

The rhythm of the newsroom every week would have been fatal if not for Friday afternoons, when we freed ourselves from work and congregated in the bar of the Hotel Continental across the street for some relaxation that tended to last until dawn. Eduardo Zalamea baptized those nights with a name of his own invention: "cultural Fridays." It was my only opportunity to converse with him so I would not miss hearing about the new books in the world, which he kept up with in his capacity as an extraordinary reader. The survivors in those *tertulias* filled with infinite drinks and unforeseeable conclusions—other than two or three eternal friends of Ulises—were those of us reporters who were not afraid to wring the neck of the swan until daybreak.

It had always surprised me that Zalamea never made any observation regarding my editorials, although many of them were inspired by his. But when the "cultural Fridays" were established, he gave free rein to his ideas on the genre. He confessed that he disagreed with the judgments in many of my pieces and would suggest others to me, not in the tone of superior to disciple but as writer to writer.

Another frequent refuge after functions at the Cinema Club were the midnight gatherings in the apartment of Luis Vicens and his wife, Nancy, a few blocks from *El Espectador*. He had been a collaborator of Marcel Colin Reval, editor-in-chief of the magazine *Cinématographie française* in Paris, who had traded his cinematic dreams for the good occupation of bookseller in Colombia on account of the wars in Europe. Nancy behaved as a magical host who could enlarge a dining room that sat four into one for twelve. They had met at a family dinner soon after he arrived in Bogotá in 1937. The only place left at the table was next to Nancy, who was horrified when she saw the last guest come in, with his white hair and the skin of a mountain climber burned by the sun. "What bad luck!" she said to herself. "I'll have to sit next to this Pole who probably doesn't even know Spanish." She was almost correct about the language, because the new arrival spoke Castilian in a raw Catalan crossed with French, and she was from Boyacá, with a short temper and a freewheeling tongue. But they got on so well after their initial greeting that they agreed to live together forever.

Their gatherings were improvised, after the great showings of films, in an apartment crowded with a mixture of all the arts, where there was no room for another painting by the young artists of Colombia, some of whom would become famous in the world. Their guests were selected from the best in arts and letters, and members of the group in Barranquilla would show up from time to time. I was made right at home after the appearance of my first movie review, and when I left the paper before midnight I would walk three blocks and oblige them to stay up all night. Maestra Nancy, who in addition to being a sublime cook was also a pitiless matchmaker, would improvise innocent suppers to connect me with the most attractive and liberated girls in the artistic world, and she never forgave my twenty-eight years when I told her that my true vocation was not to be a writer or a journalist but an invincible bachelor.

Álvaro Mutis, in the intervals he had free between his trips around the world, completed in more lofty style my admission into the cultural community. In his capacity as head of public relations for Esso Colombiana, he organized lunches in the most expensive restaurants with people who in reality were valuable and influential in arts and letters, and he often had guests from other cities in the country. The poet Jorge Gaitán Durán, obsessed with creating a great literary magazine that cost a fortune, solved the problem in part with funds from Álvaro Mutis for the promotion of culture. Álvaro Castaño Castillo and his wife, Gloria Valencia, had been trying for years to found a radio station devoted in its entirety to keeping good music and cultural programs within reach. We all kidded them on account of the unreality of their project, except Álvaro Mutis, who did all he could to help them. And so they established the station HJCK, "The world in Bogotá," with a transmitter of five hundred watts, the minimum at the time.

Television did not yet exist in Colombia, but Gloria Valencia invented the metaphysical wonder of broadcasting a fashion show on the radio.

The only repose I permitted myself in those heady times were slow Sunday afternoons in the house of Álvaro Mutis, who taught me to listen to music without prejudices of class. We would lie on the rug listening with our hearts, and with no learned speculations, to the great masters. It was the origin of a passion that had begun in the obscure little room at the Biblioteca Nacional and never forgot us again. Today I have listened to as much music as I have been able to obtain, above all romantic chamber music, which I consider the pinnacle of all arts. In Mexico, while I was writing *One Hundred Years of Solitude*—between 1965 and 1966—I had only two records, which wore out because they were played so often: the Preludes of Debussy and the Beatles' *Hard Day's Night*. Later, in Barcelona, when at last I had almost as many as I had always wanted, alphabetical classification seemed too conventional, and I adopted for my own convenience an instrumental order: the cello, which is my favorite, from Vivaldi to Brahms; the violin, from Corelli to Schoenberg; the clavichord and the piano, from Bach to Bartók. Until I discovered the miracle that all things that sound are music, including the dishes and silverware in the dishwasher, as long as they fulfill the illusion of showing us where life is heading.

My limitation was that I could not write to music because I paid more attention to what I was hearing than to what I was writing, and even today I attend very few concerts because I feel that in my seat a somewhat prurient intimacy is established with strangers sitting near me. But with time and the possibilities of having good music at home, I learned to write with a musical background in harmony with what I am writing. Chopin's nocturnes for quiet episodes, or sextets by Brahms for happy afternoons. On the other hand, for years I did not listen to Mozart after I was assaulted by the perverse idea that Mozart does not exist, because when he is good he is Beethoven and when he is bad he is Haydn.

During the years in which I have evoked these memories, I achieved the miracle, and no kind of music interferes with my writing, though perhaps I am not aware of other virtues, for the greatest surprise was given to me by two very young and diligent Catalan musicians who believed they had discovered surprising affinities between my sixth novel, *The Autumn of the Patriarch*, and Béla Bartók's Piano Concerto No. 3. It is true that I listened to it without respite while I was writing the book, because it created a very special and somewhat unusual state of mind in me, but I never thought it could have influenced me to the point where it would be noticed in my writing. I do not know how the members of the Swedish Academy discovered that weakness when they played it as background to the awarding of my prize. I was grateful in a most profound way for that, of course, but if they had asked me—with all my gratitude and respect for them and for Béla Bartók—I would have preferred one of Francisco el Hombre's spontaneous *romanzas* from the fiestas of my childhood.

In those years there was no cultural project, no book to be written or picture to be painted in Colombia, that did not pass first through Mutis's office. I was witness to his dialogue with a young painter who had everything ready for his obligatory journey to Europe but did not have the money for the trip. Álvaro had not even heard his entire story when he took the magic carpet out of his desk.

"Here's your passage," he said.

I was dazzled by the naturalness with which he performed these miracles without the slightest display of power. For this reason I still ask myself if he did not have something to do with the request made to me at a cocktail party by Oscar Delgado, the secretary of the Asociación Colombiana de Escritores y Artistas, that I participate in the national short-story contest that was about to be declared void. He said it in so unpleasant a way that the proposition seemed indecorous, but someone who overheard explained to me that in a country like ours, one could not be a writer without knowing that literary competitions are simple social pantomimes. "Even the Nobel Prize," he concluded without the slightest malice, and without even thinking about it he put me on my guard for another extraordinary decision that waylaid me twenty-seven years later.

The jury for the short-story competition was composed of Hernando Téllez, Juan Lozano y Lozano, Pedro Gómez Valderrama, and another three writers and critics from the big leagues. And so I made no ethical or economic determinations but spent the night in a final revision of "One Day After Saturday," the story I had written in Barranquilla in a burst of inspiration in the offices of *El Nacional*. After it had been lying in a drawer for more than a year, I thought it might stir a good jury. It did, and there was an extraordinary prize of three thousand pesos.

At this same time, and without any relation to the contest, Don Samuel Lisman Baum, the cultural attaché of the embassy of Israel, dropped into my office, for he had just inaugurated a publishing enterprise with a book of poems by Maestro León de Greiff: *Fifth Hodgepodge Compendium*. The edition was presentable, and I had heard good reports about Lisman Baum. And so I gave him a very much revised copy of *Leaf Storm* and sent him on his way with the commitment to talk later. Above all about money, which in the end—of course—was the only thing we never talked about. Cecilia Porras painted a new cover—which she was never paid for either—based on my description of the character of the boy. The graphics workshop at *El Espectador* provided at no charge the plate for the title pages in color.

I knew nothing else until some five months later, when Editorial Sipa of Bogotá—I had never heard of it—called me at the paper to tell me that the edition of four thousand copies was ready for distribution, but they did not know what to do with it because no one had any word from Lisman Baum. Not even the reporters on the newspaper could find any trace of him, and no one has to this day. Ulises suggested that they sell the copies to bookstores on the basis of a press campaign that he himself initiated with a note that I still have not finished thanking him for. The critical reception was excellent, but most of the edition remained in the warehouse, it never was established how many copies were sold, and I did not receive a *céntimo* of royalties from anyone.

Four years later Eduardo Caballero Calderón, who published the Biblioteca Básica de Cultura Colombiana, included a pocket edition of *Leaf Storm* in a collection of works that were sold at newsstands in Bogotá and other cities. He paid the contracted rights, meager but on time, which had for me the sentimental value of being the first I had received for a book. The edition had some changes that I did not identify as mine, and I did not concern myself with not including them in subsequent editions. Almost thirteen years later, when I passed through Colombia after the launching of *One Hundred Years of Solitude* in Buenos Aires, I found on the newsstands in Bogotá numerous remaindered copies of the first edition of *Leaf Storm* selling for a peso each. I bought all I could carry. Since then I have found in Latin American bookstores other scattered leftovers, which they were trying to sell as historic books. About two years ago an English dealer in old books sold a copy of the first edition of *One Hundred Years of Solitude*, signed by me, for three thousand dollars.

None of those incidents distracted me for an instant from the grinding of my journalist's mill. The initial success of the serialized articles obliged us to find fodder to feed an insatiable beast. The daily tension was untenable, not only in identifying and searching for topics but in the writing, which always was threatened by the charms of fiction. At *El Espectador* there was no doubt: the invariable raw material of the profession was the truth and nothing but the truth, and that kept us in a state of unendurable tension. José Salgar and I ended up so tormented by this that it did not give us a moment's peace even on Sundays, our day of rest.

In 1956 it was learned that Pope Pius XII was suffering from an attack of hiccups that could cost him his life. The only antecedent I recall is the masterful story "P. & O.," by Somerset Maugham, whose protagonist died in the middle of the Indian Ocean from an attack of hiccups that consumed him in five days, while people from all over the world were sending him every kind of extravagant remedy, but I believe I did not know the story at the time. On weekends we did not dare go too far in our excursions to the towns on the savanna because the paper was prepared to publish a special edition in the event of the pope's death. I was in favor of having the edition ready, with only a few spaces to fill with the first cables of his death. Two years later, when I was a correspondent in Rome, the resolution of the papal hiccups was still being awaited.

Another irresistible problem at the paper was the tendency to concern ourselves only with spectacular subjects that could bring in more and more readers, and I had the more modest one of not losing sight of another less-well-served public that thought more with its heart. Among the few topics that I managed to find, I have kept the memory of a simple story that caught me on the fly through the window of a bus. At the entrance to a beautiful colonial house at number 567 on Carrera Octava in Bogotá there was a sign that underrated itself: "Office of Unclaimed Letters of the National Mail Service." I do not remember at all if I ever lost anything by means of those detours, but I got off the bus and knocked at the door. The man who answered was responsible for the office with its six methodical employees, covered by the rust of routine, whose romantic mission it was to find the addressee of any letter gone astray.

It was a lovely house, enormous and dusty, with high ceilings and decaying walls, dim corridors and galleries crowded with ownerless papers. An average of one hundred unclaimed letters came in each day, and of these at least ten had the correct postage, but the envelopes were blank and did not even have the name of the sender. The employees in the office knew them as "letters for the invisible man," and they spared no effort to deliver or return them. But the ceremony for opening them to search for clues had a bureaucratic rigor that was somewhat useless, but praiseworthy.

The article, in just one installment, was published with the title "The Postman Rings a Thousand Times," and a subtitle: "The Cemetery of Dead Letters." When Salgar read it, he said: "You don't have to wring this swan's neck because it was born dead." He published it, with the correct spread, no more and no less, but you could see in his expression that he was as grief-stricken as I by the bitterness of what might have been. Rogelio Echavarría, perhaps because he was a poet, celebrated it in a good-humored way but with a remark I never forgot: "It's just that Gabo will clutch at any straw."

I felt so demoralized that on my own account—and without telling Salgar about it—I decided to find the addressee of a letter that had drawn my special attention. It was postmarked at the Agua de Dios Leprosarium and addressed to "The lady in mourning who goes to five o'clock Mass every day at the Church of Las Aguas." After making all kinds of useless inquiries of the parish priest and his assistants, I continued interviewing the parishioners at five o'clock Mass for several weeks, with no result. It surprised me that the most faithful were three very old women, always dressed in strict mourning, but none of them had anything to do with the Agua de Dios Leprosarium. It was a failure that took me a long time to recover from, not only because of self-love or the desire to perform an act of charity, but because I was convinced that behind the actual story of the woman in mourning lay another impassioned story.

As I was foundering in the swamps of writing feature articles, my relationship with the Barranquilla Group was becoming more intense. Their trips to Bogotá were not frequent, but I assaulted them by phone at any hour and in any difficulty, above all Germán Vargas, because he had a pedagogical concept of reporting. I consulted them about every problem, and there were many, or they called me when there were reasons to congratulate me. I always thought of Álvaro Cepeda as a classmate in the seat next to mine. After the cordial two-way mockery that was mandatory within the group, he got me out of the swamp with a simplicity that never failed to amaze me. On the other hand, my consultations with Alfonso Fuenmayor were more literary. He had the knowledgeable magic to save me from difficulties with examples from great authors, or to dictate to me the saving citation drawn from his bottomless arsenal. His greatest joke was when I asked him for a title for an editorial about street vendors of food who were being hounded by authorities from the Health Department. Alfonso gave me an immediate reply:

"The man who sells food does not die of hunger."

I thanked him with all my heart, and it seemed so opportune I could not resist the temptation of asking him whose it was. Alfonso stopped me cold with the truth I had not remembered:

"It's yours, Maestro."

In fact, I had improvised it for some unsigned editorial but had forgotten it. The story circulated for years among my friends in Barranquilla, whom I never could convince that it had not been a joke.

A chance trip by Álvaro Cepeda to Bogotá distracted me for a few days from the galley ship of the daily news. He came with the idea of making a film for which he had only the title: *The Blue Lobster*. It was a well-informed error, because Luis Vicens, Enrique Grau, and the photographer Nereo López thought he was serious. I heard no more about the project until Vicens sent me a rough draft of the script so that I could add something of mine to Álvaro's original idea. I added something that I do not recall today, but I thought the story was amusing, and it had a large enough dose of lunacy to make it seem like ours.

Everyone did a little of everything, but the papá by right was Luis Vicens, who imposed many of the things remaining from his first steps in Paris. My problem was that I found myself in the middle of one of those lengthy articles that left me no time to breathe, and when I managed to get free the picture was already being shot in Barranquilla.

It is an elementary work whose greatest merit seems to be its command of intuition, which may have been Álvaro Cepeda's tutelary angel. The Italian director Enrico Fulchignoni was present at one of its numerous private showings in Barranquilla, and he surprised us by the extent of his compassion: he thought the film was very good. Thanks to the tenacity and audacity of Tita Manotas, Álvaro's wife, what still remains of *The Blue Lobster* has gone around the world at daring festivals.

These things distracted us at times from the reality of the country, which was terrible. Colombia considered itself free of guerrillas after the Armed Forces took power under the banner of peace and harmony between the parties. Until the massacre of students on Carrera Séptima, no one doubted that something had changed. The military, eager for causes, wanted to prove to the journalists that there was another war going on different from the eternal one between Liberals and Conservatives. We were involved in this when José Salgar walked up to my desk with one of his terrifying ideas:

"Get ready to find out about the war."

Those of us who had been invited to find out about it, with no further details, met at five sharp in the morning to go to the town of Villarrica, one hundred eighty-three kilometers from Bogotá. General Rojas Pinilla, on one of his frequent stopovers at the military base in Melgar, was expecting our visit at the halfway point and had promised a press conference that would end before five in the afternoon, with more than enough time for us to return with firsthand photographs and news.

Those sent by *El Tiempo* were Ramiro Andrade and the photographer Germán Caycedo; there were four others whom I have not been able to recall; and Daniel Rodríguez and I from *El Espectador*. Some wore country outfits, for we had been warned that perhaps we would have to take a few steps into the jungle.

We went as far as Melgar by car, and there we were divided among three helicopters that took us along a narrow, solitary canyon with high, craggy walls in the Cordillera Central. But what impressed me most was the tension of the young pilots, who avoided certain areas where the guerrillas had taken down one helicopter and damaged another the day before. After some fifteen intense minutes, we landed on the enormous, desolate square of Villarrica, whose covering of gravel did not seem strong enough to support the weight of the helicopter. Around the square were wooden buildings with shops in ruins and residences that belonged to no one, except one that had just been painted and had been the town hotel until the terror began.

In front of the helicopter you could see the spurs of the cordillera and the tin roof of the only house just visible through the mists along the cornice. According to the officer who accompanied us, the guerrillas were there with weapons powerful enough to hit us, so that we had to run to the hotel in a zigzag and with our torsos bent over as a basic precaution against possible shots from the cordillera. Only when we reached it did we realize that the hotel had been converted into a barracks.

A colonel with battle decorations, the good looks of a film star, and an intelligent affability explained without alarm that the advance guard of the guerrillas had been in the house in the cordillera for several weeks and from there had attempted several night raids against the town. The army was sure they would attempt something when they saw the helicopters in the square, and the troops were prepared. But after an hour of provocations, including challenges over loudspeakers, the guerrillas gave no signs of life. The disheartened colonel sent a reconnoitering patrol to make certain someone was still in the house.

The tension eased. We journalists left the hotel and explored the nearby streets, including the less embellished ones around the square. The photographer and I, along with some others, began the ascent to the cordillera along a tortuous horseshoe cornice. On the first curve there were soldiers lying in the underbrush, prepared to shoot. An officer advised us to return to the square, since anything could happen, but we paid no attention. Our intention was to climb until we found some guerrilla advance guard that would save the day for us with a big news story.

There was no time. Without warning we heard several simultaneous orders and then a sharp volley from the soldiers. We threw ourselves to the ground near the soldiers, who opened fire at the house on the cornice. In the instantaneous confusion I lost sight of Rodríguez, who ran to find a strategic position for his viewfinder. The shooting was brief but very intense, and it was replaced by a lethal silence.

We had returned to the square when we caught sight of a military patrol coming out of the forest carrying a body in a wheelbarrow. The head of the patrol was very excited and did not permit us to take pictures. I looked around for Rodríguez and saw him appear, about five meters to my right, with his camera ready to shoot. The patrol had not seen him. Then I lived the most intense moment, torn between wondering if I should yell at him not to take the photograph for fear they would shoot him by accident, and the professional instinct to take it at any price. I did not have time, because at the same moment I heard the thunderous shout of the head of the patrol:

"That photograph will not be taken!"

Rodríguez lowered his camera in a slow gesture and came to stand beside me. The cortege passed so close to us we could smell the acid breath of the living bodies and hear the silence of the dead one. When they had gone by, Rodríguez whispered in my ear:

"I took the picture."

He did, but it was never published. The invitation had ended in disaster. Two more soldiers had been wounded, and at least two guerrillas who had already been dragged to the refuge were dead. The colonel changed his mood with a somber expression. He gave us the simple information that the visit was canceled, we had half an hour for lunch, and right after that we would travel to Melgar by highway since the helicopters were reserved for the wounded and the dead. The numbers of each were never revealed.

No one mentioned General Rojas Pinilla's press conference again. In a jeep for six we drove past his house in Melgar and reached Bogotá after midnight. The entire newsroom was waiting for us, for the Office of Information and the Press of the presidency of the Republic had called to report without further details that we would arrive by land but did not indicate if we were alive or dead.

Until then the only intervention by military censorship had been because of the death of the students in the center of Bogotá. There had not been a censor in the newsroom after the last one from the previous government resigned, almost in tears, when he could not endure the reporters' false items and mocking evasions. We knew that the Office of Information and the Press had not lost sight of us, and with frequency they would give us paternal warnings and advice on the telephone. The military, who at the beginning of their government displayed an academic cordiality to the press, became invisible or hermetic. But a loose end kept growing, alone and in silence, and it inspired the certainty, never proved or disproved, that the head of that embryonic guerrilla movement in El Tolima was a twenty-two-year-old boy whose name has not been confirmed or denied: Manuel Marulanda Vélez or Pedro Antonio Marín, known as "Tirofijo," or "Sureshot." Some forty years later Marulanda—consulted about this in his war camp—answered that he did not remember if in reality it was he.

It was not possible to obtain any more information. I had been longing to uncover something since my return from Villarrica but could not find a door. The Office of Information and the Press of the presidency was forbidden to us, and the unpleasant episode at Villarrica lay buried beneath military reserve. I had tossed all hope into the trash when José Salgar stopped in front of my desk, feigning a sangfroid he never had, and showed me a telegram he had just received.

"Here's what you didn't see in Villarrica," he said.

It was the drama of a crowd of boys taken from their towns and villages by the Armed Forces, without prior planning and without resources, to facilitate the war of extermination against the guerrilla fighters of El Tolima. They had been separated from their parents without time to establish whose sons they were, and many of the boys themselves could not say. The drama had begun with an avalanche of twelve hundred adults who had been taken to different towns in El Tolima, after our visit to Melgar, and placed anywhere at all and then abandoned to the hand of God. The children, separated from their parents by simple logistical considerations and dispersed in orphanages throughout the country, amounted to some three thousand, of varying ages and conditions. Only thirty were orphans who had lost both father and mother, and among these was a pair of twins thirteen days old. The mobilization was carried out in absolute secrecy, favored by censorship of the press, until the correspondent for *El Espectador* telegraphed the first pieces of evidence to us from Ambalema, two hundred kilometers from Villarrica.

In less than six hours we found three hundred children under the age of five in the Bogotá Children's Asylum, many of them with no family records. Helí Rodríguez, who was two years old, could just say his name. He did not know anything about anything, where he was or why, or the names of his parents, and he could not give any clue to finding them. His only consolation was that he had the right to remain in the asylum until he was fourteen. The budget of the orphanage was nourished by the eighty centavos a month provided for each child by the departmental government. Ten of them escaped the first week, intending to stow away on El Tolima trains, and we could find no trace of them.

At the asylum an administrative baptism was performed on many children, giving them last names from the region in order to tell them apart, but there were so many children, so alike and so active, that they could not be distinguished during recreational periods, above all in the coldest months, when they had to warm themselves by running along corridors and staircases. It was impossible for that painful visit not to oblige me to wonder if the guerrillas who had killed the soldier in combat could have wreaked such havoc on the children of Villarrica.

The story of this logistical blunder was published in several successive accounts without consulting anyone. Censorship maintained silence, and the military replied with the explanation that was in fashion: the events in Villarrica were part of a broad Communist mobilization against the government of the Armed Forces, and they were obliged to proceed using the methods of war. A line from that communiqué was enough to put into my head the idea of obtaining direct information from Gilberto Vieira, secretary-general of the Communist Party, whom I had never seen.

I do not remember if I took the next step with the authorization of the paper or if I did it on my own initiative, but I remember very well that I undertook several useless measures to make contact with some leader of the clandestine Communist Party who could inform me about the situation in Villa-rrica. The principal problem was that the military regime's wall around the clandestine Communists had no precedents. Then I got in touch with a friend who was a Communist, and two days later another watch peddler appeared in front of my desk, looking for me in order to collect the installments I had not been able to pay in Barranquilla. I paid the ones I could and said with feigned carelessness that it was urgent I talk to one of his important leaders, but he responded with the well-known formula that he had no way to reach them and could not tell me who did. But that same afternoon, with no prior warning, I was surprised to hear a harmonious and casual voice on the phone:

"Hello, Gabriel, I'm Gilberto Vieira."

Although he had been the most prominent of the founders of the Communist Party, until that time Vieira had not spent a minute in exile or in prison. However, in spite of the risk that both telephones might be tapped, he gave me the address of his clandestine house so that I could visit him that afternoon.

It was a two-bedroom apartment with a small living room crowded with political and literary books, and you climbed a steep and gloomy flight of stairs to the sixth floor and arrived breathless, not only because of the altitude but because you were aware of entering one of the best-kept mysteries in the country. Vieira lived with his wife, Cecilia, and their infant daughter. Since his wife was not at home, he kept the baby's cradle close at hand, rocking it without haste when she would cry in the very long pauses in his conversation, which dealt with politics as well as literature, though without much sense of humor. It was impossible to conceive that this ruddy bald man in his forties, with his clear incisive eyes and precise speech, was the man most wanted by the country's secret services.

From the beginning I realized that he had kept informed about my life ever since I bought the watch at *El Nacional* in Barranquilla. He would read my articles in *El Espectador* and identify my anonymous editorials to try to interpret their hidden meanings. But he agreed that the best service I could perform for the country was to continue in the same way and not allow anyone to involve me in any kind of political militancy.

He started talking about the topic as soon as I had the opportunity to disclose the reason for my visit. He was as informed about the situation in Villarrica as if he had been there, and we could not publish a word about it because of official censorship. But he gave me important facts so that I would understand that this was the prelude to a chronic war after half a century of casual skirmishes. His language on that day and in that place had more elements of Jorge Eliécer Gaitán than the Marx who was his bedside reading, as he spoke of a solution that did not seem to be the rule of the proletariat but a kind of alliance of the powerless against the dominant classes. The fortunate result of that visit was not only a clarification of what was going on in the country but also a method for better understanding it. That was how I explained it to Guillermo Cano and Zalamea, and I left the door ajar in case the end of the unfinished article ever appeared. It goes without saying that Vieira and I established a very good relationship as friends, which facilitated our contacts even during the most difficult times of his clandestinity.

Another adult drama was growing underground until the bad news broke through the wall in February 1954, and the press published the story that a veteran of the Korean War had pawned his medals in order to eat. He was only one of the more than four thousand who had been recruited at random in another of the inconceivable moments in our history, when any fate was better than nothing for the campesinos expelled at gunpoint from their lands by official violence. The cities, overpopulated by the displaced, offered no hope. Colombia, it was repeated almost every day in editorials, on the street, in the cafés, in family conversations, was unlivable. For many displaced campesinos, and numerous boys with no prospects, the war in Korea was a personal solution. All kinds of people went there, mixed together, without precise criteria, not even for their physical condition, almost in the way the Spaniards came to discover America. When they trickled back to Colombia, that heterogeneous group at last had a common characteristic: they were veterans. It was enough for some to take part in a brawl for the blame to fall on all of them. Doors were closed to them with the facile argument that they had no right to work because their minds were imbalanced. On the other hand, there were never enough tears for the countless numbers who came back transformed into two thousand pounds of ashes.

The article about the man who pawned his medals showed a brutal contrast to another published ten months earlier, when the last veterans returned to the country with almost a million dollars in cash, and when they were exchanged at the banks they made the price of the dollar in Colombia fall from three pesos, thirty centavos, to two pesos, ninety. But the prestige of the veterans fell lower the more they confronted the reality of their country. Before their return, scattered stories had circulated to the effect that they would receive special scholarships for productive careers, that they would receive pensions for life, that they would have the opportunity to stay and live in the United States. The truth was just the opposite: soon after their arrival they were discharged from the army, and the only thing many of them had left in their pockets were pictures of their Japanese sweethearts left waiting for them at the military camps in Japan where they had been sent on leave from the war.

It was impossible for that national drama not to remind me of my grandfather Colonel Márquez and his eternal wait for his veteran's pension. I had come to think that this niggardliness was retaliation against a subversive colonel in a fierce war against the Conservative hegemony. The survivors of Korea, on the other hand, had fought against the cause of Communism and for the imperial yearnings of the United States. Yet on their return they did not appear on the society pages but in the crime reports. One of them, who shot two innocent people to death, asked his judges: "If I killed a hundred in Korea, why can't I kill ten in Bogotá?"

This man, like other criminals, had been sent to the war when the armistice had already been signed. But many like him were also victims of Colombian machismo, which manifested itself in the triumph of killing a Korean veteran. It had been less than three years since the first contingent had come back, and the veterans who were the victims of violent deaths already numbered more than a dozen. For a variety of reasons, several had died in pointless fights soon after their return. One of them was stabbed to death in a brawl because he repeated a song on a tavern jukebox. Sergeant Cantor, who had honored his name by singing and accompanying himself on the guitar during breaks in the fighting,* was shot to death only weeks after his return. Another veteran was also stabbed to death in Bogotá, and to bury him it was necessary to organize a collection among his neighbors. Ángel Fabio Goes, who had lost an eye and a hand in the war, was killed by three unidentified men who were never captured.

I remember—as if it had happened yesterday—that I was writing the last installment of the series when the telephone on my desk rang, and I recognized the radiant voice of Martina Fonseca:

"Hello?"

I abandoned the article in the middle of the page because my heart was pounding, and I crossed the avenue to meet her at the Hotel Continental after twelve years without seeing her. From the door it was not easy to distinguish her among the other women who were having lunch in the crowded dining room, until she signaled me with her glove. She was dressed in her usual personal style, wearing a suede coat, a faded fox on her shoulder, and a hunter's hat, and the years were beginning to be too noticeable in her wrinkled skin, mistreated by the sun, and her dimmed eyes, all of her diminished by the first signs of an unjust old age. We both must have realized that twelve years were a long time at her age, but we bore it well. I had tried to track her down when I first came to Barranquilla, until I learned that she was living in Panama, where her sailor was a pilot on the canal, yet it was not pride but timidity that kept me from bringing up the subject with her.

I believe she had just eaten lunch with someone who had left her alone to wait for my visit. We had three fatal cups of coffee and together smoked half a pack of rough cigarettes, groping for a way to talk without speaking, until she dared to ask me if I ever thought about her. Only then did I tell her the truth: I

Cantor is the equivalent of "singer" or "songbird."

had never forgotten her, but her goodbye had been so brutal that it changed my way of being. She was more compassionate than I:

"I never forget that you're like a son to me."

She had read my newspaper articles, my stories, and my only novel, and she talked about them to me with a lucid and merciless perspicacity possible only through love or spite. Yet I did nothing but elude the traps of nostalgia with the meanspirited cowardice that only men are capable of. When at last I managed to ease my tension, I dared to ask if she had given birth to the child she wanted.

"He was born," she said with joy, "and is finishing primary school."

"Black like his father?" I asked her with the pettiness that goes with jealousy.

She called on her usual good sense. "White like his mother," she said. "But his papá didn't leave as I feared but grew even closer to me." And in the face of my evident confusion she confirmed with a lethal smile:

"Don't worry: the boy is his. As well as two daughters as much alike as if they were only one."

She was happy she had come, she entertained me with some memories that had nothing to do with me, and I was vain enough to think she was hoping for a more intimate response from me. But like all men, I also mistook the time and place. She looked at her watch when I ordered the fourth coffee and another pack of cigarettes, and stood without preamble.

"Well, baby, I'm happy to have seen you," she said. And she concluded: "I couldn't stand it anymore, having read you so much without knowing what you're like."

"And what am I like?" I dared to ask.

"Ah, no!" She laughed with all her heart. "That's something you'll never know!"

Only when I caught my breath in front of the typewriter did I become aware of the longing to see her that I had always had, and the terror that kept me from staying with her for the rest of our lives. The same desolate terror I felt many times after that day whenever the phone rang.

The new year of 1955 began for journalists on February 28, with the news that eight sailors on the destroyer *Caldas* of the Armada Nacional had fallen into the sea and disappeared during a storm when they were less than two hours from Cartagena. They had sailed four days earlier from Mobile, Alabama, after spending several months there for a mandated repair.

While the entire newsroom was listening in suspense to the first radio bulletin about the disaster, Guillermo Cano had turned toward me in his swivel chair and kept his eye on me, an order ready on the tip of his tongue. José Salgar, on his way to the printing plant, also stopped in front of me, his nerves well tempered by the news. I had returned an hour earlier from Barranquilla, where I prepared a report on the eternal drama of Bocas de Ceniza, and now I was beginning to wonder when the next plane to the coast would leave so that I could write the first story about the eight men lost at sea. But it was soon made clear in the radio bulletin that the destroyer would reach Cartagena at three in the afternoon, with no further news, for they had not recovered the bodies of the eight drowned sailors. Guillermo Cano exhaled.

"What the hell, Gabo," he said. "Our scoop drowned."

The disaster was reduced to a series of official bulletins, and information was handled with the honors required for those fallen in the line of duty, but nothing more. Toward the end of the week, however, the navy revealed that one of the men, Luis Alejandro Velasco, had reached a beach in Urabá in a state of exhaustion, suffering from exposure but certain to recover after floating for ten days on a raft without oars and nothing to eat or drink. We all agreed it would be the story of the year if we could manage to be alone with him for even half an hour.

It was not possible. The navy kept him incommunicado while he recovered at the naval hospital in Cartagena. An astute reporter from *El Tiempo*, Antonio Montaña, sneaked into the hospital disguised as a doctor and was there with him for a few brief minutes. To judge by the results, however, all he obtained from the shipwrecked sailor were some pencil sketches of his position on the ship when he was swept overboard by the storm, and some incoherent statements that made it clear he had orders not to tell the story. "If I had known he was a reporter I would have helped him," Velasco declared a few days later. Once he had recovered, and was under the protection of the navy, he gave an interview to the correspondent for *El Espectador* in Cartagena, Lácides Orozco, who could not go as far as we would have liked in order to find out how it was that a gust of wind could cause a disaster with seven men dead.

Luis Alejandro Velasco, in fact, was subjected to an ironclad commitment that prevented him from moving around or expressing himself freely even after he was transferred to his parents' house in Bogotá. Any technical or political question was resolved for us with cordial skill by a frigate lieutenant, Guillermo Fonseca, but with equal elegance he avoided essential facts regarding the only thing that interested us then, which was the truth about the adventure. In order to gain time, I wrote a series of background pieces on the return of the shipwrecked sailor to his parents' house, and his uniformed chaperones again kept me from talking to him but authorized a mindless interview on a local radio station. It became evident that we were in the hands of masters of the official art of letting the news grow cold, and for the first time I was shaken by the idea that they were hiding something very serious about the catastrophe from the public. More than a suspicion, today I remember it as a premonition.

It was a March of icy winds, and the dusty drizzle increased the burden of my regrets. Before facing the newsroom when I was overwhelmed by defeat, I took refuge in the nearby Hotel Continental and ordered a double at the deserted bar. I was drinking it in slow sips, not even taking off my heavy ministerial overcoat, when I heard a very sweet voice almost in my ear:

"The man who drinks alone dies alone."

"From your lips to God's ear, beautiful," I answered with my heart in my mouth, convinced it was Martina Fonseca.

The voice left a trail of summery gardenias in the air, but it was not Martina. I watched her go out the revolving door and disappear, with her unforgettable yellow umbrella, on the avenue stained by the drizzle. After a second drink I crossed the avenue, too, and reached the newsroom, sustained by the first two drinks. Guillermo Cano saw me come in and let out a happy shout for everyone:

"Let's see what story the great Gabo has brought us!"

I answered with the truth:

"Nothing but a dead fish."

I realized then that the pitiless mockers in the newsroom had begun to like me when they saw me pass by in silence, dragging my dripping wet overcoat, and none had the heart to begin the ritual gibes.

Luis Alejandro Velasco continued enjoying his repressed glory. His mentors not only permitted but sponsored all kinds of publicity perversions. He received five hundred dollars and a new watch to say the truth on the radio that his timepiece had withstood the rigors of the weather. The factory that made his tennis shoes paid him a thousand dollars to say that his were so sturdy he had not been able to pull them apart in order to have something to chew. In a single day he gave a patriotic speech, let himself be kissed by a beauty queen, and was shown to the orphans as an example of patriotic morality. I was beginning to forget him on the memorable day when Guillermo Cano announced to me that he had him in his office, prepared to sign a contract to recount his complete adventure. I felt humiliated.

"It's not a dead fish anymore, it's a rotten one," I insisted.

For the first and only time I refused to do for the paper what it was my obligation to do. Guillermo Cano resigned himself to the reality and sent away the shipwrecked sailor with no explanations. Later he told me that after saying goodbye to him in his office, he began to reflect and could not explain to himself what he had just done. Then he ordered the porter to bring the shipwrecked sailor back, and he called me on the phone with the unappealable notification that he had bought the exclusive rights to the complete story.

It was not the first time and would not be the last that Guillermo would become obstinate about a lost case and in the end be proved correct. I informed him, depressed but in the best possible style, that I would write the article out of obedience as his employee but would not put my name to it. Without having thought about it first, this was a fortuitous but on-target determination regarding the story, for it obliged me to tell it in the first-person voice of the protagonist, in his own style and with his own ideas, and sign it with his name. And so I protected myself against any other shipwreck on dry land. In other words, it would be the internal monologue of a solitary adventure, just as it had happened and just as life had made it. The decision was miraculous, because Velasco turned out to be an intelligent man, with an unforgettable sensibility and courtesy, and a sense of humor at the right time and in the right place. And to our good fortune, all of it was subject to a character without flaws.

The interview was long and thorough and took three exhausting weeks, and I did it knowing it was not for publishing raw but needed to be cooked in another pot: a feature article. I began with some bad faith, trying to have the shipwrecked sailor fall into contradictions in order to reveal his hidden truths, but soon I was certain he had none. I did not have to force anything. It was like strolling through a meadow of flowers with the supreme freedom to choose the ones I preferred. Velasco would come to my desk in the newsroom at three o'clock sharp, we would go over the previous day's notes, and then proceed in a straight line. At night I would write each installment that he recounted, and it was published the following afternoon. It would have been easier and surer to write the complete adventure first and publish it revised, with all the details verified in a meticulous way. But there was no time. The topic was losing immediacy with every passing minute, and another sensational news item could topple it.

We did not use a tape recorder. They had just been invented and the best ones were as large and heavy as a typewriter, and the magnetic tape would tangle like angel-hair candy. Transcription alone was a great feat. Even today we know that recorders are very useful for remembering, but the face of the person interviewed must never be neglected, for it can say much more than the voice, and at times just the opposite. I had to settle for the routine method of notes in school copybooks, but thanks to this I believe I did not miss a word or nuance of the conversation and was better able to explore in a profound way as we went along. The first two days were difficult, because the shipwrecked sailor wanted to tell everything all at once. But he soon learned, through the order and extent of my questions, and above all through his own narrative instinct and innate ability to understand the carpentry of the work.

In order to prepare readers before throwing them into the water, we decided to begin the account with the sailor's final days in Mobile. We also agreed not to end it at the moment he set foot on dry land but when he arrived in Cartagena cheered by the crowds, the point at which readers could follow the narrative thread on their own with facts that had already been published. This gave us fourteen installments to maintain suspense over a period of two weeks.

The first installment was published on April 5, 1955. That edition of *El Espectador*, preceded by advertisements on the radio, sold out in a few hours. The explosive crux of the matter was suggested on the third day, when we decided to disclose the real reason for the disaster, which according to the official version had been a storm. Searching for greater precision, I asked Velasco to tell about the storm in all its detail. By now he was so familiar with our common method that I could see a flash of roguishness in his eyes before he answered:

"The problem is there was no storm."

What happened—he specified—was some twenty hours of strong winds, typical of the region at that time of year, which had not been foreseen by those in charge of the voyage. The crew had been paid back wages before weighing anchor, and they spent it at the last minute on all kinds of domestic appliances to take home, something so unexpected that no one seemed alarmed when they ran out of space in the interior of the ship and secured the largest cartons on deck: refrigerators, washing machines, stoves. The kind of cargo prohibited on a warship, and in such quantity that it took up vital space on the deck. Perhaps it was thought that an unofficial voyage of less than four days' duration, with excellent weather forecasts, did not need to be treated with undue rigor. How many times had they made others like it, and how many more would they make without anything happening? The unlucky thing for

everybody was that winds not much stronger than those predicted convulsed the sea under a splendid sun, made the vessel
list much more than expected, and broke the lines holding a
cargo loaded in a careless way. If it had not been a ship as sea-
worthy as the *Caldas*, it would have gone down without fail,
but eight sailors standing guard on the deck fell overboard.
And so the primary cause of the accident was not a storm, as
official sources had insisted since the beginning, but what
Velasco stated in his account: an overload of domestic appliances stowed improperly on the deck of a warship.

Another issue kept under the table was the kind of life raft
available to the men who fell into the sea, of whom only Velasco
survived. It is supposed that there must have been two kinds of
regulation rafts on board that fell in with them. They were
made of cork and canvas, three meters long by one and a half
meters wide, with a safety platform in the center, and supplied
with provisions, potable water, oars, a first-aid kit, equipment
for fishing and navigation, and a Bible. Under those conditions,
ten people could survive on board for eight days even without
the fishing equipment. But the *Caldas* had also taken on a load
of smaller rafts with no supplies of any kind. According to
Velasco's account, it seems that his was one of the rafts that had
no gear. The question that will remain afloat forever is how
many other shipwrecked sailors managed to board other rafts
that did not take them anywhere.

These had been, beyond any doubt, the most important reasons that delayed official explanations of the shipwreck. Until
it occurred to them that their claim was unsustainable because
by now the rest of the crew was at home, telling the whole
story everywhere in the country. The government insisted to
the very end on its version of the storm, and made it official in
the categorical statements of a formal communiqué. Censorship did not go to the extreme of prohibiting publication of the
remaining installments. Velasco, for his part, did his best to
maintain a loyal ambiguity, and it was never learned that he had
been pressured not to reveal certain truths, and he did not ask
us to reveal them or prevent us from doing so.

After the fifth installment there had been a plan to issue an offprint of the first four installments to meet the demand of readers who wanted to collect the complete story. Don Gabriel Cano, whom we had not seen in the newsroom during those frenetic days, came down from his dovecot and went straight to my desk.

"Tell me something, my young namesake," he asked, "how many installments is the shipwrecked sailor going to have?"

We were in the account of the seventh day, when Velasco had devoured a business card as the only edible thing in his possession, and he could not tear his shoes apart with his teeth in order to have something to chew on. That meant we still had another seven installments. Don Gabriel was horrified.

"No, my young namesake, no," he responded with annoyance. "There have to be at least fifty."

I gave him my arguments, but his were based on the fact that the paper's circulation was about to double. According to his calculations, it could rise to a figure without precedent in the national press. An editorial committee was improvised, the economic, technical, and journalistic details were studied, and it was agreed that a reasonable limit would be twenty installments. That is to say: six more than the number planned.

Although my name did not appear on the printed installments, my method of working had leaked out, and one night when I went to fulfill my obligations as film critic, an animated discussion about the story of the shipwrecked sailor began in the lobby of the theater. The majority of the people there were friends with whom I exchanged ideas in nearby cafés after the movie. Their opinions helped me to clarify mine for my weekly review. As for the shipwrecked sailor, the general desire—with very few exceptions—was that the story go on for as long as possible.

One of those exceptions was a mature, elegant man wearing a beautiful camel's hair coat and a melon-shaped hat, who followed me for some three blocks after I left the theater and was returning alone to the paper. He was accompanied by a very beautiful woman, as well dressed as he, and another man who was less impeccable. He removed his hat to greet me and introduced himself with a name I did not retain. Without further preamble he told me he could not agree with the report on the shipwrecked sailor because it played straight into the hands of the Communists. I explained without too much exaggeration that I was no more than the transcriber of the story told by the protagonist himself. But he had his own ideas and thought Velasco had infiltrated the Armed Forces in the service of the Soviet Union. Then I sensed that I was talking to a high-ranking officer in the army or navy, and I was enthusiastic at the idea of a clarification. But it seemed that was all he wanted to tell me.

"I don't know if you are aware of what you are doing," he said, "but in any case you are doing a disservice to the country on behalf of the Communists."

His dazzling wife gestured in alarm and tried to move him away by the arm with a plea in a very low voice: "Please, Rogelio!" He concluded his comment with the same composure he had shown at the beginning:

"Please believe me, I permit myself to say this to you only because of the admiration I feel for what you write."

He shook my hand again and allowed himself to be led away by his distressed wife. His male companion was surprised and did not manage to say goodbye.

It was the first in a series of incidents that set us thinking in all seriousness about the risks in the street. A few days earlier, in a poor tavern behind the newspaper that served workers in the district until dawn, two unknown men had attempted an unprovoked attack on Gonzalo González, who was drinking his last coffee of the night. No one could understand what motives they might have had against the most peaceable man in the world, except that they had confused him with me because of our Caribbean manners and customs, and the two g's in his pseudonym: Gog. In any event, security at the paper warned me not to go out alone at night in a city growing more and more dangerous. For me, however, it was so reliable that I would walk to my apartment when I finished work.

One dawn, during those intense days, I felt my hour had come in a hailstorm of glass, when somebody on the street threw a brick through my bedroom window. It was Alejandro Obregón, who had lost his keys and had not found friends who were awake, or a room in any hotel. Tired of looking for a place to sleep, and of ringing the broken bell, he solved the night's problem with a brick from a nearby construction site. He almost did not greet me when I opened the door so as not to wake me altogether, and he stretched out faceup and slept on the bare floor until noon.

The crowd eager to buy the paper at the door of *El Especta-dor*, before it reached the street, grew bigger every day. People who worked in the business center would wait to buy it and read the installment on the bus. I think the interest of readers began for humanitarian reasons, continued for literary reasons and in the end for political considerations, but it was always sustained by the internal tension of the account. Velasco told me episodes that I suspected were invented by him, and he found symbolic or emotional meanings in them, for example the one about the first seagull that did not want to fly away. The story of the airplanes, as recounted by him, had a cine-matic beauty. A friend of mine who was a seaman asked me how it was that I knew the sea so well, and I replied that I had only copied down Velasco's observations with absolute fidelity. After a certain point I no longer had anything to add.

The high command of the navy did not agree. A short while before the end of the series they sent the paper a letter of protest because it had judged, with a Mediterranean criterion and in an inelegant form, a tragedy that could occur wherever naval units operated. "In spite of the mourning and grief that have overwhelmed seven respectable Colombian homes and every man in the fleet,"— the letter said—"reporters who were neophytes in this area did not hesitate to write a series overrun with nontechnical and illogical words and concepts, placed in the mouth of the fortunate and praiseworthy sailor who valiantly saved his life." For this reason, the fleet requested the intervention of the Office of Information and the Press of the presidency so that it would approve—with the assistance of a naval officer—publications about the incident in the future. It was fortunate that when the letter arrived we were at the next-to-the-last installment and could pretend ignorance until the following week.

Anticipating the final publication of the complete text, we had asked the shipwrecked sailor to help us with the names and addresses of shipmates who had cameras, and they sent us a collection of photographs taken during the voyage. There were pictures of everything, but most were of groups of men on the deck, and in the background you could see the cartons of household appliances—refrigerators, stoves, washing machines—with their prominent brand names. That stroke of luck was enough for us to deny the official denials. The government's reaction was immediate and categorical, and the supplement's circulation exceeded all precedents and predictions. But the invincible Guillermo Cano and José Salgar had only one question:

"And now what the hell are we going to do?"

At that moment, dizzy with glory, we had no answer. Every topic seemed banal to us.

Fifteen years after the story had been published in *El Espectador*, Editorial Tusquets in Barcelona published it in a book with gilt-edge covers that sold as if it were something to eat. Inspired by a sense of justice and by my admiration for the heroic sailor, at the end of the prologue I wrote: "There are books that do not belong to the person who writes them but to the one who suffers them, and this is one of those books. As a consequence, the author's rights will be for the man who deserves them: our anonymous compatriot who had to endure ten days on a raft without food or water so that this book would be possible."

It was not an idle remark, for the book's rights were paid in their entirety to Luis Alejandro Velasco by Tusquets, on my instructions, for fourteen years. Until the lawyer Guillermo Zea Fernández, of Bogotá, persuaded him that the rights belonged to him by law, knowing they were not his but the result of my decision, which had been made in tribute to his heroism, his talent as a narrator, and his friendship.

The suit against me was presented in the Civil Court 22 of the Bogotá Circuit. Then my attorney and friend, Alfonso

Gómez Méndez, ordered Editorial Tusquets to suppress the final paragraph of the prologue in future editions and not pay Luis Alejandro Velasco a *céntimo* more of rights until a legal decision had been reached. This was done. After a long court battle that included documentary, testimonial, and technical evidence, the court decided I was the sole author of the work and did not accede to the petitions submitted by Velasco's lawyer. And therefore the payments made to him up to that time by my order had not had as their foundation the recognition of the sailor as coauthor but were the result of a voluntary and free decision by the person who wrote the book. From that time on, the author's rights, also by my order, were donated to an educational foundation.

It was not possible for us to find another story like that, because it was not one of those that are invented on paper. Life invents them, and almost always by dint of blows. We learned this later, when we attempted to write a biography of Ramón Hoyos, the formidable Antioquian cyclist crowned national champion that year for the third time. We launched it to the kind of clamor learned in the series on the sailor, and we stretched it into nineteen installments before realizing that the public preferred Ramón Hoyos riding up mountains and reaching the finish line first, but in real life.

We caught sight of a minimal hope of recovery one afternoon when Salgar phoned and told me to meet him right away in the bar of the Hotel Continental. He was there with an old friend of his, a serious man who had just introduced him to his companion, an absolute albino in laborer's clothes, with hair and eyebrows so white he seemed dazzling even in the half-light of the bar. Salgar's friend, a well-known entrepreneur, introduced the man as a mining engineer who was excavating in an empty lot two hundred meters from *El Espectador*, searching for a legendary treasure that had belonged to General Simón Bolívar. His companion—a very good friend of Salgar's, and of mine from that time on—guaranteed the truth of the story. It was suspect because of its simplicity: when the Liberator, defeated and dying, was preparing to leave Cartagena and continue his final journey, it is assumed that he chose not to take with him a substantial personal treasure, which he had acquired during the penuries of his wars as a well-deserved reserve for a decent old age. When he was preparing to continue his bitter journey—it is not known whether it was to Caracas or Europe—he had the prudence to leave the treasure hidden in Bogotá, under the protection of a system of Lacedaemonian codes very typical of his time, so that he could find it whenever he needed to, from any part of the world. I recalled these reports with irresistible longing as I was writing *The General in His Labyrinth*, where the story of the treasure would have been essential, but I could not obtain enough facts to make it credible, and as fiction it seemed weak. That legendary fortune, never recovered by its owner, was what the seeker was seeking with so much eagerness. I did not understand why they had revealed this to us until Salgar explained that his friend, impressed by the story of the shipwrecked sailor, wanted to give us background to this story so that we would follow it until it could be published with comparable publicity.

We went to the site. It was the only empty lot to the west of the Parque de los Periodistas and very close to my new apartment. The friend explained with a colonial map the coordinates of the treasure in the real details of the hills of Monserrate and La Guadalupe. The story was fascinating, and the prize would be a news item as explosive as that of the shipwrecked sailor, and of greater significance worldwide.

We continued visiting the site with a certain frequency to keep up-to-date, we listened to the engineer for endless hours founded on *aguardiente* and lemon, and we felt farther and farther away from the miracle, until so much time went by that we did not have even a hope left. The only thing we could suspect afterward was that the tale of the treasure was no more than a screen for exploiting without a permit a deposit of something very valuable right in the center of the capital. Though it was possible that this too was another screen for keeping the Liberator's treasure safe.

These were not the best times for dreaming. After the story of the shipwrecked sailor, I had been advised to spend some time outside Colombia until the situation eased, because of death threats, real or fictitious, that reached us by various means. It was the first thing I thought of when Luis Gabriel Cano asked me without any preamble what I was doing next Wednesday. Since I had no plans, he told me with his customary stolidity to prepare my papers for traveling as the paper's special correspondent to the Big Four Conference that would convene the following week in Geneva.

The first thing I did was telephone my mother. The news seemed so huge that she asked if I was referring to some farm called Geneva. "It's a city in Switzerland," I told her. Without agitation, with her interminable serenity in assimilating the most unexpected upheavals from children, she asked how long I would be there, and I said I would be back in two weeks at the latest. In reality I was going only for the four days of the conference. But for reasons that had nothing to do with my will, I stayed not for two weeks but almost three years. Then I was the one who needed the lifeboat even if only to eat once a day, but I was very careful not to let the family know. Someone once tried to upset my mother with the lie that her son was living like a prince in Paris after deceiving her with the story that he would be there for only two weeks.

"Gabito isn't deceiving anyone," she said with an innocent smile, "but sometimes it happens that even God needs to make weeks that are two years long."

I never had realized that I was a stateless person, just as much as the millions displaced by violence. I had never voted because I did not have a citizen's identity card. In Barranquilla I had identified myself with my reporter's credentials from *El Heraldo*, where I had given a false date of birth in order to avoid military service, and I had been delinquent for the past two years. In cases of emergency I identified myself with a postal card* that the telegraph operator in Zipaquirá had given to me. A providential friend put me in touch with the manager of a travel agency who agreed to get me on the plane on the appropriate date by means of the payment in advance of two hundred dollars and my signature at the bottom of ten blank pages of

---

*Identification for those under eighteen.

stamped paper. This was how I learned by chance that my bank balance was a surprising amount that I had not had time to spend because of my reporter's zeal. My only expenditure, aside from personal expenses that were no more than those of a poor student, was the monthly dispatching of the lifeboat to the family.

On the eve of the flight, the manager of the travel agency chanted to me the name of each document as he placed them on the desk so that I would not confuse them: identity card, record of military service, notarized receipts from the tax office, and certificates of vaccination against smallpox and yellow fever. In the end he asked me for an additional tip for the skinny boy who had been vaccinated twice in my name, as he had been vaccinated every day for years for clients in a hurry.

I traveled to Geneva in time for the inaugural meeting of Eisenhower, Bulganin, Eden, and Faure, with no languages but Spanish and an allowance for a third-class hotel, but backed up by my bank account. I was expected to return in a few weeks, but I do not know by what strange premonition I gave everything I owned in the apartment to my friends, including a stupendous library on cinema that I had collected in two years with the advice of Álvaro Cepeda and Luis Vicens.

The poet Jorge Gaitán Durán came to say goodbye while I was tearing up old papers, and he had the curiosity to look through the wastebasket in case he found something he could use for his magazine. He rescued three or four sheets ripped in half and skimmed over them as he put them together like a puzzle on the desk. He asked me where they were from and I said it was the "Monologue of Isabel Watching the Rain in Macondo," deleted from the first draft of *Leaf Storm*. I told him it was not unpublished, because it had appeared in *Crónica* and in the *Magazine Dominical* of *El Espectador* under the same title, which I had made up for it, and with an authorization I remembered giving in a hurry in an elevator. Gaitán Durán did not care, and he published it in the next issue of his magazine *Mito*.

The farewell party at Guillermo Cano's house was so tumultuous that when I arrived at the airport the plane had already left for Cartagena, where I was to sleep that night in order to say goodbye to my family. By a stroke of luck I boarded another one at noon. It was just as well, because the domestic atmosphere had expanded since the last time, and my parents and brothers and sisters felt capable of surviving without the lifeboat that I was going to need more than they in Europe.

I traveled to Barranquilla by highway very early the next day to take the flight to Paris at two in the afternoon. In the bus terminal in Cartagena I ran into Lácides, the unforgettable porter at The Skyscraper, whom I had not seen since that time. He fell on me with a real embrace and his eyes full of tears, not knowing what to say or how to treat me. After a hurried exchange because his bus was arriving and mine was leaving, he said with a fervor that touched my soul:

"What I don't understand, Don Gabriel, is why you never told me who you were."

"Ah, my dear Lácides," I answered, more pained than he, "I couldn't tell you because even I don't know who I am yet."

Hours later, in the taxi that took me to the airport in Barranquilla under the ungrateful sky, more transparent than any other in the world, I realized I was on the Avenida Veinte de Julio. In a reflex that had formed part of my life for the past five years, I looked toward the house of Mercedes Barcha. And there she was, slim and distant, like a statue seated in the doorway, wearing a green dress with golden lace in that year's style, her hair cut like swallows' wings, and with the intense stillness of someone waiting for a person who will not arrive. I could not avoid the awful premonition that I was going to lose her forever on a Thursday in July at so early an hour, and for an instant I thought about stopping the cab to say goodbye, but I preferred not to defy again a destiny as uncertain and persistent as mine.

On the plane I was still tortured by stomach spasms of remorse. At that time there was a fine custom of putting on the back of the seat in front of you something that in plain language was still called writing materials. A sheet of notepaper with gold edges and a matching pink, cream, or blue envelope of the same linen paper, sometimes perfumed. In my few previous trips I had used them to write farewell poems that I turned into little paper doves and sent flying when I got off the plane. I chose sky blue and wrote my first formal letter to Mercedes seated in the doorway of her house at seven in the morning, with the green dress of a bride without a beloved and the hair of an uncertain swallow, not even suspecting for whom she had dressed at dawn. I had written her other playful notes that I improvised at random and had received only verbal and always elusive responses when we happened to run into each other. This was not meant to be more than five lines to give her official notice of my trip. But at the end I added a postscript that blinded me like a flash of lightning at midday at the very instant I signed it: "If I do not receive an answer to this letter within a month, I will stay and live in Europe forever." I did not allow myself time to think about it again before I put the letter in the mailbox at the desolate airport in Montego Bay at two in the morning. It was already Friday. On Thursday of the following week, when I walked into the hotel in Geneva at the end of another useless day of international disagreements, I found her letter of reply.

A NOTE ON THE TYPE

This book was set in Janson, a typeface long thought to have been made by the Dutchman Anton Janson but has been conclusively demonstrated to be the work of the Hungarian Nicholas Kis (1650–1702).

Composed by Creative Graphics, Allentown, Pennsylvania
Printed and bound by Berryville Graphics, Berryville, Virginia
Map by Paul J. Pugliese